The Wartime Sermons of Jonathan Edwards

The Wartime Sermons of Jonathan Edwards
A Collection

AUTHORED BY
Jonathan Edwards

EDITED BY
Christian Cuthbert

CASCADE *Books* · Eugene, Oregon

THE WARTIME SERMONS OF JONATHAN EDWARDS
A Collection

Copyright © 2022 Christian Cuthbert. All rights reserved. Except for brief quotations in critical publications or reviews, no part of this book may be reproduced in any manner without prior written permission from the publisher. Write: Permissions, Wipf and Stock Publishers, 199 W. 8th Ave., Suite 3, Eugene, OR 97401.

Cascade Books
An Imprint of Wipf and Stock Publishers
199 W. 8th Ave., Suite 3
Eugene, OR 97401

www.wipfandstock.com

PAPERBACK ISBN: 978-1-7252-8787-7
HARDCOVER ISBN: 978-1-7252-8788-4
EBOOK ISBN: 978-1-7252-8789-1

Cataloguing-in-Publication data:

Names: Edwards, Jonathan, 1703–1758 [author] | Cuthbert, Christian [editor].

Title: The wartime sermons of Jonathan Edwards : a collection /edited by Christian Cuthbert.

Description: Eugene, OR: Cascade Books, 2022 | Includes bibliographical references and index.

Identifiers: ISBN 978-1-7252-8787-7 (paperback) | ISBN 978-1-7252-8788-4 (hardcover) | ISBN 978-1-7252-8789-1 (ebook).

Subjects: LCSH: Edwards, Jonathan, 1703–1758 | Sermons | Theology—Early works to 1800 |Puritans—New England—History—Colonial period, ca. 1600–1775 | War—Religious aspects | Congregationalism

Classification: BX7260.E3 E39 2022 (paperback) | BX7260.E3 (ebook)

03/29/22

This volume is dedicated to the hundreds of scholars who have studied, transcribed, edited, and otherwise promoted the thought of Jonathan Edwards. Your care and attention to detail have benefited this volume and the work of so many other scholars.

Contents

Preface | ix
Acknowledgments | xi
Introduction | 1

Part 1 | British Wars Abroad

In Seeking Heaven Persons Should Behave as Valiant, Resolute Soldiers, February 1741 | 25
In Seeking Heaven Persons Should Behave as Valiant, Resolute Soldiers, Matthew 11:12 | 28
God's Care for His Servants in Time of Public Commotions, February 26, 1741 | 61
God's Care for His Servants in Time of Public Commotions, Revelation 7:1–3| 64
The Curse of Meroz, December 1741 | 86
The Curse of Meroz, Judges 5:23 | 89
Prepared to Travail and Fight, April 1743 | 107
Prepared to Travail and Fight, Exodus 13:18 | 109
Christ the Lord of Hosts, October 13, 1743 | 113
Christ the Lord of Hosts, Isaiah 47:4 | 115

Part 2 | War Comes to New England

Sin Weakens a People in War, June 28, 1744 | 127
Sin Weakens a People in War, Joshua 7:12 | 129
The Armor of God, July 1744 | 147
The Armor of God, Ephesians 6:11–13 | 149
The Duties of Christians in a Time of War, April 4, 1745 | 163
The Duties of Christians in a Time of War, 1 Kings 8:44–45 | 166
An Occasion for Praise and Thanksgiving, August 1745 | 178
An Occasion for Praise and Thanksgiving, 2 Chronicles 20:27–29 | 181
As Soldiers in War, August 1745 | 197
As Soldiers in War, 1 Corinthians 9:26 | 199

The Enemies of God's People Confounded and Broken in Pieces,
    September 19, 1745 | 212
The Enemies of God's People Confounded and Broken in Pieces,
    Isaiah 8:9–10 | 215
The Church of Christ Built on a Rock, March 13, 1746 | 229
The Church of Christ Built on a Rock, Matthew 16:18 | 232
The People of God Going Forth to War, June 1746 | 246
The People of God Going Forth to War, Nehemiah 4:14 | 248
The Fall of the Antichrist, July 10, 1746 | 258
The Fall of the Antichrist, Revelation 17:11 | 261
The Sovereignty of God's Mercy, August 1746 | 272
The Sovereignty of God's Mercy, Exodus 33:19 | 275
Walking Righteously, Speaking Uprightly, October 16, 1746 | 283
Walking Righteously, Speaking Uprightly, Isaiah 33:19 to the End | 286
God's People in Danger, November 27, 1746 | 303
God's People in Danger, Isaiah 37:28–38 | 305
Continuing Unawakened Under Divine Chastisements, August 1747 | 320
Continuing Unawakened Under Divine Chastisements,
    Isaiah 9:13–14 | 322
A Strong Rod Broken and Withered, June 1748 | 333
A Strong Rod Broken and Withered, Ezekiel 19:12 | 336

Part 3 | War Spreads to the Colonies

Warring With the Devil, April 1754 | 355
Warring With the Devil, Luke 11:21–22 | 357
God Is He Who Orders, March 5, 1755 | 359
God Is He Who Orders, 2 Chronicles 20:6 | 361
In the Name of the Lord of Hosts, July 1755 | 364
In the Name of the Lord of Hosts, 1 Samuel 17:45–47 | 367
God's People Tried By a Battle Lost, August 28, 1755 | 370
God's People Tried By a Battle Lost, Psalm 60:9–12 | 372

Appendix A: Edwards's Martial Timeline | 383
Appendix B: Index of Edwards's Martial Letters | 386
Bibliography | 387
Scripture Index | 389
Subject Index | 399

Preface

THIS COLLECTION OF EDWARDS'S wartime sermons is the result of a desire to explore how Edwards applied his theological prowess to the anxieties and fears of his congregation in Northampton during times of war. Edwards is known for wearing many different hats: theologian, historian, revivalist, exegete, philosopher, etc. While he wore each hat with distinction, I get the sense that his preferred hat was that of pastor and his other skills served his role as the shepherd of God's people. This collection of sermons uses Edwards's martial context to examine his public theology: how Edwards leveraged his theological convictions to address the needs of his congregation. I hope that these sermons shed much light on Edwards as a pastor in the midst of a world of eighteenth-century New England at war.

Most of Edwards's biographers discuss the various wars of the 1740s and 50s as the background to his thought. This volume is the first step in bringing these conflicts into the foreground. As a former Army reservist, I understand the real strain the shadow of war casts over one's life, a dynamic not fully developed in the many excellent biographies of Edwards. I hope this collection can also close the gap between the eighteenth-century context for Edwards's thought and the reality of eighteenth-century pressures on the congregation at Northampton.

People are justifiably amazed by the clarity, complexity, and scope of Edwards's "cathedral of the mind"—the integration of his metaphysics, conversionism, theology, history, exegesis, and revivalism (not to mention his ethics or aesthetics). Far from subverting an appreciation for his intellectual acumen, recognizing that Edwards leveraged these remarkable abilities toward a pastoral end, in my opinion, only increases my respect for the frontier divine. I trust that it will increase your respect as well.

Dr. Christian Cuthbert

Acknowledgments

THIS VOLUME WAS MADE possible by a host of scholars who transcribed and edited the sermons of Jonathan Edwards. Harry S. Stout and Wilson Kimnach have edited sermons which previously appeared in the letterpress edition of the *Works of Jonathan Edwards*. Craig Woods, Bryan LeBeau, Roy Paul, and Christian Cuthbert edited unpublished sermons for the Jonathan Edwards Center Global Sermon Editing Project. However, the most significant contribution comes from Ken Minkema, the executive editor for the *Works of Jonathan Edwards*, who personally edited the lion's share of the sermons that appear in this volume. The appropriate attribution is provided at the head of each sermon.

Introduction

PROVINCIAL NORTHAMPTON MAY HAVE been on the outer orbit of the British Empire, but Jonathan Edwards considered his pulpit near the center of God's redemptive plan. During the inter-colonial wars between 1739 and 1756, Edwards explicitly addressed martial events through his preaching. In almost thirty sermons preached or re-preached over a period of seventeen years covering a cluster of four conflicts, Edwards brought his brand of evangelical piety to bear on the anxieties these conflicts produced among his parishioners.[1] He designed his sermons to provide an integrated framework through which his congregation understood military action, personal piety, corporate spirituality, and God's ultimate purposes in the world. As inter-colonial warfare transitioned from distant operations to personal involvement, Edwards appropriated martial themes differently to suit his congregation's context.

In the summer of 1739, war erupted between Protestant Britain and Catholic Spain in a conflict that has curiously come to be known as the War of Jenkin's Ear (1739–48). Tensions mounted between Britain and Spain over two issues. First, both Britain and Spain were frustrated over shipping interests in the Atlantic after the Treaty of Utrecht (1713). Secondly, confusion over the border between British Georgia and Spanish Florida pushed the two European powers to formally declare war. Actual battles were few and far between and the conflict waned, though never died. Instead, the outbreak of the War of Austrian Succession folded this

---

1. It is hard to determine exactly how many sermons deserve the moniker "war time sermon." Wilson Kimnach claimed that after 1745, Edwards preached twenty-eight sermons "on the subject of war or employing war imagery" (*WJE* 25:39). This collection adopts this criterion to present the sermons contained therein. There are many sermons where martial references may be made during a time of war but are not included in this collection because this theme is not the organizing principle of the sermon.

conflict into a broader European contest. Continental powers aligned themselves around the claim of the succession of the Queen of Hungary, Maria Theresa, to the Hapsburg throne. Britain supported this claim known as the Pragmatic Solution to check the power of France and to provide support for Hanover.[2] Over the eight years of fighting that followed, allegiances shifted continuously but one axis remained constant: Britain and Austria sought to check the power of France and Spain.

Continental wars tended not to remain merely continental wars. In 1744, this contest between Britain and France spilled over into America. Open hostilities broke out on the frontiers in Maine, New York, and would soon come to Edwards's Connecticut River Valley. This transmission of war to the American frontier marks a shift between British war as the background of his preaching to the subject of Edwards' sermons. Northampton's sons were mobilized and deployed to forts throughout the western frontier as well as the far reaches of Cape Breton. The shadow of war that had fallen across the valley for generations had returned and with it, all the memories and anxieties these wars produced.

After four years of fighting across New England, in 1748 the cannons fell silent as London and Paris reached a treaty at Aix-la-Chappelle. But the fundamental unrest which drove these military conflicts continued to churn. By 1754, New France had expanded north from the Mississippi and south from Canada, threatening to encircle the British colonies. Efforts to drive a wedge between these French arms failed with the defeat of Braddock at the Ohio River. This failure endangered the survival, not only New York and New England, but Pennsylvania, Virginia, and the Carolinas. The spreading of war throughout the colonies brought a new dynamic to the conflict as well as Edwards's preaching.

Similarly, Edwards's ministry found itself in a new context. Having been dismissed from Northampton in June of 1750, Edwards accepted a call to serve as pastor of the Native settlement of Stockbridge located between the Hudson River and Connecticut River Valleys. Edwards found himself on a new frontier, preaching to a new congregation that would play a prominent role in the wars of the 1750s. Edwards's new congregation contained a handful of British families but primarily served the Mohicans of Stockbridge. This Native tribe was loosely affiliated with the

---

2. The "Pragmatic Solution" was devised by her father, Emperor Charles VI, to allow his daughter the inheritance of his kingdom. During his lifetime, Charles VI secured guarantees from the nations of Europe supporting this solution, few of which were honored after his death.

Mohawks but agreed to host a British missionary and boarding school. Edwards's preaching during this phase of his ministry reiterated many themes from his Northampton years yet with a simplicity and directness geared towards a native audience.

Edwards crafted his wartime sermons to address the specific needs occasioned by various phases of military conflict. The development of the conflict between Britain and Spain dovetailed with the burgeoning of the revivals beginning in 1740. Therefore, when fighting centered on the Caribbean and encountered mainly through the pages of the *Boston Gazette*, Edwards employed broad martial language to promote his revivalist agenda. Furthermore, this period also saw the sweeping of Whitefield's brand of piety across the colonies. Edwards, therefore, appropriated martial themes to call his congregation to participate in this brand of piety. When Britain focused her military attention on the continent, Edwards encouraged Northampton to participate through personal devotion: prayer, righteous living, etc. As a result, Edwards's commemoration of Britain's victory at the Battle of Dettingen (1743) demonstrated a perceived participation in Northampton with military events from across the globe.

The nature of Edwards's martial preaching shifted when war reached the frontiers of New England. Instead of merely leveraging military themes toward the furtherance of revival, Edwards preached on the nature of warfare, called his congregation to arms, and provided an ambitious agenda for military action. This doesn't mean that Edwards's preaching abandoned revivalism, but instead integrated themes of warfare, personal piety, revival, and God's ultimate purposes more deeply and forcefully. The personal nature of Edwards's wartime preaching came to a climax in August of 1747 after a Native war party killed Southampton resident Elisha Clark, who was working on his own property. These sermons did not merely construct theological frameworks, but served as personal, pastoral responses to the events of war. They sought to help an anxious congregation through dark times.

After his removal to native Stockbridge, Edwards recycles many of his Northampton sermons for his Mohican congregation. What at first may have been merely calls to revival using military themes with which Native warriors would have been familiar, hostilities rupture the peace between Britain and France yet again and his Stockbridge sermons take on a more practical purpose. Edwards continued to draw his sermonic material from the pages of the newspaper addressing the death of General

Braddock to make sense of God's purposes behind the defeat. The variety of purposes behind Edwards' sermons suggest that he did not rely on stock tropes for this preaching. Instead, he drew directly on the themes which worried his congregation to craft theological responses with real pastoral relevance.

To understand Edwards's pastoral purposes, one must understand the people and circumstances Edwards addressed through these sermons. War had swept through the Connecticut River Valley several times from 1670 through the 1720s and its memory set Northampton on edge. Furthermore, many of Edwards's Northampton congregation would serve as officers, soldiers, drummers, clerks, and chaplains during the King George's War; many of Edwards's Native and British congregants would serve in the French and Indian wars. Edwards' sermons addressed the people who fought as well as the families affected by the outcome of these battles. While Edwards drew heavily on his theological prowess to craft these sermons, they were often personal in tone and encouraging in purpose.[3]

British Wars Abroad

The events of 1739 provide a prologue to Edwards's martial preaching. Between March and August of that year, Edwards preached a series of thirty sermons known collectively as *A History of the Work of Redemption*.[4] This survey stretched from creation to God's consummation of history providing a context for Northampton to understand her place in redemptive history. Edwards preached these sermons to prepare his people for a deeper and more personal experience of piety which Northampton had known in 1735 known as "awakening" or "revival." As Edwards preached on this grand vision for redemption, news of the developing conflict with Spain trickled into the *Boston Gazette*. Throughout these sermons, Edwards claimed that ministers and magistrates cooperated to accomplish redemptive ends. Furthermore, Edwards demonstrated how warfare historically served to remove obstacles for the advance of the gospel.

---

3. George Marsden's excellent biography *Jonathan Edwards: A Life* and Patricia Tracy's *Jonathan Edwards, Pastor* both survey the impact of various forms of war on Edwards's ministry but neither elucidates the relationship of martial events to Edwards's thought or preaching.

4. Michael McClymond and Gerald McDermott's *Theology of Jonathan Edwards* presents a thorough and creative approach to the Redemption project.

Two events in particular inform Edwards' martial sermons between 1739 and 1744. First, the simmering conflict with Spain gave Edwards occasion to draw on military tropes and images. Disputes over shipping rights led to naval engagements across the Atlantic, though these were few and far between. Hitting closer to home, the dispute over the Florida-Georgia border organized British troops to attack the Spanish settlement of Saint Augustine. However, this conflict would culminate in a combined British and American expedition to take the Spanish stronghold of Cartagena in 1740–41. In the fall of 1740, Col. Blakeney traveled throughout the colonies recruiting an "American Foot," or regiment, who would fight alongside British regulars on an expedition in the Caribbean. Led by Virginian Col. William Gooch, 3500 Americans volunteered from all over the colonies (presumably New England) personally connecting many in Northampton with the developing conflict.[5]

Gooch and his Americans joined the British at Jamaica in January of 1741 and began preparations for an ambitious attempt to capture the Spanish fortress at Cartagena. Unfortunately, the British assault became mired down due to disease and poor supplies, decimating the British forces. To compensate, the British impressed many American volunteers into service. This proved a highly controversial action because the Americans considered the terms of their service bound to the officers under which they volunteered whereas British officers assumed they had complete control over any of his Majesty's subjects. The expedition failed and it is estimated that, of the 3500 volunteers, only one in ten ever returned home. This conflict continued to simmer, but the outbreak of the War of Austrian Succession on the continent absorbed Britain's conflict with Spain into a much larger conflict.

The second event which drove Edwards's preaching during this period was the coming of George Whitefield and the renewal of the revival experience in Northampton. After the waning of Northampton's revival in 1735, Edwards continued to press for this deep and personal piety. When Whitefield swept through the colonies in 1740, he brought a renewed wave of religious fervor. He brought this wave to Northampton in October of 1740 sparking a renewed pietistic sentiment that Edwards and other preachers would sustain through 1742. In a letter to Deacon Lyman of Goshen, Connecticut, Edwards writes,

---

5. These conflicts are treated well in Leach's *Roots of Conflict*, Peckham's *Colonial Wars*, and Parkman's *Half Century of Conflict*.

> Concerning the great stir that is in the land, and those extraordinary circumstances and events that it is attended with, such as persons crying out, and being set into great agonies, with a sense of sin and wrath, and having their strength taken away, and their minds extraordinarily transported with light, love, and comfort, I have been abundantly amongst such things.[6]

This description reflects the deep, personal—violent even—expressions of piety that attended the revivals. Such experiences visited Edwards's own house when Sarah described similar "ecstasies" under the ministry of Samuel Buell who filled the Northampton pulpit during one of Jonathan's preaching tours in January of 1742.[7]

The development of war and the rising tide of revival dovetailed in Edwards's preaching. In February of 1741, Edwards preached two sermons, *Valiant and Resolute Soldiers* and *God's Care for his Servants in Time of Public Commotions*. With the departure of Gooch's American Foot and news of naval skirmishes peppering the *Boston Gazette*, Edwards emphasized the need to take heaven as a soldier "in taking a country or kingdom." Furthermore, Edwards reminds his congregation that only the servants of God are kept safe during public calamities. Both sermons drew on the collective anxieties war produces to encourage Northampton towards personal piety.

When the tide of the expedition turned against the British over the summer of 1741, many colonists began to worry about their loved ones and neighbors fighting in the Caribbean. Many may have doubted the wisdom of volunteering for such an expedition. *The Curse of Meroz*, preached in December of 1741, reminded Northampton "it is a most dangerous thing for any of his professing people to lie still and not to put to a helping hand." Instead, as Edwards advocated in *Prepared to Trevail and Fight* (April 1743), a Christian should adopt the posture of a soldier if one wants to escape spiritual bondage. These sermons intermingled martial and spiritual language to promote an awakening experience among the members of the Northampton congregation.

Shortly after the failure to take Cartagena, Britain's focus shifted to the events on the continent and the developing War of Austrian Succession. Britain supported the claim of Maria Theresa to the Hapsburg throne for two reasons. First, it would help maintain a delicate religious

---

6. WJE 4:533.

7. For an excellent treatment of Whitefield including his attitudes towards war see Peter Choi's *George Whitefield: Evangelist for God and Empire*.

and political balance on the continent, limiting France's influence. Secondly, it helped provide a buffer zone between France and Hanover, King George's ancestral (Protestant) lands. With this objective in mind, King George II traveled to the continent to personally take command of the Pragmatic Army. On October 13, 1743, Edwards preached a sermon in commemoration and celebration of Britain's victory over the French at Dettingen. *Christ, Lord of Hosts* described God himself as the one who arbitrates individual battles. Therefore, in Edwards's theological framework, Britain's victory signals her participation in God's grand scheme of redemption.[8]

Shortly thereafter, the conflict between France and Britain would spill over into the colonies. The shadow of war in New England, according to Edwards, distracted the people of Northampton from the pursuit of revival and religious fervor waned. Edwards's promotion of revival would continue, however, with a different character than before. He moved beyond merely a personal participation in piety to a corporate participation in the grand purposes of redemption incorporating the role of warfare within those purposes.

War Comes to New England

By the time Britain declared war on France in March of 1744, preparations in New England were well underway. Governor Shirley initiated a flurry of activity, recruiting "snow-shoe men" to serve as a quick reactionary force, commissioning Edwards's uncle, Col. John Stoddard, to extend the line of block-houses (or small forts), and identifying officers to lead and fill the ranks in local militias. The news of war with France conjured troubling memories for Northampton and the Connecticut River Valley. Throughout King William's War (1688–97) and Queen Anne's War (1702–13), combined French and Indian forces descended from Canada, along Lake Champlain to Crown Point, before creeping into the valley. They surprised farmers working in their fields, women and children as they passed along byways, and set fire to whole towns. News of renewed conflict refreshed this collective memory raising the level of Northampton's anxiety.

---

8. For the best accessible treatment of the War of Austrian Succession see Reed Browning's *War of Austrian Succession*.

Unfortunately for New England, Louisbourg received news of war before Boston. Capitalizing on this intelligence advantage, the fortress on Cape Breton launched assaults on Canso and Port Royal. When news reached the desk of Governor Shirley at the beginning of June 1744, one of his first letters was to Col. Stoddard, enlisting his help and declaring that Stoddard would play a significant role in the planning of New England's response.[9] On June 28, 1744, Edwards climbed his pulpit to help his flock understand the coming conflict in his sermon *Sin Weakens a People in a Time of War*. This sermon claimed that the outcome of war was directly tied to the personal spiritual participation of its parties. Edwards saw New England's advantage lay in its commitment to a Protestant religious sentiment over and against French Catholicism. However, this sermon was a call for Northampton to not only affirm but personally express a deep religious piety. Only through such a spirituality could New England enjoy the protection of heaven.

Edwards followed this sermon with *The Armor of God* in July 1744. Echoing the themes expressed in earlier sermons, Edwards claimed that the only way to be "preserved from destruction by our spiritual enemies" one must put on the armor of God. Framing the conflict as essentially spiritual, Edwards identified the primary battlefield which would not be fought by soldiers. Instead, the laymen and civilians of Northampton participated in the outcome of battles and the war as much as those who marched across New England. Despite this flurry of activity, all seemed quiet on the western front throughout 1744.

The initial theater of King George's War centered on Cape Breton and the eastern frontier and in early 1745, Shirley targeted the most formidable fortress on the eastern coast. Acting on intelligence concerning the struggling state of the fort, Shirley proposed and eventually received the approval of the Assembly to organize an expedition against Louisbourg. By the end of March, Shirley petitioned London for Naval support and the colonies raised 2,800 volunteers to board ships and sailed for Cape Breton. It is hard to overstate the disadvantages under which these volunteers operated. A group of amateur soldiers sailing under a leader with minimal experience without the guarantee of naval support against the best constructed French fort in the New World was unenviable. However, Whitefield enthusiastically endorsed the expedition, providing a recruiting slogan that lent an air of Crusade to the mission: "Never despair,

---

9. Shirley, *Correspondence*, 127–28.

Christ Leads." Furthermore, Whitefield preached to Pepperrell and his troops before embarking on the mission in late March 1745.

On April 4, 1745, Edwards delivered the sermon *The Duties of Christians in a Time of War*. This sermon reflected a different purpose than previous wartime sermons. While many earlier sermons leveraged martial themes to promote awakening spirituality, this sermon provided a Biblical and philosophical defense for New England's actions. In his sermon *The Armor of God* the previous summer, Edwards claimed that New England's only interest was defense. Now Northampton's sons set sail on a preemptive attack against a fortress which lay far to the east. Edwards argued in *Duties of Christians* that war is not only permissible but a duty and that this war should be executed with vigor. Drawing on Enlightenment thinkers such as Grotius, Edwards presents a Just War Theory rooted in Scripture to assuage his congregation's fears and incite their prayers.

As the summer progressed, news reached Northampton that this group of untrained volunteers had taken the fortress. As Northampton's conquering heroes trickled back into town in August of 1745, Edwards preached *An Occasion for Thanksgiving*. This sermon chronicled the providences which attended the unlikely victory demonstrating the truth of earlier sermons that Christ was indeed the Lord of Hosts and controlled the outcome of battles. Between turns in weather, the timely arrival of Admiral Warren's naval support, the efforts of the God-fearing colonists, and the failures of the Catholic garrison, Edwards argued for the vindication of his claim that war was chiefly spiritual in nature. Only through the interposition of God could this group of faithful volunteers have been victorious and overwhelmingly so.

Closely following this sermon, Edwards decided to capitalize on the remarkable providences of the victory at Louisbourg. *As Soldiers in War* (August 1745) returned to the familiar theme of treating one's spiritual duties as soldiers execute their military duties. Disappointed that the shadow of war distracted Northampton from its spiritual condition, Edwards sought to leverage the visible hand of God in military events to redirect his congregation back to their spiritual state. Against the backdrop of Louisbourg, *As Soldiers in War* conflates God's purposes in advancing the Protestant cause through military action with God's purposes in the individual or local community: "To exhort all that hope hereafter to be possessed of the kingdom of heaven." The victory at Louisbourg certainly had global consequences in Edwards's thought, but it held implications for personal piety as well.

Two ideas emerged from the fall of 1745 that seem unlikely to be a coincidence. A combined French and Indian raid set out from Crown Point against Col. John Lydius's farm outside Albany, taking several captives. Col. Lydius's friend, Col. John Stoddard, suggested that an expedition be organized against Montreal and Quebec to remove the French Catholic threat form North America. This expedition would dominate Stoddard's martial imagination long after its feasibility collapsed. Secondly, Edwards preached the sermon *Enemies Confounded and Broken* claiming that if anyone moved against God's people, not alliances, preparations, nor their contrivances can save them. They will be "utterly confounded and broken in pieces." It is clear from the application that Edwards had in view the French and their Indian allies describing them as not only enemies but an antichristian kingdom. The language of total (or "utter") destruction resonates with Stoddard's idea of French removal so well that it is unlikely this resonance is coincidental.[10]

Edwards viewed New England's struggle within the broader scope of the British "Protestant Interest."[11] Over the winter of 1745–46, pro-Catholic sentiment gained a leader who organized a military challenge to the Protestant standing order. Charles Edward Stuart, a Catholic rival to the British throne, led a Jacobite uprising backed by French forces.[12] Landing in northern Scotland in Eriskay, "Bonnie Prince Charlie" or the "Young Pretender," as he is known, rallied the Scottish highlanders to depose the Protestant, Hanoverian King George II. These rebels marched as far south as Derby within 150 miles of London before their support evaporated. This struggle with French Catholics was not limited to the frontiers of New England but encroached on the British mainland, even approaching London. Edwards considered the contest with Catholicism

---

10. See Cuthbert, "'More Swiftly Propagating the Gospel,'" 153–68.

11. The term "Protestant Interest" draws on the work of Thomas Kidd and his monograph *Protestant Interest*. This work argues that after the Glorious Revolution of 1688, New England began to identify closely with the Protestant succession of British kings and their "interest."

12. The "Jacobite" movement is named after the Catholic Stuart King James II and his purported successor James Francis Edward Stuart, also known as the "Old Pretender."

in terms much broader than the safety of the Connecticut River Valley or New England, but a global contest—cosmic even.[13]

On March 13, 1746, Edwards preached *The Church of Christ Built on a Rock* developing the classic Catholic text of Matthew 16:18. This text had been used to justify the authority of the Pope, or the bearer of the keys of the kingdom, as the descendant of Peter. However, Edwards goes to great lengths to demonstrate that the foundation upon which the church is built is not merely Peter but all the prophets and apostles. This sermon turns the tide on Catholic claims to authority. Not only was Peter (and by extension, the Pope) not the foundation of the church, Edwards suggests that Catholicism is actually "the gates of hell" in Matthew's imagery. Therefore, according to Edwards, Catholicism would never be able to defeat Protestantism. While Edwards certainly had Northampton's situation in view, the broad terms of this sermon suggests that Edwards included mainland Britain and anywhere Catholicism threatened.

Stoddard's plan for organizing an expedition against French Canada progressed throughout the winter and spring of 1746 gaining the endorsement of both Governor Shirley, the Duke of Newcastle, and even King George II. Forces were assembling in Albany in preparation for a march towards Montreal while others marshaled near Boston for a naval attack on Quebec. In June of 1746, Edwards preached *The People of God Going Forth to War* outlining a Christian's duty to engage in the effort to rid North America of the Catholic threat. While Edwards claimed that military action was permissible for Christians in *Duties of Christians in a Time of War*, this sermon more forcefully emphasized not just the permissibility of war but war itself as a duty. This sermon acted as a call to arms, recruiting volunteers to fill out the ranks which Stoddard had struggled to fill.

A couple of weeks later, Edwards returned to preaching in support of the expedition to Canada in *The Fall of the Antichrist* (July 10, 1746). Edwards spoke of the French threat in terms of the cosmic struggle between the church of Christ and the kingdoms of the antichrist. The expedition to Canada (along with the Jacobite rebellion and the on-going conflict on the continent) was not merely about the safety of Northampton, Britain, or a Protestant alliance; it was a biblical struggle for the advance of the gospel, the expected ultimate defeat of the antichrist. While this contest was chiefly spiritual, according to Edwards, it manifested

---

13. For an excellent treatment of the Jacobite Rebellion of 1745 see Geoffery Plank's *Rebellion and Savagery*.

itself throughout human history. Edwards believed that New England was to play a small yet important part in the eventual defeat of these antichristian kingdoms.

In the spring of 1746, the Protestant forces struck a decisive blow in the Jacobite rebellion. On April 16, the Duke of Cumberland met the Young Pretender on the fields of Culloden outside Inverness and soundly defeated the Jacobites. Bonnie Prince Charlie fled from the battle with his life but lost the organized support of the Scottish rebels. While pockets of fighting continued for months, Cumberland effectively removed the Jacobite threat at Culloden. In commemoration of this victory, Edwards preached *The Sovereignty of God's Mercy* in August of 1746. Framing the victory at Culloden as divine mercy on the royalists and a judgment on the rebels, Edwards endorsed the idea that his brand of spirituality was inextricably linked to Britain's Protestant, Hanoverian succession. Reminders of God's merciful intervention were necessary, especially in light of the crumbling of Stoddard's planned invasion of Canada.

By the fall of 1746, rumors reached Boston of a sizeable French fleet sailing from Brest to recapture Louisbourg. In light of this threat, Edwards preached *Walking Righteously, Speaking Uprightly* on October 16, 1746. Drawing on a text wrought with nautical imagery, Edwards reminded his congregation of the promises of God to protect his people. Curiously for a Calvinist, much of Edwards's martial thought emphasizes the congregation's participation in the outcome of battles and wars through the exercise of "duties." While God ultimately decided the outcome of martial events, Edwards emphasized an individual's duty to strive, pursue, pray, and whatever else was in one's reach to participate in God's purposes. *Walking Righteously, Speaking Uprightly* reminds one that God promises protection to his people and personal conduct can put one's self in the way of such protection.

These rumors would eventually derail Stoddard's proposed expedition to Canada. Enlistments were so slow, the garrisoning of an incomplete force at Albany became logistically burdensome. Such rumors proved true when a French fleet was sighted in Jebucta (Halifax) prompting Shirley to redeploy many of these soldiers to Cape Breton. Edwards, in his sermon *God's People in Danger* preached on November 27, 1746, compared New England's situation with that of Israel under the threat of Sennacherib. The enthusiasm over the capture of Louisbourg now portended French retribution. Edwards reminded his congregation that, just as God protected Israel against Sennacherib's forces, God will preserve his people in the face of the French fleet from Brest.

During the summer of 1747, the threat of Native and French forces struck close to home. To this point, the theater of war centered on the eastern frontiers even though there had been significant movement along the western frontier. The keystone to the block-house line of defenses, Fort Massachusetts, fell to the torch in August of 1746. News of Native sightings echoed through the Connecticut River Valley for over a year, but these fears were realized in August of 1747. While threshing grain in his fields, a Native party fell on Elisha Clark of Southampton, killing him. At the end of August, Edwards preached a sermon marking this occasion: *Continuing Unawakened Under Divine Chastisement*. Edwards brought his grand vision of God's purposes back to a personal level. Edwards claimed that divine chastisements persist when men "continue unawakened and unreclaimed" by correction and "it brings 'em into great danger of utter destruction." Edwards leveraged the loss of Elisha Clark to spur Northampton to pursue the awakening for which God designed such a tragedy. Even though Edwards's theological vision transcended the individual throughout the development of his martial sermons, he never abandoned a vision for personal piety.

Northampton would lose only one more soldier during the war, but not to combat. In June of 1748, Northampton—and Edwards in particular—lost the scion Col. John Stoddard to illness at sixty-seven. Stoddard embodied Northampton life in every way possible. He served as town moderator, justice of the peace, selectman, justice for the inferior court of pleas, representative to the Massachusetts Assembly; he served on the governor's council, the commissioner of Indian affairs, as well as colonel for the western militia. Economic, legal, military, and even religious—all of Northampton's business passed across the desk of John Stoddard. For Edwards, Stoddard was a personal confidant, penning a defense of the revivals, and a benefactor directing the town council to support his nephew. However, after Stoddard's passing, Edwards lasted mere months in his pulpit before his ignominious dismissal. Edwards's eulogy, *A Strong Rod Broken and Withered* (June 1748), served not only as a personal lament, but an outline for how ministers and magistrates collaborated to advance the gospel. Edwards considered Stoddard's military role as an important pillar in defeating the antichristian forces so that the gospel could advance.

Shortly thereafter, Britain and France reached an uneasy peace at Aix-la-Chappelle. To New England's frustration, London returned Louisbourg to the French and did not settle the precipitating factors that led to war. This peace came not as the result of tactical victory but exhaustion after prolonged attrition. In other words, the forces which pit Britain and France against each other on the field of battle persisted even when the fighting did not. War between France and Britain would again visit the colonies.

War Spreads to the Colonies

The peace of Aix-la-Chappelle served as a temporary respite from intercolonial warfare. Tensions continued to mount between French and British interests through the 1750s which spread into the Ohio River Valley. New France extended her reach down from Canada into the Great Lakes hemming in several British Colonies. Furthermore, French territory extended north from Louisiana towards the Great Lakes, threatening to surround the British settlements. This brought other colonies—Pennsylvania, Virginia, and the Carolinas—into direct contact with French interests intensifying the pressure on the colonies. No longer was New France merely New England or New York's problem.

On August 8, 1751, Edwards accepted the call to serve as pastor of the remote mission town of Stockbridge. Many portray this period in Edwards's life as an almost idyllic respite from the problems of Northampton, allowing Edwards to write freely on the true object of Edwards's intellectual energies: *Original Sin*, *Freedom of the Will*, and *The Nature of True Virtue*. But this post offered Edwards no respite—no respite from the struggle with the Williams family, from salary disputes, from the intransigence of his congregation, and not from warfare. As colonial tensions mounted, Edwards found himself on a new frontier more exposed than Northampton whose residents were just as active in martial events.

Within Edwards's first couple years in Stockbridge, he re-preached *Valiant and Resolute Soldiers* twice. It is unclear if Edwards re-appropriated this sermon as a result of specific military events or if Edwards sought to connect with the warrior ethos of the Stockbridge Mohican. This sermon used martial language to promote his brand of evangelical piety among the British and Natives. Attaining the kingdom of heaven was the task of a true warrior. One, according to Edwards, has to behave as a "valiant and resolute soldier" to gain a deep and personal relationship with God. In both 1752 and 1753, Edwards exhorted his congregation to pursue the kingdom of God as a soldier takes an enemy country.

While France and Britain remained formally at peace, the signs of war were readily apparent across the frontier. The *Boston Gazette* reported the rumblings of war from Virginia and South Carolina.[14] The April 16 edition described the "Storm rising in the West" and published the first of three installments of George Washington's journal for his diplomatic expedition to the French. At the end of April, the *Gazette* published Governor Shirley's speeches to the Massachusetts Assembly highlighting the tensions along the Kennebec River to the east and Crown Point to the west. Furthermore, Shirley called for Massachusetts to send delegates to a pan-colonial conference with the Six Nations that would be known as the Albany Conference of 1754.

With these tensions mounting all around the Native community, Edwards preached the sermon *Warring with the Devil* in April of 1754. While this sermon referenced no specific military event, it was a plain and direct call for Natives to view their spiritual life in the same terms as they approach warfare. Edwards encouraged the Mohicans to defend themselves from the attacks of the devil, but his advice seemed particularly tailored to the stereotype of Natives: avoid idleness, strong drink, exercise control over one's children, and to avoid merely wandering about. These were perennial complaints the British lodged against all Native communities and became a part of Edwards' spiritual agenda for the Mohicans. The one common exhortation Edwards made to both communities concerned the need for prayer.

The British situation grew more serious over the summer. In July 1754, George Washington's forces were captured at Fort Necessity accepting terms which admitted British wrongdoing. The colonies gathered at Albany to propose a Plan of Union which was ultimately rejected but illustrated the seriousness of the British position. This position was described by a drastically worded opinion piece in the October 1 edition of the *Boston Gazette*. Outlining the religious problem of France's encroachment, the author claimed that French Papism was "an impious, absurd, blood-shedding religion, a religion as disgraceful to human understandings as it is injurious to the sacred ties of social benevolence." It decried the French encroachment in Maine and warned of attacks emanating

---

14. *Boston Gazette*, March 19, 16, April 2, 1754.

from Crown Point. Furthermore, France was in a position to connect their territories in Quebec with the Mississippi through the Ohio River Valley: "This is the great finishing stroke of their ambitious and highly to be dreaded encroachments."[15] This article represented the fears of all New Englanders, especially those who lived along the frontiers. Rumors circulated about a war party which left from Crown Point and specifically named Stockbridge as a potential target.

In November 1754, Edwards reached into his sermonic catalog to re-preach *The Sovereignty of God's Mercy*. Originally, this sermon was given in celebration of the battle of Culloden. But this seemed like an entirely different context. While still highlighting the religious context between Protestant and Catholic forces, Edwards may have struck a different chord with this iteration. Divine mercies, according to this sermon, are bestowed by the arbitrary will of God, whereas judgments are administered according to a rule. The presentation of this sermon amid Britain's—and Stockbridge's—precarious position would have served as a cautionary tale. Without one's embrace of Edwards's brand of piety, Native war-making efforts would not go well.

Shortly after Edwards re-preached *The Sovereignty of God's Mercy*, the Stockbridge Mohicans found themselves as central actors in this martial drama. In December of 1754, the Massachusetts Assembly approved the enlistment of Stockbridge Indians, three of their Native leaders received military commissions, and a company of fifty Stockbridge Indians left for Albany as scouts. Over the winter of 1754–55, all signs pointed to another wide-scale outbreak of hostilities with Stockbridge and her Native sons on the front lines. The *Boston Gazette* reported news reaching Jamaica of the expectation of war with France,[16] rumors of a French fleet arriving in Nova Scotia,[17] reports of regiments departing Britain for America,[18] and the departure of General Braddock *en route* to Virginia.[19]

In early March of 1755, Edwards preached three martial sermons that addressed these growing anxieties. First, on March 4, Edwards dusted off his sermon *Enemies Confounded and Broken*. Anticipating a widespread outbreak of hostilities, Edwards reiterated his conviction that

15. *Boston Gazette*, October 1, 1754.
16. *Boston Gazette*, February 4, 1755.
17. *Boston Gazette*, February 11, 1755.
18. *Boston Gazette*, February 18, 1755.
19. *Boston Gazette*, February 25, 1755.

the French Catholic forces would find their destruction throughout the colonies. This conviction was not the result of careful analysis of military assets, strategic positions, or tactical advantages, but the testimony of the Biblical evidence.

Edwards echoed this sentiment the following day in a sermon for a private fast, *God Is He Who Orders*. This sermon claimed that it was God and God alone who ordered all things in war "just as he pleases." God, according to Edwards, is stronger than men, wiser than the devil, and gives armies their strength. Edwards exhorted his congregation to trust in the power of God to see one's enemies "confounded and broken." This sermon resonates well with the third martial sermon delivered on the precipice of fighting, *The Sovereignty of God's Mercy*. Originally preached as a celebration of the royalist victory at the Battle of Culloden, Edwards uses this sermon to emphasize a theological point that may have been foreign to his Native listeners. This sermon echoes the thought that victory and defeat are administered by God according to His mercy and pleasure. Taken as a series, these three sermons highlight God's intent on overcoming his enemies and the spiritual dimension of physical battles.

By the summer of 1755, it became clear that this conflict was larger than New England or even the American colonies. Diplomacy on the continent intensified and nations began preparing for another global war. News reports from Boston reflected a positive outlook on Britain's prospects. Reports followed the arrival of General Braddock and his march to the Monongahela. The June 9 edition of the *Gazette* published a poem reflecting an optimistic expectation: "Too long, Britania! Gentle to her foes." Reports of robust enlistments and success in Nova Scotia filled the columns of the *Gazette*. Edwards would preach another triad of martial sermons over the summer of 1755.

In July of 1755, Edwards re-preached his classic description of war in *Duties of Christians in a Time of War*. The first time Edwards presented this sermon, New England stood on the precipice of war with France prior to the expedition to Louisbourg. With Gen. Braddock *en route* to Fort Duquesne, Gen. Shirley approaching Oswego, and Gen. Johnson departing for Crown Point, New England once again held her breath during this calm before the storm. Edwards took this opportunity to remind his British neighbors that, while this war put Stockbridge in danger, it was their duty to oppose the antichristian kingdom of France. Likewise, to his

Native congregation, this sermon would affirm the compatibility of the Christian's call to war with the Mohican warrior ethos.[20]

The second of Edwards's martial sermons that summer came later in July: *In the Name of the Lord of Hosts*. Edwards's congregation for this sermon soon marched to war under Col. Ephriam William Jr., joining Gen. William Johnson in his assault on the French outpost of Crown point. This had been the staging ground for most of the combined French and Indian assaults along the Connecticut River Valley and one of Col. Stoddard's primary targets in the previous inter-colonial war. The sermon used the story of David and Goliath as a cautionary tale illustrating victory for those who trust in God and defeat for those who don't. Edwards noted that not only do their French enemies trust in themselves, but they practice a religion "contrary to God's word" echoing the optimism of the time. While the British would win the battle in September, they would have to wait four years for the capitulation of Crown Point.

This optimism ended after Braddock's defeat and subsequent death. News of this defeat appeared as almost an afterthought in the August 11 edition of the *Boston Gazette*. This defeat was crushing to both the British war efforts as well as Edwards's optimistic expectations. After this loss, there was no previous sermon on which Edwards could fall back. On August 28, 1755 Edwards preached *God's People Tried by a Battle Lost*. This sermon brings together many of the themes of previous sermons to give a warning and an encouragement. First, the American Colonies cannot expect to win without a dependence on God; Secondly, oftentimes God humbles a people before he delivers them. Though this sermon reflected the "disappointment and confusion" of the defeat, Edwards preserved hope and optimism.

The darkness of Braddock's defeat gave way to small lights of optimism, specifically Gen. Johnson's victory at Lake George. However, in the fall of 1755, the *Gazette* reported a plethora of Indian attacks from Williamsburg to Albany and news of martial preparations on the continent. It was widely acknowledged that a rupture between England and France was imminent, marking a reversal of war's traditional trajectory. These circumstances moved Edwards to reach back into his catalog of sermons to re-preach *The Armor of God*. In the same way New England braced herself for widespread warfare prior to its original delivery (July 1744), New England prepared for a broadening of the conflict to include

20. The best modern treatment of Braddock's expedition, including a discussion of Edwards's sermon, is David Preston's *Braddock's Defeat*.

more British regulars than had ever seen American soil. As war is chiefly spiritual, according to Edwards, one's preservation is dependent on one's spiritual condition. And one's spiritual condition is dependent on "behav[ing] ourselves in the business of religion as those that are engaged in the most dangerous war."[21] No one knew if the road ahead would follow the path of Braddock or Johnson, so Edwards simplified his advice to Stockbridge: take care of your physical and spiritual safety.

Stockbridge warriors would figure prominently into British strategy in 1756. Three Stockbridge Indians received commissions: Jacob Cheeksaunkun as captain, Joseph Naunauphtaul as lieutenant, and Solomon Uhhaunauwaunmut as ensign; they were to lead a company of fifty Stockbridge Indians.[22] British North America needed all the help it could get after Britain officially declared war on France on May 17, 1756. Before the Stockbridge Indians marched with Gen. (Gov.) Shirley to Oswego, Edwards preached another sermon for their deployment. Again, Edwards reached into his oeuvre to deliver *Walking Righteously, Speaking Uprightly*. Originally preached amidst rumors of the arrival of the French fleet, New England found herself again under the pall of war. Edwards assured his congregation in Stockbridge, as he had in Northampton, that the threat of war need not trouble those who "walk righteously" and "speak uprightly." God promised not just defense, but success, in a time of war to his people. Therefore, this sermon was both an encouragement as well as a warning to the Stockbridge warriors to take their refuge in God.

Throughout the summer of 1756, the Stockbridge warriors would distinguish themselves in battle. Captain Rogers invited some of them to join his ranger unit conducting reconnaissance and scouting missions while others would operate under Gen. Shirley. Edwards used this time to complete his work *Original Sin* and visit with his daughter Esther visiting from New Jersey. Britain would lose both Fort Ontario and Fort William Henry to the French. And Edwards would lose a son-in-law.[23] Shortly thereafter, Edwards received the invitation to preside over the College of New Jersey (later Princeton University) and leave the frontier with its martial anxieties. Edwards passed away in February of 1758 in New Jersey after complications from a smallpox vaccine. Edwards never had the chance to see the glorious military victories which he expected

21. See Edwards's sermon *The Armor of God*, published for the first time in this book, on p. 150; the doctrine of this sermon, quoted here, also appears in WJE 25:722.

22. Frazier, *Mohicans*, 116.

23. Rev. Aaron Burr, Esther's husband, died September 24, 1756.

and for which he prayed. Crown Point fell to the British in the winter of 1759 and Fort Niagara fell in July of 1759. On September 13, 1759, British General James Wolfe defeated Montcalm on the Plains of Abraham defeating the French in Quebec. Finally, British forces captured Montreal on September 8, 1760. Edwards's vision of a land free of French Catholicism was to come true.

Conclusion

It is widely accepted that Jonathan Edwards was one of the great thinkers and preachers of colonial America. *A Divine and Supernatural Light*, *The Excellency of Christ*, *Sinners in the Hands of an Angry God*—these sermons stand as monuments to the genius of Edwards and as representative of an American movement. The sermons contained in this collection focused on such a specific topic as warfare may not stand as representative as some others of Edwards, but they have their significance.

First, these sermons demonstrate the personal character of Edwards's preaching. Sometimes depicted as a monolith, a stern theological statue, the picture of Edwards presented in these sermons offers the student of history a different portrait. When the shadow of war fell on Northampton and the Connecticut River Valley, Edwards concerned himself with addressing the fears and anxieties of his flock. Through these martial sermons, Edwards provided a framework within which to understand war, an encouragement of God's protection, and a prescription for ensuring one's safety. Sermons, for Edwards, were not cathedrals of the mind, but a personal application of biblical and theological truth to the circumstances of his parishioners.

Secondly, these sermons are a point of reference to explore the impact of theological ideas on the development of warfare. Most of Edwards's parishioners were either martial actors in warfare or related to those who marched off to faraway places such as Louisbourg, Albany, and beyond. One can examine the military careers of Northampton soldiers such as Maj. Seth Pomeroy, Cpt. John Baker, Zadoc Danks, or Edwards's own uncle, Col. John Stoddard, among a host of others, to see the fingerprint of Edwards's martial thought. Edwards designed his sermons to impact the lives of the people sitting in the meetinghouse pews as they marched off to war with Edwards' sermons fresh in their hearts.

Thirdly, these sermons demonstrate the grand scope of Edwards's theological vision. Edwards's application of revivalist thought to the machinations of global warfare illustrates how Edwards thought of his role in God's purposes. God's redemptive purposes, as outlined in his ambitious series *History of the Work of Redemption*, are bigger than the individual or even the congregation. Edwards claimed in these martial sermons that God's redemptive purposes moved beyond the individual, congregational, societal, or imperial. God's purpose was to create a universal kingdom through the advance of the gospel in people's hearts, and sometimes war would be the instrument of the gospel's advance.

Fourthly, these sermons illustrate the integration of Edwards's theological vision. Some scholars may label these sermons variously as political, revivalist, military, or millennial. I don't think Edwards himself made such distinctions. Theological truth, for Edwards, was a unified whole and could not be separated quite as discretely. Biblical material that addressed the nature of one's soul could be applied to the operations of nations, law, warfare, and a host of other implications. There was no area of life unaffected by the redemptive purposes of God. Many of Edwards's other sermons demonstrate the theological force which he brings to bear on various subjects: prayer, communion, the will, etc. Still, other sermons demonstrate his dramatic engagement with personal matters of the mind, the heart, and the soul. These wartime sermons bring together Edwards's personal, national, and cosmic concerns into one unified whole.

During his estimable career, Edwards probed the mystery of the human will, plumbed the depths of the majesty of God, developed a new language for traditional Reformed beliefs, and presided over an outpouring of religious fervor. Edwards brought his intellectual and pastoral prowess to bear on the events that consumed New England in his day: warfare. In this lies the genius of Edwards. His ability to operate on a grand cosmic canvas while simultaneously operating on a personal and intimate level.

Part 1

British Wars Abroad

In Seeking Heaven Persons Should Behave as Valiant, Resolute Soldiers

February 1741

A DECLARATION OF WAR between Britain and Spain in 1739 inaugurated nearly a decade of military conflict between Britain and various Catholic powers in Europe. In response to this declaration, Britain engaged the Spanish in several arenas throughout the Atlantic World. Using Gibraltar as a base of operations, Britain attacked Cadiz and Malaga on the Spanish mainland. Using Jamaica as another base, Britain moved against targets in the West Indies as far south as Porto La Plata (Argentina) but focused her expedition on the Spanish fort of Cartagena. To supplement these professional forces, Col. William Blakeney traveled the colonies recruiting American volunteer to form their own regiment commanded by Virginian Col. William Gooch. Throughout the summer and fall of 1740, a recruiting campaign swept across the colonies yielding thirty-five hundred American volunteers from eleven different colonies. These volunteers were amateurs, mostly neophytes, serving a long way from home alongside professional soldiers. By the winter of 1740–41, these volunteers were *en route* to Jamaica to join the British expedition.

Colonial involvement in Britain's war was significant for a number of reasons. First, it demonstrated the colony's attachment to their British identity: Britain's war was New England's war. The colonial identification with the British cause centered on their common "Protestant Interest" against their Catholic rivals. The third arena of this conflict demonstrates colonial identification. When London authorized attacks on Spanish holdings, James Oglethorpe, British officer and governor of Georgia, organized a series of expeditions against the Spanish city of St. Augustine in what is now Florida. Second, the integration of American volunteer forces with professional British soldiers caused widespread confusion over issues of chain-of-command, the use of British military disciple, and impressment. Third, Britain's war with Spain began to distract from another conflict boiling closer to Northampton.

In August of 1739, Whitefield arrived in the colonies preaching his dramaturgical brand of piety. While Col. Blakeney pressed his campaign to recruit volunteers for the expedition to the West Indies, Whitefield swept through New England in the fall of 1740. Edwards, having presided over a season of revival, supported this burgeoning religious reawakening in Northampton. Revival, for Edwards, was a goal towards which each Christian has the duty to press. *In Seeking Heaven Persons Should Behave as Valiant, Resolute Soldiers* represents Edwards's prescription for participating in a new, affective, and personal piety.

Against the landscape of war and revival, Edwards preached *Valiant and Resolute Soldiers* in three separate units during February of 1741. Drawing on the imagery of the expedition to the West Indies, Edwards employed martial language to promote spiritual ends. This sermon was an extended analogy, comparing the efforts of soldiers in taking a country to the efforts expected of every Christian in obtaining heaven. In the same way that the soldier must stand fast amidst the roaring of the cannon, the Christian must demonstrate resolve in the face of the devil—the roaring lion. Edwards preached a call to his congregation to make a "resolution" to devote themselves to taking heaven "by violence." This resolution requires sacrifice: "Don't expect to enter and take possession of the kingdom with a whole skin." Anyone who pursues heaven should expect to face opposition and, therefore, should "count the cost." However, heaven is so great a prize, it is worth a resolute commitment even if it requires the loss of a "right hand or a right foot or a right eye." Edwards preached *Valiant and Resolute Soldiers* to a congregation that, in Edwards's estimation, had yet to pursue "awakening" with the proper vigor.

* * * * *

This sermon was edited by Craig Woods for the Jonathan Edwards Center. The manuscript is thirty-eight duodecimo-sized leaves. Edwards's original date of February 1741 appears at the top right of the first page.

Beside it are several re-preaching notations: one in shorthand apparently for an unspecified occasion, possibly in Springfield; at Boston, October 1753; and, "Part of this to the Stockbridge Indians, June 1752" (for this last, Edwards also used a portion of his earlier sermon on Matt 11:12 [no. 177], from May 1731). According to Rev. Daniel Wadsworth's Diary, Edwards also delivered this sermon in Hartford on April 15, 1741. For the Boston re-delivery, Edwards made a number of revisions, including changes in words and phrases and excision of selected passages, concentrated in the first ten leaves of the manuscript; and for that or another of the re-preachings, he highlighted passages (especially in the first preaching unit) with vertical lines in the left margins. The "Redemption" symbol (which Edwards wrote on sermons he intended to consult for his "History of Redemption" project) also appears at the top left of the first page.

In Seeking Heaven Persons Should Behave as Valiant, Resolute Soldiers

Matthew 11:12

And from the days of John the Baptist until now the kingdom of heaven suffereth violence, and the violent take it by force.

It is supposed that John the Baptist began to preach about three years and an half before Christ began his public ministry. Before he began to preach, it was an exceeding dull and dead time among the Jews, as to the interest of true religion; but there was an extraordinary pouring out of the Spirit and general awakening attended his preaching, and a general awakening.[1] It is said that all "Jerusalem, and all Judea, and all the region round about Jordan, went out to him, and were baptized of him in Jordan, confessing their sins" [Matt. 3:5–6].

The awakening seemed to reach all sorts of persons: as the publicans, that were looked upon as some of the off-scouring of the earth;[2] and the soldiers, that commonly were a sort of men at the greatest distance from religious concern. And which is more remarkable still, the awakening reached their great men, or the Sadducees, that were men of learning

---

1. In revising for re-preaching, JE amended this passage to read: "It is evident that John the Baptist began to preach the kingdom of God some time before Christ began his public ministry. Before this, it was an exceeding dead time among the Jews as to the interest of true religion; but there was an extraordinary pouring out of the Spirit and general awakening attended his preaching."

2. In revising for re-preaching, JE deleted "off-scouring of the earth" and inserted "most wicked of men."

and were a kind of deists;[3] and the Pharisees, that were notoriously self-righteous and proud of their godliness. All sorts seemed to be deeply affected and came crying, "[What] shall we do?" John preached that the kingdom of heaven was at hand, and many of his hearers were very earnest to obtain that kingdom, and great numbers were converted.

And therefore Christ says as he does in the text, "And from the days of John the Baptist until now the kingdom of heaven suffereth violence, and the violent take it by force."

In the words, I would observe three things:

1. What the state and privilege of those that are saved is compared to: they are compared to a kingdom. The kingdom is the kingdom of heaven.[4] The privileges spoken of are the privileges, possessions and honors of a kingdom, and the country where this kingdom is, is heaven.[5] It is [not] a kingdom in any earthly country, as the kingdom of Judea, or the kingdom of Syria, or the kingdom of Egypt, or the empire of Rome, which was a kingdom that extended [to] great part of the lower world; but the kingdom of heaven.

2. We may observe what men's obtaining of this kingdom is compared to: viz., to the taking of a country or kingdom in war. When men obtain a kingdom that they are not the natural heirs of, it is most commonly done by war. Strangers seldom get the possession of earthly kingdoms any other way. So it was that the kingdom of Babylon was obtained by the Medes and Persians; and so it was that the kingdom of Persia was taken by Alexander. So it was that the kingdom of Syria, and the kingdom of Egypt, and the land of Judea, and most of the kingdoms and countries of the[6] known world, had[7] been taken by the Romans and were then in their possession, when Christ spoke the words of the text.

3. We may observe what the manner of persons' obtaining the privileges and blessings of the kingdom of heaven is compared to: viz.,

---

3. In revising for re-preaching, JE changed the foregoing part of this sentence to read: "And which is more remarkable still, the awakening reached their great men and men of learning, or the Sadduccees, that were a sort of free-thinker."

4. In revising for re-preaching, JE deleted this sentence.

5. In revising for re-preaching, JE changed the latter part of this sentence to read: "and the proper country of this kingdom is heaven."

6. In revising for re-preaching, JE inserted "then."

7. MS: "has."

to the manner of resolute soldiers taking a country or kingdom in war that is strongly defended against 'em. It "suffers violence": that supposes great opposition, and they take it by force; they will have it; they are resolved to take it; they are like resolute soldiers that will take the country they go against.

Doctrine

Persons in seeking heaven should behave in like manner as valiant, resolute soldiers do in taking a country or kingdom in which they are strongly opposed.

As particularly,

I. When they first set out and engage in this business, they must consider the difficulty of the work they undertake. Those are not commonly good soldiers that are rash and inconsiderate in their undertakings. Many that are very bold at home, and appear forward to go forth on an expedition that are unexperienced in war, and don't know nor consider what it is to fight, commonly prove miserable soldiers. When it comes to trial,[8] they are much in boasting of what they will do, and seem not to doubt but that they shall have success, and so are very forward to go; but 'tis because they don't know what they are going about,[9] they don't know what belongs to war, and therefore prove poor soldiers in the[10] battle. They become faint-hearted and soon discouraged when they enter the enemy's country.[11]

Those soldiers that are truly valiant and prove so in battle,[12] are those that courageously undertake the work they go about as being sensible beforehand of the difficulties of it. That king is very unwise that goes forth to war against another king, to enter into his country and take his kingdom from him, without considering what force he has, and what force he must encounter. Luke 14:31–33, "Or what king, going to make war against another king, sitteth not down first, and consulteth whether

---

8. "Trial" is a later insertion.

9. In revising for re-preaching, JE deleted "they don't know what they are going about."

10. In revising for re-preaching, JE inserted "field of."

11. In revising for re-preaching, JE deleted this sentence.

12. In revising for re-preaching, JE deleted this word and inserted "the engagement."

he be able with ten thousand to meet him that cometh against him with twenty thousand? Or else, while the other is yet a great way off, he sendeth an ambassage, and desireth conditions of peace. So likewise, whosoever he be of you that forsaketh not all that he hath, he cannot be my disciple."

It commonly proves a great work to conquer a kingdom, and there are many difficulties to be gone through before it can be accomplished. There must be a forsaking of friends. The soldiers that go forth on the expedition, must have the toil and fatigue of a long journey, a wearisome travail, or a dangerous voyage, and they must expect to leave their former, easy, quiet way of living at home, and to fight for their lives, and to have many hard conflicts and sore battles. It is commonly an hard thing to take one city, or to win one battle, but they must have many such hard spells before the work is finished and the work is taken.[13]

So it is a great undertaking that persons enter upon when they set out to get heaven.[14] 'Tis a very great work that they are going about, and they ought to consider the difficulties of it thoroughly beforehand, that they may be prepared to go through 'em.

II. They must as it were leave their own country, and that quietness and ease and those pleasant things which they had in their native home. When men go on expedition to take a country and kingdom, they leave their own country. Though they lived at home in ease and quietness, and slept quietly without having any enemies to molest them, or very great difficulties to encounter, yet they leave all;[15] they leave that pleasing accommodation they had at home, to go into another country.

He that goes a-warfare, don't expect to fare as he did at home. He expects hard lodging and hard fare till the warfare is over.

And if they go to take a country or kingdom, with a design to live in that country thenceforward, which is such a taking we here speak of,[16] then they take a final leave of their own country and former home.

---

13. Three blank lines appear at this point in the MS.

14. In revising for re-preaching, JE deleted "set out to get heaven" and interlineated "engage in the business of seeking time of salvation."

15. In revising for re-preaching, JE deleted this word and inserted "forsake all the quiet circumstances."

16. In revising for re-preaching, JE amended the previous part of this sentence to read: "which is such a taking of a kingdom as the text speaks of."

So those that seek heaven, should as it were forsake their native country, with all the[17] ease and quietness, and pleasant enjoyments of it that are so agreeable to corrupt nature. This world is as it were our native country, and the ease, and profits and pleasures of it, are as it were the enjoyments and accommodations of our native home. These those must forsake that would obtain heaven. Ps. 45:10, "Hearken, O daughter, and consider, and incline thine ear; forget also thine own people, and thy father's house."

So in that forementioned Luke 14:33, "So likewise, whosoever he be of you that forsaketh not all that he hath, he cannot be my disciple."

They must forsake their way of living in the gratification of their sensual appetites that they used to allow themselves in, and must endure hardness as good soldiers. 2 Tim. 2:3–4, "Thou therefore endure hardness, as a good soldier of Jesus Christ. No man that warreth entangleth himself with the affairs of this life; that he may please him who has chosen him to be a soldier."

III.[18] Resolute soldiers that go forth to take a country or kingdom that is strongly defended, won't be disheartened and discouraged by the frightful appearances and threatenings of opposition that they are like to meet with. If once, upon thorough consideration, they have listed in the service and have begun the enterprise, they won't be easily disheartened and put to flight if the enemies appear many in number, and seem to be drawn up in dreadful array and make a formidable appearance. If they seem to be of gigantic stature, and to be terribly armed and to be very dreadful in their threatenings, such things as these won't dishearten them, or deter them from their purpose; but they will go forward and meet the enemy and try it out with them. When they come to see the mouths of cannon against 'em, that won't stop 'em in their course, nor will their roaring put 'em to flight;[19] and the sight of the high walls and strong fortresses, by which the towers and cities of that kingdom are defended, won't discourage 'em. They have a strong resolution that supports 'em and carries 'em along against all these things: for they are set and resolved and violent in the matter, and are determined, if possible, let

---

17. In revising for re-preaching, JE inserted "outward, carnal."

18. In revising for re-preaching, JE inserted: "Valiant and."

19. In revising for re-preaching, JE deleted the foregoing part of the sentence beginning with "but they will go forward . . ."

what will be in the way, and whatever opposition they meet with, they will take the kingdom.

So it should be with those that seek the kingdom of heaven. Though there seem to be innumerable difficulties in the way, a vast host of enemies standing ready to pitch battle with [them], that look with a very threatening, formidable countenance;[20] though it looks like a very great attempt, and they don't see how they shall ever surmount the difficulties of it; though there be many things that seem to suggest to their minds that it will be vain for them to go forward—they shall be slain in battle; 'tis best to give over the enterprise, and return back again from whence they came—yet they must not give way to such suggestions, nor be disheartened by any discouraging appearances, but resolutely go on and encounter the difficulties, and engage with the strongest of the enemies. They must press forward as it were against the mouth of the cannon, and attack the strongest fortresses and press forward to scale the walls[21] against all the engines and batteries of the enemy. The children of Israel's taking the land of Canaan, that land of promise, was a type of taking heaven. Many of them were discouraged when they heard of the giants and high walls, and so failed, and never entered into that good land. But others were courageous,[22] and went up and took possession of the land; they were of a resolute spirit in the matter.[23]

This was the direction that was often given to Joshua and the people, as necessary for them, as they would take the land. Deut. 31:6, "Be strong and of a good courage, fear not, nor be afraid of them"; and so v. 7, "And Moses called unto Joshua, and said unto him in the sight of all Israel, Be strong and of a good courage: for thou must go with this people unto the land which the Lord hath sworn unto their fathers to give them; and thou shalt cause them to inherit it"; and v. 23, "And he gave Joshua the son of Nun a charge, and said, Be strong and of a good courage: for thou shalt bring the children of Israel into the land which I swore unto them."

---

20. In revising for re-preaching, JE amended the preceding part of this sentence to read, "pitch battle with them that appear with a threatening, formidable countenance."

21. In revising for re-preaching, JE deleted: "attack the strongest fortresses and press forward to scale the walls."

22. In revising for re-preaching, JE deleted "were courageous" and inserted "of a more resolute and courageous spirit."

23. In revising for re-preaching, JE deleted "they were of a resolute spirit in the matter."

IV. They lay out all their strength in encountering the opposition and difficulties in the way of their taking the country or kingdom. They engage the enemy in battle, and therein exert themselves to the utmost, for 'tis for their lives. There is no sort of bodily exercise that ever men are engaged in, wherein they are wont to lay out themselves more, than in encountering their enemies in a pitched battle, at least in the ancient way of fighting, which was not at a distance with guns,[24] but head-to-head[25] with swords and spears. Thus if ever men would exert themselves, and do their utmost: because life depended on the issue, and every motion and action is for life and for victory.

And so resolute soldiers, that are resolved if possible to take a city or fortress they besiege, how do they lay out themselves to batter down the walls, and how do they violently press forward to scale the walls or to enter a breach, when there is a host stands against 'em to keep 'em back, with all their might and weapons of war to oppose 'em.[26]

So those that would obtain the kingdom of heaven exert themselves. They should do what their hand finds to do with their might. They should exert all their strength in this great business, and in opposing the lusts of their hearts and the many temptations they meet with in the way.

V. Valiant, resolute soldiers, that seek to take a kingdom that is strongly defended, will bear many wounds before they will give over their enterprise. They are willing to expose themselves to wounds. They don't go into the war with a design to be tender of their flesh, or to be very careful that they don't break their skin. They will lose a great deal of blood before they will give out; yea, if they lose some of the members of their bodies, as an hand or a foot, still they will fight.[27] So it should be with them that seek to obtain heaven: they must not be tender of their worldly

---

24. In revising for re-preaching, JE amended the preceding part of this sentence to read: "encountering their enemies in war, at least in the ancient way of fighting, which was not chiefly at a distance with missive weapons."

25. Alternate reading: "hand-to-hand."

26. In revising for re-preaching, JE amended the latter part of this sentence to read: "a city or fortress they besiege, do greatly lay out themselves, do violently press forward to scale the walls or to enter a breach though an host stands against 'em with all their might."

27. In revising for re-preaching, JE amended the foregoing to read: "They will lose a great deal of blood before their courage will fail; yea, they will continue to fight though they lose some of the members of their bodies," deleting the remainder of the sentence.

interest or carnal enjoyments and inclinations; they must be willing to deny themselves, to be greatly hurt in their worldly interest, and to do things and bear things that are very cross to their natural inclination, exceeding hard to flesh and blood. Yea, they must be willing to part with a right hand, or a right foot or a right eye.

VI. Valiant and resolute soldiers that go forth to take a kingdom in which they expect to meet with strong opposition, won't give over their enterprise because they have failed in some attempts. If they were not successful at the first onset, yea, if the enemy seemed for a while[28] to gain many advantages, and they have [been] put to worse in several skirmishes, and have lost ground, and things for a considerable time seemed to go cross, and the enemy from time to time has the better: yet their courage don't soon fail. Still they will renew their attempts: they will make the battle more strong; they will correct their former errors and oversights; they will exert themselves so much the more violently.

So it should be with those that seek heaven. They should not be discouraged because[29] they have been unsuccessful hitherto, or because they seem to fail in past attempts and they seem to be further off rather than nearer, and their enemies seem to have more and more advantages against 'em. It should not discourage 'em, but should only make 'em to consider wherein they have erred and failed heretofore, and correct their former errors, and apply themselves to their work with redoubled earnestness.

VII. Resolute and valiant soldiers do and undergo all this, while they are uncertain of success. They don't know what the event[30] will be. The event of war is uncertain when they undertake so great and difficult a work, and go through those great labors and hardships. They don't know whether ever they shall take the kingdom; they don't know but instead of that, they shall lose their lives, but yet that is no prevailing objection with them. They venture upon nothing but that general encouragement, that the way to be successful is to be valiant and resolute, and that providence generally favors and succeeds such.

28. In revising for re-preaching, JE wrote "seem," but this has been treated as an incomplete insertion.

29. In revising for re-preaching, JE deleted "They should not be discouraged because" and inserted "If."

30. In revising for re-preaching, JE deleted this word and inserted "issue."

So it should be with those that seek the kingdom of heaven. Many are ready to say they could be willing to take a great deal of pains and endure a great deal of difficulty if they knew they should be successful at last, but they must be willing and not know beforehand what the event will be, but must venture on that encouragement that this is the only way to be successful: and God ordinarily succeeds those that seek the kingdom of heaven in this manner.

VIII. And lastly, valiant and resolute soldiers that go forth to take a kingdom that is strongly defended, they oftentimes resolve that they will either conquer and win the prize, or die in battle. That is what they are determined upon, that seeing they have undertaken the business, they won't return again without having accomplished [their enterprise].[31] And if they don't conquer, this shall be business they will die in. So should it be with those that seek the kingdom of heaven: they should resolve upon it, that whether they are successful or unsuccessful, yet this should be the one thing that they do, and this they will continue to do, even strive to enter in at the strait gate. And if they are not successful, death shall find 'em in the way of doing their utmost. And [if][32] they perish, they will perish striving in the use of all appointed means, and struggling and exerting themselves therein to the utmost of their power. This should be the way in which persons should seek their salvation.

Application

[*Use* I of] *Exhortation* to all, to seek the kingdom of heaven in this way. You all are probationers for the kingdom of heaven. All hope to obtain it; now has been set before you the way in which you should seek it. Don't vainly expect to obtain the kingdom of heaven easily. Let no person foolishly flatter himself that he can at any time, when he pleases, with but little difficulty, get salvation. If you enter upon the affair with such a notion, you will be very like to fail.

Those[33] that are now gone forth out of this land on expedition to the West Indies, they heard that the Spanish countries that they were going against were rich countries, that they abounded in silver and gold and many precious pleasant things. And probably they went with an

---

31. JE added "their enterprize" in revising for re-preaching.
32. JE added "if" in revising for re-preaching.
33. A later bracket precedes this paragraph.

expectation of obtaining many of these things, but they were not wise if they expected this without first going through a great deal of difficulty and hardship. They did not act prudently if they undertook the service expecting only a pleasant diversion of it, or if they expected any other than to fight, and did not go prepared to engage in many an hard and sore battle: for there is no prospect of their winning those precious things in these countries in any other way, for they are strongly fortified, and great preparations are made to oppose them.

So neither do those act prudently that undertake the business of religion, hoping to win the precious things of the heavenly country in any other way than a way of earnest strife, many sore conflicts and long-continued struggling.[34]

Whoever of you[35] think to take the kingdom of heaven, 'tis a great enterprise that you have before you. Don't undertake it without considering what belongs to war. Prepare for the toil and fatigue of a long and tedious travail, and don't think ever to obtain heaven without as it were forsaking your own country, without quitting all the slothful ease and quietness and carnal enjoyments of this world, your native country, and quitting them finally and forever. And expect no other than to meet with many things that will look dark and discouraging; don't think to win heaven without facing the enemy, yea, a mighty host of enemies, and don't think it any strange thing to see 'em appear with a terrible countenance.[36] Don't expect any other than to meet with many things in your way that will appear exceeding discouraging and dark; expect no other than to go abreast against the mouths of cannon, and don't give back for their roaring.

And be willing to lay out your strength; be willing to engage the enemy in battle, though they are very strong; don't, if possible, give the enemy an inch of ground, but violently press forward and scale the high walls of the city. And[37] don't expect to enter and take possession of the kingdom with a whole skin: expect to receive many wounds in the battle, and to leave right hands and right eyes behind. If you may but enter alive and at last have quiet possession of the kingdom, though it be with one

---

34. In the MS, a later closing bracket follows this sentence.

35. In revising for re-preaching, JE inserted: "are seeking salvation and."

36. In revising for re-preaching, after some slight emendations, JE deleted the remainder of the paragraph.

37. In revising for re-preaching, JE deleted the paragraph up to this point.

hand and one eye, think yourself well off.[38] And when you have once undertaken[39] this enterprise, don't give over because you meet with foils and disappointments. If your attempts seem to be baffled, your enemies seem to be too hard for you, yet go on, renew the battle with greater vigor than ever. And how many disappointments soever you meet with, how often soever the enemy seems to get the advantage and you seem to lose ground, don't let it discourage you, but go on striving, fighting and wrestling still, aiming at nothing less than winning the kingdom. And don't let that be a prevailing objection with you, that let you do what you will, you don't know that you shall be successful at last. What you may be sure of, [is] that if you don't go forward, you will not obtain.

There is not the least hope of your obtaining in any other way, than a way of pressing forward; that is the way to obtain.[40] You must come to this resolution, that you will take the kingdom or die in battle;[41] that if you die and perish at last, you will die sword in hand. Be obstinate (if I may so speak) in that resolution, that you will conquer or die in the conflict.

Consider,

First. The opposition is so great, that you can't reasonably expect to take the kingdom of heaven in any other way, than that of being violent. The walls of Canaan are high and built up to heaven, and there are giants that stand in the way to keep you out, as it was of old in Joshua's time. When they began to approach near the land, they were met with by Sihon, king of the Amorites, and Og the king of Bashan, who was a mighty giant as well as a king. And then they had a river to pass, and that in a great swell of its waters, for Jordan at that time overflowed all its banks. And when they had passed that river, there was a mighty combination of kings, five kings and all their hosts united in one. After they had conquered them, there was still a much greater host, a great number of kings were combined with their armies at the waters of Merom, being as the sand on the sea shore [Josh. 11].

---

38. In revising for re-preaching, JE deleted "well off" and inserted "most happy."

39. In revising for re-preaching, JE deleted "undertaken" and inserted "engaged in."

40. In revising for re-preaching, JE deleted "that is the way to obtain," and at the beginning of the next sentence inserted "Therefore."

41. In revising for re-preaching, JE deleted "that you will take the kingdom or die in battle."

So the devil and all his hosts, and the whole host of your lusts, stand in the way, to keep you from getting possession of the heavenly Canaan.

Second. The kingdom of heaven is worthy of all that be at all this pains and difficulty to take it. The country that you are called to go and take is an excellent country, a rich country; it abounds with the most precious things. If you can take it, you will be rich indeed, richer than the kings of the earth. There are more precious jewels, a thousand times, than any of the coffers of princes can afford.

It is a most plentiful country. There is a plenty of everything that you want, and a most pleasant country it is, a land flowing with milk and honey. There flow rivers of water of life, and there grows the tree of life. The whole land is a mere paradise, more pleasant than the garden of Eden. This country, if you can take it, you shall dwell in, and have the quiet possession of, and there you shall have a better rest and quietness than you had in your native home, before you went forth to war. And there you shall find balm that will soon heal all the wounds you received in battle, and shall even restore your limbs that you have lost. If you have lost a right hand or right eye, there you shall be made perfectly whole. The leaves of the tree of life shall heal you.

You may read the description of the city, the metropolis of that kingdom that you have to take, in Revelation [ch. 21].[42]

What do you think of such a city? Is not this worth striving and being violent for? All this glory shall be yours, if you take the kingdom of heaven.[43]

And you shall not only be a subject in that kingdom, but the kingdom, as a kingdom, shall be yours. You shall reign as king in that kingdom; you shall there sit on a throne, and be covered with glory.

[Christ] hath "made us kings and priests" [Rev. 5:10]. You shall reign as co-heirs with Christ, the great King of that kingdom: "heirs of God, and joint-heirs with Christ" [Rom. 8:17]; "I appoint unto you a kingdom, as my Father [hath appointed unto me]"; "I will give unto him to sit with me in my throne" [Rev. 3:21].

How great an honor and privilege will that be, to reign in such a kingdom as that. If you take the kingdom of heaven, you will have the possession [of] a thousand times better crown than the greatest monarch upon earth. It will be a crown of glory indeed. If you conquer the enemies

---

42. Three blank lines appear in the MS at this point.

43. In revising for re-preaching, JE deleted this paragraph and wrote above it, "Such is the city and such the kingdom."

that stand in the way to keep you out of that kingdom, you will obtain a better kingdom by it than Alexander did by conquering the world.[44]

Third. You are called of God to go forth, and strive to take this kingdom. 'Tis prudence for men, when they enlist to go forth on any great expedition to take some country, to see that their call is good, namely, that the country they go against is a rich country, and they shall have a great booty if they succeed. [It] would not be sufficient to move a man to undertake the difficulties and hardships of the expeditions, and to get through the fatigues and dangers of war, unless he see that his call was good. Men commonly look upon a call from their king to be a good call in such cases: but in this case, 'tis certain that you have a good call, for you have a call from God. You have as good a call as the children of Israel had to go to take Canaan. That was a great undertaking, and they would have been mad to have ventured upon it, when the inhabitants of Canaan were so many more, and mightier than they; but God called 'em, and that was warrant sufficient for them to venture to encounter the giants and kings of Canaan. Caleb and Joshua looked upon it so, and they were in the right of it.

So God calls you to go and encounter the difficulties that are in the way of your taking the kingdom of heaven. Let 'em look never so frightful, here is your warrant: God himself counsels and commands you to go and engage the enemy, and strive to take this kingdom.

Fourth. If you behave yourself in seeking heaven in the manner that has been spoken, there is great reason to think God will help you. If you give way to discouragement when you see great difficulties arise, and the enemy makes a formidable appearance and things look threatening; [if] you are faint-hearted and turn your back, or if you soon give out because of past disappointment; or are soon weary of the toil and fatigue of battle, and are tender of your flesh and over careful lest you should suffer wounds: you can't expect help from God. But if you hold your resolution to violently press forward, and quit you like men, then may you expect God's help. Thus Caleb and Joshua encouraged themselves, that God would help 'em against the Anakians. Num. 14:7–9, "And they spake unto all the company of the children of Israel, saying, The land, which we passed through to search it, is an exceeding good land. If the Lord delight in us, then he will bring us into this land, and give it us; a land which floweth with milk and honey. Only rebel not ye against the Lord, neither

---

44. In revising for re-preaching, JE deleted "did by conquering the world" and inserted "or Caesar or any of the great conquerors of the world."

fear ye the people of the land; for they are bread for us: their defense is departed from them, and the Lord is with us: fear them not." And God did help 'em wonderfully: he made the sun to stand still to help 'em, and sent down great hailstones on their enemies, so that the hailstones slew more than the swords, and discomfited their enemies before 'em.

Fifth.[45] If you are slothful, and faint-hearted and slack to go and possess the land, your carcasses will miserably fall in the wilderness. So it was with the children of Israel: they were discouraged by the difficulties they see in the way; they were discouraged with the length of the way, and the fatigues and hardships of their long travail, and had no heart to go to encounter the Anakians, or to attempt to scale the high walls of Canaan, and their carcasses fell in the wilderness, were awful tokens of God's wrath. They never enjoyed the blessings of that good land, but died miserably in the wilderness. So it will be with you, if you ben't willing to be violent for the kingdom of heaven. While others enjoy peace and rest in Canaan, and rejoice in the enjoyment of the pleasant fruits of it, are partaking of the milk and honey with which their land flows, and reigning as kings, and are feasting and rejoicing and praising God, the wild beasts, and fiery serpents and vultures of the wilderness shall be preying on your dead carcass—i.e., the devils, those roaring lions and fiery serpents, shall be preying on your poor damned soul.[46]

[II.] I have already made some general application of this Doctrine in an Use of Exhortation to all, to seek the kingdom of heaven in this way.

I would now make some more particular *Improvement* of the Doctrine.

First. By answering an inquiry persons may be ready to give, for their own instruction and direction.

Second. By putting an inquiry to the consciences of some persons for their conviction.

First. I would speak to some inquiries persons may be ready to put, for their own instruction and direction.

---

45. In revising for re-preaching, JE interlineated above the point: "5. Let it encourage you to consider how glorious that Captain of the salvation is that has undertaken."

46. In revising for re-preaching, JE added: "and shall continue so to do forever and ever." This marks the end of the first preaching unit; JE's recapitulation of the text, Doctrine, and major points covered thus far is omitted here.

Inquiry. As first, some may be ready to ask what they shall do, and to say, "How shall I go about to be thus violent to take the kingdom of [heaven]? how shall I thus exert myself, and lay out all my strength? Must I spend all my time in reading, and prayer and other religious exercises? Must not I attend my ordinary outward business? Must not I attend the business I have to do abroad, or the business I have to do in the family I belong to, and must not I take my necessary rest and sleep? How then must I behave myself as a resolute soldier, fighting with many and strong enemies to take a country or kingdom?

I would *Answer* to this *Inquiry*:

1. By showing what work you have to do, that will require as much earnestness and struggling as is used by resolute soldiers in taking a kingdom strongly defended.
2. I would show you what you have to strive and wrestle with.
3. I would show after what manner you should strive in these things.

1. I would show what work you have to do, that requires such earnestness.

Your business is thoroughly to reform your life, and to live in the strict and thorough performance of all duty.

Thorough reformation is no small matter. The ill ways that most men walk in are innumerable; even most of those natural men that are called civil and orderly persons that are not awakened. If they could be seen everywhere, and strictly and narrowly observed in all their ways and practices, open and secret, in all their talk and all their thoughts, their evil ways that they walk in would be found to be very many. You have it before you to reform all your evil ways: evil ways with your tongues, and every evil way with your hands, and evil ways in your allowed thoughts and imaginations. Every corrupt inclination must be crossed. All the sweet food of every lust must be cast away; every secret morsel of that kind must be spit out of your mouth, and every evil habit and custom must be broke off.

And particularly you must part with the sin that may be called your iniquity: the sin that so easily besets you, the sin that either by your constitution, or custom, or the temptation of your circumstances, [you][47] are

---

47. In revising for re-preaching, JE added "you."

especially inclined to, and apt to fall in with.[48] This, in your case, is one of the greatest giants that stand in the way, to keep you out of Canaan. And you must not think to conquer the host of the Philistines till Goliath is slain. If you destroy all the Amalekites and save Agag the king alive, it will be of no great service to you.

You must not do, with respect to your sins or the enjoyments of your lusts, as Pharaoh did by his pride and covetousness, that was gratified in keeping the children of Israel in bondage. The profit he had by their service gratified his covetousness, and the dominion he had over 'em gratified his pride, and he could not bear to part with those objects of his lusts. But yet sometimes when God's plagues were upon him and he feared more, he made as if he would let the children of Israel go. But he soon repented: he could not bear to part with those[49] lusts which were gratified in their bondage. You must not stand parlaying and disputing with your own conscience, as Pharaoh did with Moses, but you must actually let go your lusts. Pharaoh, when God's plagues were hard upon him, was for contriving that God might be served, without parting with his slaves. Ex. 8:25, "And Pharaoh called for Moses and for Aaron, and said, Go ye, sacrifice to your God in the land." And when he saw[50] that was not accepted, then he consented to let the children of Israel go, upon the condition that they should not go very far away.

He was not willing to part with them finally, and therefore would not let 'em go clear, but would have 'em within reach, that he might bring 'em back again, and again gratify his lusts in their bondage. But you must be willing, finally and forever, to part with all your sins, to let 'em go clear from you, without any desire of keeping 'em within sight, or having 'em within your reach that you may fetch 'em back again. You must let 'em go without any expectation of ever having anything more to do with them.

Afterwards, when God's plagues came still harder upon Pharaoh, he consented to let the men go, if they would leave the women and children. Ex. 10:8–10, "And Moses and Aaron were brought again unto Pharaoh: and he said unto them, Go, serve the Lord your God: but who are they that shall go? And Moses said, We will go with our young and with our old, with our sons and with our daughters, with our flocks and with our herds will we go; for we must hold a feast unto the Lord. And he said unto

---

48. In revising for re-preaching, JE deleted "in with" and inserted "into."
49. MS: "that which."
50. MS: "see."

them, Let the Lord be so with you, as I will let you go, and your little ones: look to it; for evil is before you."

And then after that, when God's hand pressed him still more sorely, he consented that they should go, men, women and children, provided they would but leave their cattle behind 'em; but he was not willing to let 'em all go, and all that they had, Ex. 10:24. It must not be thus with you, when God's hand presses you in convictions of conscience: you must not only be willing to part with some of your sins, but you must part with them all, little and great, and all that belong to 'em; not only the men or the principal ones, but even men, women, and children and cattle; "there must not be an hoof left behind" [Ex. 10:26].

At last Pharaoh, when it came to extremity, was willing to let the people all go, men, women, children and cattle. But he soon repented and pursued after 'em again.

It must not be so with you, but you must part with all, not only for a little while, to quiet your conscience and to ease you of present smart, and then quietly to follow after 'em again, and live in the same sins as you did before: that is the way to be overthrown in the Red Sea. But you must take an everlasting farewell of 'em.

Thus you must thoroughly reform your life, reform all sin thoroughly and finally. This requires great striving and earnestness. A person may live so as to pass among men for an honest, moral man, without so much difficulty. But 'tis not so easy a matter, to keep a conscience pure and void of offence before God.

And besides reforming and avoiding sins of commission, you must live in the strict and thorough performance of all duty, which is what requires no small degree of earnestness and striving. It requires an exceeding degree of engagedness and labor of the mind, to live in a thorough performance of all duties to God; diligently, and carefully and devoutly to attend on every ordinance and every duty of worship; strictly to keep the sabbath in God's house and at home; and to maintain a consistent search of the holy Scriptures, and a search of your own hearts; to keep up the duties of meditation, self-examination, self-reflection, religious conversation; and strictly to maintain a devout and constant worship of God in your closets, there to call upon God, to confess your sins to God, and cry to him for mercy.

And at the same time, strictly and thoroughly to observe all moral duties. To do justly by all, and not only to do justly, but to perform all duties of charity; to do duties to friends, and duties to enemies, too.

Strictly and thoroughly to observe all duties required of you in the families you belong to, towards family relations, and to carry yourself aright when you are abroad amongst your neighbors.

To govern your tongue, so as not to sin with it. To avoid all falsehood, and all bitterness, and all guile, and all evil-speaking, all unsuitable, un-Christian speech, and to govern your thoughts and imaginations, and to govern your behavior.

To do your duty in the business of your general, and also in the business of your particular calling. To behave yourself according to the rules of God's Word on all special occasions, on public occasions and private occasions, and under all the vast variety of temptations that you meet with.

Here is the work in which you are thus to lay out yourself as you have heard. And if any think, here is not work enough to require such earnestness and violence as has been spoken of, 'tis a sign they never made any great trial.

They that ben't aware of any such vast difficulties in such a business as this, 'tis a sign that they never, never went about the business in good earnest, and so are unexperienced in the difficulties of it.

Now therefore, I counsel you that have a mind to obtain heaven, earnestly to strive in this business, apply yourself to it with as much resolution, vigor and earnestness of mind, as a resolute soldier, that would take a strong city or kingdom, applies himself to war. There are duties enough, and hard duties, to employ all the force of your mind; here is work enough for you to do. Therefore, apply yourself to this work with all your might.

2. I would show you what you have to strive and wrestle with. And,

(1) You have to wrestle with your lusts. You must wrestle with your dullness and slothfulness. There is naturally an exceeding backwardness in the heart of man to a strict and diligent attendance to the work and business of religion. Man is naturally dead in sin, and when [men] go about duties of religion, they often find a strange dullness and heaviness, which as it were sways 'em down and binds their hearts, hands and tongues. This often is found in the duties of prayer, and in reading, and hearing and meditating. This is a very strong enemy that men have to conflict with, that would take the kingdom of heaven.

You must wrestle with this enemy. You must keep up a continual war with it. When it comes like an armed man, it must not be given way to. The more powerful its onsets are, the more vigorous must be the resistance.

Some, when they [are] counseled to be earnest and violent, are ready to say, "How can I be earnest, when I feel so dead and dull?" I answer, There is the enemy that you must use violence with; there is the occasion you have for earnestness. If there were no backwardness nor opposition in your heart, you would have no occasion for violence.

When your dullness comes most upon you, that is the time when the enemy encounters you. That is the time for a man to fight, when the enemy comes forth against him, and not when there is no enemy there for him to fight with. To fight when there is no enemy there, is to beat the air. The Apostle says, he did not fight "as one that beat the air," I Cor. 9:26. To do so, and to lie still or turn your back when the enemy comes, to be sure, is not the way to take the kingdom of heaven. Another giant you have to wrestle with is your pride. This lust has many ways of working, and is in all[51] a strong enemy to keep a person out of the kingdom of heaven. 'Tis to this is owing many of those evil corrupt ways that you naturally walk in, and that you must reform; and this is very opposite to many duties you have to do. The Christian religion is not calculated to suit man's pride, but exceedingly to oppose and resist it. This lust opposes men's confessing their faults; it opposes their asking counsel; it opposes their showing their ignorance. It stirs up an envious spirit. It makes men willful and high-spirited in dealings with their neighbor, and is as contrary as possible to the spirit of the gospel. So you must wrestle with a covetous spirit, which is another of the sons of Anak that {that you must overcome}, an exceeding snare to the souls of multitudes that seek salvation. It takes off their minds from eternal things, it takes up their thoughts, it draws away their cares and affections, and it draws away and consumes the strength of the mind, and makes 'em very opposite to many duties. And if it ben't constantly and violently opposed, it will quickly make the soul to be like ground overgrown with thorns, and all convictions will be choked. And men will not do those duties that are of great importance: it will hinder their doing deeds of charity, if not keep 'em from paying their honest debts and doing other deeds of justice, and in short, will dispose 'em to excuse themselves from complying with Christ's calls. One will excuse himself with his having bought a piece of land, another with his having bought cattle, and they will go away, one to his farm, and another to his

---

51. MS: "all in."

merchandise. Therefore, you must violently oppose and wrestle with such a disposition.

Again, you must wrestle with your sensual inclinations and appetites. These are oftentimes inordinate, violent things, are like giants for strength, and must be earnestly watched over and restrained, otherwise they will prove an undoing snare to the soul. This the Apostle mentions as one main thing wherein his running and fighting consisted, even his restraining his bodily appetites. I Cor. 9:25-27, "And every man that striveth for the mastery is temperate in all things. Now they do it to obtain a corruptible crown; but we an incorruptible. I therefore so run, not as uncertainly; so fight I, not as one that beateth the air: but I keep under my body, and bring it into subjection: lest that by any means, when I have preached to others, I myself should be a castaway."

So you must wrestle with a spirit of bitterness and ill will to others, that is ready to [be] stirred up by seeing others' faults, seeing them manifest an hateful, proud or spiteful spirit; and especially when they show such a spirit towards you, by talking against you, and doing you wrong. There is an exceeding proneness to bitterness, and high resentment and hatred in such cases, and great danger of contracting a seated leaven in the heart. That will be a great wound to the soul, and a vast hindrance to persons obtaining the kingdom of heaven.

You must wrestle against bitterness of spirit towards those that you have most to do with, towards any that you live with.

You must wrestle against the particular unhappiness of your temper. You must wrestle against the sins of the tongue, that natural itch there is in that member to speak evil of others.

You must wrestle against any lusts that have been strengthened by contracted habits and former bad customs.

(2) You have an host of devils to wrestle with, which are enemies that are exceeding crafty, and very mighty and very busy; that have great strength and subtlety, and will exert them to the utmost. Eph. 6:12, "For we wrestle not against flesh and blood, but against principalities, against powers, against the rulers of the darkness of this world, against spiritual wickedness in high places."

When a person begins to set his face Zion-ward, and sets about the work of seeking the kingdom of heaven, then presently a mighty host of devils is raised to oppose, and if possible, to hinder it, and the soul is plied with many temptations. Sometimes they suggest that it is not worth the while to seek salvation, but hereafter will be a more convenient season.

Sometimes, that it will be in vain for 'em to attend such and such duties: it does no good, it only makes their case worse, they have only the more to answer for. Sometimes he tempts 'em to discouragement, that let 'em do what they will, they never can obtain.

Sometimes he tells 'em that they are so wicked, that God won't show 'em mercy. Sometimes he suggests that they have no conviction, and are given over to final hardness of heart.

Sometimes, on the other hand, he flatters 'em that now they are very nigh. He tells 'em they will quickly be converted; they are now in a very good way, and mightily sooths 'em with their own good deeds and the pains they have taken.

Sometimes he stirs up blasphemous thoughts against God. Sometimes he tells persons, that 'tis not best for them to have thorough convictions. If they have, it will make 'em distracted, or it will strike 'em into a fever, or consumption or some distemper that will kill 'em. Many are the weapons and fiery darts of the devil, with which he opposes those that seek the kingdom of heaven. And many are his stratagems, and powerful are his assaults.

And many are the poor souls that are ruined by him, and fall a prey to this roaring lion. They never enter into the kingdom of heaven, but on the contrary, are carried captive by Satan, and are carried down into that lion's den.

Therefore you must wrestle with that enemy with all your might, and resist all his suggestions, whatsoever he would tempt you [with], contrary to the counsel God gives in his Word.

(3) You must wrestle against the temptations of the world. The world abounds with objects that are wont to prove a snare to the souls of men, and are a great snare to many that seek heaven, and keep from taking it.

As the devils' and men's lusts, may fitly be compared to the Anakians that stood to keep the children of Israel out of Canaan, so may worldly objects and snares be well compared to their high walls.

There is scarce any worldly objects or enjoyment, but what proves a temptation to men. Those things that are in themselves lawful have their temptation, and worldly business is a temptation, especially when men are called to engage in any extraordinary worldly business, or any business wherein there is a great deal of entanglement and difficulty.

You had need to wrestle against such temptations.

Your particular circumstances in the world may prove a great temptation to you. As if you are in higher circumstances than ordinary, are lifted above the level of ordinary men in estate and honor, that is a vast temptation which you had need to wrestle against with all your might. Or if you are very poor, and greatly pinched with want, that has great temptation, and you had need to wrestle against that.

Company oftentimes proves a temptation to persons. You may fall into company either at home or abroad, that may be such as you may have great occasion for an earnest[52] strife in your soul, to keep from being greatly wounded in your spiritual interest by 'em.

When new worldly objects [are] present, and there are changes in our worldly circumstances, they commonly tend very much to take off the mind from the business of religion, and so to prevent their entering into the kingdom of heaven. You must therefore wrestle against such things. And the ill examples of the world are great temptations, especially in a time when religion decays, as after a time of awakening, when that awakening begins to die away. Example very often ruins persons. In such cases, you had need therefore, to wrestle against such temptations with all your might.

(4) You must wrestle with God, though in a very different sense from what you must do with those spiritual enemies mentioned before. You must wrestle with him in prayer. In vain will all your wrestling with the world, the flesh, and the devil be, without God's help. The enemies that stand to keep you out of the kingdom of heaven, are too many and too mighty for you. Those giants are so great, that you are but grasshoppers in their sight; and so you would be in your own sight, if you was sensible of their strength and your own weakness. You will never get the victory if God don't help you. As the children of Israel never would have taken Canaan, if God had not fought for 'em. Therefore, you must wrestle with him for his help and blessing. When persons are seeking the kingdom of heaven, God is commonly pleased for a while to seem to deny them, and to resist them, as Christ did the woman of Canaan. He doth so for a trial of their earnestness and constancy in seeking, and to bring 'em to a sense of their own impotency and unworthiness.

God seemed to oppose Jacob for a while when he sought the blessing. He seemed to struggle against him, and to get from him and leave him. So he often is pleased, when persons seek salvation of him. He seems for a while to hide his face, to give one denial after another, and instead of showing them favor, he frowns upon them and testifies his

---

52. MS: "earnestly."

anger and turns a deaf ear to their calls. Then is a proper occasion for them to wrestle with him by prayer.

Therefore, do thus be earnest and importunate with God. Don't be slothful and slack in your prayers, but pour out your soul before him. Exert yourself, take great pains in that duty, and continue instant in prayer. Resolve that you will not let God go, except he bless you. Take no denial of God; let him deny you never so often, yet persist in importunate cries, and be the more importunate for past denials.

Thus you see what you have to wrestle with, in this great affair that is before you, of taking the kingdom of heaven.[53]

I come now, in the

3. [Third] place, to show after what manner you must strive in these things.

(1) By strongly resolving. The violence of the soldier that takes a country or kingdom where he meets with strong opposition, has its foundation in his resolution: 'tis that which carries him through such hardships and difficulties, 'tis that which makes him so vigorous and steadfast in pursuing his design.

So if you seek heaven, it should be with a strong resolution that you will, if possible, obtain it: not if you can without a great deal of difficulty, not if you can do it in a little time, but if it be possible. You must strongly resolve that you won't spare yourself, that you won't spare any of your

---

53. End of second preaching unit. After a horizontal line, Edwards wrote "Math 11. 12," followed by the Doctrine, which are omitted here. He also deleted the following transitional passage:

After some general improvement made of this Doctrine the last week, I proposed to make some more particular improvement. And,
1. I proposed to answer some inquiries persons might be ready to put for their own instruction and direction.
How shall I go about to be violent for the kingdom, as resolute soldiers are in {taking a country or kingdom that is strongly defended}?
I proposed, in answer to this inquiry, to give those that desire to be informed what they shall do to be saved, an idea of the work they had before 'em, and to give 'em to see what occasion they had for such violence, and how they should strive, by representing,
(1) The work they have to do in which they must strive;
(2) What they have to struggle and wrestle with; [and,]
(3) After what manner they must strive.
Having spoken to the two former, . . .

Apparently the delivery of this discourse resumed the following sabbath, as JE mentions "the last week."

lusts, and that if anything stands in the way of your obtaining heaven, let it be never so pleasing to corrupt nature, you will let it go. If anything proves a weight to clog and hinder you, though it looks precious as gold, you will cast it away from you. And that if at any time, anything needs to be done to promote and forward you in this design, you will do it, however disagreeable it may be to you, contrary to your ease, to your worldly profit or credit, and cross to your pride and hard to flesh and blood. You must put on the like resolution that a man under some desperate wound puts on, when he goes to have his wound lanced, or goes to have a gangrened hand or foot cut off. You must take up a strong resolution to continue steadfast and immoveable in this business, and that you will not let God go except he bless you, and that you will either conquer in this warfare or die in it; that if you do perish, you will perish in a way of doing your utmost for your salvation. If death comes upon you, and finds you without an interest in Christ, it shall find [you] violently exerting yourself to obtain one.

With such resolution should you do the work that you have to do, and with such a resolution should you wrestle with those that you have to wrestle with.

(2) Another thing wherein your engagedness in this work should be manifest, is speediness, or making haste. Persons are wont to be speedy in those affairs wherein their minds are greatly engaged, and therefore, earnestness in any work is often in Scripture represented by its a-being done early. Ps. 63:1, "O Lord, thou art my God; early will I seek thee"; Hos. 5:15, "In their affliction they will seek me early."

Success in war commonly very much depends on speediness of acting and not losing time.[54] Therefore, whatever you have to do that must be done before you die, do it now, immediately, without any delay. If you intend to get heaven, put nothing off that must be done. Eccles. 9:10, "Whatsoever thine hand finds to do, [do it with thy might]."

If you have lived in any wrong of any other person, be speedy in removing the wrong, making satisfaction. If you have wronged any in their estate, be speedy in making restitution; if you have injured 'em otherwise in any notable instance, be speedy in confessing your fault to 'em. If there be any difficult duty that lies upon your mind, and that you can't but be sensible is a duty, but quiet yourself hitherto with that, that you intend to do it but yet have put it off, be advised to put it off no longer. If you

---

54. This sentence, which JE interlineates, continues "for while," but this has been treated as an uncompleted thought.

are sensible that you as yet do not do so much as you should do for your salvation, or at least, though you hope that what pains you take will be sufficient, but yet are doubtful whether it will or no, and are suspicious whether or no it won't be necessary at last to alter your hand, don't wait to see whether it will be necessary or no, but be more earnest now; don't run on uncertainly: do as much as is possible for you to do now, that you may be sure that nothing is delayed.

(3) Another thing wherein your earnestness must appear, is by narrowly searching. He that seeks heaven has much occasion for searching and scrutiny, in order to a thorough knowledge of the state of things that concern his soul's welfare. As a general that goes on a warlike expedition to take a country or kingdom will be diligent to know the state of that country, to search and find out the strength of the enemies, where their weakness and where their strongest parts are.

So if you are indeed in good earnest in seeking your salvation, you'll find great occasion to be often on the most diligent search. There is need of a diligent search, in order to know your duty. Though the rules be plain and plentiful, yet there are so many things to blind your minds with respect to your duty, that you'll find it in many things exceeding difficult. That you may know your duty, and know the mind and will of God, you must be much in searching the Scriptures. John 5:39, "Search the scriptures: for in them ye think ye have eternal life." Searching the Scriptures implies two things: viz., [first,] reading the Scriptures a great deal, being very conversant with them; and secondly, diligently observing what you read, attending[55] to the drift and intent of the Holy Ghost in it, taking notice how what is said in the Scriptures, suits your case and how you should apply it to yourself.

And then you should be exceeding diligent and narrow in your search of your own ways, to know whether or no you don't walk in some ill way, whether you don't allow something that is not right in the sight of God, whether there be no duty omitted, and whether no evil inclination be at all indulged. 'Tis an hard thing for a man to see his own sins; men are exceeding apt to blind their own minds concerning evil ways that they walk in and allow themselves in. Ps. 19:12, "Who can understand his errors? cleanse thou me from secret faults." You had need therefore, continually to be upon that search. So you must be narrow in searching your heart, strictly observing its workings, and what principles it is that you

---

55. MS: "attended."

act from in what you do; observing the pride, the self-righteousness and other vile corruptions that are continually operating there, that you may be sensible what a wicked heart you have, what darkness and unbelief, and slothfulness and hardness, and pride and worldliness, and carnality and filthiness, and enmity and perverseness there is there.

So you should be very diligent and particular in searching your past life, as well as your present practices, that you may be sensible what a life you have lived, that you see your way in the valley, and know what you have done; should often be bringing as many particular acts of sin to mind as you can, endeavoring that none may be hid from you, and buried in oblivion.

These things you should be doing continually, and especially you should make a solemn work of doing these things before every attendance on the sacrament of the Lord's Supper.

(4) By watching. Those that go forth to war in an enemy's country to take a kingdom, are wont to keep up a strict watch. If they did not, they would soon be undone. The enemy would come upon them unawares and might surprise 'em in the night, and fall upon 'em and cut 'em off before they had time to prepare for their own defense. Or they might fall into an ambush of the enemy and be cut off as they march from place to place.

Nothing can be done in war with any safety, without keeping up the most diligent watch.

In like manner, you had need to be always upon the most diligent watch, watching over your own heart, watching against your enemies, watching lest Satan gets some advantage against you unawares, for he is always watching for an advantage. 1 Pet. 5:8, "Be sober, be vigilant; for your adversary the devil, as a roaring lion, walketh about, seeking whom he may devour"; Luke 21:36, "Watch and pray always, that ye may be accounted worthy to escape all these things that shall come to pass, and to stand before the Son of man."

You had need to keep the strictest watch over your lusts, lest some lust, some corrupt disposition, should get a-going and make great head before you are aware. When it is so, it is very much like the breaking out of fire: if it be observed at its beginning, it may be easily quenched; but if we are asleep when it begins, and it gets a-going, and gets a great head before we wake, there is great danger that it will prove ruinous and destructive.

So you should watch against the first beginnings of backsliding. Always keep an eye upon your own heart in that matter, to see if convictions don't begin to abate and you don't begin a little to relax your carefulness and earnestness, and don't begin to grow more slack; [to see] whether you don't begin to look out more after the world, after youthful vanity, having your mind less taken up at home by the great concerns of your soul, and whether company, or ill examples, or some other temptation don't begin to prevail upon you; whether some worldly object don't begin to steal away your heart, and divert the channel of your thoughts and cares another way.

(5) Another thing wherein your earnestness should be exercised, is in contriving and disposing things well for the good of their souls. Neither your contrivance nor strength signify anything, without God is pleased to show mercy: yet both are to be used. How much do men study, as well as labor, for the world, and we ought to be as wise for our souls as the men of this world are in their generation. Men that go forth to war to take a country or kingdom, are not only wont to bestir themselves vigorous, but to use contrivance. Wisdom as well as strength [are] necessary in war. The Wise Man says, Eccles. 9:18, "Wisdom is better than weapons of war." Seeing God has given you a faculty of understanding, you should improve it in religion, in disposing things wisely for the good of your soul. Christ commands his disciples to "be wise as serpents," and we should be so, not only in winning others' souls, but to save our own. [In] Jer. 4:22, the children of Judah are condemned for that, that they were "wise to do evil, but to do good they had no knowledge."

Persons' wisely contriving and disposing things for their souls' good, consists chiefly in two things:

1. In putting themselves under the best advantages for the good of their souls, to obtain all the advantages they can, and to deliver themselves as much as they can from disadvantages; to keep themselves from being exposed to temptation, as soldiers in war will contrive to keep themselves as much out of the reach of the enemy as they can. And,

2. In improving what special advantages and opportunities they have. A wise man, if he has any special advantages in his hands, will observe it and improve it; he won't let it slip.

So as you would take the kingdom of heaven, you must observe and improve all the special advantages you have in your hands, such as a time of youth, a time of the outpouring of the Spirit of God, and times of the striving of the Spirit of God with you in particular.

(6) By vigorous performing. You should not only be much in searching, and watching and contriving, but you must also be much in doing: in doing good and in seeking good. You should be, not slack and dull, but vigorous in all duties of religion: attentive in hearing, and earnest in prayer, crying mightily to God to show mercy to you. Be frequent in this duty, praying with all prayer, not only set prayers, but in ejaculatory prayer, lifting up your heart to God in short and earnest requests when about your work, when going by the way, and when lying in your bed, when you wake up in the night season. And doubtless it would be proper, for those whose circumstances will allow it, to set apart days for fasting and praying in secret. 'Tis a duty recommended by Christ, and I think it a great pity that 'tis not more attended. I would advise all those that are seeking heaven to attend it. Now and then keep such a day for your soul's good.

(7) By exactness to the rule of God's Word. You must not only be vigorous in acting, but you must be exact in all you do to Christ's commands. As it concerns soldiers in war, not only to exert themselves notably, and lay out their strength, but it behooves 'em to be very exact to the words of command, otherwise they will be apt to go into confusion, whereby the enemy will have 'em at advantage, and will make an easy prey of 'em; so you must diligently observe the words of command, as they come from the mouth of the great Captain of salvation, the Lord Jesus, and endeavor in everything to be exact.

(8) By patient bearing and waiting. Patiently bear the wounds that you receive in your warfare; don't be impatient of the self-denial, and difficulty and suffering that you meet with in the business of seeking heaven. If you think you lose many temporal advantages by it, if you think you miss of any pleasant things by it that others enjoy, if you think the trouble and labor great of continuing so long, striving and doing so much for your salvation and receiving no light nor comfort, no gracious answer to your prayers: yet you must patiently endure, you must be willing to bear this trouble and labor, and must not repent your loss of the fleshpots and onions and leeks of Egypt.

You must be content to bear the fatigues of your wilderness travail, and the fatigues of war, till God is pleased to give you rest in the good land.

Thus I have endeavored to show you how and wherein you must strive and be violent for the kingdom of heaven, as valiant and resolute soldiers are violent that go forth to take a country or kingdom, where they meet with great opposition.

And now can anyone imagine, that here is not work enough to require such earnestness and vigor as has been spoken of? Is here too little to be done, to need that those that seek the kingdom of heaven should behave themselves in like manner as a resolute soldier, in taking a kingdom that is defended against 'em by many and strong enemies, and high walls and strong fortresses?

Thus, you that have lately been stirred up to seek heaven, and are inquiring what you shall do to be saved, see what you have before you. This, this is the business you must apply yourself to and pursue. Seek heaven in this way, and then 'tis probable you will obtain. If you would really take and have possession of that glorious kingdom, seek it in this way. Lay aside every weight, and let this be your business; hither turn your thoughts, and your cares and desires, and here employ your strength, and in this improve your time.

You that seem to be concerned for your salvation, what have you sat here for today hearing the Word, but that you might be instructed what you should do, how you might seek your salvation? Now therefore you have been told: go, and do likewise. Now you have heard, go and apply yourself to the practice of what you have heard. Don't be like a man that looks in the glass, and then goes away and straitway forgets what manner of man he was. Don't only think of those things tonight and tomorrow, or this week, but let those things be with you henceforward, and put 'em in practice as long as you live.

And thus strive to enter in at the strait gate, and press into the kingdom of God. Thus scale the high walls of that glorious city, the new Jerusalem that cometh down from God out of heaven.

I come now, in the

Second place, to put an *Inquiry* to the consciences of persons for their conviction.

To those that have been seeking conversion a great while and have not obtained, I would put it to the consciences of such, whether or no they have sought salvation in anywise in such a manner? They that have sought a great while to enter in at the strait gate and han't been able, and see others enter in while they remain without, are ready to ask, What is the matter? Why should so many others obtain, when I can't obtain? But examine your manner of seeking; thoroughly consider after what manner you have been spending your time, and it may be then you won't wonder.

And particularly compare your way of spending that time wherein you have been seeking salvation, with that way of seeking that has been described. I know that all fail in many particulars, but when you consider what your way has been of behaving yourself in this business in general, has[56] it been in any measure like that of valiant and resolute soldiers in taking a country or kingdom wherein they meet with strong opposition? Did you, upon deliberate consideration and pondering the difficulties of it, enter upon it with resolution, to go through with all? And have you come to that fixed engagedness of mind, that you have stood ready to part with all that is sweet to flesh and blood, and entirely to renounce your worldly interest, and make it stand by and give place, whenever it should stand in the way of this affair? Have you had a heart to sell all? Have you been constant and steadfast, holding your resolution, nothing giving back for discouraging and dark appearances? Have you been in a way of exerting the utmost strength of your mind, and doing what your hand found to do with your might? Have you willingly exposed yourself to deep wounds and great crosses in your corrupt inclination and carnal interest, and even to the parting with a right hand or a right eye? Have you kept up your resolution under all disappointments, and gone on to renew your attempts with greater vigor, though you have often failed?

And [have you] been willing to go on still in this, though you have been uncertain of success with a fixed determination of mind, that you would either take the kingdom of heaven, or die and perish in a way of earnest striving and struggling for it? Or have you not exceedingly failed of coming up to anything like such a method of seeking as this?

And more particularly,

1. Has there not all this while been an Achan in your camp, to hinder you from taking Canaan? something that has never been thoroughly reformed, some ill, corrupt disposition in you, that is from time to time given way, and is to this day almost as often an occasion, and temptation is renewed? Is there not something in your behaving yourself that God all this while sees, that is very offensive to him, that you don't in good earnest go about to correct?

As long as 'tis thus, there is no likelihood that ever you would take the kingdom. You must not expect to succeed in battle, till you have put away this evil, and slain this Achan, and all his children and his cattle, and burnt him, and all that belongs to him, with fire.

---

56. MS: "General & has."

The children of Israel could not take Canaan, till Achan was slain. They went out as you do against their enemies, hoping for success, but it was in vain. They were smitten down before their enemies, and they never would have had success if they had not slain Achan as God told 'em, Josh. 7:12.

Inquire whether or no your pride is not some way allowedly indulged, or else a greedy, violent spirit after the world, or a close spirit, or a spirit of ill will against your neighbor, or a neglect of rendering to everyone his due, or some fleshly appetite inordinately indulged.

2. Inquire whether or no there is not some practice that you have lived in hitherto, that you have had many parlays and debates with your own conscience about, [that] you often have been raising in your own mind about it. 'Tis something you are very much inclined to, but have now and then an inward disturbance about it, and then you search about for a ground to quiet your conscience, and to satisfy yourself that there is no hurt in it; but in the meantime live in it, but to this day are not fully satisfied of the lawfulness of it, so but that you are forced to renew your dispute with conscience. The debate between your inclination and your conscience is still carried on.

If it be so, then consider how hurtful this must needs be to you, to keep up such a debate with your own conscience. It appears that your conscience is not fully easy, by the renewing of those debates so often. And why will you yet go on? Is it not better to have done with it, and so set your conscience fully at ease? Is [it] not best to be on the sure side in this matter? If you was violent as valiant and resolute soldiers that go to war, you would never have disputed this point so long.

If a valiant general that is about to take a city or kingdom, has one in his camp that he doubts whether be a friend or an enemy, doubts whether he han't secretly a design to {betray his plans, would that general not immediately confront such a traitor}?

3. Is there not something that you live in neglect of, that you have been often at a loss whether you ought not to do it? something that is much against your inclination, and is what you hate to do, but yet are at a loss whether 'tis not your duty? Surely you ought not to live thus, you ought to come to some determination. If you find yourself undetermined in your own thoughts, you should ask help, seek advice of others, and make haste and come to a determination. If you was violent for the kingdom of heaven, you would do thus.

4. In all your endeavors to take the heavenly Canaan, don't you let the biggest giants, that stand to keep you out of it, alone? This is oftentimes the case with those that go to take the land of Canaan: they encounter the lesser enemies, they reform their lesser sins, a great many of 'em, but there are some particular sins that are above all others dear to 'em, that they let alone. The sin of their constitution, or that they have been most addicted to, or most exposed to in their case, is the champion of their enemies. 'Tis that enemy that has greatest strength against 'em, and therefore is among their enemies as Goliath was among the Philistines.

Such sins are oftentimes spared by those that try to take the kingdom of heaven. They reform other practices, but they don't reform this. The special iniquity of some men is pride, or very high spirit which disposes 'em to deep resentment and ill will. With others, the principal giant that stands to keep 'em out of the kingdom of heaven, is worldliness. With others, it is sensuality. And there is a great variety as to the particular sins that are especially dear to men. Those sins are often spared, as Saul spared Agag, the king of the Amalekites, though we may suppose he slew thousands of lesser men. So Herod, when he heard John the Baptist preach that the kingdom of heaven was at hand, he did many things. But there was one iniquity that [was] exceeding dear to him, that he would not part with: he loved Herodias, and could not bear to put her away.

Inquire whether it ben't so with you? As long as it is, in vain do you fight with your enemies. It is in vain for you to imagine you shall take the kingdom of heaven.

You should take the course that David did, by which he was successful: he went forth in the first place against the champion, he slew the giant, and then all the rest were an easy prey. And as the Syrians did, 1 Kgs. 22:31, "But the king of Syria commanded his thirty and two captains that had rule over his chariots, saying, Fight neither with small nor great, save only with the king of Israel."

If you would behave like a valiant, resolute soldier that is resolved to take the kingdom, then[57] strike directly at the tallest giant that stands in your way in the first place; pitch battle with him.

And to conclude, let every one that seeks heaven, attend to the things that have been [said], and let your practice be accordingly. We all hope for heaven; we all must obtain the kingdom of heaven: for all that don't take heaven, perish miserably and everlastingly in hell. And the gate will

---

57. MS: "that."

be shut, the walls will be high, and giants will be in the way. Therefore, 'tis in vain for us to think to obtain heaven in any other way than that of striving and wrestling, and fighting and suffering grievous wounds, and running through many and great difficulties. Some may imagine[58] they have entered; some may imagine that they are converted, that were never violent for heaven, never strove or struggled much, either before or since: but vain are their imaginations. So it used to be of old: the kingdom of heaven suffered violence, and those that took it, took it by force. And so it is still, and so it will be, as long as there is any such thing as escaping hell, and taking the kingdom of heaven.

---

58. MS: "Image."

God's Care for His Servants in Time of Public Commotions

February 26, 1741

THE VARIED AND COMPLEX theaters in which Britain and Spain fought soon entangled the American colonists. Gov. Oglethorpe had already recruited a small force to take St. Augustine in Florida, but America's most substantial involvement would come in the West Indies. In June of 1740, London sent Col. William Blakeney with £200,000 sterling to recruit American volunteers for an all-American regiment supplementing British regulars. Blakeney's campaign progressed alongside a burgeoning awakening throughout the summer of 1740. After the arrival of George Whitefield in September, the American regiment sailed 3500 strong to Jamaica under the command of Col. William Gooch. The colonies shared a rising expectation of Protestant success over the Spanish Catholic forces, an expectation paralleled by the progress of revivals throughout the colonies.

As the American regiment, known as "Gooch's Foot," sailed to fight for the Protestant Interest, Whitefield traveled throughout New England finding himself in Northampton in October by Edwards's request. Even though revivals were already underway, the British itinerant's preaching fueled a dramatic response to the gospel. Northampton, including Edwards's own children, experienced to the emotional power of Whitefield's preaching. Edwards's conviction that God drove the wheels of providence did not allow him to see the advance of the gospel and the progress of the British expedition in the West Indies as disconnected happenstance.

Compounding the complexity of his providential interpretation was the news which broke in the January 26 (1741) edition of the *Boston Gazette* announcing the death of the Holy Roman Emperor, Charles VI. This event portended a much broader conflict most likely involving Britain's ancient rival, the French. Edwards preached *God's Care for His Servants in Time of Public Commotions* on February 26, 1741 in observance of the fast day proclaimed to spiritually prepare New England for the coming conflicts. The text Edwards chose reflects the sense of the impending danger to the British Empire: the image of four angels holding back the winds that would descend with judgment on the earth (Rev. 7:1–3). These angels, Edwards claimed, were to be understood symbolically allowing his congregation to interpret their work in light of God's providential purposes across the globe. Despite the dangers inherent in the world, Edwards assured the people of Northampton that God will take "thorough and effectual care" of his people during times of public calamities. This doctrine was not merely a statement of comfort for the church but a call for the people to take refuge in a personal relationship with Christ.

Edwards preached *God's Care for His Servants in Time of Public Commotions* to call Northampton to pursue a safety which can only come through the sealing work of God. Edwards claimed that those who are in Christ are "out of reach of all the changes and tumults of this world." News of war stretching from la Plata, Argentina to Cartagena portended dark days for the New England frontier. As all colonists understood, wars that begin in Europe rarely ended there. Edwards's martial language leveraged fear of these various "commotions" to further fuel the revivals arising throughout the colonies. Edwards called on his congregation to examine themselves to determine whether they truly were servants of God. If not, Edwards cried, "Fly for shelter! Fly to the Lord Jesus Christ." Only as servants of Jesus could be assured of their safety in an increasingly dangerous world.

* * * * *

This sermon was edited by edited by Harry S. Stout and Nathan O. Hatch for the Work of Jonathan Edwards. The manuscript is twelve duodecimo leaves. On the top of the first page Edwards wrote, "Fast for success in the war, Feb. 26, 1740, 41." A re-preaching symbol appears in the upper-left-hand corner, but there is no indication of when the sermon was re-preached. The handwriting is hasty in appearance, but the text is nonetheless nearly fully written out; only in later portions of the Application does Edwards resort to a somewhat telegraphic form of composition.

God's Care for His Servants in Time of Public Commotions

Revelation 7:1–3

And after these things I saw four angels standing on the four corners of the earth, holding the four winds of the earth, that the wind should not blow on the earth, nor on the sea, nor on any tree. And I saw another angel ascending from the east, having the seal of the living God: and he cried with a loud voice to the four angels, to whom it was given to hurt the earth and the sea, saying, Hurt not the earth, neither the sea, nor the trees, till we have sealed the servants of our God in their foreheads.

THE PRINCIPAL THING TO be observed in these words, is the remarkable orders or commands sent from heaven, that is contained in them. Concerning which, these four things may be observed:

This is an account of a vision that the apostle John [had], representing something that was to come to pass in the course of God's providence towards his church and towards the world of mankind. And in this vision we may observe,

1. Who are the actors in the vision. They are said to be "four angels standing on the four corners of the earth." We are not to understand that this represents anything in fact literally agreeable to this vision, or that it signifies that there should be at any certain time really four angels standing on the four corners of the earth, as was represented in this vision. 'Tis but a visionary and symbolical representation. Angels are the ministers of God's providence, and therefore when great dispensations of providence are represented in this book, angels are introduced as

bringing to pass those things that are figures and symbols of real events that should come to pass.

2. We may observe what is represented as the business and office of these angels. They have the care and management of the four winds of the earth, which represents to us the ministry of the angels in those things that cause great commotion and tumults in the world. As the winds cause a great commotion in the air, so that oftentimes all is in a storm, and as they are very changeable, sometimes blow from one quarter of the heaven and sometimes from another, and are not at the command of men but under the ordering and disposal of divine providence; so the great changes, commotions and revolutions that are in the affairs of the world of mankind are sometimes attended with great uproar and come as if with a mighty storm, and are very changeable, and are in the hands of God. And God makes use of the ministration of angels in regulating those events. The wind is often made use of in Scripture.

We may observe the special commission that those angels had received, which was "to hurt the earth and the sea," to signify public changes and commotions. So in Is. 27:8, "In measure, when it shooteth forth, wilt he debate with it. He stayeth his rough wind in the day of the east wind"; and Is. 32:2, "A man shall be an hiding place from the wind." So Jer. 4:11–12, "A dry wind of the high places in the wilderness toward the daughter of my people, not to fan, nor to cleanse. Even a full wind from those places shall come unto me: also will I give sentence against them."

3. We may observe the special commissions that those angels had received, which was to hurt the earth and the seas by the four winds. It is said in the 2nd verse that to them "it was given to hurt the earth and the seas," i.e., they had power given them to bring great public calamities upon the world of mankind. And it has a special reference to those great tumults and dreadful calamities which the Roman Empire was subject to after Constantine the Great.

In the latter part of the foregoing chapter is foretold the destruction of the heathen empire in the days of Constantine, which is set forth as a kind of coming of Christ to judgment. Verse 12, "And I beheld when he had opened the sixth seal, and, lo, there was a great earthquake; and the sun became black as sackcloth of hair, and the moon became as blood." While Constantine reigned, the world had peace and the church of God had rest; but after him there followed great commotions, very destructive wars and dismal calamities in the world. There seems to be respect to these calamities, when it is represented here as though those four angels had commission to hurt the earth and the sea by strong winds.

4. We may observe what those four angels were seen doing. They were "holding the four winds of the earth, that the wind should not blow on the earth, nor on the sea, nor on any tree." It is represented as though the strong winds were ready to blow upon the earth and {and sea and trees}, and to bring great destruction, and needed to be held or restrained. Which signifies as much as that the wickedness of the world was such, that terrible calamities by God's justice were ready to come upon the earth. Justice called for them; God's wrath hung over the earth, but was as it were restrained and withheld for some time. The angels held the four winds, lest {they should blow on the earth, the sea and the trees}.

5. We may observe the charge that these angels received, which was still to hold the winds for some time longer. There is an angel sent, a messenger of God, with his orders to them, and he cries to the four angels that held the four winds with a loud voice. He delivers his errand with great earnestness, as though it was of great importance, and what God had given a very strict charge about, not to hurt the earth, nor the sea, nor the trees as yet, to hold the winds and keep 'em back, and by no means to let 'em go.

6. We may observe for whose sake these four angels did what they did and received this strict charge. It was for the sake of the servants of God, lest they should be hurt. 'Tis true the world was full of wickedness, and their wickedness cried for vengeance, but there were a number of the servants of God mingled here and there with the wicked. The winds therefore must by no means be let go as yet, lest they should be hurt. God had rather that the wicked that deserved calamities should escape them than his servants should suffer, and therefore nothing must be done; their commission must not be executed till those were secured.

7. We may observe what benefit God's servants should receive hereby. They should be sealed in their foreheads, i.e., they should as it were have God's mark set upon them, that when the overflowing scourge should come it might not come nigh them, that it might be as it was in Egypt when the destroying angel went forth: he saw the mark upon the doors of God's people and passed over 'em. So there was a seal to be set upon the foreheads of God's servants, that when public calamities should come they might be known, and the destroying angel might let 'em alone and by no means hurt 'em. Agreeable to the charge God gave to the angels in Ezek. 9:4–6, "And the Lord said unto him, Go through the midst of the

city, through the midst of Jerusalem, and set a mark upon the foreheads of the men that sigh and that cry for all the abominations that be done in the midst thereof. And to the others he said in mine hearing, Go ye after him through the city, and smite: let not your eye spare, neither have ye pity: slay utterly old and young, both maids, and little children, and women: but come not near any man upon whom is the mark; and begin at my sanctuary."

Doctrine

In the time of great public commotions and calamities, God will take thorough and effectual care that his servants shall be safe.

In speaking to this Doctrine, I would,

I. Mention some things tending to confirm this truth.

II. I would take notice of the ways in which God is wont to preserve them and keep 'em out of the reach of harm.

I. I would endeavor to establish this truth. And to that end, I would do two things:

First. I would mention some things that do confirm that God will take great care that his servants shall be safe in times of public commotions and calamities. And,

Second. This care shall be effectual to that end.

First. I would mention some things that do show that God will certainly take great care {that his servants shall be safe in times of public commotions and calamities}, or that show that God's heart is sufficiently engaged in this matter, and that he will not be slack but thorough in it.

1. God is their God. His mercy and love are theirs; they have a great interest in his heart. Yea, if I may so say, they have possession of his heart. God has given himself to them, as he has given 'em his heart. They are entirely dear to him and precious in his sight. They are his jewels. Will not God take thorough care to preserve his jewels safe? If an house be on fire and the householder goes about to save his goods, after the lives [of his family], his first care will be [to] save that which is most precious in his house. If [he] have ever a cabinet of jewels in the house, he will soon run to that and take care to set that out of the reach of the flames. So when the world is as it were on fire by public commotions and wars, the Great Householder will take care to secure his jewels; he won't lose his treasure, that he does in

a special manner set his heart upon. They are his children: and will not the Householder, when the house is on fire, use thorough endeavors to save his children? Yea, they are represented as the apple of God's eye. Zech. 2:8, "He that toucheth you, toucheth the apple of mine eye."

What is there that men are more careful of in times of tumult and danger than they are of themselves? And of all the members, what are men more quick to guard and defend than their eyes? So God keeps his servants. Deut. 32:10, "He kept him as the apple [of his eye]." As Jehovah is their God, so his infinite wisdom is theirs, and therefore if he have wisdom enough to contrive that they[1] shall be safe in time of public calamity, they shall be safe. And his almighty power is theirs, and therefore he will surely use it to secure them.

2. Public commotions that shake the state of mankind don't shake the love of God to his servants. However great and general those commotions may be—though they may shake and overturn the state of kingdoms and vast empires; though they make vast alterations in the world—yet they will not shake God's love to his servants. His love to them is not so easily shaken. God loved them before they had a being, yea, before the foundation of the states and kingdoms in the world. His love has stood firm from all eternity hitherto; it was the same yesterday that [it] is today; it has remained the same through all past ages and all past changes of the world, and will be the same forever. When the days shall come that there shall not only be a great commotion in the state of mankind, but heaven and earth shall be shaken and shall pass away with great noise, still God's love will remain; he loves them with an everlasting love.

3. God's covenant with them is more stable than the foundation of states and kingdoms. 'Tis an everlasting covenant that is "ordered in all things, and sure" (2 Sam. 23:5). God has once sworn by his holiness, and he won't alter the thing that is gone out of his mouth (Ps. 89:34). He has often promised that he will preserve them safe and happy through all changes and troubles. Is. 3:10, "Say ye to the righteous, it shall be well with him." In Ps. 91:4, he promised that he will do with them in times of public commotion and calamity as a bird does to shelter her young in her nest from the rain in a time of storm: "He shall cover thee with his feathers, and under his wings shalt thou trust; his truth shall be thy shield and buckler."

He has promised that when they pass through the waters, he [will be] with them, and through the rivers, and they shall not overflow them;

---

1. MS: "there."

and when they walk through the fire, they shall not be burnt, neither shall the flame kindle upon them (Is. 43:2). If there comes a time of famine or a time of dreadful calamity and destruction by war, God has promised to preserve them from the power of the sword, and from men that are furious as the wild beasts of the earth, and from all destruction. Job 5:19–22, "He shall deliver thee in six troubles: yea, in seven there shall no evil touch thee. In famine he shall redeem thee from death: and in war from the power of the sword. Thou shalt be hid from the scourge of the tongue: neither shalt thou be afraid of destruction when it cometh. At destruction and famine though shalt laugh: neither shalt thou be afraid of the beasts of the earth."

These promises stand here, and cannot be removed. God's covenant will remain not only when states and kingdoms are[2] overthrown, but when the everlasting mountains and perpetual hills are removed. Is. 54:10, "For the mountains shall depart, and the hills be removed; but my kindness shall not depart from thee, neither shall the covenant of my peace be removed, saith the Lord that hath mercy on thee."

4. We may argue from those things that God has done for them. He has purchased them by his own blood (Acts 20:28). And we may be sure he'll take thorough care not to lose that which he has purchased at so dear a rate. And besides, he has delivered them out of great calamity in their commotions, when they were involved in such difficulties and surrounded with such enemies that one would have thought they never could be extricated. He has saved 'em from strong enemies, from armies of devils, and he that has done this will doubtless take care to save 'em from the wrath of man.

These things confirm that God's heart is sufficiently engaged to take thorough care to defend his servants in time of public commotion and calamity. I would now,

Second. Mention some things that do evince that this care will be effectual.

1. This God who is their God, and is thus engaged for them, is he that orders and governs all the public commotions that are in the world. None of the ferments and quarrels and uproars that are in nations, or between one nation and another, come to pass without his ordering. Those changes that God has ordained of old in his eternal counsels shall come

---

2. MS: "&."

to pass, and no others; and they shall come to pass no otherwise than just as he has determined. Their manner, nature and extent, and all their circumstances and their whole issue, is ordered by him.

And everything that appertains to 'em is in God's hands. There is not one that is an agent in such commotions, whether he be little or great, can get out of God's hands. He governs the spring of every motion and guides and limits it just as he will. The hearts of kings are in his hands, and he turns 'em as he will. And so the power and lives of kings is in his hands: when he will he pulls 'em down from their thrones, and when he will he stops their breath.

Whenever there is any calamity or trouble in any public society, city or kingdom, 'tis God that orders it. Is. 45:7, "I make peace, and create evil: I the Lord do all these things." And Amos 3:6, "Shall the trumpet be blown in the city, and the people not be afraid? shall there be evil in the city, and the Lord hath not done it?"

God has the government of the motion of the wheels on which the world goes. In the 1st chapter of Ezekiel, the world is represented as God's chariot in which he rides, that moves on the wheels of providence, and drawn by cherubims. The pavement of this chariot is there represented to be the firmament, and the seat of the chariot, where God sits and rides, is the heaven of heavens above the firmament, as you may see in 26th verse of that chapter. And God, who rides in the heavens, has the government of all the motions of the wheels, as 'tis said there in the 20th verse: "Whethersoever the spirit was to go," the wheels went. And we are told in the 33rd chapter of Deuteronomy that God rides in this chariot of the world, in his seat above the firmament, in the help of his people. Verse 26, "There is none like unto the God of Jeshurun, who rideth upon the heaven in thy help, and in his excellency in the sky." And ['tis] therefore said in the consequence that is drawn in the next verse but one, "Israel then shall dwell in safety alone."

The Lord Jesus Christ that died for them has the government of the world committed to him, and 'tis committed to him to that end, that he may govern it for their good. He is made "head over all things to the church" (Eph. 1:22).

If there be great wars, and nation rises up against nation, and there be mighty armies gathered together to encounter one another, what then? 'Tis Christ who is the Lord of armies: he is the Lord strong and mighty, the Lord mighty in battle, and he is with his people to defend 'em, and can dash the most potent princes and their biggest armies in pieces.

He has created the smith that makes their weapons of war, and he hath said that no weapon shall prosper against them. Is. 54:16–17, "Behold, I have created the smith that bloweth the coals in the fire, and that bringeth forth an instrument for his work; and I have created the waster to destroy. No weapon that is formed against thee shall prosper; and every tongue that shall rise against thee in judgment thou shalt condemn. This is the heritage of the servants of the Lord, and their righteousness is of me, saith the Lord."

God's people dwell in Zion where they are safe, and in vain are all weapons of war used against them there, for there God breaks "the arrows of the bow, the shield, and the sword, and the battle." Ps. 76:3–5, "There brake he the arrows of the bow, the shield, and the sword, and the battle. Thou art more glorious and excellent than the mountains of prey. The stouthearted are spoiled, they have slept their sleep: and none of the men of might have found their hands."

The nations may make a great tumult and may come against [God's] people like the rolling of the raging waves of the sea, but all will be in vain. Is. 17:12–13, "Woe to the multitude of many people, which make a noise like the noise of the seas; and to the rushing of nations, that make a rushing like the rushing of mighty waters! The nations shall rush like the rushing of many waters: but God shall rebuke them, and they shall flee far off, and shall be chased as the chaff of the mountains before the wind, and like a rolling thing before the whirlwind."

2. God's servants are in Christ who is in heaven, out of the reach of all the changes and tumults of the world. They have fled for refuge to Christ, and he is in Scripture represented as their hiding place. Ps. 32:7, "Thou art my hiding place." They are united to Christ in such a manner, that the life and happiness of both Christ and them is but one in the original of it, as 'tis with a vine and its branch. And therefore if Christ be out of reach, their life and their happiness is out of reach; and if his life be safe, theirs is so too. John 14:19, "because I live, ye shall live also." Christ, in carrying the children of Israel out of Egypt when there was such a great army pursued 'em with swords and other weapons of war, was compared to an eagle carrying her young in her flight, who carries them high and therefore carries them safe and out of reach of men here below. But Christ, the Savior of his people, is higher than the flight of an eagle: he is in the heaven of heavens; and because he is the Redeemer and surety and vital head of believers, they are as safe as if they were there too: for their life is there hid with him. Col. 3:3, "your life is hid with Christ in God."

3. The river that supplies them never fails in times of the greatest public calamity and trouble. The Holy Spirit, in his blessed influences and comforts, is compared to a river supplying the New Jerusalem, or the spiritual City of God. Rev. 22:1, "And he showed me a pure river of water of life, clear as crystal, proceeding out of the throne of God and of the Lamb"; "rivers of living water," or "water of life," viz., the Holy Spirit, as Christ interprets. John 7:38–39, "He that believeth on me, as the scripture hath said, out of his belly shall flow rivers of living water. (But this spake he of the Spirit, which they that believe on him should receive: for the Holy Ghost was not yet given; because that Jesus was not yet glorified.)" This river is that which supplies God's servants with soul refreshment and comfort, and this river is never dry. And therefore it is that they have no need to be afraid, however great public commotions and troubles arise, yea, though the very earth should be removed. Ps. 46[:1–2], "God is our refuge and strength, a very present help in trouble. Therefore will not we fear, though the earth be removed, and though the mountains be carried into the midst of the sea."

This water may well be called living water upon that account, that the spring that supplies it, which is the love of God, is a living spring, a spring that never fails. And therefore the river flows plentifully in the time of the greatest drought, and the trees that are planted by such a river will flourish and look green when other trees are scorched and burnt up with heat. So are those that trust in the Lord: they need not be afraid of a drought and heat. Jer. 17:7–8, "Blessed is the man that trusteth in the Lord, and whose hope the Lord is. For he shall be as a tree planted by the waters, and that spreadeth out her roots by the river, and shall not see when heat cometh, but her leaf shall be green; and shall not be careful in the year of drought, neither shall cease from yielding fruit."

It has sometimes been the way of enemies that have besieged cities, to turn the course of those streams of water that have run through those cities, to distress the inhabitants with thirst. But the enemies that presume to besiege the church of God can't dry up the waters of that City, but their waters shall not fail; they shall forever be supplied from a never-failing, inexhaustible, infinite fountain.

4. We may argue from what God has done for his church in ages past in times of public calamity, [as in the] old world {and in} Egypt.[3]

Having thus mentioned some things to confirm the truth of the Doctrine, I come now, in the

---

3. This point is squeezed in at the end of the previous paragraph. JE most likely would have expanded on it extemporaneously.

GOD'S CARE FOR HIS SERVANTS IN TIME OF PUBLIC COMMOTIONS 73

II. Second place, to show how God preserves his [people] in safety in times of public commotions and calamities.

First. God does sometimes remarkably distinguish his servants from others in outward preservations. So God preserved David at a time when the land was all involved in war and bloodshed, in the time of Absalom's rebellion.

So God wonderfully preserved Jeremiah when the king of Babylon's armies invaded the land and destroyed. Jer. 39:11–12, "Now Nebuchadnezzar king of Babylon gave charge concerning Jeremiah to Nebuzaradan the captain of the guard, saying, Take him, and look well to him, and do him no harm; but do unto him even as he shall say unto thee."

So also God remarkably preserved the Christians that were in Jerusalem in the time of the second destruction by the Romans. Christ to that end gave 'em a sign whereby they might know when the destruction of it was nigh, that they might timely make their escape out of that accursed city. Luke 21:20–21, "And when ye shall see Jerusalem compassed with armies, then know that the desolation thereof is nigh. Then let them which are in Judea flee to the mountains; and let them which are in the midst of it depart out; and let not them that are in the countries enter thereinto." And accordingly they did so, as approved histories do give account. When they saw this sign, they fled [to] a certain village in the mountains called Pella, and were saved: whereby there was some resemblance in the distinction that was there made between Christians and others, of that distinction that will be made at the day of judgment; for only those that believed in Christ will give so much credit to his word as to fly and leave all that they had in Jerusalem, without so much as turning back out of the field to take their clothes. So that when that sign of Jerusalem's being compassed with armies first appeared, there was at once a remarkable separation made between believers and unbelievers.

Second. Sometimes, if they seem to suffer outward calamities in one respect, God more than makes it up to 'em in other outward good things. So Daniel, who was a servant of God, he was not preserved from the captivity as Jeremiah; he was carried captive as the other Jews were. But God showed[4] him great mercy in the land of his captivity, and exalted him there to great honor and outward prosperity.

---

4. MS: "but he was Grant G. shewing."

Hananiah, Mishael and Azariah[5] were also carried captive into Babylon, and there were cast into a fiery furnace; but it proved the way for their outward advancement. So Jacob suffered with others the difficulties of that public calamity of famine that in his days was in all lands, but it proved a means of great outward blessings to him and his family: it was a means of his seeing his son Joseph again that he thought was dead, and seeing him in great prosperity and honor, and living in plenty and ease with him the rest of his days.

Third. Let what will befall them outwardly, nothing can deprive them of their real happiness. What has any man to fear but a being made unhappy? But this, those that are true servants of God cannot be. They may be deprived of their outward substance, their bodies may be wounded and mangled, but they can't be hurt. The apostle Peter in a time of persecution says to the Christians, 1 Pet. 3:13, "who is he that will harm you, if ye be followers of that which is good?" And therefore a true servant of God has nothing to fear from men in a time of war and of great temporal destructions, though it is true they don't know but their bodies may be killed—because when man has done that, he can go no further. Luke 12:4, "Be not afraid of them that kill the body, and after that have no more that they can do." But their happiness don't depend upon their outward estates, or upon the ease or life of their bodies. Let what will become of these, they have an eternal inheritance, everlasting mansions that Christ has provided for 'em, meat that perishes not, and durable clothing. Sword or famine may be the means of separating soul and body, but they can't separate them from Christ. If men kill them, what do they do to them but send 'em to their rest and glory? They are indeed, though undesignedly, the instruments of their gain. For death is gain to them, and "blessed are the dead that die in the Lord" [Philip. 1:21, Rev. 14:13]. Nothing can hurt them, for their inheritance is incorruptible and undefiled, undiminished, untouched, reserved in heaven for 'em.

Fourth. God will take care that they shall be subject to no outward suffering but such an one and in such time and circumstances as shall contribute to their real happiness. They shall not only not be deprived of their real happiness, but they shall suffer no danger with respect to it in times of public commotion and calamity. Yet nothing shall befall

---

5. The Hebrew names of Shadrach, Meshach, and Abednego, who were cast into the fiery furnace by Nebuchadnezzar but survived (Dan. 3).

them but what shall advance their happiness, nothing but what they shall have cause to rejoice in. If they are persecuted, they shall not be hurt but benefited by it, as gold is refined in the fire. And Christ, who sees things as they are, bids 'em rejoice and be exceeding glad in their persecutions (Matt. 5:12). Their suffering for a moment will work out for them "a far more exceeding and eternal weight of glory" (II Cor. 4:17).

And there shall nothing in the manner, measure, continuance, or any circumstance of their sufferings be allowed that shall in the least hurt their real interest, but all to advance it. They are in happy circumstances, for all things shall work together for their good.[6]

Application

To put persons upon examining themselves, whether or no they are some of God's servants. 'Tis now a time of no small commotion in the world. 'Tis the more suitable that we should closely apply what has been said on this subject to ourselves and diligently improve it for our own benefit at this time, because of the present state of things and aspects of divine providence with respect to the world in general, and our nation and land in particular, in that affair which [is] the special occasion of the appointment of this day. We live at such a time in the age of the world, it is come to be that time of day that 'tis not to be expected that the state of the world will remain a great while as it now is.

If we consider what things are past, how much that is foretold in Scripture is already fulfilled, and how things now are in the world and have been for a considerable time, and what things are foretold yet to be, 'tis reasonable to expect commotions and changes. There are many things seem to forebode great changes in the state of religion in the church of God, and what is in the womb of Providence we can't tell. But the Scripture seems to be very plain and full in it, that that flourishing, happy state of the church that is to be in the latter days will not be introduced without exceeding great strugglings and tumults and overturnings, so great that there never was any to be compared to 'em.

---

6. The first preaching unit ends here. In large letters JE made the notation, "two Hours & two Bells," which may mean that the congregation was to reconvene in two and a half hours, possibly following a midday meal or an event associated with the fast day, such as a militia muster. The restatement of the text and Doctrine at the beginning of the second unit is omitted.

The struggles that the church will then have with her enemies will be as the last, travailing pains of a woman in travail, just before the birth of the child.

'Tis true we don't know that any of us that are here present shall live to see that last and greatest conflict which the church will have with her enemies, though we know not how soon it may be. But this is certain: that what now appears, calls aloud to us to prepare for all events. 'Tis now a time of no small commotion in the world, and especially in our nation that is now involved in war. And there is an appearance of nothing else than of the calamities becoming much greater and far more extensive.

And though at present we don't feel much of it, yet we know not how soon we may. The circumstances of the present war is such, and such are our circumstances, that we in this land are loudly called upon to prepare to feel the effects of war.

Therefore, in the

First place, let all examine themselves whether or no they are some of God's servants. You see how highly such are privileged above all others, what great and effectual care God takes of them, to secure them from all hurt in all public commotions and calamities. 'Tis the servants of God that are thus favored. This is what the angel that has the seal of God cries with so loud and earnest a voice: "Hurt not the earth, nor the sea, nor the trees, till we have sealed the servants of our God in their foreheads." He don't say, "till we have sealed the professors of godliness," or "till we have sealed such as cry, 'Lord, Lord,'" or "till we have sealed all such as have had great affections and great joys, and boast of their great experiences," but "till we have sealed the servants of our God." If you ben't a servant of God, if you seem to be religious, your religion is vain. If you have been never so much affected with sorrow or joy, and whatever experiences you think you have had, you are not marked out for one of God's, to be reserved as one of his children and his jewels. And that you may know whether you are truly God's servants, inquire,

1. Whether or no you serve God as your only master, or are you one that goes about to serve two masters. Have you forsaken all your former masters that once you served, that you might give yourself up wholly to the service of God? Have you not only refrained but renounced your lusts, your old masters? The children of Israel could not serve God till they were gone from their old taskmasters. "Let my people go," says God time after time, "that they may serve *ME*." Now they served the Egyptians, and till they were let go from them, they could not perform that service

of God that he sought of them. Pharaoh proposed that they should serve God and continue to serve the[7] Egyptians too (Ex. 8:25).

But Moses objected against complying with Pharaoh's proposal in this matter, that the serving of God and sacrificing to him that which he required, and their continuing among the Egyptians in slavery to them, were inconsistent one with another; that the Egyptians their taskmasters would abhor that service that God required, and would not tolerate it, but would kill God's worshippers. And therefore there was a necessity of a separation to be made between Israelites and Egyptians in order to God's being served. So the service of God and our continuing still in the service of our lusts are inconsistent one with another. As Christ says, "No man can serve two masters" [Matt. 6:24].

Inquire therefore whether you have truly forsaken your old masters, whatever lusts you formerly served, whatever lusts you formerly were mainly under the dominion of. Was it sensuality? Was it pride, and an affectation of your own honor? Or [inquire] if it was worldliness.

If you would know whether you are truly a servant of God, inquire strictly whether or no you have forsaken Mammon, or are you not to this day, notwithstanding all your pretenses to experience of a work of conversion, more of a servant of your worldly interest than you are of God? Don't you go about to serve God and Mammon, like the Samaritans who worshipped the God of Israel? 2 Kgs. 17:33–34, 41, "They feared the Lord, and served their own gods, after the manner of the nations whom they carried away from thence. Unto this day they do after the former manners: they fear not the Lord, neither do they after their statutes, or after their ordinances, or after the law and commandment which the Lord commanded the children of Jacob, whom he named Israel. . . . So these nations feared the Lord, and served their graven images, both their children, and their children's children, as did their fathers, so do they unto this day."

Be not deceived with a vain hope of being converted. If that be what you are chiefly concerned about and engaged in, to serve your worldly designs and interests, to see to make things out for yourself in this world, how to accomplish and bring about such and [such] worldly designs: and this be more your care and what takes up your heart, more than the service of God, and that for the sake of which 'tis your manner to make the service of God give place, you are none of those that have the seal of God

---

7. MS: "their old."

set on your forehead, nor will you be owned for one of his, nor are you at all secure from those dreadful judgments that shall come on the wind.

If you are one that is commonly more concerned to serve worldly designs and interests than to serve God, then either you are in the gall of bitterness and bond of iniquity, and you are a notorious hypocrite; or else you know better what are signs of godliness than God himself, and God did not know how to give us good rules.

Does [not] Christ say expressly, "He that comes to [me], and hatest not his father, and his mother, [. . . cannot be my disciple]" (Luke 14:26); 1 John 2:15, "He that loves the world, the love of the Father is not in [him]"; and Jas. 4:4, ["Whoever therefore will be a friend of the world is the enemy of God"]?

2. Do you serve God in what you do in religion, or do you only serve yourselves? Is it only or chiefly out of fear of hell, or that you may have good evidence? Inquire how has it been: han't fears carried you further than anything else ever did? While you was under fears of hell and thought yourself in danger of it, was you not willing to do a great deal more in religion than you are since? How does your hope work? Your joys and comforts?

3. Do you take God's service as a task, or as your entertainment and delight? Do you see the beauty of holiness? Are you sensible of the sweetness of it and happiness there is in it? Ps. 119:111, "[Thy testimonies have I taken] as my heritage." 1 John 5:3, "This is the love of God, that we keep his commandments: and his commandments are not grievous."

4. Have you that grace that overcomes that opposition you meet with in God's service, so that you do persevere in a way of universal obedience? Those are the servants [of God] that have Christ's seal and his name set upon their foreheads. Rev. 3:12, "Him that overcometh will I make a pillar in the temple of my God, and he shall go no more out: and I will write upon him the name of my God, and the name of the city of my God, which is New Jerusalem, which cometh down out of heaven from my God: and I will write upon him my new name."

5. Inquire whether you have God's seal set upon you. Have you his image and superscriptions set on your heart? Seals of old used to have the person's name engraven on it, and his image.

Have you the spirit and temper of a Christian? This is the image and superscription [of God. This is] the temper of Christ.

Second Use is of *Exhortation*.

[*Exh.*] 1. To such as are in a Christless condition, to make haste to get an interest in Christ, that you may be some of those servants of God that God will take such effectual care to preserve in times of public commotion and calamity. You know not what you are born to; you know not what you are to see in the world. We have, ever since our childhood, lived in a country which has been in a great measure in quietness, not subject to those great commotions and revolutions and extraordinary troubles which have been in many other lands. It has been with this land hitherto as it was sometimes said of Moab, Jer. 48:11–12, "not emptied from vessel to vessel." But that we have enjoyed such ease and quietness hitherto, is no sign that it will be so still. God seems, if we may judge from the aspect of things, to be coming forth to do something great in the world, and 'tis not likely that this land will be unconcerned or will have no share in the changes that are coming, whatever they be. God is shaking his hand over us. We read of those that, when God's hand is lifted up, will not see (Is. 26:11); but it there follows, "they shall see."

You know not what you are to see, what troubles and tumults and great trials God may bring upon this land. Now is your time to prepare; now is your time to get into a refuge before the storm comes.

When God was about to bring that terrible storm of thunder and hail upon the land of Egypt, notice was given of it beforehand, that those that would take warning might seasonably get under shelter. And some, they took warning and fled into houses; but others, that did not take warning, they were miserably destroyed (Ex. 9:18–25). They were surprised abroad without any shelter or hiding places in that dismal storm, with hailstones and lightning and thunders upon their heads, and fire round about 'em: and then it was too late for 'em to flee; there was no escape for them; it came upon 'em unawares and were soon disabled from flying to any refuge, and so perished miserably.

So it may be with you, if you don't take warning. Now you are warned therefore: Fly for shelter! Fly to the Lord Jesus Christ, who is an hiding place from the wind and covert from the tempest! Now you may fly, now the door stands open!

Don't be like the wicked of the old world, who would not believe Noah when he told 'em {that God would destroy the world with a flood}.[8]

All that are out of Christ lie miserably exposed. There is no safety for 'em. They are utterly unprovided for public calamities and troubles. They

---

8. No Scripture account tells of Noah warning others about the impending deluge, though in 2 Pet. 2:5 he is called "a preacher of righteousness."

have no security from any public judgments. When a land is filled with the grievous calamities of war, and the sword of the enemy prevails, it may be compared to the stormy seasons that we have in the winter. Christ is said in the 25th [chapter] of Isaiah, 4th verse, to be "a refuge from the storm, [. . .] when the blast of the terrible ones is as the storm against the wall"; and in the 4th [chapter] of Isaiah, 6th verse, he is called "a covert from storm and from rain."

How badly would you been off in those terrible stormy seasons that we have had this winter,[9] if you had no shelter or covert but had remained abroad, exposed to the force of the terrible winds and tempests. How miserably would you have perished. But you may possibly see worse storms than these, and be exposed to perish much more miserably, if you are out of Christ: for there is no other refuge that will defend persons in a time when the overflowing scourge passes through.

The four angels do as it were now stand, holding the four winds of heaven from blowing upon this part of God's earth. Though the winds seem of late to have threatened us—we hear of their vehement struggling and tumultuousness at a distance—but yet they are held back hitherto from us. They han't yet a commission given to {hurt the earth and the sea}, and it may be 'tis for that end, that God may first set his seal upon the hearts of his elect servants, those that are chosen to obedience through sanctification. We see that the angel that has the seal of the living God is very busy: his sealing work goes on in these American plantations; many are sealed daily in one place and another, have God's mark set upon their foreheads. So we hear it has been in Pennsylvania, and in Carolina and Georgia, and in the Jerseys and New York, and in Boston and some of the towns adjacent; and something of this sealing work has lately been carried on here and in one of the neighboring towns.[10]

It may be 'tis to prepare 'em for the storm. It may be this work now goes on, and God's elect servants are now sealed, because the four angels have commission to hurt the earth and the sea, and the four winds are

---

9. In his journal, Northampton hatmaker Ebenezer Hunt recorded that the winter of 1740–41 saw an "Abundance of cold, rainy weather. About Nov. 20 the great river froze over, & some days after there was a great rain which occasioned the greatest flood the first week in December that has been known for 35 years. After the flood ceased, there were four weeks of excessively cold weather; the eaves of the houses scarcely dropped all the time. Then we had a great thaw followed by cold weather until late in the spring." Judd MSS, Mass. Series, vol. 1, p. 25, Forbes Library.

10. A reference to the revivals set off by the itinerations of George Whitefield, followed by other controversial preachers such as Gilbert Tennent.

going to be let loose upon this part of the earth, and God is taking care that his elect may not be hurt.

If this should prove to be the case, how miserable will all such be as shall then not be found amongst the sealed!

When we read of the locusts that came upon the earth, to whom "is given power as the scorpions of the earth have power," in the 14th [chapter] of Revelation, 3rd [and] 4th verses, we there read that they are commanded to hurt none "but only those men that have not the seal of God in their foreheads."

When the four angels let loose the four winds, and when God lets men loose to rage and destroy, they have power given 'em to hurt those men that are found without the seal in their foreheads. It is in their commission to hurt them; yea, they are let loose to that very end, that they might hurt 'em, that God by them might chastise 'em and punish 'em, and might pour out the vials of his wrath upon them. The four angels had it given to 'em to hurt the earth and sea to that end, that they might plague the men that have not the seal of God.

And so when God brings great public calamities upon the earth by wars and tumults, it is to that end. God sometimes lets loose foreign enemies to come into a professing country, that are like locusts and scorpions to waste and destroy; and when it is so, it is in wrath against all such as han't the seal, for they shall suffer God's wrath by 'em.

How much therefore does it concern you to seek now that you may have the seal of God also set upon your forehead, and that you may get into the refuge before the storm. When you see many flying for refuge and Christ is calling in one and another, cry earnestly to him that you also may be effectually called. How sorrowful does your case appear, that you have been passed by so long. The angel of the covenant, that has the seal of the living God, has been doing his work now for a considerable time; he has sealed a great number. What numbers were sealed six years ago, and then you was passed over. The angel that set God's seal upon the foreheads of others passed you by then, and when he seemed to have done the work that he had then, you were left. When that angel departed, great numbers of your neighbors appeared with their heavenly Father's name written on their foreheads; but you yet remained without that name written on you. And since that, the angel with the seal of God has gone to other places and there has been carrying[11] on his work of

---

11. MS: "carry."

sealing the elect servants of God, and has sealed multitudes far and near, and now at length has come round hither again and renewed his work—especially among the younger generation, those that were not grown to years of discretion when he was here before—and has been setting God's seal upon the foreheads of one and another: but still he has passed you by, and you remain to this day without that seal of God; you han't God's mark upon you; you are none of his.

After the angel with God's seal has gone through a place, oftentimes destroying angels follow. And when they come, they smite everyone that has not the mark. See Ezek. 9, from the 2nd to the end of the 6th verse: And behold, six men came from the way of the higher gate, which lieth toward the north, and every man a slaughter weapon in his hand; and one man among them was clothed with linen, and with a writer's inkhorn by his side: and they went in, and stood beside the brazen altar. And the glory of the God of Israel was gone up from the cherub, whereupon he was, to the threshold of the house. And he called to the man clothed with linen, which had the writer's inkhorn by his side; and the Lord said unto him, Go through the midst of the city, through the midst of Jerusalem, and set a mark upon the foreheads of the men that sigh and that cry for all the abominations that be done in the midst thereof. And to the others he said in mine hearing, Go ye after him through the city, and smite: let not your eye spare, neither have ye pity: slay utterly old and young, both maids, and little children, and women: but come not near any man upon whom is the mark; and begin at my sanctuary. Then they began at the ancient men which were before the house.

Therefore if you should still be passed by as you have been hitherto, and should be found without the mark of God when the destroying angels come with slaughter weapons in their hand, what will you do, or which way will you turn? The destroying angels won't pity nor spare you. See, their orders are to go through the city and smite: "Let not your eye spare, neither have ye pity; slay utterly old and young, both maids and little children, and women." They will strike you with a mortal stroke, and there[12] will be none to save you; there will be no protection given you, and no refuge for you.

If you han't the seal of God set upon you, and han't his name as it were written on your forehead, you have the devil's name written there.

---

12. MS: "th."

You are marked as some of his, and go about every day with that black mark upon you. You carry about with you the devil's brand.

If you han't God's image and superscription stamped upon your heart, you have the devil's image, and in the day of God's visitation Christ won't own you as one of his, but will say, "Depart, I know you not." And there will be no restraint laid on the devil and his instruments; they'll find you with their mark, and they will seize you as their proper prey.

And how inexpressibly miserable will you be if God should visit the land with the sword of a conquering enemy, that should subdue and enslave the inhabitants of the land.

Such public calamities commonly prove the overthrow of great multitudes. Sometimes a land, when invaded and overrun with a foreign enemy, is as it were sealed with blood: and then what becomes of those that han't the mark? How thick do the souls of such descend into hell—many thousands sent thither sometimes in a few days.

If we should see such a day in this land, what will your worldly possessions signify to you without an interest in Christ? What you have may be taken from you. If your life should be preserved, you might in one day be stripped of all that you have in the world.

And what a miserable case would you be in, if there should come a time of persecution in the land, and you should have that trial, that you must either openly renounce your religion and go over to the profession and constant practice of the popish religion, or else must die a cruel death. What would you do in such a trial without an interest in Christ? What a dreadful case would you be [in], and what danger of the issue's being your being sealed up forever in a state of damnation. You would not be prepared for death, nor would there be any likelihood that you would withstand the great temptation. Natural men have no principles that are ordinarily sufficient to {withstand such a trial}.

And if you openly renounced {your religion}, the consequence in all probability would be your damnation, and much more dreadful damnation.

Therefore now bestir your[selves]. This is your opportunity, now while there is respite, and while the angels that have power to hurt {the earth and the sea} are still holding back the winds. Now is the sealing time, and now Christ calls and invites you, and now there is a door of mercy set open before you. Hear what God says to you in the 2nd chapter of Zephaniah, 1st, 2nd, [and] 3rd verses: "Gather yourselves together, yea, gather together, O nation not desired; before the decree bring forth, before the day pass as the chaff, before the fierce anger of the Lord come upon you, before the day of the Lord's anger come upon you. Seek ye the Lord, all ye meek of the earth, which have wrought his judgment; seek righteousness, seek meekness: it may be ye shall be hid in the day of the Lord's anger."

If you may have God's seal and his image stamped upon your heart, then you will be happy. They that are truly in Christ, they need not be afraid of evil tidings. If there should come a great storm to hurt the earth and the sea, Christ, with infinite kindness and love, says to 'em, as in Is. 26:20–21, "Come, my people, enter thou into thy chambers, and shut thy doors about thee: hide thyself as it were for a little moment, until the indignation be overpast. For, behold, the Lord cometh out of his place to punish the inhabitants of the earth for their iniquity."

And in Christ's chambers they are safe. Let the nations of the world tumultuate and rage never so much, or if all the world should be filled with confusion and wars and the most dreadful uproars, yea, if heaven and earth should all go to wrack, if the mountains should be carried into the midst of the sea, and the earth should be broken to pieces with earthquakes, and the stars of heaven should fall to the earth, and the whole visible world should be all wracked into one ruinous heap, yet they need not fear; they are safe and out of reach. Whatever becomes of this world, they will appear joyful on Mt. Zion with their Father's name written in their foreheads (Rev. 14:1).

Exh. 2. I would exhort those that profess godliness earnestly to such a preparation for public commotions and calamities. And particularly, let all prepare for persecution. None knows but he shall have that trial. It has been a common trial.

(1) Set your hearts less upon the world.

(2) Be more in the exercise of a self-denying, suffering spirit now. "If you have run with the footmen, [and they have wearied thee, how canst thou contend with horses? and if in the land of peace, wherein thou trustedst, they wearied thee, then how wilt thou do in the swelling of Jordan]?" (Jer. 12:5).

(3) Earnestly seek that you may have God's seal more sensibly set upon you. Seek that seal of the Spirit in your heart. Eph. 1:13, "Ye were sealed with that holy Spirit of promise"; 4:30, "grieve not the Spirit of God, by which ye were sealed." You will need clear evidence.

Exh. 3. Let parents be hence exhorted to be very painful and diligent in instructing and educating your children, that they may be some of

God's sealed ones. You have been the instruments of bringing of 'em into this evil, sinful, troublesome world, where is abundance of commotion and tumult and great calamities, and you know not what your children are born to, as they are very young. It is much more likely that they may live to see great commotion and changes in the world.

Considering the age in which they are born, it would not be strange if they should live to the ordinary age of men and see[13] great changes in the world. And if great commotions should come, and an overflowing scourge should pass through while they are very young and even in their childhood, the destroying angels won't pity nor spare 'em if they are in their sins. You see that in the 9th chapter of Ezekiel they are commanded to smite little children that have not the mark of God set upon them. If you love your children, it concerns you a great deal more to take care and pains that they may be safe in Christ and have God's seal set upon them, than to provide earthly things for 'em.

You perhaps are taking a great deal of pains that you may have something to leave to your children for their outward supply when you are dead, when, if they should live, they may see those times that it will prove of no service to 'em. It may be all swept away at once by a destroying, persecuting enemy.

If such troubles as those should come, your estates or portions that you lay up for 'em will stand 'em in but little stead. What they will need then will be God's grace in their hearts and his name written on their foreheads. How will your consciences hereafter accuse you, if your children should be taken from you to be instructed in the popish religion, {or if they} should be carried captive to Canada.[14] Therefore don't neglect their souls. Be abundant in counsels and warning them, and never let 'em alone, nor let God alone for 'em, till you have hopeful evidence.

---

13. MS: "& not see." JE interlineated "not" earlier in the sentence but did not delete this second occurrence, so it is omitted here to prevent a double negative.

14. JE may be referring to his cousin Eunice Williams, the "unredeemed captive," who in 1704 had been taken by Indians to Canada, where she remained and converted to Catholicism; she had visited her family in Longmeadow with her Indian husband in 1740. See Demos, *Unredeemed Captive*.

The Curse of Meroz

December 1741

THE EXCITEMENT OF THE recruiting campaign of summer 1740 quickly gave way to the realities of war in 1741. The American regiment of thirty-five hundred soldiers arrived in Jamaica in the winter of 1740–41 to join the British regulars. Early reports of the campaign were favorable, but by April of 1741, sickness had taken its toll and the campaign stalled without taking Fort Lazaro. General Thomas Wentworth admitted, "we cannot give a pleasing account concerning Cartagena."[1] Disease and sickness had literally decimated the British ranks; the British navy replenished its losses by impressing soldiers from the American regiment. This reorganization of forces was controversial among the Americans because they saw the terms of their enlistment limited to the officers under whom they volunteered. Of the thirty-five hundred enthusiastic volunteers who left New York for glory and plunder, less than three hundred returned home. In light of British setbacks, introspection and caution replaced the optimism of Edwards's martial sermons of February 1741.

While Britain languished in the West Indies, the awakenings built momentum back in New England. Edwards preached *The Curse of Meroz* to draw clear "battle lines" between those who supported God's work and those who did not. In the Biblical examples of Deborah and Barak, God cursed Meroz because "they came not to the help of the Lord, to the help of the Lord against the mighty." These battle lines were beginning to emerge in the burgeoning revivals. The itinerancy and rhetoric of Whitefield drew large crowds and much controversy. On September

---

1. *Boston Gazette*, July 6, 1741.

1741, Edwards delivered Yale's commencement address later published as *Distinguishing Marks of the Spirit* where, instead of endorsing one faction in the controversy over another, he tried to cobble together a coalition from the various factions. While Edwards did much to carve out a moderate position, he failed to quell the objections of the "Old Light" established or satisfy the enthusiastic thirst of "New Light" itinerates such as James Davenport. *The Curse of Meroz*, on the one hand, was a call to embrace the revivals and those who did not oppose the work of the Lord.

When Edwards preached *The Curse of Meroz* in December of 1741, Britain's struggles in the West Indies were widely advertised. The general theme of the sermon draws on martial language, however it seems as if Edwards included not-so-veiled references to American's involvement in Cartagena. One example includes his use of Judges 5 where Edwards drew parallels between the Biblical story and Blakeney's recruiting campaign of the previous year: "Deborah and Barak, with whom great part of the people Israel joined themselves and willingly offered themselves to assist in this war without either being pressed or hired." Military service, in this text, is voluntary without the need for impressment. Therefore, Britain's practice of impressing soldiers into naval duty, according to Edwards's suggestion, became one of the reasons for her failure.

The trajectory of American involvement in the West Indies paralleled the course of the revivals in late 1741. Both began with much promise in 1740 but had lately faltered, opening divisions which threatened the success of each. Edwards's view of history and providence allowed him to see these parallel trajectories as part of a single divine program to advance the gospel through the outpouring of the Spirit as well as the advance of the Protestant cause abroad which paved the way for further outpourings of the Spirit. Therefore, *The Curse of Meroz* drew on both the martial and revival contexts to further the advance of the gospel at home and abroad.

* * * * *

This sermon, a single preaching unit in length, consists of twenty-two duodecimo leaves. At the top of page one is Edwards' date, "Dec. 1741." There is no shorthand to indicate a re-preaching, but that Edwards preached this sermon again is evident by the later changes, both interlineations and cross outs, which are distinguished by their darker ink. The sketchy nature of the sermon, particularly the application, is a further indication of how Edwards was altering his preaching style in the months after Whitefield preached in Northampton. As in his lectures and the preceding two sermons, Edwards is clearly moving in this sermon toward an outline style that allowed greater room for "freedom" in the pulpit.

On the eleventh and twelfth leaves is found the beginning of an Application for another sermon. It is written upside down relative to the text of the sermon on Judg. 5:23, and it is crossed out but still legible. These two pages lack an expansion of the headings, an illustration of how Edwards blocked out the major heads of his sermons beforehand.

The Curse of Meroz

Judges 5:23

Curse ye Meroz, said the angel of the Lord, curse ye bitterly the inhabitants thereof; because they came not to the help of the Lord, to the help of the Lord against the mighty.

THIS IS PART OF the song of Deborah and Barak, which they sung on occasion of the glorious victory {over Sisera, the captain of the army of Jabin, king of Canaan}.

The land [of Israel] before this victory were in distressing circumstances. They were greatly oppressed by the Canaanites, were brought into miserable bondage and slavery by them and were cruelly used, and their enemies were exceeding strong and powerful. Chapter 4:2–3, "And the Lord sold them into the hand of Jabin king of Canaan, that reigned in Hazor; the captain of whose host was Sisera, which dwelt in Harosheth of the gentiles. And the children of Israel cried unto the Lord: for he had nine hundred chariots of iron; and twenty years he mightily oppressed the children of Israel." This distress is represented, vv. 6–7: "In the days of Shamgar the son of Anath, in the days of Jael, the highways were unoccupied, and the travelers walked through byways. The inhabitants of the villages ceased, they ceased in Israel, until that I Deborah arose, that I arose a mother in Israel." [Verse] 11, "They that are delivered from the noise of archers in the places of drawing water, there shall they rehearse the righteous acts of the Lord, even the righteous acts toward the inhabitants of his villages in Israel: then shall the people of the Lord go down to the gates."

They were delivered by a glorious work of God that he wrought for his people Israel by the hands of Deborah and Barak, with whom great part of the people Israel joined themselves and willingly offered themselves to assist in this war without either being pressed or hired. It was a common cause that nearly concerned them all, and therefore they voluntarily, when called thereto by Deborah and Barak, went forth to the war in great multitudes, being animated to it by the Spirit, that same Spirit that moved Deborah and Barak to undertake in this glorious cause. See v. 2, "Praise ye the Lord for the avenging of Israel, when the people willingly offered themselves." Verse 9, "My heart is toward the governors of Israel, that offered themselves willingly among the people. Bless ye the Lord."

But yet there were some particular parts of the land the inhabitants of which did not offer to promote this glorious work. They were not animated as others were, were not willing to follow Deborah and Barak to the war without wages, and therefore, let their brethren fight the Lord's battles and jeopard their lives while they indolently stayed at home. They chose not to put themselves to the toils and difficulties of the war; but had rather indulge their sloth and sleep in a whole skin at home, and more of the same spirit that the children of Israel were [of] in Egypt, who said to Moses when {being pursued by Pharaoh}, "Let us alone, that we may serve the Egyptians" [Ex. 14:12]. So these did practically say, "Let us alone."

Thus it was particularly with the tribe of Reuben, the inhabitants of Gilead, and the tribes of Dan and Asher. Verses 15–17, "And the princes of Issachar were with Deborah; even Issachar, and also Barak: he was sent on foot into the valley. For the divisions of Reuben there were great thoughts of heart. Why abodest thou among the sheepfolds, to hear the bleatings of the flocks? For the divisions of Reuben there were great searchings of heart. Gilead abode beyond Jordan: and why did Dan remain in ships? Asher continued on the sea shore, and abode in his breaches." And also the town of Meroz, who thereby brought that heavy curse upon themselves that we have in the text. Wherein I would observe:

1. By whom it is that this curse is denounced: [the] captain of the Lord's hosts. Josh. 5:13–15, "And it came to pass, when Joshua was by Jericho, that he lifted up his eyes and looked, and, behold, there stood a man over against him with his sword drawn in his hand: and Joshua went unto him, and said unto him, Art thou for us, or for our adversaries? And he said, Nay; but as captain of the host of the Lord am I now come. And Joshua fell on his face to the earth, and did worship, and said unto him, What saith my lord unto his servant? And the captain of the Lord's host

said unto Joshua, Loose thy shoe from off thy foot; for the place whereon thou standest is holy. And Joshua did so."

2. The greatness of the curse {pronounced against Meroz}.

3. Who they were that were thus bitterly cursed. [Meroz is] supposed to be a city near Kedesh, the place whence Barak [came].

4. The sin that brought this bitter curse, viz., not putting to their hand to assist and forward the victory that was obtained {over Sisera}. Two aggravations are mentioned:

(1) That it was the work of God. That victory and deliverance that was thereby procured for the children of Israel was a glorious work of God that he wrought for his people and against his enemies. It is all along represented as a work of God. {The children of Israel} cried to the Lord {and God sent them Deborah}, a prophetess. {It was accomplished} by those that were very feeble in comparison of their enemies, enemies exceeding strong. {They were} poor slaves {who were} under great disadvantages. {They were} unarmed, {as we read in} v. 8: "was there a shield or spear seen among forty thousand in Israel?"

This song represents it as the glorious work of God. It was not by the strength of the people but a remarkable and most visible hand of God. Verse 20, "They fought from heaven; the stars in their courses fought against Sisera." The inhabitants of Meroz are blamed that they came not to the help of the Lord. The expression is remarkable, for though God stands in [no] need of man's help, yet he is pleased to make use [of] the endeavors of men in carrying on his work, and as it were makes use of their help as a king that goes forth to war is helped by his soldiers.

(2) Another aggravation of their sin mentioned, is the power of their enemies, and the great need there was upon that account for all to join and assist one another to their utmost in this great work. The case was more extreme, the distress of Israel the greater and more badly calling for help, and there was the more need of the help of all.

Doctrine

When God remarkably appears in a great work for his church and against his enemies, it is a most dangerous thing for any of his professing people to lie still and not to put to an helping hand.

It is a thing that exposes to the curse of the angel of the Lord, i.e., of Jesus Christ and to his bitter curse. Here I would:

I. Briefly mention some reasons of the Doctrine, and then proceed to the Application.

II. Observe what evils they will expose themselves to.

I. *Reasons.*

First. Christ's people are his army, and he may well highly resent it if, when he in a remarkable manner leads the way, they won't follow him to the battle. Christ is often spoken of in Scripture as the Lord of hosts or armies, the Lord mighty in battle and the captain of the salvation of his people. Thus when he appeared to Joshua. And his people are his soldiers; his church is his army. So the church is represented in Cant. 6:13, "Return, return, O Shulamite; return, return, that we may look upon thee. What will ye see in the Shulamite? As it were the company of two armies."

And all God's visible people do professedly belong to this army. By their profession they have listed under this captain. And therefore it may well be highly resented if they don't resort to him when he in a remarkable manner orders his honor to be displayed, and if they refuse to follow him when he in an extraordinary manner orders his trumpet to be blown, and gloriously appears going forth against his enemies. Amongst men, martial laws are exceeding severe, and if any soldier in such a case should refuse to follow his general, he would immediately be shot down or thrust through with a sword.

When Christ appears remarkably going forth against his enemies, he as it were blows the trumpet, as Ehud did when he had slain Eglon, king of Moab. And God's Israel should be gathered after Christ as they were after him. Judg. 3:27–28, "And it came to pass, when he was come, that he blew a trumpet in the mountain of Ephraim, and the children of Israel went down with him from the mount, and he before them. And he said unto them, Follow after me: for the Lord hath delivered your enemies the Moabites into your hand. And they went down after him, and took the fords of Jordan toward Moab, and suffered not a man to pass over."[1]

Second. God at such a time appears in peculiar manifestations of his glory. And therefore, not to follow him at such a time is to cast great contempt on him. 'Tis very heinous at any time not to be much affected with the divine glory, and argues a mean and low thought of God; but

---

1. On the significance of this biblical imagery, see *The Blowing of the Great Trumpet* (no. 620, WJE 22:436–47).

especially not to be animated at a time when God does in a very unusual and extraordinary manner display his glory.

A subject that stood in the way and should not appear to bow before his king, when he appeared riding in triumph or in a magnificent procession in all his majesty and magnificence, would be looked upon as casting great contempt on his prince and would be thought unworthy to live; he would perish from the way. So if a person should stand by on a king's coronation day and should be a spectator of the solemnity of his coronation, and should appear silent and mute when all the multitude were crying, "God save the king," he would soon be taken notice of and would not be suffered to stand long on his feet, but would be smitten down for his open contempt.

At a time when [God] remarkably appears going forth {against his enemies}, he gives peculiar manifestations of glory {and} majesty {in it}. And therefore, according as the displays of God's glory before our eyes are greater, a proportionably greater curse do we expose ourselves to if we are not affected and animated by it.

Third. God at such a time appears in a remarkable exercise of kindness to his people, whereby all such as are his people are laid under high obligations to join with him. He don't only appear in a glorious manifestation of his majesty, but also of his love to his people. When God remarkably appears in a great work for his church and against his and their enemies, if those that are of it, his church, will sit still and won't come and join with their Lord and savior in such a work of goodness and grace to them, they will make themselves guilty of the most extreme and intolerable ingratitude. They will sin against their own mercies and their own happiness. As if the citizens of a city that is besieged by an enemy should sit still and refuse to arise and open their gates to a glorious deliverer, that appears in mighty power and fervent love to fight for them and save their lives, to raise the siege of their enemies and to set 'em [at] liberty.

Fourth. At such a time as that wherein God {appears in a glorious manifestation of his majesty}, there is no such thing as being neuters. There is a necessity of being either for or against the King that then gloriously appears. As it would be if a king should come into one of his provinces that had been opposed by an enemy, where some of the people had fallen off to the enemy and joined with them against their lawful sovereign and against his loyal subjects, and the lawful sovereign himself should come into the province and should ride forth there against his enemies, and should call upon all that were on his side to come to gather themselves to him. There would be no such thing in such a case as standing neuter. They that lay still and did not come to the king, might justly be looked upon as his enemies and treated as some that were undoubtedly rebels. And in the day of battle, when the two armies join, there is no such thing as being of neither party. All must be of one side or the other.

So when a king is crowned and there are public manifestations of joy on that account, there is no such thing as standing by an indifferent spectator. All must appear as loyal subjects and express their joy on that occasion, or be accounted enemies. So it always is when God, in any great dispensation of his providence, does remarkably set his King on his holy hill of Zion, and when Christ does in an extraordinary manner come down from heaven to the earth and appears in his visible church in a work of salvation for his people. So it was when Christ came down from heaven in his incarnation and appeared on earth in his human presence: there was no such thing as being neuters, neither of his side nor against him. Those that sat still and did nothing, and did [not] declare for him and come and join with him, were justly looked upon as his enemies. As Christ says, Matt. 12:30, "He that is not with me[2] is against me; and he that gathereth not with me scattereth abroad."

So it is in a time when Christ is remarkably spiritually present as well as when he was bodily present, and when he comes to carry on the work of redemption in the application of it as well as in the imputation. And therefore,

Fifth. They that don't join with Christ in such a work must expect to be sharers with his enemies. For the time that we speak of is a time when [Christ] remarkably appears going forth against his enemies, and that, as supposed in the Doctrine, Christ then remarkably goes forth to execute vengeance on his enemies. And therefore all such as at that time don't appear on his side, but rather against him, must expect to share in that remarkable vengeance he executes on his enemies at that time.

But as has been now observed, all that ben't with him are against him. All that on such an occasion don't arise and follow the captain must be looked upon as on the enemies' side, and accordingly, must expect to have the weapons of the glorious conqueror turned against them, and to fall

2. MS: "us."

amongst the rest of his enemies that at that time he destroys. Thus when Christ appears to destroy the spiritual Babylon, 'tis loudly proclaimed to Christ's people to come out of her, that {they be not partakers of her sins}. Rev. 18:4, "And I heard another voice from heaven, saying, Come out of her, my people, that ye be not partakers of her sins, and that ye receive not of her plagues"; i.e., "Come out of the city of my enemies, come and join with me and don't join with mine enemies, lest ye partake of their plagues."

Sixth. At such a time God appears especially determined to put honor upon his Son, and therefore, they that won't glorify him actively must expect that he will be glorified upon them in their suffering. God had much in his heart to glorify his dear and only begotten Son. He has sworn that every knee [shall bow], and there are some special seasons that [he] appoints [to] that end, wherein he comes forth to fulfill that promise and oath.

There are some special seasons when God did in a more remarkable manner set his King on his holy hill of Zion. Such a time is spoken of in the second Psalm, when God should be about to give him the heathen for his inheritance [vv. 6–12].

When such a time [comes], it will be everyone's wisdom, whether they be great or small, to kiss the Son, to come and join with him. And those that refuse must expect that he will be angry and that, as he rides forth in the chariots of his power, they shall be smitten and shall perish from the way, and that he will dash 'em in pieces with his rod of iron. Ps. 2:7–9, "I will declare the decree: the Lord hath said unto me, Thou art my Son; this day have I begotten thee. Ask of me, and I shall give thee the heathen for thine inheritance, and the uttermost parts of the earth for thy possession. Thou shalt break them with a rod of iron; thou shalt dash them in pieces like a potter's vessel"; as much as to say, "I am determined upon it that my Son shall be honored. It is my declared decree {that he shall be honored by those that oppose him}." There seems to be an allusion to a king's riding forth in triumph in a solemn procession.

Seventh. Such a time is always spoken of as a resemblance of a day of judgment. There are often in Scripture predictions of times when Christ shall come and remarkably appear in the world, to destroy the kingdom of his enemies and to {judge the world}. And such seasons are almost always spoken of in language adapted to the day of judgment, as though they were all types of the great day of Christ's coming: so that great gathering in of the elect that accompanied the destruction of Jerusalem; so the pouring out of the Spirit at the destruction of Antichrist; so the glorious gospel times, [spoken of] in Psalms. Ps. 9:6–8, "O thou enemy, destructions are come to a perpetual end: and thou hast destroyed cities; their memorial is perished with them. But the Lord shall endure for ever: he hath prepared his throne for judgment. And he shall judge the world in righteousness, he shall minister judgment to the people in uprightness."

Such a time is like a day of judgment on this account. Thus it is foretold, Ps. 110, "The Lord said unto my Lord, Sit thou at my right hand, until I make thine enemies thy footstool. The Lord shall send the rod of thy strength out of Zion: rule thou in the midst of thine enemies. Thy people shall be willing in the day of thy power, in the beauties of holiness from the womb of the morning: thou hast the dew of thy youth. The Lord hath sworn, and will not repent, Thou art a priest for ever after the order of Melchizedek. The Lord at thy right hand shall strike through kings in the day of his wrath. He shall judge amongst the heathen, he shall fill the places with the dead bodies; he shall wound the heads over many countries. He shall drink of the brook in the way: therefore shall he lift up the head."

Eighth. At such a time, the enemies of Christ do greatly exert themselves to hinder his work, and therefore, surely his professing friends are loudly called upon to exert themselves to promote it. Surely it will be provoking to God if his pretended friends will stand by and see his enemies greatly and vigorously exerting themselves against his cause and kingdom, and they sit still and not put to their hand to promote it.

If they have any true friendship to Christ in them, to see the violent opposition of enemies would have a great tendency to animate them and excite their zeal. That is the nature of true friendship. This is mentioned as a great aggravation of the sin of the inhabitants of Meroz: that the enemies of the Lord were mighty against his work.

Ninth. At such a time, there are glorious examples to animate the friends of Christ. Of those that do greatly exert themselves {to promote his work}, there always is a Spirit poured out on a number. Some jeopard their lives {for Christ's sake}. This will be a great aggravation [of the sin of those who do not greatly exert themselves]: to stand by and see their brethren. This was a great aggravation of the sin of the inhabitants of Meroz. Verses 14–15, "Out of Ephraim was there a root of them against Amalek; after thee, Benjamin, among thy people; out of Machir came down governors, and out of Zebulun they that handle the pen of the writer. And the princes of Issachar were with Deborah; even Issachar, and also Barak: he was sent on foot into the valley. For the divisions of Reuben there were great thoughts of heart." Verse 18, "Zebulun and Naphtali were a people that jeoparded their lives unto the death in the high places of the field." Angels and men were jointly engaged. It is always so.

II. What curse they will expose themselves to.

First. To have no part in the blessing.

Second. To be sealed up in hardness and lewdness.

Third. To be set forth as visible monuments of God's displeasure in this world.

Fourth. To an aggravated punishment hereafter.

Application.

Use I may be of *Warning*, to warn all to take heed to themselves that they don't make themselves guilty by that which is spoken of in the Doctrine at this day when God remarkably appears in a great work for his church and against his enemies.

First. [We] can't lie still at such a time as this. Now God is going forth {against his enemies}. We are his professing people {and belong to his army}. Let all take heed to themselves that they don't expose themselves to the curse of the inhabitants of Meroz by lying still and not putting to an helping hand.

There are a great many here present that do make an explicit profession of an experience {of grace}, profess to find in themselves evidences of being true and sincere friends of God. In them it will be especially aggravated and especially dangerous {if they refuse to follow him}. You that call yourselves true saints, if your practice is such as not to help forward this great work, you hinder vastly more than others. Dull, sleepy, carnal saints are especial clogs to the work.

Let such inquire how it has been: whether they, when they take a view of the state of religion and the things which God has been doing since this great work began here seven years ago, and view their own practice and the consequence of it, whether this work has been promoted, its reputation and purpose advanced, {or whether they have lain still and not put to an helping hand}; and how it has been this year.

If it has been so hitherto, it must not be any longer. You must rouse up yourself. It grows more and more intolerable. The trumpet sounds louder and louder to call you [to] battle, {and you must rouse up yourself}. It is insufferable for those that call themselves true saints to continue still, loitering at home, slumbering and sleeping.

Second. Particularly, let all take heed to themselves that they don't do those things that have a direct tendency to hinder this work rather than to help it forward. Indeed, dullness and inactivity only[3] has a tendency {to hinder this work}. "He that is not with me is against me" [Matt. 12:30]. But there are other things that are positive that have a more direct tendency, and these may be either in a person's talk or behavior. Talk may be such as has a considerable tendency to {hinder the work, to} create suspicions. What wounds the reputation of a work wounds the work itself. And so a person's practice may be such as exceedingly tends {to hinder this work rather than to help it forward}: to move those things that tend to youthful vanity; to do anything that[4] tends to contention, as to enter into any broil.

[*Use* II may be of] *Motive.*

First. The work of God in Israel, spoken of in the text, was a type of that very work of God that is to be wrought for his church in the latter days that we are expecting, and which seems to be now beginning. There is a great work of God often foretold, wherein {Christ triumphs over his enemies}.

This great battle of Deborah and Barak with the Canaanites—that the inhabitants of Meroz are cursed for not joining—was designed for a type of this very thing. I prove it thus: when that great battle between Christ and his enemies, wherein {he will destroy his enemies}, is foretold, {it is shadowed forth in the history of Israel}. Rev. 16:16, "And he gathered them together into a place called in the Hebrew tongue Armageddon." Verse 19 of the context, "The kings came and fought, then fought the kings of Canaan in Taanach by the waters of Megiddo."

---

3. MS: "only dullness and inactivity."

4. Here appears a deleted heading for the Application of another, apparently discarded sermon: "II. To encourage drooping saints more considerably to rely and rest [on Christ] under all their difficulties, to fly to Christ, and more considerably fully to rest and rejoice in him." Because JE turned the page over before continuing the sermon on Judg. 5:23 on it, this second deleted head appears first (see following note).

[The] Canaanites [are] types of the spiritual enemies of the church. Deborah [is] a type of the church, Barak a type of the ministry.

Second. The circumstances of the inhabitants of Meroz [are] more especially parallel with the circumstances of the inhabitants of this town.[5] That is supposed to be the reason why the inhabitants of Meroz brought a greater curse {upon themselves: because they did not greatly exert themselves to promote the work of the Lord}. There were others that did not join {in battle}. Verses 15–17, "And the princes of Issachar were with Deborah; even Issachar, and also Barak: he was sent on foot into the valley. For the divisions of Reuben there were great thoughts of heart. Why abodest thou among the sheepfolds, to hear the bleatings of the flocks? For the divisions of Reuben there were great searchings of heart. Gilead abode beyond Jordan: and why did Dan remain in ships? Asher continued on the sea shore, and abode in his breaches."

Third. Consider that curse denounced against the Ammonites and Moabites and Amalekites, because they did not join and lend an helping hand in the time of that great work of God {when the Israelites were led out of Egypt}, but opposed. Deut. 23:3–4, "An Ammonite or Moabite shall not enter into the congregation of the Lord; even to their tenth generation shall they not enter into the congregation of the Lord for ever: because they met you not with bread and with water in the way, when ye came forth out of Egypt; and because they hired against thee Balaam the son of Beor of Pethor of Mesopotamia, to curse thee." [And the] Amalekites, Ex. 17:14–16, "And the Lord said unto Moses, Write this for a memorial in a book, and rehearse it in the ears of Joshua: for I will utterly put out the remembrance of Amalek from under heaven. And Moses built an altar, and called the name of it Jehovah-nissi: for he said, Because the Lord hath sworn that the Lord will have war with Amalek from generation to generation." They were related to the Israelites, which made their crime the more aggravated.

Fourth. Let the instance of Reuben and Gad and the half tribe of Manasseh [be considered], when God was bringing the children of Israel into Canaan [Num. 32:20–23].[6]

---

5. Here appears the first head of the discarded sermon that JE used to construct the present sermon: "Application. *Use* I. To invite those that [are] heavy laden sinners to come to Christ."

6. JE deletes with an "X": "This is what I observe from it: that all Israel were strictly required to join in that great affair; nothing would excuse 'em. Num. 32:20, etc."

Fifth. Let it be considered what befell those who were unbelieving and would not join with Gideon, at a time when God wrought a great work for Israel, and against their enemies, by him.[7]

Sixth. [Consider] how Christ represents the hard-heartedness, manifested by silence, at the time when he made his solemn entry into Jerusalem. Luke 19:37–40, "And when he was come nigh, even now at the descent of the mount of Olives, the whole multitude of the disciples began to rejoice and praise God with a loud voice for the mighty works that they had seen; saying, Blessed be the King that cometh in the name of the Lord: peace in heaven, and glory in the highest. And some of the Pharisees from among the multitude said unto him, Master, rebuke thy disciples. And he answered and said unto them, I tell you that, if these should hold their peace, the stones would immediately cry out." This solemn, public, joyful entry was a designed representation of the glorious time prophesied of in Zech. 9:9, "Rejoice greatly, O daughter of Zion; shout, O daughter of Jerusalem: behold, thy King cometh unto thee: he is just, and having salvation; lowly, and riding upon an ass, and upon a colt the foal of an ass." Matt. 21:5, "Tell ye the daughter of Sion, Behold, thy King cometh unto thee, meek, and sitting upon an ass, and a colt the foal of an ass."

Seventh. Consider what we are told of Christ's going forth against his enemies at the time of the introduction of the glorious times of the church, in the 19th chapter of Revelation.

Eighth. [Consider] what a mark of infamy is set on the elder brother, that would not join in the rejoicings on occasion of the return of the prodigal son. So if you stand abroad, dumb and finding fault, you will be guilty of the very same thing.

Ninth. Consider how, when God wrought a great work for his church in bringing 'em out of Babylon and restoring and rebuilding Jerusalem, how all were required to assist is rebuilding Jerusalem. Neh. 2:20, "we his servants will arise and build." See Nehemiah, ch. 3. In Jerusalem, not only public persons but private persons were to put to their hand and act in their sphere. Verse 10, "And next unto them repaired Jedaiah the son of Harumaph, even over against his house. And next unto him repaired

---

7. JE later inserted, "It is observed how multitudes in Israel came to the help of the Lord on that occasion (Judg. 7:23–24). But the men of Succoth and Penuel [did not come to the help of the Lord] (ch. 8:6–17)." JE then added a sixth point, changing the numbering of the following points accordingly: "*Sixth.* [Consider] how it was resented in Israel when the men of Jabesh-gilead did not come to their help against the open enemies of God (Judg. 21:10)."

Hattush the son of Hashabniah." Verse 23, ["After him repaired Benjamin and Hashub over against their house. After him repaired Azariah the son of Maaseiah the son of Ananiah by his house."] [Verse] 28, "From above the horse gate repaired the priests, every one over against his house." [Verse] 30, "After him repaired Hananiah the son of Shelemiah, and Hanun the sixth son of Zalaph, another piece. After him repaired Meshullam the son of Berechiah over against his chamber." Those that did not dwell at Jerusalem yet were to help in the building.

They were exceeding diligent and laborious, put not off their clothing. Chapter 4:21–23, "So we labored in the work: and half of them held the spears from the rising of the morning till the stars appeared. Likewise at the same time said I unto the people, Let every one with his servant lodge within Jerusalem, that in the night they may be a guard to us, and labor on the day. So neither I, nor my brethren, nor my servants, nor the men of the guard which followed me, none of us put off our clothes, saving that every one put them off for washing." [They held a] weapon in one hand. Chapter 4:17, "They which builded on the wall, and they that bare burdens, with those that laded, every one with one of his hands wrought in the work, and with the other hand held a weapon." A mark of infamy [was] set on those that did not assist. Neh. 3:5, "And next unto them the Tekoites repaired; but their nobles put not their necks to the work of their Lord."

Tenth. Consider the dreadful curses denounced against them that should not join with God's people in the glorious times of the Christian church, in Zech. 14. Against those that should not join, vv. 16–19, "And it shall come to pass, that every one that is left of all the nations which came against Jerusalem shall even go up from year to year to worship the King, the Lord of hosts, and to keep the feast of tabernacles. And it shall be, that whoso will not come up of all the families of the earth unto Jerusalem to worship the King, the Lord of hosts, even upon them shall be no rain. And if the family of Egypt go not up, and come not, that have no rain; there shall be the plague, wherewith the Lord will smite the heathen that come not up to keep the feast of tabernacles. This shall be the punishment of Egypt, and the punishment of all nations that come not up to keep the feast of tabernacles." Against those that should oppose at that time, v. 12, "And this shall be the plague wherewith the Lord will smite all the people that have fought against Jerusalem; their flesh shall consume away while they stand upon their feet, and their eyes shall consume away in their holes, and their tongue shall consume away in their mouth."

Thus abundant has God been in warning us of the great danger of {opposing him in such times}.

Eleventh. Let it be considered how much persons will be in the way of God's favor and blessing by cheerfully and vigorously exerting themselves to promote so great a work. What a mark of honor does God put upon those that cheerfully came to the help of the Lord against the mighty, when Deborah and Barak went forth. Verses 14–15, "Out of Ephraim was there a root of them against Amalek; after thee, Benjamin, among thy people; out of Machir came down governors, and out of Zebulun they that handle the pen of the writer. And the princes of Issachar were with Deborah; even Issachar, and also Barak: he was sent on foot into the valley. For the divisions of Reuben there were great thoughts of heart."

What great notice is taken of those that cheerfully put themselves to great hardship and expense, trouble and hazard, to promote this work. Verse 9, "My heart is toward the governors of Israel, that offered themselves willingly among the people. Bless ye the Lord." Verse 18, "Zebulun and Naphtali were a people that jeoparded their lives unto the death in the high places of the field." Here is a blessing upon the great men, rulers, judges. [Verses] 9–10, "My heart is toward the governors of Israel, that offered themselves willingly among the people. Bless ye the Lord. Speak, ye that ride on white asses, ye that sit in judgment, and walk by the way." [Verse] 15, "And the princes of Issachar were with Deborah; even Issachar, and also Barak: he was sent on foot into the valley. For the divisions of Reuben there were great thoughts of heart." Scribes, [v.] 14: "out of Zebulun they that handle the pen of the writer." And not only so, but the common people. And what a great blessing is pronounced even on a woman for the hand she had in promoting this affair. Verses 24–27, "Blessed above women shall Jael the wife of Heber the Kenite be, blessed shall she be above women in the tent. He asked water, and she gave him milk; she brought forth butter in a lordly dish. She put her hand to the nail, and her right hand to the workmen's hammer; and with the hammer she smote Sisera, she smote off his head, when she had pierced and stricken through his temples. At her feet he bowed, he fell, he lay down: at her feet he bowed, he fell: where he bowed, there he fell down dead."

What particular notice is taken in Scripture of David's helpers when he came to the throne after a long-continued low and afflicted state. And what marks of honor are put upon them, in 1 Chron. 12:23–31:

And these are the numbers of the bands that were ready armed to the war, and came to David to Hebron, to turn the kingdom of Saul to him, according to the word of the Lord. The children of Judah that bare shield and spear were six thousand and eight hundred, ready armed to the war. Of the children of Simeon, mighty men of valor for the war, seven thousand and one hundred. Of the children of Levi four thousand and six hundred. And Jehoiada was the leader of the Aaronites, and with him were three thousand and seven hundred; and Zadok, a young man mighty of valor, and of his father's house twenty and two captains. And of the children of Benjamin, the kindred of Saul, three thousand: for hitherto the greatest part of them had kept the ward of the house of Saul. And of the children of Ephraim twenty thousand and eight hundred, mighty men of valor, famous throughout the house of their fathers. And of the half tribe of Manasseh eighteen thousand, which were expressed by name, to come and make David king.

And particular notice is taken of those that had understanding of the times. Verse 32, "And of the children of Issachar, which were men that had understanding of the times, to know what Israel ought to do; the heads of them were two hundred; and all their brethren were at their commandment." There are some that in the time of a glorious outpouring {of God's Spirit} are like the Pharisees. They don't understand these times. {They are} always at a loss, stumbling, and so do nothing to help forward [God's work]. And so a mark of honor is set upon those that were hearty and engaged in coming and joining in the affair of turning about the kingdom to David. Verse 33, "Of Zebulun, such as went forth to battle, expert in war, with all instruments of war, fifty thousand, which could keep rank: they were not of double heart." And v. 38, "All these men of war, that could keep rank, came with a perfect heart to Hebron, to make David king over all Israel: and all the rest also of Israel were of one heart to make David king."

Now these are the times when [God] is turning about the kingdom to the spiritual David.

Let these things effectually warn and excite us.

Now the armies which are in heaven are going forth, the stars in their courses.

Use [III.] Here I would mention some particular things that persons should avoid and do, as they would not expose themselves to the curse of the inhabitants of Meroz.

First. If at any time you are of a doubtful mind concerning the work that is carried on in any parts of the land, avoid a being forward to express your troubles or to talk after such a manner that others may plainly know[8] your doubts. [This is a] very foolish thing. It may be of very ill consequences, ill consequences to yourself. [It may] keep you from any share {of God's work}. [It may] keep you miserably back. After you have expressed it, you will be prejudiced that way, loath to own the contrary, hard to come back.

[This kind of activity] tends to beget doubts in the minds of others, to cause 'em to doubt of the whole work instead of coming to the help of the Lord. You will hinder [it]. They that throw out hints that tend to bring the present great work of God under some suspicion, don't consider what they do. 'Tis a wonder they can't have so much prudence as Gamaliel. If they are in doubt, it would be a much more proper course for them to go and discourse with those that may probably enlighten them. 'Tis inconceivable what such persons aim at.

They had need to be well satisfied that these and those things are not of God before they give any hint against them. If Christ was now upon earth as he once was, men had better[9] throw out hints and suspicions against him.

Those that talk doubtfully of the work, because of extraordinary terrors and exceeding joys that in some respects carry persons beyond themselves, talk in the dark, object against they know not what. I dare appeal to the consciences of everyone that has done so, whether they were not, at that time when they did so, in cold and dead frames, or had had for a long time any remarkable income of the Spirit of God into their souls.

'Tis no wonder at all that some are carried something beyond themselves, {that their} cup overflows. Those that are ready to object against extraordinary comforts would do well to consider the instance of Michal [2 Sam. 6:16–23].

There is a strange restlessness in an opposing spirit. When men give way to a disposition to speak against the work that is carried on in the land, or to speak suspiciously {of it}, they seem to be urged on. They can't be at rest unless they vent themselves, though it be at such times and places as tends to no good in the world.

Second. Persons insisting much on the blemishes that attend this work, looks as if they were disposed to find what fault they can, and glad to find blemishes to observe; looks as though they were out of humor with the work itself, and therefore would object what they could. If they

---

8. MS: "shew."

9. In an obsolete meaning, "rather."

greatly rejoiced {in the work}, they would not love to speak of the blemishes. Who loves, in a day of great joy and gladness, to insist on those things that are uncomfortable, that attend the affair [of] the bridegroom on the wedding day?

And would it not be very improper on a coronation day to insist on the blemishes of the king's family?

If the substance of that work that is carried on in the land be a work of God, 'tis a joyful day indeed. We, if we are the friends of Christ, ought to be swallowed up with joy. This is a day of rejoicing with Christ himself, and shall not we rejoice with him? He calls together his friends and neighbors.

[There is] joy in heaven over one sinner {that repenteth} [Luke 15:7]. So great an event as the conversion of so many souls is worthy to receive our attention, far beyond {the conversion of one sinner}.

We have an account how that, in Nehemiah's time, many of the people wept at the faults that were found amongst the people. Neh. 8:9–10, "And Nehemiah, which is the Tirshatha, and Ezra the priest the scribe, and the Levites that taught the people, said unto all the people, This day is holy unto the Lord your God; mourn not, nor weep. For all the people wept, when they heard the words of the law. Then he said unto them, Go your way, eat the fat, and drink the sweet, and send portions unto them for whom nothing is prepared: for this day is holy unto our Lord: neither be ye sorry; for the joy of the Lord is your strength."

Much insisting on the blemishes of the work greatly tends to hinder it, for whatsoever tends to wound the reputation of the work tends [to] hinder it. 'Tis principally in these two ways that the work of God has been opposed in the land: talking suspiciously and doubtfully of great part of the work; insisting much on the blemishes.

They will own there is a work of God but, if one were to judge by their actions, they are more displeased than they were before.

The Jews in Christ's time owned his miracles to be the works of God.

There are undoubtedly imprudences and errors that attend the work of God, and always will be. No other are to be expected. But must we therefore always harp upon them? 'Tis true, proper endeavors should be used to correct the errors there[10] are. And if you think you can do anything towards it, then take a proper course in order to it. But your speaking against and finding fault with many things that attend this

10. MS: "they."

work, tends to make others stumble at the whole, for persons of weak capacities don't know how to distinguish. Besides, you'll shut religion out of your own heart.

'Tis to be feared some persons find fault and object to show their knowledge, that others may take notice how discerning they are and think them wiser than others that are imprudent. 'Tis difficult to conceive of any other end they should have in it. While they talk so much of imprudences, they themselves are guilty of the greatest imprudence.

Third. Take heed you don't retain the accursed thing, old rancor. This won't help, but hinder. The whole congregation were hindered.

Fourth. You must freely and voluntarily go through great difficulties and self-denial. So did the children of [Israel]: [they] willingly offered themselves; jeoparded their lives.

Fifth. Let every soul avoid stirring up any contention. Take heed in the management of public affairs.

Sixth. Let everyone promote it in his own sphere.

Seventh. Let all God's people cry earnestly to God.

[I] conclude with a word of awakening to Christless sinners: you are all enemies [of Christ], especially foolish sinners.

Prepared to Travail and Fight

April 1743

AFTER BRITAIN'S FAILURE TO take Cartagena, the war effort continued in the West Indies but the focus began to shift to the continent. Since the death of the Holy Roman Emperor (Charles VI) in January of 1741, armies and alliances began shifting across Europe. Charles had no male heir, so he made an agreement with the powers in Europe to exchange Austria's financial interests in the Indies to allow his daughter Maria Theresa rights of succession to his throne. This agreement, known as the "Pragmatic Sanction," held widespread support during his lifetime, but when Charles VI passed, many European powers saw it as an opportunity to further their own interests. Throughout 1741 and 1742, news of troop movements, diplomatic alliances, and open battle in Prague and Silesia filled the columns of the *Boston Gazette*. War with Spain did not end but was absorbed into a broader European conflict.

The War of Austrian Succession centered on Austria, Bavaria, and Prussia; however, Britain and France still held significant interests in the developing conflict. French troops supported Bavaria to ensure French leadership in a balanced Europe whereas Britain sent an army led by King George II himself. Britain's interests in this war were complex. The "Pragmatic Army" positioned itself to protect the Protestant Hanovarian lands and to check the influence of the French. Neither Britain nor France had formally entered the war, yet the gravitational pull of these ancient rivals drove the war's direction.

As the Pragmatic Army began its march across the Rhine, Edwards instructed his parishioners with the sermon *Prepared to Travail and*

Fight. Relying on imagery of the Exodus, Edwards drew a comparison between Israel's deliverance from physical bondage with her deliverance from spiritual bondage—bondage from sin and bondage to the law. The Christian, in Edwards's analogy, could achieve this deliverance by travailing and fighting as a soldier. The Christian is to travail by attending his daily business of preparing a heart for Christ. Furthermore, the Christian is to fight as a soldier for this deliverance because he will meet with special opposition in this endeavor. Conversion is not the end of the work of the Christian. Instead, conversion is the beginning of the practice of Christlikeness: repentance, love, humility, hope, and joy. Drawing on the martial events reported by the *Boston Gazette*, Edwards compared the Christian life to that of a soldier: "be careful that you understand . . . Christian warfare and what it is to be good soldiers."

Echoing the language of *Valiant and Resolute Soldiers*, Edwards encouraged his congregation to take sides during the emerging conflicts both within New England and the global Protestant Interest. This sermon is a call to pursue the type of personal, spiritual reformation Edwards promoted in the revivals. This pursuit, according to Edwards, should be undertaken as a soldier "travails and fights" in war. Because Edwards's view of providence connected the progress of the gospel with the advance of the Protestant cause, his sermons like *Prepared to Travail and Fight* leveraged the news of war to promote revival. As Britain engaged in the defense of the Protestant Interest in Europe, so also battle lines began to solidify in the struggle for souls, churches, and communities in New England.

* * * * *

This sermon was edited by Christian Cuthbert for the Jonathan Edwards Center. The manuscript is six duodecimo-sized leaves. LL. 5–6 were made from a discarded letter from Sarah Pierpont Edwards, dated March 17, 1743 (Letter B17). Edwards's text is outlinish throughout, consisting in large part of key words or phrases upon which he would extemporize.

Prepared to Travail and Fight

Exodus 13:18

And the children of Israel went up harnessed out of the land of Egypt.

1. The thing described.
    Two things observable:
    (1) Leaving Egypt.
    (2) Entering on their journey towards Canaan.
2. The description.
    [They] were encamped in the wilderness like an army.

Doctrine

When God truly delivers men from spiritual bondage, they go forth prepared both to travail and to fight as soldiers to war.
   I. How persons are delivered from spiritual bondage.
   II. How that all [that are delivered go forth prepared both to travail and to fight as soldiers to war].

   I. How [persons are delivered from spiritual bondage].

First. What work that is by which they are delivered.
Answer. Conversion.
Not conviction.
[Conviction] may work reformation.
[But] not any other change.

Though there may be many great alterations in one respect and another.

Second. What they are delivered from bondage to.
Two sorts of bondage:
1. Bondage to sin.
2. Bondage to the law.

1.[Bondage to sin].
A soul in conversion is delivered from bondage to sin and Satan.
[Sin] is not in reigning power.
[Though it] may be great power.
[A converted soul] has the victory.
[A converted soul] enjoys liberty.

2. Bondage to the law.
Bondage to the will of God.
Prisoners of justice.

II. How those that are delivered [go forth prepared both to travail and to fight as soldiers to war].

First. What is meant by [the] travailing and fighting they are prepared for.
Sometimes the whole that a Christian has to do, is represented by one of these.
But as there were those two things that were before the children of Israel, so they represented things appertaining to the great work and business of Christians that were somewhat diverse.
1. What is implied in their being prepared to travail.
This respects especially the conflict and daily business of a Christian, at all times and in all circumstances.
[Travailing] has respect to those things in this daily business of a Christian.
(1) The respect it bears to the terms of his motion.
From which [it arises].
Prov. 16:17, "The highway [of the upright is to depart from evil]."
An heart prepared.
To which [it pertains].

(2) The labor.
A true Christian has a heart prepared.
(3) The progress.
[The true Christian seeks a] heart prepared.
[He does] not rest in what is past.
Not resting in what he meets with by the way.
2. What is implied to being prepared to fight.
This more especially [has] respect to what they have to do when they meet with more special opposition.

Second. How they are prepared.
1. They are sincerely willing.
2. There is a foundation laid for their being steadfast in this willingness.

Application

[*Use*] I. Hence the great error of those that think their work is done when they are converted.
[They] put off the harness.

Use II of *Self-Examination.*
If that be the manner of persons, thus to flatter themselves, 'tis a greater argument of hypocrisy, and that they are in a state of nature, a thousand times.
Ezek. 33:13, "when I shall say to the righteous that he shall surely live."
These make their experience a preparation for sin.
If this therefore be the case [with you], take heed.
The nature of the experience of Christians all tends to practice. All engage the mind.
Things that precede conversion.
Their convictions tend to practice.
Humiliation.
Comfort.
Their discoveries [tend this way].
[They] mourn for past transgressions.
[They are] careful and exact as to [the] future.

[They] look backward and forward.
[They are] jealous [of themselves].
[Their] hearts [are] tender.
Their faith leads to practice.
Repentance.
Love.
Humility.
Hope.
Joy.
The experience of hypocrites rests on itself.
Therefore, examine [yourselves].

And particularly examine whether, now you suppose yourself delivered from spiritual bondage, you go forth prepared to travail and fight.

Neh. 4:17, "[They which builded on the wall, and they that bare burdens, with those that laded, every one with one of his hands wrought in the work, and with the other hand held a weapon]." Ch. 2:20, "[Then answered I them, and said unto them, The God of heaven, he will prosper us; therefore we his servants will arise and build: but ye have no portion, nor right, nor memorial, in Jerusalem]."

But here be careful that you understand the Christian warfare, and what it is to be good soldiers.

[Our] enemies are chiefly within.

[True Christians are] never so much in the exercise of humility, meekness and love, as when they acquit themselves best.

The more [one is] like a little child, the better [the] soldier.

[Observe] an holy pusillanimity.

[*Use* III of] *Exhortation.*

Go up harnessed, as soldiers go forth to war.

Hypocrites put on the harness to defend themselves from doubting.

They that would take away their hopes, are all the enemies they fight with. Ministers {try to take away their false hopes, but they resist}. Scripture {may take away their hopes for a time, but it} lasts no further.

What cause there is [to travail and fight].

How glorious their reward.

Christ the Lord of Hosts
October 13, 1743

BRITAIN SOUGHT TO LIMIT French influence on the continent and bring a balance to the interests in Europe. Towards this end, Britain engaged continental powers diplomatically, financially supported Austria, committed her forces to armed conflict, and King George II himself traveled to lead the Pragmatic Army personally. Marching along the River Main, the Pragmatic Army stumbled upon a well-positioned French force at Dettingen. As British forces struggled to form lines of battle, the French made two tactical blunders leading to their improbable defeat. Edwards preached *Christ the Lord of Hosts* as a commemoration of King George's victory on the continent against the French. French blunders were interpreted as signs of divine providence demonstrating God's care for the advance of the Protestant Interest foreshadowing the colonial victory at Louisbourg. The General Assembly called for a day of thanksgiving for Thursday, October 13th, allowing Edwards to fit Britain's victory into his providential framework. *Christ the Lord of Hosts* demonstrates sustained reflection on the character of God and his providential control of the world with particular respect to military activity.

The central claim, reflected in the title, is that Jesus Christ is the Lord of hosts or armies. With his characteristic thoroughness, Edwards considered the breadth of the meaning of "hosts" in the Bible: national armies, the heavenly bodies, the angels; Christ is even considered Lord of the demonic armies, although "in a different sense." As the Lord of all armies, Christ is in complete control of the outcome of every battle. Therefore, history (particularly military history) became yet another canvas upon which God could manifest his glory. Continuing this trajectory, Edwards brought the sermon from the level of the cosmic and national activities into his meetinghouse. Northampton should not expect military victories if she opposed the work of Christ. This final step tied Edwards's thought to the other major theme of the decade: revival.

The church in this sermon is sometimes called "the church militant," referring to her opposition to Christ's enemies and her march towards the kingdom of God. Therefore, the church is one of the armies which Christ, "captain of salvation," has as its head. Christ uses his church as an army to oppose various enemies in the world—spiritual and temporal—clearing the way for the advance of the gospel. Drawing on imagery in Ezekiel, Edwards stated: "The church of God, as it shall be in the latter days, when it shall revive as from the dead is represented as a great army." This passage connected the idea of "revival," the church's function as an army, and the latter days. Given the coverage of European developments in the *Boston Gazette*, it would have been hard for the congregation to understand this sermon apart from the military realities encompassing the British Empire.

* * * * *

This sermon was edited by Bryan LeBeau for the Jonathan Edwards Center. The manuscript, an assortment of duodecimo-sized foolscap, odd-shaped fan paper, and a portion of a discarded letter, is sixteen leaves, but incomplete at the end, as evidenced by an incipit "7." at the bottom of the last extant leaf.

Christ the Lord of Hosts

Isaiah 47:4

As for our redeemer, the Lord of hosts is his name.

THERE WERE OF OLD two noted cities in the world, Jerusalem and Babylon.

As one prospered and flourished, [the other declined].

The destruction of Babylon is here foretold. Two things are intimated in the text, with relation to the destruction of Babylon. One is that [God] had the disposal of the military power that was concerned in it, [the] hosts of Babylon [and the] hosts of their enemies.

The other {thing intimated in the text, is} that God was concerned therein as the redeemer of his church, ch. 44:26–27, and [ch.] 45: {a type of that redemption was seen in} Cyrus.

Observations:

1. Who is spoken of: {viz.,} the true God, {and} especially Jesus Christ.

2. What appellation is here ascribed to him: "Lord of hosts," or armies.

3. After what manner this appellation is given him: as a name proper to him. We have often the like expression, chs. 48:2, 51:15, 54:5; Jer. 10:16 and 31:35 and 32:18, 50:34, and 51:19.

I would, first, show how Christ is the Lord of hosts or the Lord of armies; and then, secondly, show what is implied in its being said that is his name; and then [make] Application.

I. Show in what respects Christ is said to be the Lord of hosts or armies. And in this I shall wholly limit myself to the holy Scripture as my guide, and shall mention those things only that the Scripture calls by the name of armies or hosts, and which the Scripture represents

First. He is the Lord of those

Those multitudes, when thus commissioned of God, are in Scripture represented as armies. Prov. 30:27, "The locusts go forth all of them by bands."

And in the 1st and 2nd chapters of Joel, the Prophet speaks of multitudes of devouring insects—palmer worms, locusts, canker worms and caterpillars—that are there represented as God's armies. Joel 2:11, "The Lord shall utter his voice before his army: for his camp is very great."

Whether by those locusts and caterpillars, etc., is meant literally those kinds of insects, or whether thereby {other creatures are intended}, it alters not the case as to what I now observe herefrom: viz.,

It appears that armies of men, and those vast companies of insects, are in Scripture-account fitly compared one to another. So again, v. 25: "I will restore to you the ears[1] that the locusts hath eaten, the cankerworm, and the caterpillar, my great army which I sent among you."

God, as the Lord of these hosts, gives them being. He sends 'em forth, arms them, gives their commission [to] go to do his business.

[He] leads them. [As is] intimated, Prov. 30:27, "[the locusts have] no king." He restrains {them}, rebukes [them], calls 'em off. [They are] wholly at his disposal. [The] hand of God [is] remarkably visible in them.

Though they are weak, yet the power of God appears in them. [There is] no resisting {them}, no strength [can stand] against them. What could Pharaoh [do]?

Because God is thus the Lord of these, therefore {they are} called his army, Joel 2:25.

Second. Christ is the Lord of the armies of mankind, that go forth to war one with another.

The greatest things of an external nature, that are done in the world of mankind from age to age, are accomplished by armies. Most of the great outward changes and revolutions [are accomplished by armies].

The strength of kings, nations and empires lies chiefly in their armies, or in their military force. And great have been the events of war from one age to another. Great have been the changes that have been

---

1. MS sic; KJV: "years."

accomplished. Such is the calamity and misery of fallen man, that war is a thing that is almost continually carried on {in this world}. And the state of the world of mankind, by means of it, is continually fluctuating and changing.

But the Lord Jesus Christ, as he is the person whom the Father hath made King of Kings {and Lord of Lords}, and hath committed the government {of the world into his keeping}, so he has set him at the head of all those affairs. [God has] committed to his disposal all the events of war, {and has} made him Lord of armies. [Christ has the] kingdom given to him. {He has been} appointed heir of the world, head of all principalities and power. And God hath sworn that to him "every knee should bow" [Philip. 2:10], {and he shall make} his enemies {his} footstool [Ps. 110:1].

All revolutions by war are to be in subordination to the designs of His kingdom. Ezek. 21:27, "[I will] overturn, overturn, overturn [it]."

He therefore, in all these affairs, as it were sits at [the] helm.

[He] holds the reins.

[He] evermore holds the balance in his hands, turns the scales just as he pleases.

[He] has the hearts of kings and the great men of the world, that have the power of peace and war.

Whenever armies are gathered, 'tis he that musters the host, Is. 13:4.

[They] come at his call. Is. 7:18, "[the Lord shall] hiss for the fly [that is in the uttermost part of the rivers of Egypt]."

[They shall] go forth to do his business; no more shall be done.

God is pleased to make his overruling providence more conscious and evident in governing and ordering the events of war, than many other things. All things are subject to {God's overruling providence}. But 'tis observable {that 'tis especially so} in things of greatest importance.

Oftentimes, [God] remarkably disappoints the most crafty devices and strategems. Job 5:12–14, "He disappointeth the devices of the crafty, so that their hands cannot perform their enterprise. He taketh the wise in their own craftiness: and the counsel of the froward is carried headlong. They meet with darkness in the day time, and grope in the noonday as in the night." Ps. 33:10–11, "The Lord bringeth the counsel of the heathen to nought: he maketh the devices of the people of none effect. The counsel of the Lord standeth for ever, the thoughts of his heart to all generations."

[God] gives strength and courage. When he has work to do, [he] remarkably spirits and animates men. Is. 45:5, "[I] girded thee, though thou hast not [known me]." And [he] oftentimes wonderfully assists. Joel

2:7–8, "They shall run like mighty men; they shall climb the wall like men of war; and they shall march every one on his ways, and they shall not break their ranks: neither shall one thrust another; they shall walk every one in his path: and when they fall upon the sword, they shall not be wounded."

And sometimes, [men] are remarkably disappointed. Eccles. 9:11, "I returned, and saw under the sun, that the race is not to the swift." Sometimes, [God] strangely takes away the courage of the most valiant.

The most potent princes have been used as God's weapons. Is. 10:15, "Shall the axe boast itself against him that heweth therewith? or shall the saw magnify itself against him that shaketh it? as if the rod should shake itself against them that lift it up, or as if the staff should lift up itself, as if it were no wood."

Oftentimes, it has pleased God to use a small force [to defeat a large one].

The greatest preparations have commonly been disappointed.

Sometimes, things take a sudden turn. Suddenly, [God] puts an end to the prosperity and success of the greatest warriors, and destroys them. [He] uses them, [then] casts them out of his hands.

And so the events of war are wholly of him. [God] pulls down one, and sets up another.

And [it is] all to accomplish his design. Prov. 19:21, "the counsel of the Lord, that shall stand." Prov. 16:9, "man's heart deviseth his way: [but the Lord directeth his steps]."

[Sometimes, it is] quite other purpose that they design, even in their victories. Is. 10:6–7, "[Howbeit he] thinketh[2] not so."

It is in vain to use art or strength to hinder his design.

If men gather together and associate themselves, [it is in vain]. Is. 8:9–10, "Associate yourselves, O ye people, and ye shall be broken in pieces; and give ear, all ye of far countries: gird yourselves, and ye shall be broken in pieces; gird yourselves, and ye shall be broken in pieces. Take counsel together, and it shall come to nought; speak the word, and it shall not stand: for God is with us."

Mighty armies [are in vain]. If God blows upon them, [they fall]. Is. 37:7, "[I will] send a blast upon him."

And if God pleases, a few shall be succeeded.

---

2. KJV: "meaneth."

Third. Christ is the Lord of the militant church, that is often spoken of in Scripture as God's hosts.

That part of the church of God that is on earth, is called his church militant. [The church are as] soldiers. [They have] many and great enemies to conflict with. And God is pleased to appoint them to be his army, to overcome the armies of hell, for the greater glory of his power and the greater triumph over [them]. Ps. 8:2, "Out of the mouths of babes and sucklings hast thou ordained strength because of thine enemies, that thou mightest still the enemy and the avenger." "[God hath] chosen the weak things [of the world to confound the things which are mighty]." The church of God on earth is often represented in Scripture as his army. Cant. 6:4, "terrible as an army with banners."

The congregation of Israel that went forth out of Egypt, were in the form of an army. [They were] harnassed. [They are] often spoken of as an host, or as a company of hosts. Ex. 12:41, "And it came to pass at the end of the four hundred and thirty years, even the selfsame day it came to pass, that all the hosts of the Lord went out from the land of Egypt." So Deut. 2:15, and many other places.

The church of God, as it shall be in the latter days, when it shall revive as from the dead, is represented as a great army, Ezek. 37:10.

Christ is the Lord of this host. [He is the] head of the church. He is, in an eminent manner, the captain of this army. Josh 5:13–15, "And it came to pass, when Joshua was by Jericho, that he lifted up his eyes and looked, and, behold, there stood a man over against him with his sword drawn in his hand: and Joshua went unto him, and said unto him, Art thou for us, or for our adversaries? And he said, Nay; but as captain of the host of the Lord am I now come. And Joshua fell on his face to the earth, and did worship, and said unto him, What saith my Lord unto his servant? And the captain of the Lord's host said unto Joshua, Loose thy shoe from off thy foot; for the place whereon thou standest is holy. And Joshua did so."

David's army represented this army, 1 Chron. 12:22, as David was the head of that army.

This host is called "the host of heaven," Dan. 8:10, and v. 11. Christ is called "the prince of the host." In like manner, in the 19th [chapter] of Revelation, the church is represented as an army in heaven, and Christ their captain.

Christ is the Lord of this host in a peculiar manner, as everyone of the army is his by a peculiar propriety: as he has purchased {them}, as [they are] united strictly {to him}, as they all are willingly subject to him {and} trust in him, [and are] all under the influence of his Spirit in their spiritual warfare. All depend entirely on his leading and guidance. {All depend} on his strength. [This is] the army that fights with him. And [this is] the army that will triumph with him.

Fourth. He is the Lord of the host of the visible heavens, consisting

They are fitly compared to an host or army because of their multitude, and also because of their order and the exact regularity of their motion. As in an army, every soldier has his place appointed him, and in a well-disciplined army all are regular and exact in their motions, all keeping their proper distance without breaking rank or file, or interfering one with another, and all exactly observing the words of command.

So it is.

God is the Lord of this mighty and splendid host. He hath made the heavens and earth, and all the hosts. Ps. 33:6, "By the word of the Lord were the heavens made; and all the host of them by the breath of his mouth."

He knows 'em, every one. Ps. 147:4, "He telleth the number of the stars; he calleth them all by their names." He has appointed every one his station. He leads the hosts in their regular motions, Is. 40:26. He is the glorious leader that gives them the word of command, and whose command they constantly obey without once transgressing it. Is. 45:12, "I have made the earth, and created man upon it: I, even my hands, have stretched out the heavens, and all their host have I commanded." The Second Person in the Trinity, in particular.

Fifth. He is Lord of the hosts of angels. [He is the Lord of the] good angels, [the] hosts of the heaven of heavens. The good angels are often represented as an host or hosts in Scripture. Gen. 32:2, "This is God's host." Ps. 103:21, "Bless ye the Lord, all ye his hosts; ye ministers that do his will." Ps. 148:2, "Praise him, all his angels: praise him, all his host." Luke 2:13, "And suddenly there was with the angels a multitude of the heavenly host."

As the sun, moon, and stars {are called the} host of heaven, so these. 1 Kgs. 22:19, "the host of heaven standing by him"; "army of heaven," Dan. 4:35.

[Angels are] fitly represented as an host.

[They are a great] multitude.

[They are described as having] great strength, mighty men of valor.

[So in their] business: [they are] ministers of Gods providence, especially to defend and assist God's militant church, [acting as] ministering spirits.

They defend [the militant church]. Ps. 91:11–12, "give his angels charge concerning [thee]." Ps. 34:7, "The angel of the Lord encampeth [around them that fear him, and delivereth them]." Cant. 3:7–8, "threescore valiant men are about it."

They improve their great strength in resisting the enemies of the church. Judg. 5:20, "[They] fought from heaven; the stars in their courses [fought against Sisera]." So in Rev. 12, Michael and his angels. [They are] like an host for their order. Their preparation [is] to execute the wrath [of God], as a company of soldiers armed, as a flame of fire.

Christ is the Lord, [as he is] Creator.[3]

Christ [is the Lord] as God-man, the head of the angels. He is the glorious captain. [Command is] committed by the Father unto him, as a king commmits soldiers to the care and command of a general. This is that Michael. Him they adore. His word and will they obey.

Also, [Christ is] the Lord of the host of evil angels, though in a different sense. These [too are] represented as an host., Rev. 12:7.[They are represent as] "legion" [Mark 5:9].

[Christ is] Lord by sovereign, irresistible, uncontrollable dominion over them. Though they are not united to him, and he is not their head, yet he rules 'em by his mighty arm. They accomplish nothing but what he permits and orders in infinite wisdom.

II. Show briefly what is intended when it is said, "the Lord of hosts is his name." Two things are taught us in it:

First. That God's glory much appears in it.

God's name is to express his glory. [His] name in Scripture signifies "honor."

[His name signifies the] glory of his supreme dominion and strength.

Princes gain dominion. The great empires of the world have commonly this way been established, and they maintain their dominion by this. Rebellions are suppressed. Their kingdom is defended from the power of other kingdoms. He that is the lord of the military force of any

---

3. JE wrote "Eph.," but his reference is uncertain.

kingdom, he thereby has all the power of dominion in that kingdom in his hands. Since therefore Christ is the Lord of all the hosts of the universe, [this] shows that there is no power or might against him; [it is] in vain to fight against him. [This shows] that all power is derived from him.

It shows how far Christ is exalted above earthly princes, in that he is the Lord not only of the hosts of one particular country or kingdom, but of the whole earth; not only the armies of the earth, but of heaven: sun, moon and stars. {It shows that he is Lord} not only [of the] visible heaven, [but of the invisible].

Second. Another thing taught us in this, is that this is peculiar to him.

Names are for distinction. 'Tis the divine prerogative thus to be the Lord of armies.

None but God is the Lord of all the armies of the universe. And none but God is Lord of any one army in the sense that he is.

And this honor is given to Christ as God-man, as it never [was], and never will, be given to any other. As the Father hath committed to him the governing of the universe, and set him at the head of all principality and power, so he hath made him captain of all his hosts in a manner that he never did any other: and herein has given him honor infinitely greater than ever he gave any mere creature.

Application

I. Hence, what praise and glory belongs to Jesus Christ.

We have observed how his glory appears in this. How may it excite admiration and praise in our souls, when we consider that he that was once a little infant, {is the Lord of hosts}.

He is the person spoken of, Ps. 24[:8], "The Lord strong and mighty, the Lord mighty in battle."

The consideration of the victories he hath obtained, should excite our praise.

Princes esteem their victories their greatest glory.

II. Hence we learn all the praise of preservations, deliverances and victories in a just war belong to him.

For as has been observed, [Christ has committed to his disposal all the events of war].

III. Hence how little reason a nation has to expect any continued success in war, when there great prevails a contempt of Christ and the gospel.

If it be so that a nation [that] has enjoyed the gospel long, have apostatized, [and] religion is much out of credit, become very unfashionable and looked upon below the great men; if Christ has but little honor from most of the rulers; infidelity and apostasy very much prevails; those doctrines especially that may be said, by way of eminency, to be evangelical, [are neglected,] and vice and wickedness of life prevails; if many of those that are in power are governed by their private interest; places of public trust are bought and sold or disposed of to serve private designs; and God is visibly much neglected in the management of public affairs: [then how little reason has that nation to expect any continued success in war].

It is a thing unknown in history, that a nation has prospered for any long time [when Christ and the gospel are held in contempt].

IV. Hence the madness of fighting against God.

"[Who would set the] briars and thorns [against me in battle?]" Is. 27:4]. Prov. 11:21, "[Though] hand join in hand, [the wicked shall not be unpunished]."

V. Hence the safety of the church of God, and of all such as trust in him.

The church may well glory as she does, Ps. 46: "God is our refuge and strength, a very present help in trouble. Therefore will not we fear, though the earth be removed, and though the mountains be carried into the midst of the sea: though the waters thereof roar and be troubled, though the mountains shake with the swelling thereof." [God] casts her enemies "into a dead sleep" [Ps. 76:6]. Is. 54, latter end: "[Behold, I have] created the smith [who bloweth the fire of coals in the fire, and that bringeth forth an instrument for his work," Is. 54:16. 2 Kgs. 6:13, etc., "[Fear not: for] more are they that are with us [than with them]."

Part 2

War Comes to New England

Sin Weakens a People in War

June 28, 1744

BREAKING FOR WINTER CAMP of 1743–44 signaled a new phase of intercolonial warfare. Events on the continent consumed Britain, absorbing her engagement with Spain into The War of Austrian Succession (1740–48). Britain had been involved on the continent for some time, but this winter marked a shift from Britain and France fighting as auxiliaries of the Austrian and Bavarian forces to the primary actors vying for influence on the continent. During the course of the winter of 1743–44, open conflict between Britain and France became inevitable.

At the end of March 1744, Governor Shirley addressed the Massachusetts Assembly predicting "a great probability of an immediate rupture with France."[1] Shirley proposed immediate measures to improve the readiness of Massachusetts: the calling of a quick reactionary force known as "snow-shoe men" and improved fortifications on the frontiers.[2] What Shirley could not have known was that this rupture had already occurred. The French at Louisbourg had received notice of French and British declarations of war before Boston and launched a successful campaign to reduce Canso in May of 1744. Shirley responded by rallying the troops, logistically as well as inspirationally. In a speech to the Assembly on May 31st, he proclaimed, "We have good ground to hope for the favorable assistance of divine providence in so just a cause."[3] Edwards disagreed.

1. *Boston Gazette*, April 3, 1744 (citing a speech given on March 22).
2. Shirley, *Correspondence*, 115.
3. *Boston Gazette*, June 5, 1744.

In this sermon, Edwards used Joshua 7:12 to warn the people that their sin could bring judgement instead of protection: "neither will I be with you anymore, except you destroy the accursed thing." Sin, according to Edwards, rendered New England vulnerable two ways. First, it has the tendency to erode the discipline and capabilities of the troops exposing them to danger. Secondly—and more importantly—sin deprived a community of their most sure defense: the protective hand of God. Edwards continued to apply this Biblical teaching to "the present circumstances of our own nation and land." Facing Catholicism's two greatest powers, Spain and France, Edwards tried to identify the conditions under which exposed God's people to destruction. Often, destruction came after God prompted a great work among his people who then turned their back on God. Two recent experiences of awakening demonstrated this principle exposing them to God's destructive hand. There was no Scriptural precedent, according to Edwards, for any of God's people to persist in a state of spiritual obstinacy and continue to enjoy the proactive hand of God.

Sin Weakens a People in War responded to New England's personal entrance into the widening intercolonial conflict. Most throughout New England understood that wars which begin on the continent soon drew the colonies into war with the potential to produce casualties. Concerns about the expansion of hostilities allowed Edwards to lead his congregation towards the safety of the sealing work of God's Spirit. Only through a collective turning away from sin and towards Christ could the community be assured of their safety in a time of fear and uncertainty.

* * * * *

This sermon was edited by Christian Cuthbert for the Jonathan Edwards Center. The manuscript is twenty-three duodecimo-sized leaves. Edwards titles it, "Fast on Occasion of the War with France, June 28, 1744." Leaf nine is made of a salvaged piece of paper containing notes in another hand, possibly that of one of Edwards' students. Another leaf is made from a discarded letter by William Gray to Edwards, Feb. 2, 1744 (Letter B39). Shorthand notations on the first page indicate that Edwards preached "The doctrinal part the second time from Is. 30:12–13." And a further notation states that the sermon was re-preached in March 1755.

Sin Weakens a People in War[1]

Joshua 7:12.[2]

Therefore the children of Israel could not stand before their enemies, but turned their backs before their enemies, because they were accursed: neither will I be with you any more, except you destroy the accursed thing from among you.

[THE CHILDREN OF ISRAEL were an] excellent generation.
God had done great things for them.
But [Achan had taken the "accursed thing" from Jericho].
[When they were defeated at Ai, they were] greatly surprised.
This is part of what God says: a reason given of what was past, and a threatening as to what is future.

1. A reason given of what is past: viz., why they could not stand before their enemies of the city of Ai.

(1) The more immediate cause: God's departing from 'em, and cursing them.
They were greatly surprised.
They had great success before, against much more powerful enemies.
They seemed to have been strangely and unaccountably weakened and dispirited.

---

1. Also referred to as "Fast on Occasion of the War with France, June 28, 1744." *Boston Evening-Post*, June 11, 1744, p. 4: "On Friday last, His Excellency the Governour, with the Advice of His Majesty's Council, and at the Desire of the Hon. House of Representatives, was pleased to issue out a Proclamation, appointing Thursday the 28th Day of *June* Instant to be observed as a Day of Fasting and Prayer throughout this Province, on Account of the War, &c."

2. "The doctrinal part the second time from Is. 30:12–13."

(2) The procuring cause: that the "accursed thing" was found among them.

Implied [in the text].

2. A threatening as to what is future.

Herein something expressed, and something implied: expressed, in that God would be with 'em no more; implied, that in consequence of this, they should have no more success in war, but [God would not be with them any more].

Doctrine

Sin, above all other things, weakens a people in war.

This may be well inferred from the text, both from the fact it refers to, and from the threatening denounced.

Sin, above all other things, weakens a people in war, and lays 'em open to their enemies, two ways:

I. By a natural influence.

II. By God's judicial disposal.

I. {Sin weakens a people in war,} by a natural tendency and influence.

First. When vice prevails much among a people, it tends to enfeeble both their bodies and minds.

In a degenerate time among a people, sensuality is wont to prevail. Many give up themselves very much to a sensual, intemperate, luxurious way of living. Which has been the case of late in our nation.

[Sensuality] greatly enfeebles the bodies of men.

Those that give themselves over to sensual delights and an extravagant way of living, are commonly but miserably fitted to go through the hardships and fatigues of war.

[Sensuality] enfeebles their minds.

As it were enervates the mind, destroys its stability and firmness, introduces an habit of indolence, negligence and inactivity.

Causes 'em to be of an effeminate, mean spirit.

It was observed of the ancient Romans.

And it has been observed of our nation.

Sin enfeebles the minds of a people. It intimidates their minds by guilt.

Prov. 28:1, "The wicked flee when no man pursues: but the righteous is bold as a lion."

[The righteous] look death in the face with courage.

[They] meet it with thoroughness in the way of this duty.

Religion leads to trust in God; that givest the truly firmest and best courage.

How bold did this make David, when he went against Goliath. 1 Sam. 17:44, etc.,

And the Philistine said to David, Come to me, and I will give thy flesh unto the fowls of the air, and to the beasts of the field. Then said David to the Philistine, Thou comest to me with a sword, and with a spear, and with a shield: but I come to thee in the name of the Lord of hosts, the God of the armies of Israel, whom thou hast defied. This day will the Lord deliver thee into mine hand; and I will smite thee, and take thine head from thee; and I will give the carcasses of the host of the Philistines this day unto the fowls of the air, and to the wild beasts of the earth; that all the earth may know that there is a God in Israel. And all this assembly shall know that the Lord saveth not with sword and spear: for the battle is the Lord's, and he will give you into our hands.

[So] Caleb and Josh. Num. 14:9, "Only rebel not ye against the Lord, neither fear ye the people of the land; for they are bread for us: their defense is departed from them, and the Lord is with us: fear them not."

They have a reasonable fearlessness, a sure foundation of courage.

Second. Sin impoverishes a people.

The wealth of a people under God is very much their strength.

When it is corrupt time in a nation or land, luxury and sensuality is wont greatly to prevail, as was observed before. And these have a tendency to destroy that laudable industry, whereby their substance is increased.

That vice, luxury and vanity of mind {that prevails in a corrupt time}, tends to indolence and negligence, and a vain and unprofitable way spending of time, whereby a people is impoverished.

[This is] agreeable to frequent observations of the Wise Man. Prov. 13:18, "Poverty and shame shall be to him that refuseth instruction." Prov. 23:21, "the glutton and the drunkard shall come to poverty: and drowsiness shall clothe a man with rags." Prov. 28:19, "he that followeth vain persons shall have poverty enough." Prov. 6:26, "by means of a whorish woman a m[an] is brought to a piece of bread."

And constant experience shows that the prevalence {of sin impoverishes a people}.

Third. It makes [rulers] unfaithful and treacherous to the public, and regardless of the public interest.

When it is a very corrupt time, and wickedness abounds among a people, the disease is commonly seated very much in the head, and rulers and officers that have the management of the public affairs of a people are infected. Whereby they become unfaithful to the community {interest}, and for the sake of this oftentimes neglect, yea, betray and sell the public interest.

Whereby they become their worst enemies.

Rulers are the keepers of the city. But if they are treacherous, and open the gates to the enemy, they prove their worst enemies.

[That people would] better have a hundred foreign enemies.

Fourth. It sets them at variance one with another.

As the strength of a building consists in the several parts being well-joined together, so the like strength of a community consists in their firm union.

[So] when disunited. Matt. 12:25, "Every kingdom divided against itself is brought to desolation; and every city or house divided against itself shall not stand."

But it is the prevalence of sin that [causes disunion].

This introduces the causes of contention, selfishness, pride, covetousness, injustice, unfaithful[ness].

[It introduces] a disposition to contention, destroys love.

[It] causes a disposition to anger, wrath and malice.

II. Sin, above all things, weakens a people in war by God's judicial disposal.

God is provoked.

His displeasure procured.

Makes him their enemy.

Brings his wrath and curse upon them.

And this will show how greatly sin weakens a people in war, and exposes 'em to their enemies, if the following things be considered:

First. Sin deprives a people of their main defense from their enemies, viz., the protection of heaven.

The Word of God teaches that God's protection is the only sure defense. Ps. 127:1, "except the Lord keep the city, [the watchman waketh but in vain]."

Ps. 33:16–17, "There is no king saved by the multitude of an host."

And reason teaches the same.

They that have God's protection, as every virtuous and religious people have, they have a sure defense.

God is for 'em, and who can be against 'em [Rom. 8:31].

The eternal God is their refuge [Deut. 33:27].

"He rideth on the heavens in their help" [Deut. 33:26].

God appoints salvation for walls and bulwarks [Is. 26:1].

They may laugh at the power of the enemy.

Is. 33:16–17, "They shall dwell on high: their place of defense [shall be the munition of rocks]."

God is able effectually [to protect them].

Experience shows that there is no other sure defense in a time of war.

[The walls of Babylon [were] thirty-five feet high, eighty-seven feet thick, [surrounded by a] vast ditch filled with water, [having] gates of brass.

[But God "will] break in pieces [the] gates of brass," Is. 45:2.

[So he did with] Zerah the Ethiopian. 2 Chron. 14:9, etc., "And there came out against them Zerah the Ethiopian with an host of a thousand thousand, and three hundred chariots; and came unto Mareshah. Then Asa went out against him, and they set the battle in array in the valley of Zephathah at Mareshah. And Asa cried unto the Lord his God, and said, Lord, it is nothing with thee to help, whether with many, or with them that have no power: help us, O Lord our God; for we rest on thee, and in thy name we go against this multitude. O Lord, thou art our God; let no man prevail against thee. So the Lord smote the Ethiopians before Asa, and before Judah; and the Ethiopians fled."

[So with] Xerxes.

Commonly the greatest, vastest preparations have been baffled.

But sin deprives [a people of this protection].

Second. God more generally manifests his judicial hand in this world by punishing a people or public society for their sins, than he doth particular persons.

Reason [shows it].

Experience shows it. [So the] history of past ages.

History shows it to be so with heathen nations, but 'tis so more especially with a visible people of God. Ps. 94:10, "He that chastises the heathen, shall not he correct?"

A visible people of God are a people in covenant with him. His covenant with them as a people consists much in promises and threatenings of temporal calamity.

The threatenings in the Books of Moses of temporal judgments, are principally national.

The temporal prosperity or calamity of a visible people is much more constantly and exactly agreeable to their moral state.

As it was in Israel.

Amos 3:2, "You only have I known."

Third. God is wont in a special manner to show his hand in the government of the world, in disposing the events of war. Which is one reason why God is so often called by the name of "The Lord of hosts," or "Lord of armies." As Isai 47:4, "As for our redeemer, the Lord of hosts is his name, the Holy One of Israel"; and 48:2, "For they call themselves of the holy city, and stay themselves upon the God of Israel; The Lord of hosts is his name."

And [this is] one reason why God is said to be "a man of war," Ex. 15: 3.

Fourth. Destruction by the sword of the enemy, is a most just and meet recompense for the rebellion of a people against God. 'Tis just that a people that will be enemies to God, should suffer from the hands of enemies themselves.

There is in sin a mortal enmity against God. 'Tis an opposition to God's dominion, yea, and to his being.

It is, in its nature, to oppose the life of God.

How just therefore is it, that God should punish them by suffering their enemies to take away their lives.

And as 'tis the nature of sin to excite enmity against God, so it also excites in them an enmity against their neighbors. When wickedness prevails among a people, hatred, envying, revenge and contention prevail.

As all holiness is summarily comprehended in charity, so {wickedness is comprehended in enmity}.

Now how just is it that God should so order it, that they that delight in enmity and war with their fellow creatures, should have enough of it.

Fifth. God has often threatened in his Word that he will punish the wickedness of a sinful people, by giving them into the hands of their enemies.

These are the punishments chiefly insisted on by Moses in the books of Leviticus, Numbers and Deuteronomy.

[And] by the prophets.

Sixth. It has ever been the most ordinary way of God's destroying a sinful, rebellious people, to do [it] in war by the sword of the enemy.

[So it was with the] seven nations of Canaan.

In the time of the Judges.

[So the] Ten Tribes.

[This was how God] destroyed the kingdom of the Two Tribes.

[And] the kingdom of Assyria.

Babylon.

So a war thus executed the destruction threatened by the prophets against Egypt, {against} Ethiopia, {against the} land of Moab, {against the} children of Ammon, {against the} Philistines, {and against} Tyre and Sidon, for their wickedness.

So he executed threatened punishments upon Elam, and on [the] empire of Persia.

[So] Grecia.

Jerusalem in the apostles' days.

{So God executed threatened punishments on the} Roman monarchy.

[So he will execute] temporal judgments on Antichrist.

The sword of enemies is one main instrument of God's vengeance in this world.

Such as God has made use of as great instruments of destroying nations in war, called God's "battle axe, Jer.³ 51:20, etc.; [the] rod of God's anger, Is. 10:5; "[the] overflowing scourge," Is. 28:15.

The sword of the enemy is called the sword of the Lord. Jer. 12:12, "for the sword of the Lord shall devour from the one end of the land even to the other end of the land: no flesh shall have peace."

It being therefore thus, their chief defense is God's protection.

God [is wont] more generally to punish a people [in such circumstances].

[God is wont] in a special manner to show his disposing hand in the government {of the world}, by disposing the events of war.

And destruction by the sword, being so just and meet.

And God, having so often threatened; and it having been found by the experience of all ages that this is God's most common way; and sin being that which brings God's displeasure on a people: it must needs be so.⁴

Application

I would now apply this Doctrine to the present circumstances of our own nation and land; and to lead you to such an improvement of it as may be proper for the occasion and business of this day, which is appointed on occasion of the war the nation is engaged in with many and powerful enemies, to the calamities of which war this land in a special manner lies greatly exposed.

And this I would do in the following method:

I. I would observe that it has very visibly and remarkably [been] owing to the protection of heaven, that our nation and land have not been destroyed before now by the same kind of enemies with those that we are now exposed [to].

The nations that have chiefly from time to time acted the part of enemies, and by which the nation has been threatened with destruction

---

3. MS: "Isai."

4. L. 9v. contains notes in another hand, possibly by Samuel Hopkins or another of JE's students, consisting of references to three biblical passages: Ezra 9:6, Ezek. 36:26, and Deut. 9:22–28.

more than any other foreign enemies for several ages past, are the nations of France and Spain

These have often sought our ruin.

But God has not given us up.

And it has very visibly been owing [to God's protection that we have not been conquered].

[So] in Queen Elizabeth's time.

God wrought a marvelous deliverance when the nation was brought to the brink of ruin.[5]

Again, when through the influence of France the nation was again greatly exposed in the latter part of Queen Anne's reign.[6]

And since that, many plots and attempts for bringing in the Pretender, the King of France assisting.[7]

Perhaps no nation can parallel ours, for the wonders of divine mercy

If the Lord had not been on our side, [we would have been lost].

Not chiefly the vigilance or strength of the nation.

And we in this land have [in] times past been marvelously preserved from destruction by the Indians: the same kind of enemies that we are now afraid of.

II. To consider under what circumstances a visible people of God have usually been in, by the Scripture account, before a great destruction by the sword of their enemies.

First. Such destruction has come after a people have continued long in their degeneracy, after many means used to reclaim 'em.

[So the] Ten Tribes, 2 Kgs. 17:12–15.

[And] the tribe of Judah.

For the most part from Solomon's time.

Especially from the beginning of the reign of Manasseh.

Prophets are often expostulating with the people concerning their long continued [degeneracy]. Jer. 4:14, "How long shall thy vain thoughts [lodge within thee]?" Is. 57:10, " Thou art wearied in the greatness of thy way; yet saidst thou not, There is no hope: thou hast found the life of thine hand; therefore thou wast not grieved."

Before the destruction by the Romans.

---

5. Probably a reference to the defeat of the Spanish Armada in 1588.

6. Referring to Queen Anne's War.

7. Referring to the efforts by the Jacobites in Scotland to restore the Stuart family to the throne in 1715.

Second. It has been usual that the visible people of God have been the subjects of extraordinary calls and warnings a little before such destruction.

So before the destruction of the Ten Tribes by the sword of {the Assyrians}.[8]

Hosea.

Amos.

[So the kingdom of] Judah.

Many prophets, especially the prophet Jeremiah.

Destruction in their war with the Romans, [prophesied] by Christ and other apostles.

But especially a little before (Christ's crucifixion}.[9]

Epistle to the Hebrews.[10]

Third. The Scripture gives an account, in several instances, of God's extraordinary striving with a people by his Spirit, not long before {they are destroyed}.

Josiah's time.

Apostles' time.

Extraordinary call.

Extraordinary opportunity.

Bring in his elect.

Fourth. After such an outpouring of the Spirit, there have followed an uncommon degree of obduracy and hardness of heart in those that have not been the subjects of the saving benefit of it.

After the outpouring {of the Spirit} in Josiah's [reign, the kingdom was taken over by the Egyptians].[11]

Jer. 5:3, " O Lord, are not thine eyes upon the truth? thou hast stricken them, but they have not grieved; thou hast consumed them, but they have refused to receive correction: they have made their faces harder than a rock; they have refused to return."

[We have] a more awful instance, Jer. 44:15–19.

Then all the men which knew that their wives had burned incense unto other gods, and all the women that stood by, a great multitude, even all the people that dwelt in the land of Egypt, in Pathros, answered

---

8. Under Shalmaneser, c. 772 BCE; see 2 Kgs. 17–18.

9. See Christ's prophecy concerning Jerusalem in Matt. 23.

10. Possibly a reference to Heb. 12:22.

11. See 2 Kgs. 23 and 2 Chron. 35.

Jeremiah, saying, As for the word that thou hast spoken unto us in the name of the Lord, we will not hearken unto thee. But we will certainly do whatsoever thing goeth forth out of our own mouth, to burn incense unto the queen of heaven, and to pour out drink offerings unto her, as we have done, we, and our fathers, our kings, and our princes, in the cities of Judah, and in the streets of Jerusalem: for then had we plenty of victuals, and were well, and saw no evil. But since we left off to burn incense to the queen of heaven, and to pour out drink offerings unto her, we have wanted all things, and have been consumed by the sword and by the famine. And when we burned incense to the queen of heaven, and poured out drink offerings unto her, did we make her cakes to worship her, and pour out drink offerings unto her, without our men?

Vv. 25–26, "Thus saith the Lord of hosts, the God of Israel, saying; Ye and your wives have both spoken with your mouths, and fulfilled with your hand, saying, We will surely perform our vows that we have vowed, to burn incense to the queen of heaven, and to pour out drink offerings unto her: ye will surely accomplish your vows, and surely perform your vows. Therefore hear ye the word of the Lord, all Judah that dwell in the land of Egypt; Behold, I have sworn by my great name, saith the Lord, that my name shall no more be named in the mouth of any man of Judah in all the land of Egypt, saying, The Lord God liveth."

In the apostles' days. Rom. 11:7, etc., "the election hath obtained, and the rest were blinded."

Acts 7:51, etc., "Ye stiffnecked and uncircumcised in heart and ears, ye do always resist the Holy Ghost: as your fathers did, so do ye. Which of the prophets have not your fathers persecuted? and they have slain them which shewed before of the coming of the Just One; of whom ye have been now the betrayers and murderers: who have received the law by the disposition of angels, and have not kept it.

Acts 28:25, etc., "And when they agreed not among themselves, they departed, after that Paul had spoken one word, Well spake the Holy Ghost by Esaias the prophet unto our fathers, saying, Go unto this people, and say, Hearing ye shall hear, and shall not understand; and seeing ye shall see, and not perceive: for the heart of this people is waxed gross, and their ears are dull of hearing, and their eyes have they closed; lest they should see with their eyes, and hear with their ears, and understand with their heart, and should be converted, and I should heal them."

Fifth. A spirit of strife and contention did most dreadfully prevail.

Before the destruction by the sword of the Chaldeans, called "briars," "thorns," "scorpions." Ezek. 2:6, "And thou, son of man, be not afraid of them, neither be afraid of their words, though briers and thorns be with thee, and thou dost dwell among scorpions."

Jer. 9:4–5, "for every brother will utterly supplant, and every neighbor will walk with slanders. And they will deceive every one his neighbor, and will not speak the truth: they have taught their tongues to speak lies, and weary themselves to commit iniquity."

Of a most violent spirit.

How violent their behavior towards Jeremiah.

And one towards another.

Ishmael kills Gedaliah and all the Jews that were with him [2 Kgs. 25:25].

Before the destruction by the Romans.

A violent spirit against Christ, {against the} apostles, and all Christians.

In Antioch of Pisidia. Acts 13:45, "But when the Jews saw the multitudes, they were filled with envy, and spake against those things which were spoken by Paul, contradicting and blaspheming."

[In] Thessalonica. Acts 17:5, "But the Jews which believed not, moved with envy, took unto them certain lewd fellows of the baser sort, and gathered a company, and set all the city on an uproar, and assaulted the house of Jason, and sought to bring them out to the people."

[Paul was] followed to Berea, v. 13.

[In] Corinth, Acts 18:12.

Not only {a violent spirit} against Christians, but "contrary to all men." 1 Thess. 2:14–16, "For ye, brethren, became followers of the churches of God which in Judaea are in Christ Jesus: for ye also have suffered like things of your own countrymen, even as they have of the Jews: who both killed the Lord Jesus, and their own prophets, and have persecuted us; and they please not God, and are contrary to all me: forbidding us to speak to the Gentiles that they might be saved, to fill up their sins alway: for the wrath is come upon them to the uttermost."

[They] began dreadfully to quarrel one among another.

III. How far these circumstances agree to this land at this day.

[We have] long been departing from God.

[Though we have lived] under many means.

[We have had] extraordinary warnings by the preaching of the Word.

Extraordinary strivings by his Spirit.

How many things soever to be found fault with.

Yet none can deny that there has been a great awakening: [there has been an] extraordinary call, [great] opportunity, [which has] gathered in great numbers of the elect.

No such general work.

[It] has [been] followed [by] an uncommon obduracy, hardness of heart: insensibility, desperate prejudices. [There] never [was] such a time.

[We have] reason to fear great numbers [have been] deluded. They are hardened in their delusion.

Many remain under the influence of a false spirit.

A spirit of error came in: Quakers, Anabaptists {and, it is} to be feared, deists.

Others [have been] hardened another way.

In this town [there was] never such a time, wherein the town so universally seemed to be so far from any manner of appearance of a work of awakening, or conviction of sinners.

And as to a spirit of contention.

IV. Take notice of some of the circumstances of our nation and land that show how visibly we stand in need of the divine protection and help in the war.

[*First.*] As to the nation.

[Our] enemies [are] many and powerful: the two greatest papist monarchies that are in the world; either of them singly much greater than the dominion of the King of England.

Our nation very much weakened and exposed by their misunderstandings and mutual jealousies, {and by} uneasinesses one towards another, and great intestine divisions, that there seems to be at present no prospect of the removal of.

Have hitherto been greatly disappointed in the war with Spain.[12]

And though the nation is in alliance with some other nations that have lately had great success in war, yet this success has seemed to be more owing to an uncommon interposition of divine providence.

---

12. A reference to the failed invasion of Cartagena.

[*Second.*] As to this land. There is scarce any part of the king's dominion so much exposed.

V. It may be reasonably expected to be the event.

And under this head, to express what it appears to me from the analogy of God's dispensations—I would be far from being positive in things of this nature; God's judgments are a great deep—it is reasonable to suppose either that we are near some very extraordinary day of mercy, or that we are near a day of great judgment and wrath.

If God spares us.

It appears to me he will do otherwise. [This] has been usual in former ages, agreeable to Scripture instances.

[It is] otherwise than he has been commonly wont to do with a visible people.

Especially on account of the late extraordinary dispensation.

And our present circumstances.

If God has mercy on that part of the risen generation that remain in sin, so as to carry on any great work among them, [that would not be as God has commonly done].

No such instance in Scripture.

Probably no age can parallel.

We have long continued departing from God before this.

But sinning against the Holy Spirit is highly aggravated {and provoking to God}.

If God is now about to make way for the destruction of Antichrist, it may be [some extraordinary dispensation is at hand].

When that time comes, God will doubtless go out of his usual way.

But however, so much we may undoubtedly determine, that it will be presumption for us to expect success or safety in the present war, unless we forsake our evil ways. What says God in the text? "Neither will I be with you any more, except ye destroy the accursed from among you."

It is now some time since God has lift up the sword against us, but has hitherto withheld the stroke.

He therein deals mercifully by us, as being slow to anger, as it were loath to give us up, still waiting to give us opportunity.

'Tis no sign that God will not smite us with that sword with great severity, unless we put away the accursed thing.

Before God destroyed Jerusalem by the Romans, he proceeded in like manner.

There are some things at present that have a very fair, pleasant aspect with respect to the war as it concerns us in this land, that give hopes that we shall not be so much exposed to the calamities of this war.

But we know not how soon the scene may change.

It will [be a] presumption for us to promise ourselves {that we shall not be exposed to calamities}, unless we repent.

The scene may soon greatly change, and the pleasing prospect vanish away.

It is often so.

We may take the fair prospect. There is as an offer of God to us, joined with his threatening.

We may have a line of fortifications on our frontiers, but if our sins remain we shall still lie open, and shall be like a city without walls.

We may have some nations of Indians on our side, but we shall have God against us.

One government may join with another, but let us remember that, Prov. 11:21, "Though hand join in hand, [the wicked shall not be unpunished]."

Whatever the present prospect is, the event will be just as God pleases.

We may devise and contrive what we will for our own safety.

God can baffle all our wisest projects.

We shall be in danger of trusting to an arm of flesh, and so neglecting to make our peace with God.

We have long enjoyed the blessing of peace.

There are perhaps no professing countries but those that are more lately settled in America, but have had their turn to pass under the trial of persecution.

'Tis spoken of as the common lot of professing lands, Rev. 3:10, "Because thou hast kept the word of my patience, I also will keep thee from the hour of temptation, which shall come upon all the world, to try all them that dwell [upon the earth]."

Whatever the state of things with regard to this war may be within the land, it would be no strange thing if, before the finishing of this war with the two powerful nations we are engaged with, we should be invaded by sea. 'Tis not unlikely the war may continue long, and none but God knows what may be before the end of it. The world seems to be ripe for great things, and God seems to be warning us to prepare for them.

[So] earthquakes: and one very lately coming with the proclamation of war. God is shaking the land, perhaps to warn us to prepare for a more dreadful shaking in the political and ecclesiastical state of the land.

It is with us as it was with Moab of old. Jer. 48:11–12, "Moab hath been at ease from his youth, and he hath settled on his lees, and hath never been emptied from vessel to vessel, neither hath he gone into captivity: therefore his taste remained in him, and his scent is not changed. Therefore, behold, the days come, saith the Lord, that I will send unto him wanderers, that shall cause him to wander, and shall empty his vessels, and break their bottles."

And unless those warnings hit and shake our hearts, 'tis to be feared whether God won't shake and unsettle us in a more awful sense.

The darkest thing that attends our circumstances, is [our] sinful, corrupt state; and if we continue obstinate under all the warnings and threatenings we are the subjects of, it will look yet much more dark—as though the blow would come, and a very dreadful blow, and such an one as we never yet received.

VI. What is thus the wisest course for us to take, that we may be protected and blessed during the present war?

In general, it is to destroy the accursed thing, and to be thorough in it.

But more particularly,

First. If we would act a wise part, we shall not be prevented of putting away the accursed thing, by any trust in any arm of flesh.

We shall not be in this respect as[13] it often is with sailors in a storm.

We are not yet brought ashore.

Second. If we would be wise, we shall thoroughly search out the accursed thing, that we may destroy it.

Consider the state of the land.

[Consider the] state of the town.

[Consider] our own state and ways.

This is a work of great difficulty.

If we don't search, 'tis to be feared that God will search us in the same manner as he threatened, Zeph. 1:12–13, "And it shall come to pass at that time, that I will search Jerusalem with candles, and punish the

---

13. MS: "For."

men that are settled on their lees: that say in their heart, The Lord will not do good, neither will he do evil. Therefore their goods shall become a booty, and their houses a desolation: they shall also build houses, but not inhabit them; and they shall plant vineyards, but not drink the wine thereof."

Third. It is our wisdom to be speedy in this.

We have delayed long enough.

Till the sword is lifted up.

[Till the] rod [is] held over us.

Surely, 'tis time.

Zeph. 2:1–3, "[Gather yourselves together, yea, gather together, O nation not desired; before the decree bring forth, before the day pass as the chaff, before the fierce anger of the Lord come upon you, before the day of the Lord's anger come upon you. Seek ye the Lord, all ye meek of the earth, which have wrought his judgment; seek righteousness, seek meekness: it may be ye shall be hid in the day of the Lord's anger."

Let young and old speedily [do this].

Let our young people consider.

Fourth. It is our wisdom, especially to seek these two things: righteousness and meekness.

We see Second Table duties chiefly insisted on by the prophets, in order [to secure God's temporal blessings].

More than sacrifices and other ordinances.

Our external duty to God chiefly consists in these.

God, in a national covenant, promises prosperity to external duties.

These are two main duties, and may be so understood as to comprehend all.

War seems to be a fit punishment of those sins that are contrary to these: unrighteousness, sins contrary to meekness.

Now God is so ready to appear for the defense from those that rise up against them, or those that practice those duties.

Ps. 45:3–4, "Gird thy sword upon thy thigh, O most mighty, with thy glory and thy majesty. And in thy majesty ride prosperously because of truth and meekness and righteousness; and thy right hand shall teach thee terrible things.

If [we] would comply with these duties, we should be defended, and all dark clouds would vanish away. If our public fasting was followed {with reformation}, that promise would be fulfilled to us, Is. 58:8–9, "Then shall thy light break forth as the morning, and thine health shall spring forth speedily: and thy righteousness shall go before thee; the glory of the Lord shall be thy reward. Then shalt thou call, and the Lord shall answer; thou shalt cry, and he shall say, Here I am. If thou take away from the midst of thee the yoke, the putting forth of the finger, and speaking vanity."

The Armor of God

July 1744

BY JULY 1744, A shot had yet to be fired in New England, but the specters of previous wars cast a pall over the Connecticut River Valley. Memories of wars past echoed in the anxieties of Northampton and prompted a flurry of preparations in expectation of another wave of conflict. The *Boston Gazette* continued to relay news from towns like Ratisbon, Genoa, and Stockholm, however, reports began to focus on local preparations after the declarations of war. Governor Shirley proposed initial preparations in his speeches to the assembly and correspondence with the Duke of Newcastle.[1] In early June, Governor Shirley wrote to Edwards's uncle, Col. John Stoddard, to accelerate those preparations. He asked Col. Stoddard to raise a scouting party and impress soldiers to defend the frontier. The very next day, Shirley penned another letter to Stoddard instructing him to lead a diplomatic delegation to Albany in order to secure the assistance of the Mohawks.[2] Preparations seemed to progress quickly.

The awareness of these preparations frame his sermon, *The Armor of God*. Edwards did not merely use themes of war to press his revivalist agenda nor did he present his theory on Just War. Instead, Edwards drew on the immediacy of martial preparations and the anxieties over impending attacks to drive home spiritual lessons. Edwards highlighted the gravity of their precarious position on the frontier. Northampton's enemies were great, powerful, and numerous enjoying many advantages

---

1. *Boston Gazette*, April 3, 1744.
2. Shirley, *Correspondence*, 127–28.

in warfare. The only sure protection, according to Edwards, was the protection of God secured by "great care and vigilance."

In the Application, Edwards compared strategic vulnerabilities to one's spiritual vulnerabilities. One must take the same great care and vigilance in defending spiritual vulnerabilities as Northampton was currently taking care to protect themselves from combined Native-French attacks. When a watchmen spies the enemy approaching the town, they run and call "Arm! Arm!" Why, according to Edwards, would one not react with the same urgency when there is a threat to one's spiritual well-being? Edwards specifically mentions one defensive measure, leveraging it for a spiritual lesson. Shirley commissioned John Stoddard to repair and construct new forts along the western frontier. Edwards highlighted "the great folly of men" who do not exert any effort to secure themselves in a "spiritual fortress."

Military preparations begun in and around Northampton became the backdrop for Edwards's pastoral goals. Edwards revealed his pastoral purposes by drawing on the martial anxieties of his congregation to cultivate a desire for spiritual awakening. As the war continued to inch closer to Northampton, the martial events of the frontier provided an opportunity for dramatic and personal calls to piety.

*****

This sermon was edited by Christian Cuthbert for the Jonathan Edwards Center. The manuscript is twenty-two duodecimo-sized leaves. Edwards dated the booklet at the top of the first page, "July 1744." To the left of the date is a re-preaching notation, "+ Nov. [17]55," and to the right is the Redemption symbol. Portions of the manuscript were made from repurposed children's writing exercises and from a bill of goods.

The Armor of God

Ephesians 6:11–13

Put on the whole armor of God, that ye may be able to stand against the wiles of the devil. For we wrestle not against flesh and blood, but against principalities, against powers, against the rulers of the darkness of this world, against spiritual wickedness in high places. Wherefore take unto you the whole armor of God, that ye may be able to withstand in the evil day, and having done all, to stand.

AFTER INSISTING ON PARTICULAR duties and when he[1] had finished his exhortations in that respect, [he] closes his exhortation in the text and following verses with direction to that which is absolutely necessary in order to a thorough and proper performance of those duties he had insisted on. Which in substance is that, viz. that in the performance of those duties, they should behave themselves with like caution, vigilance, and vigor that persons are wont to do in war with the most powerful and violent enemies.

And in the text may be observed three things: a direction, end, and reason.

1. The direction: which is to do our utmost for our defense in our spiritual warfare.

This direction is expressed:

(1) More specially, v. 11, "Put on the whole armor of God"; and in other words, v. 13, "take to you the whole armor of God."

---

1. I.e., the apostle Paul.

(2) 'Tis more universally expressed: having done "all to stand." Which implies a direction to do the utmost that is in our power for our own defense[2] and safety in all respects.

2. The end why we should do thus: that we may be able to stand against the wiles of the devil.

And v. 13: "That we may be able to withstand in the evil day."

3. The reason given why we should use such means to such an end, viz., that our enemies are so powerful: "for we wrestle not [against flesh and blood, but against principalities, against powers, against the rulers of the darkness of this world, against spiritual wickedness in high places]."

Doctrine

In order to our being preserved from destruction by our spiritual enemies, we had need to behave ourselves in the business of religion as those that are engaged in the most dangerous war.

The following reasons may be given of this doctrine:[3]

I. Our spiritual enemies are very numerous.

There is a vast army of devils that seek the destruction of the souls of men. No other than they can be intended in Rev. 9:16. Speaking of the army that is listed under the king whose name is Abaddon and Apollyon—i.e., Satan—it is said, "the number of the army of the horsemen was two hundred thousand thousand," the greatest particular number that is mentioned anywhere in the Bible upon any occasion whatsoever. We are far from having reason to conclude that this is intended as a designation of the precise number of the fallen angels. But so much we may infer: [it was] a vast and innumerable multitude; [we] can't reasonably suppose that the number is less.

'Tis not usual nor ever to be found in any instance in Scripture, that visionary representations of the things of another [world] exceed the truth. Nor is it to be found anywhere in Scripture, that when a certain and particular great number is put for an uncertain to signify a vast and inconceivable multitude.

---

2. A piece of Mary Edwards's copy book.

3. A shorthand notation at this point reads: "From hence three leaves preached the second time." This part of the sermon is made from a discarded receipt.

Jude 14, "[And Enoch also, the seventh from Adam, prophesied of these, saying, Behold, the Lord cometh] with ten thousands of his saints."

Num. 10:36, "Return O Lord to the ten thousand thousand of Israel."

So those wicked spirits that are the enemies of our souls are exceedingly numerous. Besides the lusts in our own hearts we have to conflict with, which are very numerous, especially considering that each single person, has so many lusts, so many spiritual enemies in his heart to conflict with; which would be looked upon as vast odds in any temporal war.

II. Our spiritual enemies are very powerful.

This is signified in the text: "[For we wrestle] not [against] flesh and blood [but against principalities, against powers, against the rulers of the darkness of this world, against spiritual wickedness in high places]."

That which is flesh and blood, or they that have mortal bodies, are very weak and feeble in comparison of pure spirits. Thus, when God represents the weakness of the Egyptian forces, he [reminds us of their mortality].

Is. 31:3, "[Now the Egyptians are men and not God; and their] horses flesh and not spirit.

[It signifies the] great power [of our spiritual enemies, that] they are further called "principalities and powers."

"Rulers of the darkness."

"Spiritual wickedness in high places" [Eph. 6:12]

Mighty potentates.

By their strength, they are rulers of the world, as to the evil of it; rulers of the darkness of the world. But they fell. They were mighty angels; lost their holiness and all their spiritual strength, but not their natural strength, at least not to such a degree but that they still remain mighty and powerful beings. [They are] represented by the giants of old:

Goliath.

roaring lion [1 Pet. 5:8].

Leviathan [Is. 27:1].

strong man armed [Luke 11:21].

great dragon [Rev. 12:3].

Our lusts, [though] naturally in reigning [position], never have mastered all rational principles in the soul.

[They] are strong in the best.

III.[4] [Our spiritual enemies] have great advantages against us.

Our internal enemies have great advantage; our external enemies, those numerous, cruel spirits, have great advantage {over us} on this account. As when one nation goes to war with another nation, 'tis a vast advantage {for them} if they have a great number of friends in the midst {of them}.

Traitors stand ready to open the gates, to receive 'em and assist 'em when an invasion is made. And a nation with whom this is the case, lies under unspeakable disadvantage.

Especially if those traitors lie hid, which is very often the case with men.

[Our spiritual enemies have] great advantage against us, by reason of our circumstances in the world. [The] world is full of those things that give them advantage; ['tis] full of their snares. We walk in the midst of them. We are in the enemy's country, where they have open access; [where they] pass and repass, and have filled [the country] full of traps and snares and ambuscades. We are like men whose way and business is in the woods in an Indian war, where the enemy is thick, and skulks behind the thickets, laying wait for them.

IV. There is no such thing as escaping [spiritual enemies] without conquering.[5]

All must engage, and not only so, but conquer or die.

In other wars, comparatively few are obliged actually to engage. {But here, there is} no escaping by flight.

V.[6] They ever have been, and still are, exceedingly successful enemies of mankind.

Indeed, they are not successful enemies of God and Christ, nor of the elect in all ages.

[So] in the old world.

[They were able to] destroy the bigger part.

For a great many ages together, all nations, excepting one, were subdued under him,[7] and enslaved to him.

And still most of the nations of the world, and the far greater part of those few remaining nations, [are subject to the] dreadful havoc [these

---

4. MS: "8." That JE jumps from "2" to "8" suggests that he originally had more material in the doctrinal section, which he took out.

5. MS: "9."

6. MS: "10."

7. I.e., Satan.

enemies] make from day to day. No country, province, city, or town; no fort that man can build; no condition, rank, or degree escape.

[They have had] successfulness against the greatest kings, conquerors.

[They are] the most politic and crafty.

VI.[8] We can't expect that God should help us against these enemies in any other way, than that of our own great care and vigilance.

However many strong {spiritual enemies attack}, yet God can easily protect us, and subdue [them]. But we have no reason [to trust in his help].

He has often commanded us to use our utmost [care and vigilance].

[He] has given no encouragement.

Though all dependence be on him, yet he has so ordered that our own vigilance {is necessary}, as of persons engaged in war {whose vigilance} is no less necessary. [God] has often represented the necessity of it in his Word. Particularly in I Cor. 9:24 to the end: "Know ye not that they which run in a race run all, but one receiveth the prize? So run, that ye may obtain. And every man that striveth for the mastery is temperate in all things. Now they do it to obtain a corruptible crown; but we an incorruptible. I therefore so run, not as uncertainly; so fight I, not as one that beateth the air: but I keep under my body, and bring it into subjection: lest that by any means, when I have preached to others, I myself should be a castaway."

Application

Use I of *Instruction*.

If it be so, that in order {to expect being preserved from destruction by our spiritual enemies}, we had need to behave {ourselves in the business of religion as those that are engaged in the most dangerous war}, then hence we learn how great a degree of stupidity, negligence and folly with respect to the business of religion the bigger part of those that sit under the gospel are guilty of. For how far are they from behaving {as those that are engaged in the most dangerous war}?

Particularly, the folly and negligence of the bigger part {of those that sit under the gospel}, appears in the following things:

8. MS: "11."

First. That their minds are no more taken up about it. When one people is engaged in war with another people, especially if it appears to be a very dangerous war, their minds {are taken up about it}.

We now see it in this land since we have had the news that our nation have entered into a war with France, by which we in this land are exposed. How much has the land seemed to be affected with it, [their] minds taken up, especially in those parts of the land that are much exposed?

How much does the war seem to be the subject of people's thoughts? How much is it the subject of conversation—persons showing how much they think of it, by their talking so much of it. "Out of the abundance of the heart the mouth speaketh" [Matt. 12:34].

But how little is said about things that concern our spiritual warfare? How much are those things neglected in men's conversation, and in their minds?

How eager do persons seem to be to hear any news relating to the war? And to take notice of every event and circumstance that seems either smiling or frowning? And how forward to inquire?

How far are they from being so ready to inquire after those things?

How far are men from being so eager to hear the things that do appertain to their spiritual warfare? And how dull and negligent do they generally appear, when the great things that concern it are declared and proclaimed in the name of the great King {of heaven and earth} in the preaching {of the Word}? Little regarding {the minister}, or not at all: many sleeping, and others, regarding it[9] no more than if they were asleep, have their thoughts [in] the meantime engaged about other things, and wandering to the ends of the earth.

Second. Men's exceeding stupidity in things pertaining to their spiritual enemies, appears in that they are no more alarmed at the appearance of danger from those enemies.

How easily do we become sensible of danger in a time of war with temporal enemies?

[There is] no need of great pains in arguing and reasoning with men, to convince {them with} long, particular, labored discourses, to point out the ways by which their enemies might come at them and among them. Eloquent speeches, labored with utmost skill that men are capable of to make men sensible, [are not necessary].

---

9. MS: "it."

Men are easily sensible. They think readily enough of ways {to take measures}.

Some men are more eminently exposed to eternal destruction by their spiritual enemies than others, by reason {of their exceeding stupidity in things pertaining to their spiritual enemies}. But how hard a thing is it to make 'em sensible of it.

Commonly, those that are most in danger, are least sensible.

How far otherwise is [it] among men in a state of war with temporal enemies. Some are more exposed than others in the skirts of a town—those that live in our new towns and settlements on the frontier: and how readily are they sensible of it.

And if there are any signs of the approach of the enemy, any tracks discovered in the woods, what an alarm does it give. How does it awaken the town. But with regard to the enemies of our souls, how far is it otherwise, though there be many plain and evident signs of an approach.

[So with signs of the approach] of a great army: yea, that they are just upon us; yea in the midst of us: and this be proclaimed never so loudly.

If a company of Indians in a time of war be discovered near a town, and one comes in and gives information of it, what a stir does {it cause}. How do men run to their arms. {How do we see} men running about streets, calling loudly one upon another.

But if a messenger comes in the name of God, [how is it otherwise].

If one that is set as a watchman in time of war discovers the approaches of the enemy, and gives notice of it, blows the trumpet and discharges his gun, or cries, "Arm! Arm!" {what an alarm does it give}.

But if one that is set as a spiritual watchman {should come, how far is it otherwise}.

If persons in the time of war hear the noise of guns in the night, though it seems to be at a great distance, [how are they alarmed].

If now we should have the news of four or five persons killed, {how would we be moved}.

How would men be affected, we may judge by what has appeared already, though hitherto we have heard of no one person killed in New England by the enemy.[10] And especially how would persons, particularly all that live in exposed places,[11] be moved with it, if we heard that the

---

10. This would change before the end of the war, as in the slaying of Elisha Clark by Indians.

11. MS: "Persons."

Indians {had captured any, and} roasted 'em alive, or [put them to] some other very cruel death, many days a-killing [them].

If that was their known way and manner; [if] it was known that they gave no quarter, but burned all {in their path, how would we be affected}.

What terror would the news [bring] of their being on our borders, and having proceeded, though but in a very few instances, thus to execute.

But 'tis our general profession that the bigger part that die go to hell, and but few are saved.

There are doubtless many scores of persons in one week in New England, take one week with another through the year, and from year to [year, that have died painful deaths at the hands of enemies]. And we profess to believe that what the damned suffer is immensely more dreadful. And this [is] what multitudes are greatly exposed to, vastly more than persons in the most exposed places generally have been exposed to {painful deaths} in times of the hottest war.

Men dread falling into the hands of the Indians, and being slain or led into captivity by them.

But how many are there that are wretched captives [of Satan].

Men would have a great dread indeed of falling into the hands of Indians, if they expected {to be used} cruelly {and put to death}.

But how little dread do they seem to have of falling into the hands of devils, {who are called} cruel spirits, roaring lions, bloodthirsty serpents, forever tormenting [their prey], without being ever glutted.

Third. The great stupidity and folly of persons with respect to their spiritual enemies, appears in that they use no more vigilance or watchfulness to escape them.

In a time of war, great care is taken to keep up a good watch, especially in places that are peculiarly exposed. They can't lie down easy in their beds, or give sleep to their eyes, till they are [sensible a watch][12] is set for their defense; and will neither sleep, nor work, nor eat, nor drink in quietness without watch or word.

But how negligent are many that are greatly exposed to eternal death by their spiritual enemies? If any watch against those enemies, they set no spiritual watch in their own hearts. They sleep, and eat and drink, and work and play, and visit and divert themselves without any watch kept, or a very unsteady [one], and thus from day-to-day, and from month-to-month and from year-to-year.

---

12. Conjectural reading of line where MS is damaged.

In a time of war, persons are afraid to be conversant in dangerous places or go in exposed roads, and will not needlessly venture themselves in the thickets that lie nigh the enemy's country, and choose the safest places to dwell in and to work in.

But {how do they expose themselves to death by their spiritual enemies}.

[There are] places where many have fallen. Agreeable to that, Prov. 9:17–18, "[Stolen waters are sweet, and bread eaten in secret is pleasant. But he knoweth not that the dead are there; and that her guests are in the depths of hell]"; and Prov. 2:18–19. "[For her house inclineth unto death, and her paths unto the dead. None that go unto her return again, neither take they hold of the paths of life]."

If persons in a time [of war] are necessitated to expose themselves, or to go into places of danger, what extraordinary and strict vigilance do they maintain. But how {negligent are they when exposed to spiritual enemies}.

Sometimes, persons are necessitated to expose themselves to temptation. Some kinds of business are attended with greater temptation. Sometimes, persons are obliged to [go] amongst [temptations]. But [how negligent are they when they must go amongst spiritual enemies].

In a time of war, besides watch and word kept at home, we are very sensible that 'tis our prudence to send out scouts at a distance to discover the distant approaches of the [foe], that we may not be surprised by the enemy unawares, and so taken at disadvantage; but may have such timely notice of them as to provide against them, while they are yet at a distance. And this great caution we think needful, because life is concerned.

But how far are most men from using such precautions against their spiritual enemies, wherein the life of their souls is concerned. If we were sensible of the thousandth part of the misery we are in danger of from our spiritual enemies, and the degree in which we are exposed thereto, we should take as much, and much more pains and care to discover the least approaches of the enemy.

[We must take] caution, lest [we be] surprised. [We must take care] to observe every road by which they might have access, and to prepare beforehand and seasonably to be in a [state of] readiness.

Fourth. The great folly of men in neglecting their own safety from spiritual enemies, appears in that, [that] there is no more care taken by them to secure them in a spiritual fortress.

In a time of war, we are sensible of the necessity of fortresses.

Great pain is used.

Great care taken.

Men will neglect to till their fields to build forts; and persons in exposed towns will retire from their own houses from night to night, to lodge in a fort with wives and children, though they have but a hard lodging attended with many inconveniences. But how negligent are men that are greatly exposed {to be mindful} of their spiritual fortress which God has provided, [with] ready-built gates set upon strong and sure [posts, which] are far better entertainments for 'em than at home: glorious accommodation, a place of rest, a place of daily feasting and rejoicings, all at free cost. This refuge is nigh at hand.

And there is no other [refuge]. All that remain out, from one generation after another, not one escapes.

People are careful to make provision for their safety in time of war by building forts, though there be no appearance of immediate dangers: no mischief yet done, no enemy heard of that is approaching, though there seems to be at present promising appearance.

Yet because life [depends] on the case, [they] provide for all events.

But how far otherwise, when it is a time of health with 'em, and so see no immediate danger of falling into the hands of those terrible enemies: death, Satan and the wrath of God.

Fifth. Men's stupidity with respect to their spiritual warfare, appears in that they take no more care to arm themselves against their spiritual [enemies].

This is what we are exhorted to in the text—"Put on the whole armor of God"—and this is what is exceedingly neglected by most that sit under [the gospel].

What care is there in a time of war, especially [among] such are much exposed, to get arms and ammunition. We stand in need of spiritual armor. [God's people stand in need of] a shield of faith, to establish their hearts in a firm belief. [They have need to] get more acquainted with the Word of God, strengthen their resolution, arm their minds with prayer, and take care and pains that their minds may be kept always in a calm, peaceful frame and so be stored with the preparations.

Men are sensible that they are in a poor case in war, in case of an attack.

Arms are more necessary then than ordinary raiment at such a time.

So are men in a miserable condition, as to their spiritual warfare, without spiritual armor.

Luke 22:36, "he that hath no sword, let him sell his garment, and buy one."

Sixth. Men's negligence and senselessness, with respect to their spiritual warfare, appears in that no more care is taken for the establishing and maintaining union among visible Christians to strengthen themselves for their common defense. It seems we are sensible how much it [is necessary].

Disunion and division exceedingly weakens a people. [It] exposes [them] to the enemy, and in nothing more than in the spiritual warfare. And union exceedingly strengthens a people in war. But how much is this neglected with regard to the spiritual warfare. How few seem to be sensible of the import.

It is little pains [that are] taken. How little are used. How many make-hates [are there] instead of one peacemaker. How easily and needlessly do persons fall, and continue in variance, and widen it more and more, not considering how they lay themselves open to spiritual and eternal enemies by it.

Seventh. {Men's negligence and senselessness, with respect to their spiritual warfare, appears} in that there is no more care taken to make friends with those that are able to help and defend them.

[They] are careful to make alliances, [and] send abroad to that end. In the war, care has been taken by this province [to make alliances].

Eighth. [Men's negligence and senselessness, with respect to their spiritual warfare, appears] in that they are so unwilling to be at expense for the safety and good of their souls. What great charge do a people willingly put themselves [to]. What charge is the country at.

But is there such a forwardness in the public to {be at expense for our safety}. If what will be now expended in one year, should have been expended in ten for the advancement of the kingdom of Christ and promoting the good of souls, as it might have been prudently laid out, might probably [have] been the means of the eternal good of multitudes of souls, and of saving many from being eternally destroyed by the spiritual enemy.

And particularly, if one half so much had been laid out for the instruction of the Indians, it might [have been better spent]; and also been the most effectual means to secure ourselves from being hurt by 'em in temporal war.

Particular persons, besides bearing their part of the public charge, many of them put themselves to great charge; many as it were forsake all.

They consider that they had better have their habitation and their lands than lose their lives. But how few will be persuaded to this, though in the most extreme necessity, for the sake of their eternal salvation?

Ninth. [Men's negligence and senselessness, with respect to their spiritual warfare, appears in] that they are no more speedy and seasonable in the means they use for their own defense.

As soon as we heard that war was proclaimed with France, [we were speedy and seasonable in securing means for our defense].

And [so] when an alarm is made, and notice given of the approach of an enemy.

But men, in the concerns of their souls, have to do with the Father of Lies, [with their] deceitful lusts.

And yet [they] trust to their flattery [and] promises, by which they have deceived millions, though they never fulfill [them]. [The devil and their lusts] make promises on purpose to ensnare, yet [they] trust [them] as [to] be their friends, yield themselves wholly to 'em, {and} be governed by them.

Tenth. [Men's negligence and senselessness, with respect to their spiritual warfare, appears in their] folly, in that they are so ready to trust their enemies.

In a time of war in this land, we have to do with Indians, that are many of 'em found to be a very treacherous, deceitful kind of people, little to be depended on. And therefore, {we are ready to trust them}. Though {they are deceitful, yet} they speak fair.

Last *Use* of *Exhortation.*

First. To behave in the business of religion with like vigilance and earnestness that persons are wont to do [in time of war].

We are abundantly told the necessity of it. [The] business [of religion] is often compared to a warfare. Christ has told us that "the kingdom of heaven suffers violence" [Matt. 11:12].

Though the enemies are invisible, and so we are ready to neglect, yet the time will soon come when we shall see 'em. And if we neglect {them, we} shall fail. They are more dangerous for being invisible. We have heard what is the madness of the generality of men, and the consequence of it is such as might be expected. The far bigger part {will go to hell}.

Therefore, let me now warn you, that you ben't guilty of this madness. Consider how you behave yourself now in this time of war.

[Are] you concerned?

Affected?
Full of thoughts?
Talk?
Vigilant?
[Are you] sensible of need of arms?
Forts?
Watches?
Scouts?
Cautions?
[Are you] sensible of the need of expense?
Of union?
Alliance?
Trust in enemies?
And will not your own conscience reproach [you]?

Consider, life is concerned in the latter case as well as the former, and in an infinitely more important sense.

You must maintain your war against Satan's temptations, and {you must} maintain a daily war against your lusts and indwelling sin, in like manner as [maintaining a war against temporal enemies].

[Consider,]

1. We have no positive gains in view in this temporal war. We are concerned but only [in] our defense.[13]

2. Let it be considered that by being thorough in the business of religion, we shall best consult our safety and defense with respect to this temporal war.

Sin above all things weakens [a people in a time of war].[14] So virtue, and religion, and walking with God above all things strengthens. The land can no way so effectually consult [its own good] as by reformation.

And particular persons {can strengthen a people}, as by seeking meekness and righteousness and charity.

So that both consult the safety of our souls and our outward safety.[15] If we would expend our goods in pious and charitable uses, it would tend more [to our safety].

---

13. See the sermon preached *A People of God Going Forth to War*.

14. See sermon entitled, *Sin Weakens a People in a Time of War*.

15. Towns such as Deerfield and Northfield had been settled and abandoned after King Philip's War and recently resettled; Southampton was a new town and a target of French and Indian activity (cf. see "after Elisha Clark was Killed").

Dan. 4:27, "by showing mercy to the poor, if it may be a lengthening of thy tranquility."

We get nothing by withholding. We see how many ways God can take from us.

Second Exh. Not to trust in your own endeavors in your spiritual warfare, but trust to Christ as the captain.

You have heard how God is the Lord of Hosts.[16]

[It is] great sin and folly to trust in an arm of flesh in a temporal war. More so still in a spiritual war, where we are so much weaker, and our enemy so much stronger.

Third Exh. Take care for the safety of others from their spiritual enemies.

Don't be treacherous. How would it be resented if any in a time of war should be treacherous, and should secretly betray his friends? How many side with the devil?

Take care for the safety of those committed to your care.

How greatly do we reckon them to blame that are set as watchmen, and are not faithful? Let parents {take care for the safety of their children}. How are men concerned for their families?

If you neglect the souls of your children, it will be the way, both in a spiritual and literal sense, to bring up your children for the sword. You will expose your children to the like judgment that Eli [had]. 1 Sam. 2:32, "[And thou shalt see an enemy in my habitation, in all the wealth which God shall give Israel: and there shall not be an old man in thine house]."

---

16. Cf. *Christ Lord of Hosts*.

The Duties of Christians in a Time of War

April 4, 1745

AFTER ALL THE PREPARATIONS and speculations of 1744, the winter of 1744/45 remained quiet. Following the initial attacks on Canso and Annapolis Royal during the summer of 1744, New England settled into the winter to consider their response. In the meantime, two British men taken by the French from Canso returned from their captivity in fortress Louisburg claiming the fortress was low on supplies, and in disrepair. Shirley secretly proposed to the Assembly an expedition to take the beleaguered outpost, but the assembly would not give their blessing. However, word of Shirley's proposal leaked and pressures from merchants convinced the Assembly to shift their support to the ambitious expedition. Preparations took on a religious dimension when George Whitefield threw his support behind the expedition, providing a recruiting slogan, and preaching to Col. Pepperrell and his men before departure.

Thirty-one members of the Northampton community joined the expedition including Major Seth Pomeroy adding a personal connection to Edwards's thanksgiving sermon preached on April 4, shortly after the expedition had departed for fortress Louisburg. *Duties of Christians in a Time of War* was an atypical sermon for Edwards in a couple respects. First, Edwards did not use a traditional "doctrine" to outline his message, but organized it around four propositions. Second, unlike earlier revival sermons, Edwards did not use war simply as the background for this sermon but its subject providing a philosophical and Biblical foundation for warfare. As the war moved into a new phase, so did Edwards's martial preaching.

Drawing on Enlightenment language and concerns, Edwards presented the expedition as a necessary defensive measure even though it was initiated by the New England. This may have been in part a result of Edwards's claim in *The Armor of God* that Britain's only aim in this war was defensive. Extrapolating from the principle of self-defense, Edwards claimed it is permissible for societies to use preemptive action defend themselves. Moving from philosophical to Biblical themes, He explained that the sixth commandment necessitated warfare to curb the loss of life: "The sixth commandment is so far from forbidding [self-defense] that the design of the command plainly requires it."

Edwards then moved from just causes of war (*jus ad bellum*) to proper conduct within war (*jus in bello*). Drawing on the thought of Hugo Grotius, Edwards provided his congregation with a standard of conduct: "If it be a duty [of a people] to wage war, 'tis a duty to prosecute it with vigor."[1] Northampton shared Europe's understanding of "vigorousness" but adapted it to a uniquely American context. Fighting a "skulking" enemy in the forests and mountains of the frontier required different technology and tactics than the green fields of France.

While Northampton's sons sailed to Louisburg, Edwards expected those remaining to participate in the war spiritually in the same way that troops take up weapons on an expedition. The duty to defend one's country is shared by those who march and those who do not. Edwards believed that the deciding factor of any battle was the intervention of God, therefore, it was the Christian's duty to participate in the battle through prayer. This spiritual participation allowed Edwards to integrate the personal piety of his revivalist agenda into his just war theory.

* * * * *

This sermon was edited by Wilson Kimnach for the *Works of Jonathan Edwards*. The manuscript of this sermon is, unlike most sermons of the period, written in single-column format. This would suggest that Edwards expected to develop the material more fully on paper and that he probably viewed the sermon as an especially important one. The twenty-leaf booklet is duodecimo, though oblong (4 1/2 inches tall by 3 inches rather than the usual roughly 4 inches square), and the paper is generally good, including two letter covers. The sermon is fairly well written out,

---

1. Hugo Grotius was a seventeenth-century thinker that wrote about warfare and theology. *On the Rights of War and Peace*, 282, 301.

although the hand is uneven in neatness, the first few pages of the Application being more regular in handwriting and even in development than the material before and after it.

There are a number of later additions to the manuscript, notably a list of the doctrinal propositions squeezed in around the original first proposition (but omitting the fourth proposition). These additions and modifications probably were made in conjunction with a re-preaching of the sermon indicated on the manuscript: "July 55." The most probable occasion for this re-preaching was the expedition to Crown Point, since that directly involved Stockbridge. Edwards wrote *In the Name of the Lord of Hosts* (see below, pp. 682–84) for the Indian congregation in July, and this sermon may have been re-preached to the English congregation at the same time.

The Duties of Christians in a Time of War

1 Kings 8:44–45

If thy people go out to battle against their enemy, whithersoever thou shalt send them, and shall pray unto the Lord towards the city which thou hast chosen, and toward the house that I have built for thy name: then hear thou in heaven their prayer and their supplication, and maintain their cause.

SOLOMON ACTED UNDER THE special and immediate influence [of God]. 1 Chron. 28:[19], "All this, said David, the Lord made me understand in writing by his hand upon me, even all the works of this pattern." [He] specifies many particular cases of special need of divine favor and help. Solomon in the text asks God's favor and help for his people. Of which may be observed:

1. The business or exercise, viz., going out: "Go out to battle against their enemy." What Solomon here has a special respect to is their leaving their own habitations, going forth from amongst their friends on a warlike delegation, as appears by the words that next follow: "whithersoever thou shalt send them." In which words may be observed,

2. Their call to this business [and] whether the call spoken of is the call of God.

3. The duty that the people should attend in order to obtaining God's help in such a case.

4. The manner of their performance of this duty.

5. The favor and regard that Solomon prays that God would have to his people in such a case.

6. The help he asks for them in the fruit of this favor.

[Doctrine]

There are four propositions that I would [take] particular notice of that are contained or implied in these words.

Prop. I is, *A people of God may be called of God to go forth to war against their enemies.*[1] This will appear by the consideration of these two things:

First. It is lawful and a duty in some cases for one nation to wage war with another. Reason and the light of nature shows it; it follows from the law of self-preservation. If it be lawful for a particular person, when assaulted, to stand in his own defense and to wound and kill another to preserve his own life, the very same principles that prove the lawfulness of one will [prove the other]. If it be lawful for a particular person to defend himself with force, then it is lawful for a nation or people. [A nation is] made up of particular persons, [and when] particular persons are endangered, [they] can't be defended without [the efforts of others]. [What is] lawful for one [is lawful for the nation]. Then [it is] doubtless lawful to help one another. [The] ends of public societies show it, which is mutual help. [The] ends of society especially require mutual help when the destruction of the community is threatened. The argument for the lawfulness of opposing force to force for the defense of public societies is more forcible than for the defense of particular persons, as the public good is more important. If it were so that all public societies must be restrained from opposing force to other nations that commit rapine and violence towards them, the whole world of mankind would be open to be laid waste. For there have [been] many nations [that] appeared forward to subdue and enslave [other nations]. The sixth commandment is so far from forbidding [self-defense] that the design of that command plainly requires it. The very same principles on which is manifest the lawfulness and necessity of civil magistracy and of human laws, forcibly to maintain the rights of mankind in society and to use the civil sword for the punishment of those that violate those rights that are within the society, will prove the lawfulness of war. [The] power of the sword [is], Rom. 13:4, "to execute wrath upon him that doeth evil." Those that violate the rights {of mankind in society} are punished by the civil sword only as acting the

---

1. In revising for re-preaching, JE interlineated a fragmentary list of propositions: "Prop. 2. G. & he only [...]. Prop. 3. Tis the [...]. This is plainly implied."

part of enemies. If there should, instead of a single offender, arise a great number—as in a public riot or mob or rebellion—'tis lawful [to punish them]; and this is the same thing with here, if a particular town or city or province [should offend]. This is war. If war be lawful to defend a society from domestic enemies, then doubtless if a particular man should come from a foreign country and should set himself to do mischief, [he should be similarly punished]. Thus the light of nature [justifies war]. But besides, God has abundantly shown his approbation: directing, encouraging, commanding, [and] ordering the affairs of war, [and] rewarding [the defenders of the people]. And that God approves [of some war] appears not only from the Old Testament, but the New. The New Testament approves of the civil magistracy, and of the magistrates' using the sword to restrain open violence with force. Rom. 13:1–4,

Let every soul be subject unto the higher powers. For there is no power but of God: the powers that be are ordained of God. Whosoever therefore resisteth the power, resisteth the ordinance of God: and they that resist shall receive to themselves damnation. For rulers are not a terror to good works, but to the evil. Wilt thou then not be afraid of the power? do that which is good, and thou shalt have praise of the same: for he is the minister of God to thee for good. But if thou do that which is evil, be afraid; for he beareth not the sword in vain: for he is the minister of God, a revenger to execute wrath upon him that doeth evil.

Christ and John the Baptist were often concerned with men of military employment and never condemned them: when the soldiers came to John the Baptist, [he told them, "Do violence to no man, neither accuse any falsely; and be] content with your wages" [Luke 3:14]. [The] centurion. Matt. 8:8, "The centurion answered and said, Lord, I am not worthy that thou shouldest come under my roof: but speak the word only, and my servant shall be healed." Cornelius. Acts 10:1, "There was a certain man in Caesarea called Cornelius, a centurion of the band called the Italian band."[2] Paul, defended by a military force. Acts 23:17–23, 27–30, "This man was taken of the Jews, and should have been killed of them: then came I with an army, and rescued him, having understood that he was a Roman. And when I would have known the cause wherefore they accused him, I brought him forth into their council: whom I perceived to be accused of questions of their law, but to have nothing laid to his charge

---

2. JE only cites the verses that introduce the stories of the centurion and Cornelius; in preaching the sermon, he may well have read the complete passages.

worthy of death or bonds."[3] By these things it appears that in some cases it is not only lawful but a duty [to take up arms]. Those words of Christ, John 18:36, "If my kingdom were of this world, then would my servants fight," do imply that it is lawful and necessary to fight for the maintenance and support of temporal kingdoms. If there should be [attacks upon] earthly kingdoms, or kingdoms of this world, [they must be defended].

Second. If it be a duty for a people to wage war for the defense of the community, then it is their duty to prosecute [that war] in such a manner as tends most effectually to obtain this end, not barely to stand on their defense when their enemies actually assault them. [To] not sufficiently defend [may] greatly expose 'em; [they should] not merely [attempt] to stand to defend [themselves] when assaulted by robbers or pirates. If it be a duty of [a people to] wage war, 'tis a duty to prosecute it with vigor. [The] sixth commandment requires it, [as it] tends most to save the lives of the innocent, [and is in fact] soonest to bring the war to an end. The good of the community, and especially the maintaining its rights, is the end of war; this end therefore must govern the management of it.

Inq. When a people may be said to be called of God. This general inquiry may be best answered by[4] these two more particular inquiries:

Inq. 1. When the authority of a community are called of God. I answer, first, in two cases:

(1) When the rights of the public society are so invaded [that] preservation of the community or public society requires it. [People] ought not to be forward to enter into war; [the] occasion should be important, [even] be so that the public preservation requires [it, as] when the society is invaded. When another nation do declare war with them unjustly, or when they do that which is equivalent, [or] when another nation do in some very notable instances invade their rights and do persist in it, the upholding of the rights and privileges of the society requires it. When the destruction of the society is threatened more immediately or remotely, the overthrow of the rights [of the people] tends to overthrow the society itself.

(2) When a people are obliged to it by the tenor of a just alliance or covenant, entered into with another people for their mutual defense and preservation, still the same law of self-preservation will in this case

---

3. JE deletes: "The Prophecies shew the same thing. plainly implied in many of the Prophecies that G. would deliv. his People in this."

4. MS: "Answered in answered."

warrant [their taking up arms]. In this case, two nations or communities do so far forth become one in things that appertain to that covenant, if self-preservation be lawful and necessary for a nation, then it is lawful for nations to unite together with other nations in such a manner as shall tend to this end.

Inq. 2. When particular persons are called of God.

Answ. When they are called by those that are in authority, unless it be notoriously manifest that the war is unjust. In ordinary cases, particular subjects are not called to inquire. God has not made them judges. It is not practicable, and therefore, unless it be plain and notorious [that the war is unjust, particular persons should act as called by God]. Sometimes the professed and declared design of a war is plainly unjust, as when the declared design is persecution. But when this is not the case, and persons are particularly required by the civil authority, and when the call of the civil authority is not particular but only general—leaving it to particular persons to judge for themselves and follow their own voluntary determinations, as in gathering of an army of volunteers—then persons should look on themselves as called of God according to[5] the best judgment they can make to be marked out in providence, as the properest persons to engage in the business that the civil authority calls [them] to, considering their particular circumstances [and] qualifications.

Prop. II. *'Tis God, and he only, that determines the event of war and gives the victory.* I shall here mention three things that make this manifest:

First. It appears from the nature of the business, it depending on so great variety of incidents that the event of war depends upon [that] which men can't foresee or determine. Health or sickness [greatly qualify men's efforts, and they depend] very much on the wind and weather, [as] when military forces go forth by land, and especially when they go forth by sea. [It also depends] on the frame of mind that those that are engaged are in, in the time of action, especially those that are the commanding officers. Men han't at all times equal courage. Presence of mind is especially [important] in some particular persons in the hurry and confusion of battle. The particular thoughts that are suggested to the mind at that time [are critical]: one wary thought [or] one oversight may lose a battle. [The

---

5. MS: "according as they seem to be marked out in p thems. according to."

outcome] depends on a multitude of particular occurrences in the time of action. One stroke of the sword or one blow of a ball, discharged and directed of providence, may decide the event of a battle, and so of the whole war, if it so happens that a general or some other persons of great importance be slain.[6]

Second. By the prerogatives which God so often assumes and challenges [the wills of men].

Third. It appears by facts and experience: events happening so often in an unforeseen [and] unthought of [way], so many incidents that have great and determining influence that were not conceived of, the greatest strength and best preparations so often defeated, the sudden and extraordinary changes and turning of the scale, the weak and few prevailing so often against the many and mighty.

Prop. III. *When a people are called to go forth to war, 'tis their duty, by prayer and supplication, to look to God for help to maintain their cause.*
First. 'Tis our duty in all our concerns and undertakings to make known our requests and commit our ways to God. Ps. 37:[4–]5, "Commit thy way unto the Lord, and he shall give thee the desires of thine heart." Prov. 16:3, "Commit thy works unto the Lord, and thy thoughts shall be established." Prov. 3:6, "In all thy ways acknowledge him, and he shall direct thy paths." Phil. 4:6, "In everything by prayer and supplication."

Second. The vast importance of this business does especially require it. The liberties, life, and religion, and all [the welfare] of a people depend upon it.

Third. This is an honor especially due to God when we engage in this business, because it is a business wherein, as has been shown already, God does especially interpose and show his disposing hand.

Prop. IV. *God is ready in such a case to hear the prayers of his people, and give 'em success, when they offer up their prayers in the manner that he has appointed.* This is evident by this prayer of Solomon with its

---

6. For re-preaching, JE added: "And then this is a business which above all others seems to determine the state of the world."

circumstances:[7] First, when [people pray] in the manner that he has appointed, then [God hears their prayers]. Second, show that God is ready.

First. When? This is expressed in the text. Therefore, I would answer this inquiry by showing what may be supposed to be typified by the children of Israel's praying towards [the temple]. It was doubtless typical.

1. [The people's praying] towards the temple [typified] looking to Christ and trusting in him.

2. Towards the city which God had chosen.

(1) In union with God's people or with the saints; continuing in peace and friendship with them. Jerusalem was the city of peace: "city compact together" (Ps. 122:3). "In the bond of peace" (Eph. 4:3). "Charity, which is the bond of perfectness" (Col. 3:14). "The whole being fitly formed together and compacted" (Eph. 4:15–16). "I will therefore that men pray everywhere, lifting up holy hands, without wrath" (1 Tim. 2:8) Continuing in the worship and service of God, [they are] cleaving to God's people in this respect.

(2) Seeking the prosperity of Jerusalem or the church of God, not from private views.

(3) Continuing in the way of duty, which is the way to heaven. Jerusalem [is] a type of heaven. In the original it is: "By the way of the city." A people must continue in God's way, otherwise God will not hear their prayers. Hearing prayers is often promised to the obedient. 1 John. 3:22, "And whatsoever we ask, we receive of him, because we keep his commandments." Refusing to hear prayer [is] often threatened to the disobedient. Ps. 66:18, "If I regard iniquity[8] in my heart, the Lord will not hear me." Prov. 28:9, "He that turneth away his ear from hearing the Lord, [even his prayer shall be abomination]." Is. 1:15, "And when ye spread forth your hands, I will hide mine eye."

Second. Show that God is ready to hear [the prayers of his people] and to give success when {they offer up their prayers in the manner that he has appointed}.

1. God has often promised to hear all the prayers of his people that are offered after this manner. John 15:7, "If ye abide in me, and my words abide in you, ye shall ask what ye will, and it shall be done unto you." So

---

7. The introductory clause appears to be a later addition to the head.
8. MS: "If I regard Judg."

John 14:13–14 and 15:16. "Nigh to his people in all that they call upon him for" (Deut. 4:7).

2. There are special evidences that God is ready to hear the prayers of his people thus duly offered up in such a case.

(1) This is especially agreeable to one of the offices that Christ executes for his people that trust in him, viz., that of their king. [He is also:] Captain of their salvation. Captain of the Lord's host.

(2) This is agreeable to multitudes of promises that God has made to a covenant people in the Scripture. All promises of temporal blessings imply promises of the preservation of the church of God in the world. War is that by which the church of God has been especially endangered; Satan has sought to overthrow it this way. Therefore, the many promises made of defense of God's people. Besides, there are many particular promises of this very nature:[9] Lev. 26, Deut. 8:16 to the end, Deut. 28:7.

Application

These things that have been said point forth our duty and interest with respect to that important and hazardous enterprise of a warlike nature that is the occasion of the appointment of this day of fasting and prayer. What has been said shows us in whose hands we are with respect to this undertaking and all affairs of this nature, and in whose hands those are that are gone forth from amongst us on the expedition that has been undertaken, [and] who will order everything. And what has been said shows what it is that the Lord of hosts expects of us on this occasion, and what duties it concerns us to attend and perform as we would have success in it. It greatly concerns this land with one accord, all sorts of persons in it—magistrates, ministers and people; young and old—to go to [the] God of armies and pour out their prayers and supplications to him, that he would appear for us and maintain our cause in this undertaking. It is of vast importance to us that the expedition should be succeeded on many accounts. This province have put themselves to a very great expense, and before the affair is finished the expense will doubtless be yet vastly greater—doubtless several hundred thousand pounds—and it would be a great and sore judgment upon us to have all this expense frustrated. And besides, if the enterprise should be defeated, the defeat will probably be attended with the loss of much blood and [the] expense of many lives: to the filling of many families and

---

9. MS: "nary." Conjectural reading.

many of our towns, yea, the province in general, with mourning through the bereavement of friends and neighbors. There will probably be many made widows and many children fatherless, and many parents bereaved of dear children, and some of those that were the flower of our land cut off.[10] Besides, the place that our forces are gone against has been a great annoyance to us. The people of this land have been more annoyed from this particular place than any other whatsoever since the commencement of the present war, and if this design is defeated there is a prospect of their being still a much greater annoyance to us. Projections have been formed and preparations been making, as we have had credible information, to annoy us from thence with a much greater force than heretofore; and if we fail in this enterprise, that will strengthen them and expose us to them many ways. We shall be greatly weakened by it: we shall be weakened as we shall be greatly impoverished and less able to be at the expense of a vigorous defense and opposition for the future, and shall [be] weakened in numbers and shall be greatly weakened as it will tend to dishearten us. If we should have occasion hereafter to go forth against the enemy, it will probably be with far less courage and so under much greater disadvantage; on the other hand, our enemies—not only in that place but in Canada, and others of the same nation in other places—will be irritated; and not only irritated but encouraged, and will be much more likely to come against us and invade and annoy us both by sea and land. And then, besides the vast expense we shall have been at in this expedition without gaining anything to compensate it, we shall be under a necessity of being at yet a further great expense to defend ourselves from our annoyed and encouraged enemies. So that if we fail in this design, it may probably be in a great measure our undoing. On the other hand, if it pleases God to give us success, very great are the appearing advantages. 'Tis to be hoped that we may see most of our friends that are gone forth returning with rejoicing. We shall [be] delivered from a strong fortress that has been very much the nest and resort of our enemies, and shall have a very strong place in our possession that is so situated that we shall thereby be probably under vast advantages against our enemies in Canada, to restrain them and distress [them], and prevail against them by hindering supplies being sent to them. And our enemies that we have

10. See the prayer bid of Northampton's John Baker and his wife (in note to sermon on Zech. 8:20–22, no. 857, Feb. 1747, published as *The Suitableness of Union in Extraordinary Prayer for the Advancement of God's Church*, WJE 25:197–209) to sanctify the death of their son at Louisburg. This and other similar documents validate the realism of JE's wartime rhetoric.

most reason to fear will probably be much weakened and disheartened, and will be much more afraid to molest us, lest we should [be] provoked to prosecute the advantage we have gained and go on with our conquests till we have subdued the neighboring country of our enemies. Our sea coasts will be much less exposed and our enemies under much less advantages to disturb us in our business on the sea, in our trade and fishery; and our eastern settlements in particular would be much less exposed. That tribe of Indians[11] in the eastern parts that are at war with the English would probably be much discouraged, and [the] English at Annapolis that have several times been invaded the year past would probably be much less disquieted. These things show how greatly it is our interest to seek to God on this occasion in such a manner as has been spoken of: to look to God and cry to him, sensible of our own unworthiness and hoping in his free mercy only through Christ the mediator, and trusting in him as the captain of the Lord's host to defend us and fight our battles for us; and particularly to pray to God by the way of the city which God has chosen, as the expression is in the text, in the way of turning from our iniquities and in the way of obedience to the commands of God and making religion our great business, and the way of peace one with another. Without this, there will be no preparedness in us for such great mercies as that which are now seeking of God. God's manner is first to prepare the hearts of men before he hears. "Lord, thou hast heard the desire of the humble: thou wilt prepare their heart, thou wilt cause thine ear to hear" (Ps. 10:17). Our provocations have been very great:[12] if we don't turn from our evil way, we can't pray with the spirit of prayer—we shall not look towards God's holy temple in our prayer. There is no true praying in the name of Christ without repentance of sin, for Christ is the savior of sinners. As long as we continue in the worship of idols, we shall trust in idols to deliver [us] and look to them [for our strength]. They that are devoted to the creature trust in the creature. This will not be such a fast as God has chosen: our fasting and praying will be but mocking.

[*Exh.*] Before I conclude, I would mention two things to excite all to seek to God for success in that warlike enterprise that is the occasion {of our fast}.

---

11. I.e., the Abenaki.

12. JE drew a long dash here, indicating he may have enumerated some of New England's "provocations."

First. How God has blasted us in such like enterprises heretofore, as we have reason to think, for want of this [spirit of prayer].

Second. How many remarkable instances we have in it of the success of faith and prayer in warlike undertakings. The first I shall mention is in that great pattern of believers, Abraham, called in Scripture the father of all them that believe, that we have an account of [in] Gen. 14. The giants could not stand before them. Thus God "gave the nations before him," as is said, Is. 41:[2]. Another instance is that of the people of Israel against Amalek, Ex. 17:9–13,

And Moses said unto Joshua, Choose us out men, and go out, fight with Amalek: tomorrow I will stand on the top of the hill with the rod of God in mine hand. So Joshua did as Moses had said to him, and fought with Amalek: and Moses, Aaron, and Hur went up to the top of the hill. And it came to pass, when Moses held up his hand, that Israel prevailed: and when he let down his hand, Amalek prevailed. But Moses' hands were heavy; and they took a stone, and put it under him, and he sat thereon; and Aaron and Hur stayed up his hands, the one on the one side, and the other on the other side; and his hands were steady until the going down of the sun. And Joshua discomfited Amalek and his people with the edge of the sword.

Joshua taking the city of Jericho; Heb. 11:30, "By faith the walls of Jericho fell down." Joshua's prevailing against Ai, Josh. 7 and 8. Joshua's prevailing against the Amorites, Josh. 10:12–14, "Then spake Joshua to the Lord in the day when the Lord delivered up the Amorites before the children of Israel, and he said in the sight of Israel, Sun, stand thou still upon Gibeon; and thou, Moon, in the valley of Ajalon. And the sun stood still, and the moon stayed, until the people had avenged themselves upon their enemies. Is not this written in the book of Jasher? So the sun stood still in the midst of heaven, and hasted not to go down about a whole day. And there was no day like that before it or after it, that the Lord hearkened unto the voice of a man: for the Lord fought for Israel." Gideon, [in] Judg. 7, [who attacked] a great multitude (v. 12) after leave had been given to all [those] fearful and afraid to depart (v. 3). Jephtha [in] Judg. 11, [and] Sampson [in] Judg. 16. Jonathan [among the] vast multitude, 1 Sam. 13:5 [and] 1 Sam. 14:6. David [and] Goliath, 1 Sam. 17. David [and] the Amalekites, 1 Sam. 30, with 400 men (vv. 8–10). David [and the] Philistines, 2 Sam. 5, [at the] latter end. Asa against Zerah, 2 Chron. 14:9–15. Jehoshaphat against the Moabites, 2 Kgs. 3:11, [and] against the children of Moab and Ammon and Mount Seir, 2 Chron. 20—a wonderful instance: [they] kept a fast [v.3], [confessed,] "we know not what to do," [but they] trusted in God (vv. 12–13). How graciously were they answered: vv. 15–16, "And he said, Hearken ye, all Judah, and ye inhabitants of Jerusalem, and thou king Jehoshaphat, Thus saith the Lord unto you, Be not afraid nor dismayed by reason of this great multitude; for the battle is not your's, but God's." Vv. 23–29,

For the children of Ammon and Moab stood up against the inhabitants of mount Seir, utterly to slay and destroy them: and when they had made an end of the inhabitants of Seir, every one helped to destroy another. And when Judah came toward the watch tower in the wilderness, they looked unto the multitude, and, behold, they were dead bodies fallen to the earth, and none escaped. And when Jehoshaphat and his people came to take away the spoil of them, they found among them in abundance both riches with the dead bodies, and precious jewels, which they stripped off for themselves, more than they could carry away: and they were three days in gathering of the spoil, it was so much. And on the fourth day they assembled themselves in the valley of Berachah; for there they blessed the Lord: therefore the name of the same place was called, The valley of Berachah, unto this day. Then they returned, every man of Judah and Jerusalem, and Jehoshaphat in the forefront of them, to go again to Jerusalem with joy; for the Lord had made them to rejoice over their enemies. And they came to Jerusalem with psalteries and harps and trumpets unto the house of the Lord. And the fear of God was on all the kingdoms of those countries, when they had heard that the Lord fought against the enemies of Israel.

[So] Hezekiah against Sennacherib, 2 Kgs. 19:14, etc., [and] the Jews against their enemies in Esther's time. Esther 4:16–17, "Go, gather all the Jews that are present in Shushan, and fast ye for me, and neither eat nor drink three days, night or day: I also and my maidens will fast likewise; and so will I go in unto the king, which is not according to the law: and if I perish, I perish. So Mordecai went his way, and did according to all that Esther had commanded him." See the success in the beginning of the ninth chapter. Such abundant encouragement is there in the Word of God. These instances show that 'tis God that disposes, and how ready he is to appear, and as it were delights to bestow great mercies of this kind and bring wonderful things in subduing mighty enemies and strong cities, and breaking the greatest power of the enemy, in answer to the believing prayers of his people that walk in his ways.[13]

13. For a more apocalyptic interpretation of the events addressed in this sermon, see JE's letter to the Rev. William McCulloch in WJE 16:219–21. The two interpretations emphasize the diverse requirements of pastoral leadership and philosophical theology.

An Occasion for Praise and Thanksgiving

August 1745

NEW ENGLAND'S AMBITIOUS EXPEDITION was fraught with concerns: would the weather hold out? Is colonial leadership up to the task? Will the British navy support this operation? The optimism of the April 4th fast day led to the dribble of news concerning the volunteer's advance on the grand battery.[1] However, the positive reports in 1741 concerning the colony's advance on Cartagena proved discouraging which may have cast a shadow over reports from Cape Breton. The *Gazette* interspersed updates from Cape Breton with stories of French atrocities in the War of Austrian Succession as well as news of George Whitefield's revivals.[2] However, reports remained positive culminating in the July 9th report of Louisbourg's formal surrender.

Reports of a colonial victory at Louisbourg trickled in and the *Boston Gazette* ran descriptions of the siege, the governor's announcement of victory, and personal accounts of the battle.[3] These testimonies recounted the improbable events of the siege. Despite a march launch for the expedition, the volunteers enjoyed unseasonably warm weather including favorable winds and a lack of ice. These amateur soldiers and sailors were soon joined by Commodore Warren, a British captain sailing from the

---

1. *Boston Gazette*, May 21, 1745.

2. One example comes from the July 2nd edition of the *Boston Gazette* (1745) which reported the martyrdom of a Protestant minister in France whose head was displayed on a pike. Another from the *Boston Gazette*, July 30, 1745, recounting the story of Marshall Malebois who instituted an arbitrary death penalty for those "committed an insult."

3. *Boston Gazette*, July 23, 1745.

Caribbean who supported New England's operations. Despite New England's lengthy hiatus in Canso, they maintained the element of surprise sending the French defenders into a panic resulting in poor tactical decisions. For example, despite having a numerical advantage, the French abandoned the grand battery allowing the colonists to take advantage of both a superior positions as well as French provisions. As the French were forced into poor tactical decisions, the British seemed to employ excellent martial wisdom. The British abandoned a direct assault which may have shifted the momentum of the battle to the French in favor of a more patient and successful siege strategy. The siege continued for seven weeks with a remarkable lack of casualties concluding with France's formal surrender.[4] The providential character of New England's victory was evident to and celebrated by all in the colonies.[5]

Edwards read the various reports in the *Gazette* with enthusiasm, however, after August 8th when many Northampton men had returned (including Maj. Seth Pomeroy), Edwards supplemented the published accounts with personal testimony from his congregation. *An Occasion for Praise and Thanksgiving*, preached in August of 1745, is a thanksgiving sermon re-telling the battle through spiritual eyes. Using a text describing Israel's triumphant return to Jerusalem after battle, Edwards exhorted his congregation to imitate Israel's example of praise and thanksgiving. According to Edwards, those who do not offer praise to God after such a victory are "ungrateful and stupid." The capture of Louisbourg was a victory worthy of much praise because it robbed the French of a base of operations from which they could launch attacks on Cape Breton, molest trade and supply in the North Atlantic, and support their Abenaki allies along New England's eastern frontier.

Edwards's presentation of these providences which attended victory underscores his conviction that war is chiefly spiritual. Praise and thanksgiving, therefore, is the proper response of the church after God fought on their behalf. As developed in other sermons, Edwards used the victory at Louisbourg to illustrate the role of spiritual duties in warfare.

This sermon conceded, in fact, Governor Shirley was right when he claimed that "we have good Ground to hope for the favorable Assistance

---

4. Edwards claims in his letter to "A Correspondent in Scotland" that, save one ill-fated assault, the amateur British militia suffered less than twenty casualties. WJE 16:194.

5. These details of the battle reflect the content of Edwards's letter to "A Correspondent in Scotland" which drew on a number of published and personal accounts. WJE 16:179–97.

of the divine Providence in so just a Cause."⁶ Edwards bore witness to the visible and remarkable hand of God in this expedition. This sermon also served as a demonstration of themes Edwards' sermons developed: God controlled the outcome of battles and wars. The themes of spiritual duty in times of war may not have been explicit in this sermon but served as the sub-text to Edwards's application of Biblical examples to the events of Louisbourg. Whereas the *Curse of Meroz* and *Valiant and Resolute Soldiers* drew on Joshua 7 and the Biblical concept of "the accursed thing," here Edwards illustrated this idea in the positive. Asa, in 2 Chron. 15:8, enjoyed military victory only after destroying idols. The visible and remarkable hand of God moved because of New England's (and Northampton's in particular) spiritual participation in the contest between the Catholic French and Protestant British.

* * * * *

This sermon was edited by Christian Cuthbert for the Jonathan Edwards Center. The manuscript is eighteen duodecimo-sized leaves, though the final two seem to contain collateral materials that are written on a fragment of discarded letter. At the top of the first page, Edwards titled the sermon: "On Occasion of the Return of our soldiers from Cape Breton. Aug. 1745."

---

6. *Boston Gazette*, June 5, 1744. Cf. *Journals of the House of Massachusetts*, 21:8–11.

An Occasion for Praise and Thanksgiving[1]

2 Chronicles 20:27–29

Then they returned, every man of Judah and Jerusalem, and Jehoshaphat in the forefront of them, to go again to Jerusalem with joy. [And they came to Jerusalem with psalteries and harps and trumpets unto the house of the Lord. And the fear of God was on all the kingdoms of those countries, when they had heard that the Lord fought against the enemies of Israel.]

HERE WE HAVE AN account of the circumstances of the people's return from the triumph God had given 'em over their enemies.

1. Observe whither they returned: to Jerusalem.
2. The state they returned in: a state of prosperity.
3. The ground and reason of this their rejoicing: God had made 'em to rejoice, by fighting against the [enemy on their behalf].
4. The duty there performed, agreeable [to the circumstances].

Doctrine.

When any [of] God's people have been forth to war, and God has remarkably appeared to fight for them, and return 'em to the people and house of God in prosperity, it is an occasion that requires much praise and thanksgiving to God.

I. I would observe how God sometimes remarkably appears to fight for his people that go forth to war, and returns 'em to the people and house of God in prosperity.

1. "On Occasion of the Return of Our Soldiers from Cape Breton, August 1745."

II. [I would] show that this is an occasion [that requires much praise and thanksgiving to God].

Why.

Of whom.

I. I would observe how {God sometimes remarkably appears to fight for his people that go forth to war, and returns 'em to the people and house of God in prosperity}.

As God has declared himself to be the captain of {his people}.

There is scarce any age of the world but affords many instances of God's appearing remarkably to fight for his people against their enemies. The Scriptures contain many instances. [God] often has made his arm bare [Is. 52:10]. He governs all things. But in this matter, he often shows his hand more visibly. And especially in defense of his church and people, [God] doth it many ways, wonderfully stirring up his people to go against their enemies, to engage in great and difficult and hazardous enterprises.

[So] Ehud. Judg. 3:15, "But when the children of Israel cried unto the Lord, the Lord raised them up a deliverer, Ehud the son of Gera, a Benjamite."

[So] Deborah.

David against Goliath.

Jonathan. 1 Samuel, ch. 14.

Wonderfully stirring up others to come to the assistance of those that have first undertaken.

To Ehud. Judg. 3:27, etc., "And it came to pass, when he was come, that he blew a trumpet in the mountain of Ephraim, and the children of Israel went down with him from the mount, and he before them. And he said unto them, Follow after me: for the Lord hath delivered your enemies the Moabites into your hand. And they went down after him, and took the fords of Jordan toward Moab, and suffered not a man to pass over. And they slew of Moab at that time about ten thousand men, all lusty, and all men of valor; and there escaped not a man. So Moab was subdued that day under the hand of Israel. And the land had rest fourscore years."

Deborah. Judg. 5:9, "My heart is toward the governors of Israel, that offered themselves willingly among the people. Bless ye the Lord." [Vv.] 14–15, "Out of Ephraim was there a root of them against Amalek; after thee, Benjamin, among thy people; out of Machir came down governors, and out of Zebulun they that handle the pen of the writer. And the princes of Issachar were with Deborah; even Issachar, and also Barak:

he was sent on foot into the valley. For the divisions of Reuben there were great thoughts of heart." [V.] 18, "Zebulun and Naphtali were a people that jeoparded their lives unto the death in the high places of the field."

It was strange they should be ready in such a case. [The] Canaanites [were] exceeding strong, ch. 4:3. They[2] [were] without arms, ch. 5:8.

[God remarkably appeared] in wonderfully preserving and conducting them in their way. Is. 5:25–27, "Therefore is the anger of the Lord kindled against his people, and he hath stretched forth his hand against them, and hath smitten them: and the hills did tremble, and their carcases were torn in the midst of the streets. For all this his anger is not turned away, but his hand is stretched out still. And he will lift up an ensign to the nations from far, and will hiss unto them from the end of the earth: and, behold, they shall come with speed swiftly: none shall be weary nor stumble among them; none shall slumber nor sleep; neither shall the girdle of their loins be loosed, nor the latchet of their shoes be broken." Joel 2:7–9, "They shall run like mighty men; they shall climb the wall like men of war; and they shall march every one on his ways, and they shall not break their ranks: neither shall one thrust another; they shall walk every one in his path: and when they fall upon the sword, they shall not be wounded. They shall run to and fro in the city; they shall run upon the wall, they shall climb up upon the houses; they shall enter in at the windows like a thief."

[God remarkably appeared in] taking away courage from their enemies. Ex. 23:27, "I will send my fear [before thee, and will destroy all the people to whom thou shalt come, and I will make all thine enemies turn their backs unto thee]." Deut. 11:25, "[There shall no man be able to stand before you: for the Lord your God shall lay the fear of you and the dread of you upon all the land that ye shall tread upon, as he hath said unto you]." Josh. 2:9, "[And she said unto the men, I know that the Lord hath given you the land, and that your terror is fallen upon us, and that all the inhabitants of the land faint because of you.]" Is. 37:26–27, "[Hast thou not heard long ago, how I have done it; and of ancient times, that I have formed it? now have I brought it to pass, that thou shouldest be to lay waste defensed cities into ruinous heaps. Therefore their inhabitants were of small power, they were dismayed and confounded: they were as the grass of the field, and as the green herb, as the grass on the housetops, and as corn blasted before it be grown up."

---

2. I.e., Israel.

[God remarkably appeared in] confounding their enemies in their counsels. Job 5:11–13, "To set up on high those that be low; that those which mourn may be exalted to safety. He disappointeth the devices of the crafty, so that their hands cannot perform their enterprise. He taketh the wise in their own craftiness: and the counsel of the froward is carried headlong." Is. 8:9–10, "Associate yourselves, O ye people, and ye shall be broken in pieces; and give ear, all ye of far countries: gird yourselves, and ye shall be broken in pieces; gird yourselves, and ye shall be broken in pieces. Take counsel together, and it shall come to nought; speak the word, and it shall not stand: for God is with us."

[God remarkably appeared in] giving them courage and strengthen[ing] them against them, Ps. 118:9. [The] Spirit of the Lord came upon Othniel, Judg. 3:9–10.

{And upon} Gideon: "Go in this thy might." Judg. 6:14, "And the Lord looked upon him, and said, Go in this thy might, and thou shalt save Israel from the hand of the Midianites: have not I sent thee?" [The] Spirit of the Lord {came upon} Gideon. Judg. 6:34, "But the Spirit of the Lord came upon Gideon, and he blew a trumpet."

[So] Jephthah. [Judg.] 11:29), "Then the Spirit of the Lord came upon Jephthah."

[And] Sampson. [Judg.] 13:25, "And the Spirit of the Lord began to move him at times in the camp of Dan between Zorah and Eshtaol."

Supposing those that are small in strength and under great disadvantages, to prevail against strength that is much greater than theirs.

[So] Abraham.

[And the] children of the people in going to Jerusalem, to the house of the Lord, to offer praises.

Application

I come now to apply what has been said to ourselves, who have now that occasion of praise and thanksgiving that is spoken of in the Doctrine, in that God has been with those that have lately been forth to war from among us, and has remarkably fought for them, and has returned so many of 'em to their native land and their friends, and to the people and house of God, in prosperity. God in this matter has wrought for us, that does in a peculiar manner call for our praises and thanksgivings to his name. So that if we are not thankful to him on such an occasion as this, we shall show ourselves very ungrateful and stupid indeed.

First. Consider the great importance of the mercy.

[Louisburg is a] place that had been a great annoyance to us.

[It is] so situated as to give great advantage to our enemies to distress us, especially by sea.

[It] would in all probability have been a much greater annoyance.

[Consider the] great projections [made, the] great preparations, both by sea and land.

If we had failed, [we] should have been greatly weakened.

[And our] enemies greatly encouraged.

[They] would have had great advantages against us.

[They] would have improved it to the uttermost.

[They would have been] both enraged and encouraged.

[It would have] encouraged the Indians, tended very much to have prompted 'em. {It would have} encouraged those that hitherto have forborne to molest us to take up arms.

[It] probably [would have] made those that appeared friendly to become cold towards {us}, and show more of an inclination to join with the prosperous side.

But now, [this victory] tends to discourage 'em.

[It] has already that effect, as we hear.

It will tend to fasten those Indians to us that have appeared friendly.

[The capture of Louisburg is] of great importance, as it tends at once to free our seacoasts, and all the seacoasts in North America, from our enemy's privateers and ships of war.

[It makes] sailing much less dangerous.

[The capture of Louisburg] greatly weakens the French nation.

[It is] a great loss to them, by reason of the vast expense they were at in building and fortifying.

[This victory] tends to strengthen and enrich our land and nation.

[It] turns the stream of a very valuable branch of trade to our nation, by which the French nation were wont to reap vast, vast wealth, and in which an innumerable multitude of his subjects were enlarged, and by which they subsisted.

[This loss] greatly weakens the French in this war, as it exposes them to us.

[It] exposes Canada.

[It gives us the] key to that country.

[It] gives us vast advantages against that land, by which we have been principally annoyed in time of war.

[This victory serves] to restrain distress, and even reduce it.

[The capture of Louisburg is] of great importance, as it is a place of great strength.

Much the greatest thing that has been done by the nation in the present war.

[It is] of great importance, by reason of the great expense we have been at.

If the design had been defeated, [we] probably must have borne it, and not only so, but put to much great [expense].

Second. [Consider] the visible hand of God that has appeared in this event, in a remarkable series of providences by which it has been brought about.

[It was] put into the hearts of our governor and the government, though so great and expensive an undertaking. ['Tis] remarkable.

[The proposed expedition was] carried by a single vote in the House of Representatives among fourscore.

Several [were] absent that were known to be against [the expedition]. One that had been against [it] in the Council, [was] for it in the House.[3] Forming the expedition at such a time. If [they] had delayed longer, [it would have failed].

If [it had been undertaken] the last year, the place [was] not so strong.

[It is] wonderful that we did not know the strength of the place.

[It was] a mercy [that] we did not know the strength.

[It was a] mercy it was so strong.

It seemed to be a very adventurous, and I had almost said rash undertaking, but it was a mercy that we were so adventurous.

In so stirring persons up, and, spiriting them.

Such men of note.

Men of religion.

Fearing God.

[The] principal officers [of the land].

Stirring up soldiers willing to offer themselves in a wonderful manner, [even] some that seemed most backward.

---

3. Trumbull, *History of Northampton*, 2:112–13.

Favorable weather in February and March while preparing for the expedition, such as rarely happens.

But about six weeks before [they] actually sailed.

Giving such a spirit of prayer.

A spirit to look to Him, and trust in him.

Some of the principal officers [of this spirit], as I was knowing.

To our rulers, our governor, many of the people.

[It was a mercy our plans remained] wonderfully concealed, concealed from Canada. Otherwise, [the French] might probably have overthrown the design.

[It was a mercy that they remained] concealed from the people of the place. Though our forces were hindered, and lay just by, over a time.

[It was a mercy that they were] prevented from discovering themselves by opposite winds.

[That] all [were] preserved from the small pox, which was then in Boston.

[That they were] preserved all in their passage. Not one vessel failed, [Though it was a] stormy time of year, not one storm [appeared] to scatter the fleet, [and so they were] preserved from the enemy.

[The] Connecticut forces narrowly escaped—about eighty sail.[4]

None died by the way. But one died there.

In sending us assistance, when we had no reason to depend [on it].

And if we had not, dreadful would have been the consequence.

[There was] assistance, when it looked as though we should have none, after a denial.

[It was] wonderfully ordered that, presently after Commodore Warren had sent a denial, [assistance was given].[5]

Much greater assistance than was expected.

If we had had [the] assistance that we expected only, what would have been the consequence?

Orders came to the *Elthan* but an hour or two before she was to have sailed for England.[6]

---

4. It is difficult to verify these numbers. The journal of Roger Wolcott is defective before the Connecticut contingent's arrival on Cape Breton. Robert Emmert Wall Jr.'s article "Louisbourg, 1745" (*William and Mary Quarterly* 37.1, March 1964) states that the expedition included fifteen naval vessels and close to one hundred troop transports (p. 75).

5. Shirley, *Correspondence*, 224.

6. Edwards relates many details about the siege, some of which come from the

The best assistance [arrived]. The chief commander [was] the most active, brave and successful of any.

[It was wonderfully ordered,] that this assistance should receive orders so early.

If [he] waited till the ministry had heard the news, it would have been too late to have prevented the *Vigilant* [from being sent home].

Preserving the packet boats[7] that were sent home: not cast away nor taken. Preserving every vessel in their way thither, transports, men of war and packet boats. None [were] taken nor cast away till they arrived, [though it was the] stormy season.

That the government at home should be so wonderfully spirited [and] send forth so speedily.

[That they] should come just at such a time after the ministry, and particularly the Lords of the Admiralty, were changed.

Circumstances of the first landing.[8]

If they had gone when they intended, [they] could not have lived there on shore [because of the] bad weather.

[They were] prevented till Commodore Warren came, and Connecticut forces; and till the time was come that God intended for the weather [to improve].

[They were] prevented from landing in the night, as they had been ordered. [They were] prevented by the wind's falling.

[The wind had] come out to hinder; that was in mercy.

That so few [of the enemy] came out: but eighty-eight; that they came openly, and discovered them[selves, when they] might have laid an ambush.

So many of the enemy killed, [and] none of our soldiers, though fences so much in number.

[our] enemies [were] struck with dread.

[They] deserted the grand battery, their chief fortress of all. Without this, [it is] not likely we should have succeeded.

---

reports of the siege from the *Boston Gazette* (July 16, 23, and August 13, 1745); other details would have come from the various Northampton volunteers which had returned home including Maj. Seth Pomeroy. Edwards's uncle, Col. John Stoddard, may have also provided some additional details through his network of correspondence.

7. Packet boats were medium-sized vessels designed to transport passengers and mail.

8. These circumstances are described in a letter from William Pepperrell to Gov. Shirley (*Correspondence*, 222–26 as well as the *Boston Gazette* (July 23, 1745).

[The French] endeavored to deprive us of the use of their arms, but in vain.

[They] left balls behind.

So that our enemies built a strong fortress for us, and [their] arms [were] chiefly made use of by our forces.

Discovering the grand battery to be empty, just as they did.

If the grand battery had not been taken, [we would not have succeeded].

God wonderfully ordered things with respect to another battery the enemy were about to build on the lighthouse point. [God] caused 'em to provide artillery.

[It was] discovered to our soldiers.

This battery our soldiers erected gave chief advantage.

[It was a blessing] that the enemy were sent out against {the battery} at the lighthouse. Hereby, [they were] weakened.

This led our enemies into the pit that they had digged.

Not only in these instances, but in delivering up their naval strength: the large ship of war with all its strength and stores.

So strengthening us.

Without this supply of ammunition, [we] could not have carried on the siege.

If that one ship had got into the harbor, it would have defeated [us].

Hereby, we [were] greatly strengthened.

And so other forces that they sent against us: several of their privateers were taken, and a great number of their vessels [with] their stores from time to time.

This provision supported the army; {it} could not have subsisted without what the enemy brought.

Those that came against our people by land from time to time [were defeated].

All this [at] a time when our enemies were in the midst of their designs and endeavors against us.

Annapolis [was] besieged.[9]

If Annapolis had been destroyed, five or six thousand French inhabitants under that government would have taken up arms.

So preserving the lives from being taken away by sickness.

---

9. Shirley, *Correspondence*, 225–27.

[God's] wonderfully preserving from being destroyed by the fire of the enemy, many thousand great shot and bombs.

Giving courage.

Intimidating and weakening the hands of our enemies.

Enemies restrained {thereby}, though more in number and under greater advantages.

[We were] favored as to the weather, never so since the place was settled, as our enemies observed. If the weather had been foggy as usual, it must have scattered the fleet, and given opportunity to the enemy to get into the harbor.

[They were] prevented from making an assault by scaling the walls. It had been determined [it would not succeed].

The government at home [was] wonderfully stirred up to add to their assistance, as if they had messengers sent to 'em to tell 'em.

The timing of everything was wonderful, [such as] when our forces had lost their large mortar.

Wonderful was the success.

The weakness of forces: unexperienced, many of 'em, sick and unfit for service.

The strength of the place.

The number of the enemy.

The circumstances of delivering up the city were wonderful, so as to save our lives:

Just after they had determined.

Taken without the loss of a man.

Just before the season changed.

Just before an army came.

Our enemies themselves observed that God fought for the English.

This place, since it has been taken, has proved hitherto a snare to the enemy, and has brought wealth to the English.

The taking of St. Peters, as the Major General informed me, [was] attended with some remarkable circumstances.[10]

If I remember right, the fortifications [were] considerable.

Some attempts disappointed.

Preparations the enemy were making [were] considerable.

At last, taken without the loss of a man.

We in these parts [are] greatly distinguished.

---

10. The taking of St. Peter's is mentioned in Shirley's *Correspondence* (279) though not the providential circumstances.

In this town in particular.

The whole is wonderful, from beginning to the end.

No parallel in history.

We live in a day of wonders

[We have] great reason to think that God is now about to fulfill prophecies.

Jer. 50:37–38, "a sword is upon her treasures, and they shall be robbed. A drought is upon her waters, and they shall be dried up."[11]

So again, Is. 15:6—, "For the waters of Nimrim shall be desolate: for the hay is withered away, the grass faileth, there is no green thing. Therefore the abundance they have gotten, and that which they have laid up, shall they carry away to the brook of the willows."

Hos. 13:15, "his spring shall be dry, and his fountain shall be dried up: and he shall spoil the treasure of all pleasant vessels."[12]

s2 Sam. 12:27, "[I have] fought against Rabba, and taken the city of waters."

God oftentimes having thus fought for his people that have gone forth to war, returns them to {to the people and house of God} with joy.

So Abraham.

[So] Joshua, ch. 10:43.

David {returned} to Jerusalem with the head of the Philistine, {Goliath}, 1 Sam. 17:54.

So [also] Jehoshaphat {returned from battle} [2 Chron. 19].

II. When God hath thus remarkably appeared {to fight for his people}, it is an occasion that requires much praise and thanksgiving to God.

How many of the sacred songs that are recorded in the holy Scriptures are songs that were sung and penned on [such] occasions.

[So the] song of Moses.

Of Deborah and Barak.

[And] many of David's songs.

['Tis] foretold often that God's people, on future occasions of this nature, should abound in thanksgivings and songs of praise to God.

In the Old Testament:

Is. 25, and five first verses: "[O Lord, thou art my God; I will exalt thee, I will praise thy name; for thou hast done wonderful things; thy

---

11. An allusion to the sixth vial of Revelation 16. Sixth-vial imagery is central to JE's understanding of eschatology as well as warfare.

12. Another sixth-vial allusion.

counsels of old are faithfulness and truth. For thou hast made of a city an heap; of a defenced city a ruin: a palace of strangers to be no city; it shall never be built. Therefore shall the strong people glorify thee, the city of the terrible nations shall fear thee. For thou hast been a strength to the poor, a strength to the needy in his distress, a refuge from the storm, a shadow from the heat, when the blast of the terrible ones is as a storm against the wall. Thou shalt bring down the noise of strangers, as the heat in a dry place; even the heat with the shadow of a cloud: the branch of the terrible ones shall be brought low]."

And [the] last verse, with ch. 26:1, "And the fortress of the high fort of thy walls shall he bring down, lay low, and bring to the ground, even to the dust. In that day shall this song be sung in the land of Judah; We have a strong city; salvation will God appoint for walls and bulwarks"; with vv. 4–6: "Trust ye in the Lord for ever: for in the Lord Jehovah is everlasting strength: for he bringeth down them that dwell on high; the lofty city, he layeth it low; he layeth it low, even to the ground; he bringeth it even to the dust. The foot shall tread it down, even the feet of the poor, and the steps of the needy."

Many of the Psalms are prophetical, and represent the rejoicing and praises of God's people on occasion of future victories.

In the New Testament:

[They] sing the song of Moses and the Lamb, Rev. 15:3.

Ch. 19[:6], "Alleluia: for the Lord God omnipotent reigneth."

Though the war shall be chiefly spiritual, yet undoubtedly there will be also a great temporal destruction of the open enemies [of God].

First. [The] *Reason.*

Second. Who they are that ought to be much [in praise to God].

First. [The] *Reason* [is] twofold:

[1.] The importance of the mercy.

To those that went forth and more immediately engaged [their lives].

Their lives, and so their all in the world, is immediately concerned.

[They] fought for their lives.

Their lives, in the case spoken of, are not merely preserved, as they might be in captivity.

But preserved to receive the comfort of a joyful return; to enjoy the privileges of God's people; to a state of rest and quietness; [to] rejoice with their friends.

[It is] of great importance to their country.

[It is of great importance] to the church of God:

Defense.

Prosperity.

Great are the consequences of war.

Some are mentioned in the text.

2. Because God hath made his hand so visible in this mercy.

That is supposed in [that] God often makes his hand particularly visible in such an affair. God's goodness in their preservation is the more to be acknowledged because the dangers of war [are] especially so many and great.

Second. Who they are [that ought to be much in praise to God].

1. Those that went forth and were immediately engaged, and are thus returned.

They are the immediate spectators.

[They are the] more immediate subjects of the mercy [of God] in many respects.

[They are] subjects of the wonderful preservation.

[They are] immediate subjects of the mercy of God in being returned.

[They are] honored to be the instruments [of God].

2. It should be an occasion of much {thanksgiving} to the near friends of those [who went forth].

As they that are especially concerned in them, and so in the mercies they have been the subjects of.

3. God's people in general, whose enemies they were that God fought against.

They are all nearly concerned.

All should praise {God}, as they ought to rejoice in the safe and prosperous return of their soldiers that have been engaged.

But in the first place, ministers and civil rulers.

So it was in Judah.

God's ministers [should give praise], because 'tis their business to which God has appointed them, to preside over God's people in all their public religion and acts of worship.

And rulers, because it belongs to them chiefly to conduct a people in such affairs.

[They] have the ordering [of such things].

They are their head.

'Tis they first that make war, that lead and command others.

And therefore, as they lead them in the war, and so are the leading instruments, so 'tis fit they should also lead in {praising God}.

That was beautiful, that Jehoshaphat, who was in the forefront of the people in the battle, should also be in the forefront of [the people in giving thanks and praise].

[. . .]¹³

[So the] children of Israel, [after the defeat of the] giants.

Deborah.

Gideon.

Asa against Zerah, 2 Chron. 14:9.

Though but wounded men [remained among them], Jer. 37:10.

[Though the enemy had] strong fortresses, cities walled up to heaven.

The strongholds of Zion.

[The] Jebusites merely ridiculed [Israel's] attempt {to remove them from Jerusalem} [Josh. 15:63].

[But we see God] wonderfully and unexpectedly appearing for his people's help when appearances are very dark.

[As in] Hezekiah's time, {when facing} Sennacherib's army, Is. 27.

[In] Esther's time.

[And in] Jonathan's time.

[When the] great host compassed Elisha round, 2 Kings, ch. 6:15, [his servant asked,] "Alas, master! what should we do?"

[Yet we see God] preserving them in great danger.

Ps. 18:29, "By thee I run through a troop."

[God preserves them] by wonderfully governing the seasons in favor, and causing the sun, winds and clouds as it were to fight for them.

So the winds at the Red Sea. Ex. 14:21, "the Lord caused the sea to go back by a strong east wind." Ch. 15:10, "Thou didst blow with thy wind."

[God preserved his people by stopping] the sun in Joshua's time [Josh. 10].

Clouds sometimes have been made remarkably to fight against {God's enemies} and for his people, Job 38:22–23, "Hast thou entered into the treasures of the snow? or hast thou seen the treasures of the hail, which I have reserved against the time of trouble, against the day of battle and war?"

[So] against the Amorites.

---

13. One or more leaves of the MS is apparently missing.

Against the Amorites in Deborah's time. Judg. 5:21, "[The] river Kishon swept them away," with v. 4.

[So God's] destroying enemies when they are secure, and think themselves furthest from danger:

Pharaoh's chariots and horses.

The Jebusites in the strongholds of Zion.

The Babylonians.[14]

[God preserves his people from their enemies by] turning their own warlike preparations and instruments against themselves:

Goliath.

Benaiah [slew] the Egyptian. 2 Sam. 23:21, "plucked the spear out of his hand, and slew him with his own spear."

Ps. 7:15–16, "He made a pit, and digged, and they are fallen into the ditch which they had digged."

Haman, the enemy of the Jews, [was] hanged on his own gallows.

Beating down one another, 2 Chron. 20:23.

[The] Midianites, Judg. 7:22.

[The] Philistines, 1 Sam. 14:23.

[God preserves his people by] by making use of events, in themselves very small. So the shining of the sun on the water, on the occasion of the destruction of the army of the Moabites. 2 Kgs. 3:22, etc., "And they rose up early in the morning, and the sun shone upon the water, and the Moabites saw the water on the other side as red as blood: and they said, This is blood: the kings are surely slain, and they have smitten one another: now therefore, Moab, to the spoil. And when they came to the camp of Israel, the Israelites rose up and smote the Moabites, so that they fled before them: but they went forward smiting the Moabites, even in their country."

[God] sometimes makes their enemies to confess that God fights for them.

Sermon Appendix[15]

[We were] marvelously kept from the knowledge of the strength of the place, and number of inhabitants, under the greatest advantage to know and the strictest enquiries.

---

14. Ex. 14:28; Josh. 15:63; Jer. 51.

15. JE may have meant the information on the last double leaf, which provides more details about the preparations for the expedition against and assault upon Louisburg, to have been inserted in the early part of the Application. But lacking a cue to confirm this speculation, the concluding material is presented as an appendix.

Within two months from the resolution of the government, the whole military force [departed] under sail.

The determination of the court [came on] January 29, [and] the General gave the signal for sailing, March 21.

There was not the loss of a day while preparing for the expedition either by snow, rain or cold. Some who have prepared an account of the weather for more than twenty years past, have been surprised to behold the difference between the months of February and March this year and the foregoing ones. This a continued cause of good weather. These are continually intermixed with storms of snow, or rain, or severity of cold.

Great numbers of soldiers [were] in Boston when the small pox was there. 'Tis thought the time was never known when so many persons, in so many different parts of the town, were taken ill with this sickness, and it was notwithstanding stopped in its progress. Which is the more worthy of special notice because, if it had prevailed, it would unavoidably have put an end to the intended expedition.

So considerable a military force [was] carried to the place they were bound for, without the loss of a man, or meeting with the least disaster.

[The] nearest battery within less than thirty rods of the wall.

[Our forces were] preserved wonderfully when erecting their battery at the lighthouse, though continually played upon by cannon and bombs. While getting their heavy cannon out of the water up the high rocks, in sight of the enemy, and but one was slain.

[There] coming a large supply to Boston of those very provisions that were wanted, just as our forces were ready to sail, and without which they must have been delayed.

Intercepting the pacquet[16] from France to the Commandant [was another providence].

Had Commodore Warren come to Boston as he intended, he would probably [have] been too late to intercept the *Vigilant*. A vessel, therefore, is accidentally cast in his way at sea, giving him certain information upon which, though in want of water and provision, he went on.

---

16. Referring to a collection of letters, or orders, contained in a pouch.

As Soldiers in War

August 1745

THE CELEBRATION OF THE defeat of Louisbourg spread quickly through the British world, drawing the attention of king and parliament. This improbable victory captivated the religious sensibilities of New England, drawing providential praise even from Charles Chauncy, one of the few areas of agreement between he and Edwards. God visibly fought for New England. As volunteers came trickling back into their communities, more tales of God's hand poured from their providential interpretations of their expedition. The significance of this event certainly was not lost on Edwards. His celebratory sermon for the return of Northampton's sons presented a picture of God's superintendence. God directed soldiers, officers, and even the wind and waves to orchestrate a victory for the British Protestants.

Using 1 Corinthians 9:26 as his text, Edwards described the opposition that one could expect in trying to obtain the kingdom of heaven. Those that fight for the kingdom do not fight, as the text states, like one beating the air, instead they fight the "strongest enemies" which make "the most ardent opposition." Edwards drew a comparison between the struggle for the Christian life with the struggle against Louisbourg in particular. One should strive for heaven like a soldier takes an enemy city. Using the imagery of strongholds, Edwards compared the fortification of Louisbourg to the spiritual sins of unbelief, pride, darkness, and even "the Romish church." Edwards also applied Biblical images such as the "high tower" to evoke a Biblical understanding of contemporary events.

The focus of the sermon shifted from the nature of the fortress to be conquered to the weapons used to defend such a stronghold. Edwards compared the devil's weapons to "great and small shot" which can "kill a man as well as a cannon bullet." The enemy deploys these weapons in a "constant struggle" and wields them in a manner "active, violent, and obstinate in [the] fight." By comparison, according to Edwards, the people of God are weak, insects in fact. The only chance for victory is for the Captain of the host, Christ himself, to appear and lead his people to victory. Here, Edwards made the connection to Louisbourg explicit, comparing the struggle "in the last expedition" to the Christian discipline necessary to win the heavenly city. This discipline required the skills of a soldier who faces great opposition.

As Soldiers in War was not a theoretical exploration of the Scriptures nor did it merely draw on martial themes as background to make a theological point. Edwards preached to "you that are here present that went forth in the late expedition against that strong city." He preached to the people who knew the struggles against a fortified city firsthand, and to those who heard of these struggles from eyewitnesses not two months removed from the battle. Edwards used the battle of Louisbourg as a backdrop and leveraged the emotion tied to that victory to promote a personal attachment to the evangelical principles of the revivals continuing the themes he developed in his previous martial sermons.

* * * * *

This sermon was edited for the Jonathan Edwards Center by Ken Minkema. The manuscript is eighteen duodecimo-sized leaves, the inner leaves made of fan paper with the outside leaves made of sturdier paper. Within the Application, between leaves 12 and 13, is a lacunae, probably of one double leaf. At the end of the sermon, Edwards writes notices for the observance of the Lord's Supper and baptism.

As Soldiers in War

1 Corinthians 9:26

So fight I, not as one that beateth the air.

THE APOSTLE, IN THE preceding part of the chapter, gives an account what great endeavors he used in the work and business of his Lord and Master. In this latter part of the chapter, he gives the reason of it, and improves it to stir up the Corinthians that he wrote to [to] the like earnestness in the business of religion. In the text and context, the Apostle shows the reason why he was so earnestly engaged {in the business of religion}, and why others ought to be so, in two things:

1. By representing the greatness of the work, comparing it to two things: running and fighting.

2. By representing the greatness of the reward. V. 25, "[Now they do it to obtain a corruptible crown; but we an incorruptible]."

With regard to the text, we may observe two things:

1. What the business of religion is compared to in them: [viz.,] fighting.

2. What manner of fighting: viz., fighting with the strongest enemies, and those that make the most ardent opposition.

Not as those that "beat the air." Air is a weak thing; it easily yields to a stroke, makes no resistance, is easily repelled. When a man fights with a shadow that has no substance, then he fights with nothing but the air.

But the Apostle says that he did not fight as one that beat the air. 'Tis a figure of speech, representing the contrary to the highest degree. Not the air, not shadows, but the strongest [enemies].

[The enemies are] represented as stronger than any temporal enemies. Eph. 6:12, "For we wrestle not against flesh and blood, but against principalities, against powers, against the rulers of the darkness of this world, against spiritual wickedness in high places."

Doctrine

In the business that must be done in order to our salvation, we had need to behave ourselves as soldiers in war, where they meet with great strength and mighty opposition.

'Tis not so, only with regard to the pains that sinners had need to take in order to their conversion; but with regard to the whole business Christians are called to, in order to their actual arriving at a state of eternal blessedness.

What the Apostle is speaking of here, is not [an occasional struggling]. And where the work we are called to is compared to running, wrestling and fighting, {a constant struggle is} generally signified.

'Tis a great mistake in any to suppose that they have occasion for striving and violence in religion, only before they are truly religious at all. Where there is one exhortation in the New Testament to sinners {in regard to the pains they had need to take} in order to conversion, there are ten.

But the important truth contained in the Doctrine, may be illustrated by the consideration of the following things:

I. Paradise, or a state of life, is like a city that is taken from us by our enemies.

We were in possession [of it]; that was a state of life and happiness. It was as it were a glorious city. By guile and subtilty, we resisted not, when we ought to have resisted.

We are conquered, have been brought under the power of our enemies, made prisoners, miserable captives. Our enemies have as it were driven us out, away from this glorious city, into a wilderness, a land that brings forth briars and thorns, to have our dwelling with wild beasts, where we are in a poor, lost, in a pining, famishing condition.

II. According to the state that things are in as we are naturally, this city is as it were in the possession of our enemies.

Not that our enemies that have conquered us, and deprived us of a state of life, and driven us out of paradise, are themselves in the enjoyment of a state of life, or of the blessings of paradise. {On the contrary,} they are in a state of misery. Yet 'tis all one to us, as though they had the possession of it. As to what concerns them, they have not the possession; but as to what concerns us, it is just all one, as if they had the possession as to what concerns us: for they have driven us out, and stand in the way to keep us out, as enemies do that are in possession of a city. ['Tis] typified by the land of Canaan's being {in the hands of Israel's enemies, especially} the city of Zion.

And though our enemies have not the enjoyment of the blessings of a state of life for themselves, yet thus far they look upon it as their possession, that they glory in it as their conquest; they glory in it, as what they have yet gotten from us, and keep from us. They have no true happiness in their conquest, yet they look upon it their honor and glory, and what gratifies their pride and haughtiness, and they have really set up a kingdom upon the ruins of our welfare. Babylon, which of old was the head city of the kingdom of the devil, was built, as is supposed, about the same spot of ground where the garden of Eden had been, upon the same River Euphrates.

A state of life is like a city that the devil has conquered, and takes from us and casts us out, and he has as it were set up his throne on our ruins. He has set up a kingdom in this world, to reign as god of this world.

So that he has as it were exalted himself, and cast us out of that high and heavenly city we dwelt in at first, and taken possession of it himself. According[ly], fallen angels are called "spiritual wickedness in heavenly places," Eph. 6:12.

And Satan, in being conquered by Christ, is represented as being cast down from heaven. Luke 10:18, "[I beheld Satan as] lightning fall from heaven." Rev. 12:3, "And there appeared another wonder in heaven; and behold a great red dragon, having seven heads and ten horns, and seven crowns upon his heads"; and [vv.] 7–9, "And there was war in heaven: Michael and his angels fought against the dragon; and the dragon fought and his angels, and prevailed not; neither was their place found any more in heaven. And the great dragon was cast out."

III. The enemies that have taken this city from us, and that stand in the way to keep us out of it, are very numerous, and of great ability in war.

IV. Those enemies of ours have as it were strongly fortified the city against {us}.

In representing our spiritual enemies as having built strong fortifications against us, we represent things as the Scriptures represent them: for we read of their strongholds. II Cor. 10:4, "For the weapons of our warfare are not carnal, but mighty through God to the pulling down strongholds." What those strongholds are, we are told in the next verse: "casting down imaginations, and every high thing that exalteth itself against the knowledge of God" [II Cor. 10:5].

By the evil thoughts and imaginations of the hearts, are in Scripture-style often meant the corrupt habits of the mind. One of these strongholds of Satan is the natural darkness and blindness of the mind. By this, the devil makes his kingdom and interest strong; by this, he maintains his power over the hearts of men. Hence, we read of the power of darkness, and the devils are called the rulers of the darkness of this world, and the kingdom of Satan is called the kingdom of darkness [Rev. 16:10].

Another stronghold of the devil, is unbelief and the atheism that is in the heart. 'Tis said, "the god of this world has blinded the minds of them that believe not, lest the light of the glorious gospel should shine into them" [II Cor. 4:4]. A desperate spirit of unbelief, is like a strong castle Satan has erected to keep men out of heaven.

Another stronghold {of the devil}, is that spirit of pride, self-righteousness and self-exaltation {that is in the heart}. And this is indeed that wherein the strength of Satan's interest in the heart chiefly consists, and is his strongest castle. The corruption of the heart seems to be so strong. This is what the Apostle has chief respect to in that, II Cor. 10:4, as appears by his words: "For the weapons of our warfare are not carnal, but mighty through God to the pulling down of strongholds."

This proud, self-exalting spirit that is in the hearts [of men], is as it were the devil's high tower. The chief fortifications they had of old were towers, that were very high and lasting buildings, as appears by Judg. 8:9. "When I come again in peace, I will break down this tower"; v. 17, "And he beat down the tower of Penuel, and slew the men of the city." Ch. 9:51, "But there was a strong tower within the city, and thither fled all the men and women, and all they of the city, and shut it to them, and gat them up to the top of the tower."

Hence God is called "the high tower" of the saints. 2 Sam. 22:3, "The God of my rock; in him will I trust: he is my shield, and the horn of my salvation, my high tower." "The name of the Lord [is] a strong tower"

[Prov. 18:10]. The Apostle seems to have respect to fortifications that were high towers, when he speaks of casting down iniquity and every high thing [Ps. 36:12].

The pulling down the pride of men, is prophesied of in Is. 2, under the representation of the hand of the Lord's being upon every high tower. Vv. 12 and 15: "For the day of the Lord of hosts shall be upon every one that is proud and lofty, and upon every one that is lifted up; and he shall be brought low: [. . .] and upon every high tower."

And the tower of Babel was a type of this great interest of the devil's kingdom, as it was built to gratify men's pride. "Let us build a tower, whose top may reach unto heaven, and make us a name," Gen. 11:4.

Again, those strong habits that are naturally in men, covetousness and sensuality, are strong fortifications of the devil that he has built to keep men from taking the kingdom of heaven.

So are the evil habits that men contract by custom in sin, and that guilt and hardness of heart that is induced by striving against light and {the strivings of God's Spirit}. So are the increase of prejudices mankind are under against God, and against the truth and holiness, by education, and the evil, established customs of nations and sects. Thus Satan fortified himself of old in the heathen world exceedingly, [and] fortified himself amongst the Jews in Christ's and the apostles' times. [Thus Satan] fortified himself in the Romish church {of old}.

At this day in New England, [Satan fortifies himself] by many false notions many have of religion: [in some, by] a great inclination to regard impressions; in others, by a strong prejudice against all vital religion. ['Tis] typified by the high walls of the cities of Canaan, [and by the] high walls of Babylon of old, that chief city of Satan's kingdom.

V. These enemies that stand to keep us out of heaven, have many terrible weapons and means that they use to repel us and destroy us.

His temptations are called "fiery darts," Eph. 6:16, signifying that they are mortal weapons, or weapons that carry death in them; and not only so, but that they tend to a most terrible and tormenting death, as when one is tormented to death with fire.

The devil has many kinds of weapons with which he fights with men, to hinder their taking the kingdom of heaven, and with which he destroys them. There are the flattering and alluring objects of lusts, with which he destroys men secretly, that are like daggers hid under his skirts. And there are the frowns, bitter reproaches and terrible persecutions of the world, with which he fights more openly to affright men from the heavenly city, and to destroy them eternally. There are in many places human laws and the edicts of princes, forbidding the profession and practice of the true religion under terrible penalties, with officers vested with great power to execute those laws. Those are as it were the devil's artillery and roaring cannon.

There are evil examples that the devil makes use of to decoy and allure men, while he lays an ambush for their destruction. And there are horrid, blasphemous suggestions that he sometimes casts into the minds of men, that are like red hot balls thrown in. And there are many contrivances he has to befog and bewilder men as it were with a thick smoke, in which he fights against them in the dark.

And [the devil] has many contrivances to deceive men, and lead 'em into places of danger, and make 'em think they stand on solid, firm ground, when indeed the ground is hollow, and there are mines underneath to blow 'em up.

And there are many shows that [the devil] often makes of his strength and of his warlike preparation, and trophies of past conquests to dishearten and discourage men, to prevent their being violent for the kingdom of heaven, and to cause 'em to give over the war, and so finally to destroy them.

And the devil has as it were both great and small shot with [which] he kills men. Sometimes he tempts men to great sins, and others he flatters that such and such sins are little sins, and so encourages 'em to allow themselves in the commission, and so destroys 'em as effectually as if they went on in a course of murder or blasphemy, as a small shot will kill a man as well as a cannon bullet.

VI. These enemies that stand {to keep us out of heaven}, are exceeding active, violent and obstinate in [the] fight.

[They are] active, [but] not flesh and blood. [Their] spirits are more active. Once, [they] were a flame of fire. [The devil] eggs on by a desperate malignity of spirit.

[These enemies are] exceeding violent, as they have great strength. They mightily exert themselves.

[They are] constant, [exerting themselves] night and day.

[They are] vigilant, watching all opportunities, observing advantages.

[The devil is] obstinate. [He] never will give out, as long as the least remains that 'tis possible for him to do. They are desperate enemies.

VII. We are weak.

They are much stronger than we. [We] are as insects in comparison. [We are] not skilled and versed in war as they are. As was said to David with regard to Goliath: "[Thou art not able to go against this Philistine to fight with him: for thou art but a youth, and he a man of war from his youth," 1 Sam. 17:33]. [We have] no weapons or ammunition of our own fit to oppose to theirs. Goliath came with a coat of mail, an helmet of brass and greaves of brass, a target of brass and a spear whose staff was a weaver's beam; but David came without armor.

VIII. Yet notwithstanding all these things, there is opportunity for us again to retake that glorious city, or paradise, or state of life that we lost.

A glorious Captain appears to lead us. Though we are weak and unskillful, yet he [is mighty and skillful]. He has provided arms for us. There is a possibility. There is great hopes, if may be. [When we] take it, [it will be] vastly more glorious than when we lost it. And we are called to go and follow this Captain, and fight and strive.

IX. 'Tis expected and required that we should exert ourselves in this war, in some measure answerable to those things that have been mention[ed].

The strength {of our enemies is great}, yet {we must exert ourselves}. That was the case in the last expedition {against Cape Breton}. But how reasonably is this required.

['Tis] in some measure according to the importance and difficulties {of the cause}. Men are willing to exert themselves mightily. If there be anything at all for us to do, 'tis fit that it should be so, as David, that we earnest[ly assert ourselves].

Application

Use I of *Information*. Hence, we may undoubtedly infer that but few are saved.

If this that has been spoken of be the narrow way to life, [then] all must go [in it]. ['Tis] work that all must do, or never will obtain the prize.

Then, undoubtedly, there are but few. Though 'tis not for us to determine concerning individual persons who {are saved and who are not}, yet thus far we may determine: that if it was a common thing for men to be thus engaged {in the business that must be done in order to their salvation}, there would be more appearance of it than there [is]. If a country or town be full of those that are thus engaged {in the business of religion}, there will be more appearance of it.

The face of the world plainly shows that the bigger part of professors are not chiefly devoted to the business of religion, but that other pursuits are what they are ordinarily more engaged in; and those with whom it is so, are not in the way of salvation. If those words of Christ are true, {then} "ye cannot serve God and mammon" [Matt. 6:24]. That which a man chiefly serves, that is a man's god.

Many seem to have a poor, low notion of Christian practice or a Christian discipline, as though it consisted in negatives. The reason is, we are very ready to embrace principles that suit ourselves, {and that} agree to our own state and practice. But only to live a morally honest life, is far from being a Christian life, according to the description everywhere given of it in the New Testament; {it} is not running the race, {and fighting the good fight}.

Use II of *Exhortation*. To exhort all that hope hereafter to be possessed of the kingdom of heaven, not to fight as those that beat the air, but to behave yourselves in the business of religion, which you are called to attend through your whole life, as soldiers that go war to take a strong city, where they meet with mighty opposition.

Let it appear real, that this is absolutely necessary, {and} that the possession of heaven is not to be obtained in any other way: for it is certainly so, if the Scriptures are a good rule. If the Scriptures are intelligible, there is no other way. They everywhere thus represent [it to be so]. There is no way that I can devise, how they can have any other construction. To interpret all those passages of Scripture as mere hyperbolical figures of speech, is the way wholly to make the Scriptures of none effect: therefore, let none hope that he shall [argue otherwise]. ['Tis] without any foundation in the Word of God; yea, contrary [to it].

If the doctrine of God is true, this is the way that tends to life; and if the Scriptures are true, there is but one way. Therefore, if you hope for heaven in any other way, one of these two things will come to pass: either you will perish, or the word of God will perish. But "heaven and earth shall pass away, but God's words shall not pass away" [Matt. 24:35]. Better not hope for heaven at all, than live all your days in a vain hope, a hope without any Scripture-grounds.

Truly, I do verily believe that the notion many have of the way to heaven, is exceeding different from that which the Scripture lays out. And that it is so, that if all the Scripture means by that running and wrestling {and fighting}, be no more than what is found in them: that [then] it was never worth the while for the apostles to set forth the pains and earnestness of the Christian life in such strong terms; that it tends only to deceive and mislead the minds of their readers, and that really their words fall to the ground and prove of none effect.

We have now something more than common in providence, to make us sensible to the meaning of such descriptions as the Scriptures give of the life and business of a Christian: because we have something unusual to make us sensible what belongs to the business of a soldier, that goes forth to war, where he meets with great strength and violent opposition.

You that are here present that went forth in the late expedition against that strong city, Louisburg, you can tell something what belongs to war; and consequently, you are under special advantages to tell what belongs to the life of a Christian, and what the Apostle means in the words of the text, and in other texts where he compares the business of a Christian to {a soldier in war that meets with great strength and mighty opposition}. You know what hardships soldiers are obliged to endure that go forth to war, and what a different way of living it is from lying in ease and quietness at home. You forsook your own country, and the ease and comfortable and pleasant enjoyments you had here, to go a long journey over land and sea, not knowing whether ever you should return again. [You know] what poor lodgings had you: at best but a poor tent, just to keep out the rain and shelter you from the injuries of {the weather}; and many of you, it may be, at least oftentimes lodging in the open air, and suffered a great deal of cold and other inconveniences. And what hard fare had you: [you] had no great varieties of food, not much to please and gratify your appetites; it was only that which was for necessity. And you had but few accommodations.

And what made you contented with such provision and such accommodation, was that it was to be but for a little while; your place in the camp, you knew, was no abiding place, no fixed [habitation]. [You were] but sojourners there. And you knew what was to be aimed at, was only the prosecuting the great end that you went there for, viz., taking the city, and that if you could but take the city at last, it was not worth the while to be very careful about your way of living. You did not much mind your hard lodging and hard fare; {you} hoped it would be better after victory was obtained. [You] did not set your heart on your tent; you knew it was but a tent. You was not very careful about ornaments to adorn your tents, to make a great show in the camp; you knew it was not your home.

And is not this exactly agreeable to what we are taught in the Word of God concerning the life of a Christian: {that we should} forsake all, [be] content with hard fare? that here we have no abiding place, but tents or tabernacles? [that we should] not set our hearts [on this world], because we are sojourners? that what we should set our hearts upon is success in our great business {of gaining salvation}? If we have food and raiment, what is of necessity, we should be therewith content.

While you that went forth on the late expedition was engaged in your warfare, seeking to take that strong city that you went against, you did not make much of property; all things were as it were common. You lived on a common stock; and if one had more provision than he needed, he was willing to give to him that wanted. For what you aimed at, was to promote that grand design of taking the city, and not to hoard up a stock of provision in your tents, as if you was to live there always. You considered the having much provision, or little, was but of little [. . .].[1]

[. . .] ministers.

Did not you that were concerned in the late siege, find it necessary not to be easily affrighted at the appearance of danger, or to be easily driven back when danger appeared, notwithstanding resolutely to press forward, and that speedily, and not to stand to think of the difficulties? So is it necessary [in the business of religion].

How necessary was perseverance. The siege held long, longer than was expected. Seeing you had put your hand to the plow, [it was necessary] not to give way to a hankering disposition after your old enjoyments at home, not to give way to a discouraged spirit.

[It was necessary,] when you found things looked dark, and found temptations to discouragement, not to give way to them, but to rouse yourselves. [It was necessary to] cast such thoughts out of your mind.

How terrible would have been the consequence, if you had given way {to temptation}, if you had sank down, {and} turned your back, never taken the city; and not only so, but greatly exposed yourselves. And how agreeable is this [to Scripture representations of the Christian life].

---

1. There is apparently a lacuna in the MS at this point of at least one double leaf.

[You] went nowhere unarmed, had your arms about you night and day. [You] stood ready to help one another. If any one needed help, {you did what was} necessary to promote the common design. {And} this is agreeable to what the rules of the gospel require of all Christians.

You find it necessary to encourage one another, and put one another forward. So should Christians do.

You had at last come to an agreement to storm the city, though therein your lives would have been greatly exposed. [You] run almost against the mouths of their cannon. And this is the way wherein the Scripture teaches us that the heavenly city {is to be taken}.

We must as it were lose our lives, hate our own lives, resolve to conquer or die. "The kingdom {of heaven} suffers violence" [Matt. 11:12].

'Tis to be hoped that some of you put your trust in God, {and} earnestly sought to him. There was an appearance of an extraordinary spirit of prayer, and you found it was not a vain thing: God has shown himself a prayer-hearing God, [who] remarkably fought for you.

This shows the way in which you ought to strive and use your own labor and diligence in endeavoring {for salvation}: viz., in a dependence {on God}, earnestly seeking to him {for grace}.

And [this] also shows the encouragement [God gives]. God is as ready; yea, there are greater encouragements {for this than for anything else}.

Christ is the captain of his people's salvation in a temporal war. Christ's power appeared gloriously in the victory, but much more gloriously in the spiritual victory.

God appeared for you from time to time, in times of special need, and gave you help in those things wherein you needed it most. So he is wont to do].

God led your enemies into their own snare, and the pit. So is he wont to do. The officers did not think it prudent to suffer the French to dwell with the English, after taking the city of Louisburg; {they were} carried clear off the ground.

And let me on this occasion press it on those that have lately had experience of the business, and what belongs to fighting in order to take a strong city, to improve it for themselves. Learn from what you have to do, in order to your taking heaven, and never forget it; be often thinking of [it] to stir you [up.] You have a greater business to do; your greatest business is not over. You have a stronger city, and a more glorious city, to take, more and strong enemies to conquer. ['Tis] a work of infinitely greater importance. You have now seen that which may be improved to excellent purpose for your instruction, quickening and encouragement in that spiritual warfare.

And I will also press the same on all others that have now opportunity to learn what belongs to a warfare, by what they hear from you. If you do not now realize it, that you have so great a work before you, you'll see the truth of those things hereafter, and will be convinced that the conquering an earthly city is a very tittle in comparison.

And here, I would mention some things further to excite all to look on themselves as soldiers that {meet with great strength and mighty opposition} in seeking the kingdom of heaven:

First. How glorious will be the acquisition, if you take the heavenly Zion, {not only a} strong city, but a glorious city, typified by Zion of old. The habitations will be yours: exceeding magnificent, vast riches, [and] glorious ornaments. All shall be yours.

'Tis a royal city, and the throne of heaven shall be yours. [You] shall reign there.

You that lately fought against Louisburg, with what joy did you enter the city. Though the riches were not your own, did it make you as [it] were to forget all your fatigue? The wealth of the city was not your own, and though you had but poor lodgings there, [and] conquered it not for yourselves, [with what joy did you enter in]?

With what unspeakably greater joy will you enter {into the heavenly city}, if you conquer.

Secondly. You must conquer or die in this spiritual warfare.

[There is] never but one opportunity only: this time of life. [Do not] fall and be a prey to your enemies. They give no quarter; [they are] implacable, exceeding cruel.

Third. Consider, you have had sufficient information, both of the strength and importance of the place you are to take.

Christ has not failed of informing [you].

Fourth. Though there be as much need of earnestness, vigilance and violence {in a spiritual war}, as in a temporal war, yet there is much more to uphold and support you under it.

Fifth. If you once get possession, 'tis certain the enemy will never get possession again.

[The] English intend to make Louisburg strong[er] than ever. [So the heavenly city is] a thousand times more strongly fortified for you than for your enemies.

Sixth. You shall go home. [You shall not be in a] strange land, [or in your] enemy's country no longer.

Seventh. If you conquer, when once you have taken and entered this glorious city, there will be an eternal end to your warfare.

When you take the city, there [is] not an end to fighting. All was peaceable then; [but you are only] free from all impresses for two years. But [in heaven, there shall be peace] forever and ever, everlasting peace. ['Tis a] city of peace. [You will have] no more fatigues, no more breaking of your rest, no more alarms of war, no lurking enemies nigh you, no more hard fare; [no more] wounds, [nor] sweat and blood, [but] everlasting triumph. There you shall live, there you shall rest, there you shall sing. There ye shall reign and feast and rejoice, forever and ever.[2]

---

2. At the close of the sermon, JE wrote "SACRAM[EN]T" and "BAPTISM," either as reminders to observe them following the service, or to announce them to the congregation for a coming sabbath.

The Enemies of God's People Confounded and Broken in Pieces

September 19, 1745

THE CAPTURE OF LOUISBOURG proved to be the opening salvo of an ongoing conflict instead of the knock-out blow. New England's new found control over the north Atlantic and the St. Lawrence seaway secured British control over shipping, trade, and fishing, weakening Quebec and Montreal. Celebrations thanking God for his visible workings, however, were short lived. New England turned her resources to protecting themselves from Native and French sorties. The French successfully ingratiated themselves with the eastern Abenaki including the Norridgewocks and Penobscots but were less successful in penetrating the western tribes of the Iroquois and Huron. Instead, they formed religious communities outside Montreal and Quebec—Lorette, Cagnawaga, and St. Francis—that served as refuges for Catholic converts from these western tribes. While the eastern Abenaki fought along the St. George's River (modern day Maine), these communities of Mohawk and Huron provided most of the warriors for the various small unit expeditions into Edwards's Connecticut River Valley.

New England expected the trajectory of this war to follow that of the previous wars: outbreak of hostilities on the continent leading to transplantation of hostilities to the colonies with combined French and Native units ambushing outlying communities. Now that war had come to North America, Native groups were to play a significant role. The threat of combined French and Native attacks on frontier outposts brought many unpleasant memories back to the community. Through *The Enemies of God's People Confounded and Broken in Pieces*, Edwards addressed the fears brought about by the vivid memories of past conflicts of the soldiers that would fight in the war.

Edwards relied on a triumphal verse to launch his sermon: God's enemies would be "broken in pieces" (Isa 8:9–10). The assurance of success in this war was God's presence which could overcome whatever preparations, alliances, or contrivances the enemy might have. This posture echoed Edwards' conviction that war is chiefly a spiritual endeavor.

Edwards identified the French in this sermon as not just the enemy, but an "antichristian" force and, therefore, "the policy of [the] antichrist shall never prevail to overcome the Protestant church." This language suggested Edwards saw Britain's enemies in terms stronger than the vacillating political alliances of the European wars. These Native groups were not just the enemies of Britain in Edwards's cosmic framework, but they were the enemies of God himself. Because Edwards understood France and her Indian allies in Biblical terms, he was able to apply Biblical precedent to this present war. The examples of Gideon, Asa, and Jehoshaphat became the template for New England's struggles against antichristian kingdoms. Edwards compared France with their Native allies to the infamous Babylon.

Preached as a fast day sermon in anticipation of war reaching New England, *The Enemies of God's People Confounded and Broken in Pieces* echoed many of Edwards traditional themes. By combining an emphasis on spiritual duty and eschatology, Edwards demonstrated the comprehensiveness of his vision. He integrated his understanding of the awakenings with the present wars at home and abroad into God's cosmic purposes. This integration allowed Edwards to challenge his congregation pastorally to both fulfill their spiritual duties while, at the same time, rest assured in the knowledge of their ultimate victory by God's "special mercy."

* * * * *

This sermon was edited for the Jonathan Edwards Center by Ken Minkema also known as "Fast on Occasion of the Proclamation of War with the Indians." The manuscript is nineteen duodecimo-sized leaves, including a discarded prayer bid and a fragment of a letter. Edwards notes the occasion of this sermon at the top of the first page: "Fast on occasion of the Proclamation of war with the Indians septem. 19. 1745." Perpendicularly in the left margin beside the text he also noted the re-preaching, "+ March 4 1755," during the French and Indian War. For this redelivery, he made some minor additions and deletions.

The Enemies of God's People Confounded and Broken in Pieces

Isaiah 8:9–10

Associate yourselves, O ye people, and ye shall be broken in pieces, [and give ear, all ye of far countries: gird yourselves, and ye shall be broken in pieces; gird yourselves, and ye shall be broken in pieces. Take counsel together, and it shall come to nought; speak the word, and it shall not stand: for God is with us].

1.[1] WHO THEY ARE to whom they direct their speech and utter themselves in the text: their foreign enemies.

2. The number: "all ye of far countries."

3. What the affair is concerning, which God's people here utter themselves, viz., concerning the hostile purpose that they entertained against them. This appears by the context, [and] appears plainly in the text. This purpose of theirs is referred to when it is said, "Speak the word."

What people here express concerning the purpose of their enemies, viz., their confidence of its disappointment.[2]

---

1. In revising for re-preaching, JE inserted a new point: "1. Who they are that are here represented speaking: the church or people of God, or daughter of Zion." He then renumbered the following heads accordingly.

2. LL. 1–2 made from a salvaged marriage bann, which reads:
These may Certifie that the Intention of marriage between Caleb Wright and Sarah Strong both of Northampton was Entred with <me> on the 24th day of August Last and on the next day the parties were published by posting Up their Names and Intentins at the Usual place In Northampton.
Attest Saml Mather Town Clerk
Northampton Sep. 6th 1745.

4. The means the foreign enemies use, and preparations they make use [of], to accomplish this purpose. [They are] fourfold:

[(1)] Associating themselves, uniting; uniting one with another; several nations entering into a combination, and getting together.

[(2)] Strengthening themselves with armor.

[(3)] Taking counsel together.

[(4)] Doing what in them lies to bring their counsels to effect, and put their designs in execution: "speak the words." When all is ready, they shall speak the word. By the word that they speak, may be understood the word by which they utter their determination and resolution; so "word" is often taken: word of promise to themselves, and one to another; word of threatening, word by which their wish is expressed and curse denounced against [their foes]. ['Tis a] word of command.

5. What God's church here expresses concerning this purpose of her enemies, and their preparations and means to effect, viz., that all shall be disappointed: "[it shall] come to nought, [the] word "shall not stand." ['Tis a word] of determination; ['tis a word of] promise.

6. The manner in which they shall be disappointed, [viz.,] utterly, [as] signified in various expressions—"broken in pieces," "come to nought"—[and] by the repetition [of them].

7. She expressed her confidence of the certainty of their [confederacy] being thus disposed, [by the] solemnity of expression, [and by] repeti[ti]on.

8. The reason given why they are so confident.

Doctrine

If God be with a people whose destruction is sought by foreign enemies, how numerous soever those enemies are, whatever their desires and wishes, and whatever their designs are; whatever their counsels and contrivances are, and whatever their alliances; whatever their warlike preparations, and whatever their resolutions; and whatever their endeavors and whatever their hopes, they are likely to be utterly confounded and broken in pieces.

I. How God is said to be with a people.

II. Show that when is thus with them, their foreign enemies are like to utterly {fail}, how many soever they are, and whatever their designs are, etc.

I. How God is said to be with a people.

First. What is implied in his being with a people.

Second. What is the foundation of a people's enjoyment of this benefit.

First. What is implied [in his being with a people].

Three things [are implied]:

1. His being with a people in covenant relation.

[They are a] people in covenant, visible people, [with the] means [of grace]. [They have a] tabernacle in the midst of them.

[They have a] covenant union and obligation.

2. His being with them by his Spirit.

3. In the exercises of his power and wisdom for them in his providence.

Secondly. [What is the] foundation [of a people's enjoyment of this benefit].

['Tis] twofold:

1. God's sovereign, electing love.

2. Jesus Christ's being for them as the great Immanuel.

This is what the Prophet had been speaking of. All benefits to mankind are through Christ, [including] public benefits. Christ is for a people, or many among [them], mediator. His being thus for many among them,[3] he is the great foundation spoken of, v. 14 of [the] context.

Christ is the foundation of God's being with mankind, by appearing as their Immanuel, or appearing as united with them, in four respects:

[(1)] Undertaking.

[(2)] Incarnation.

[(3)] Substitution.

[(4)] Intercession.

II. Show that when God is thus with a people whose destruction is sought by foreign enemies, how many soever, [whatever their] wishes, {whatever their} designs, {whatever their} counsels and contrivances, {whatever their} alliances, {whatever their} warlike preparations, {whatever their} resolutions, {whatever their} endeavors, {whatever their} hopes, they are like to be utterly confounded and broken in pieces.

3. In revising for re-preaching, JE drew a large "X" through this paragraph up to this point.

First. How numerous soever.

Uniting of their strength don't bring their strength to any nearer or equally with God's.

All nations before him as nothing, all the inhabitants of the earth. Is. 40:15–17, "Behold, the nations are as a drop of a bucket, and are counted as the small dust of the balance: behold, he taketh up the isles as a very little thing. And Lebanon is not sufficient to burn, nor the beasts thereof sufficient for a burnt offering. All nations before him are as nothing; and they are counted to him less than nothing, and vanity." {V.} 22, "It is he that sitteth upon the circle of the earth, and the inhabitants thereof are as grasshoppers; that stretcheth out the heavens as a curtain, and spreadeth them out as a tent to dwell in." {V.} 23, "That bringeth the princes to nothing; he maketh the judges of the earth as vanity." "Though hand join in hand, [the wicked shall not be unpunished: but the seed of the righteous shall be delivered," Prov. 11:21]. Ps. 33:16, "There is no king saved by the multitude of an host."

It is like the confounding of a great number of briars and thorns. Nahum. 1:7–10, "The Lord is good, a strong hold in the day of trouble; and he knoweth them that trust in him. But with an overrunning flood he will make an utter end of the place thereof, and darkness shall pursue his enemies. What do ye imagine against the Lord? he will make an utter end: affliction shall not rise up the second time. For while they be folden together as thorns, and while they are drunken as drunkards, they shall be devoured as stubble fully dry."

Though there may be very many, yet God has larger hosts. 2 Kgs. 6:15–16, "And when the servant of the man of God was risen early, and gone forth, behold, an host compassed the city both with horses and chariots. And his servant said unto him, Alas, my master! how shall we do? And he answered, Fear not: for] more are they that are with us [than they that be with them]."

{So it was} in Gideon's time, [and in] Asa's time. 2 Chron. 14:9–12.

And there came out against them Zerah the Ethiopian with an host of a thousand thousand, and three hundred chariots; and came unto Mareshah. Then Asa went out against him, and they set the battle in array in the valley of Zephathah at Mareshah. And Asa cried unto the Lord his God, and said, Lord, it is nothing with thee to help, whether with many, or with them that have no power: help us, O Lord our God; for we rest on thee, and in thy name we go against this multitude. O Lord, thou art our

God; let no man prevail against thee. So the Lord smote the Ethiopians before Asa, and before Judah; and the Ethiopians fled.

1 Kgs. 20:27, "[And the children of Israel were numbered, and were all present, and went against them: and the children of Israel pitched before them like two little] flocks of kids."

[God gives his people victory] by many or by few.[4]

[*Second.*] If they act as if they would hide their counsel from the Lord. "Woe to them that seek deep [to hide their counsel from the Lord, and their works are in the dark, and they say, Who seeth us? and who knoweth us?" Is. 29:15].

If they make use of deceit and lying, [God will sweep away the] refuge of lies. Is. 28:15–17, "Because ye have said, We have made a covenant with death, and with hell are we at agreement; when the overflowing scourge shall pass through, it shall not come unto us: for we have made lies our refuge, and under falsehood have we hid ourselves: therefore thus saith the Lord God, Behold, I lay in Zion for a foundation a stone, a tried stone, a precious corner stone, a sure foundation: he that believeth shall not make haste. Judgment also will I lay to the line, and righteousness to the plummet: and the hail shall sweep away the refuge of lies, and the waters shall overflow the hiding place."

Third. Whatever their designs, God's purposes shall stand. Prov. 19:21, "There are many devices in man's heart, but the counsel of the Lord, that shall stand."

God's designs were first established, and man's designs don't change them. Job 23:13–14, "But he is in one mind, and who can turn him? and what his soul desireth, even that he doeth. For he performeth the thing that is appointed for me: and many such things are with him."

However evil the designs of the enemies of a people, yet if God be with them, they are quite safe. It was a terrible destruction that Pharaoh intended [Ex. 14], [and] that Rabshakeh intended [2 Kgs. 18].

Fourth. Whatever their counsels and contrivances are, he knows all their designs, though very secret, though concealed with great craft and deceitful strategies and lies from men

---

4. At this point in the MS (L. 5v.) JE writes, "* next p. but one," but there is no corresponding cue.

He has seasonable notice; knows the thoughts of their hearts. [He] hears their secret consciences, though far off from the people against whom [they counsel and contrive].

However deep their schemes, {and} however subtil, still he has the government of the world {in his hands}. [He] is wiser than they; foresees things they can't foresee. All incidents, the motion of every wheel, [God] has all in his hands. Ps. 33:10–12, "The Lord bringeth the counsel of the heathen to nought: he maketh the devices of the people of none effect. The counsel of the Lord standeth for ever, the thoughts of his heart to all generations. Blessed is the nation whose God is the Lord; and the people whom he hath chosen for his own inheritance." Job 5:12–13, "He disappointeth the devices of the crafty, so that their hands cannot perform their enterprise. He taketh the wise in their own craftiness: and the counsel of the froward is carried headlong."

[God] disappoints the device of the crafty, whatever their desires and wishes. [He disappoints those who] pray to their false gods. Is. 19:3–4, "And the spirit of Egypt shall fail in the midst thereof; and I will destroy the counsel thereof: and they shall seek to the idols, and to the charmers, and to them that have familiar spirits, and to the wizards. And the Egyptians will I give over into the hand of a cruel lord; and a fierce king shall rule over them, saith the Lord, the Lord of hosts." [He disappoints them, even when they pray] to the true God. Ps. 18:40–41, "Thou hast also given me the necks of mine enemies; that I might destroy them that hate me. They cried, but there was none to save them: even unto the Lord, but he answered them not."

[So he does to those who would] curse God's people, [as] Balaam [Num. 22].

Fifth. Whatever their alliances are. Is. 54:15, "Behold, they shall surely gather together, and not by me: whosoever shall gather together against thee shall fall for thy sake."

God is in all countries; rules over all nations and all kings. When Joshua invaded Canaan, many kings were combined together. Josh. 10:3–4, "Wherefore Adonizedec king of Jerusalem, sent unto Hoham king of Hebron, and unto Piram king of Jarmuth, and unto Japhia king of Lachish, and unto Debir king of Eglon, saying, Come up unto me, and help me, that we may smite Gibeon: for it hath made peace with Joshua and with the children of Israel." And [ch.] 11, at the beginning. [There were] so many against David, 2 Sam. 8:5. So Pekeh and Rezin [2 Kgs. 15]. So in Jehoshaphat's time; 2 Chron. 20:1, "It came to pass after this also, that the children of Moab, and the children of Ammon, and with them other beside the Ammonites, came against Jehoshaphat to battle."[5]

Sixth. Whatever their warlike preparations, or whatever fortresses [they build], God is "more glorious and excellent than the mountains of prey," Ps. 76:4. Deut. 33:29, "Happy art thou, [. . . thou shalt] tread on [their] high places." [Their] wall [is] to fall down flat. [The] walls of Babylon were no security.

He is a rock. Deut. 32:4, "He is the Rock, his work is perfect: for all his ways are judgment: a God of truth and without iniquity, just and right is he."

[He provides the] arms and weapons of war. Is. 54:16–17, "Behold, I have created the smith that bloweth in the coals, [and that bringeth forth an instrument for his work; and I have created the waster to destroy. No weapon that is formed against thee shall prosper; and every tongue that shall rise against thee in judgment thou shalt condemn. This is the heritage of the servants of the Lord, and their righteousness is of me, saith the Lord]."

"He breaks the bow," Ps. 46:9.

Pharaoh had great warlike preparations; [so] the Canaanites in Deborah's time [Judg. 4–5].

Seventh. Whatever their resolutions, how strong soever, God can weaken them, take away their courage. Their hearts are in his hands.

[They shall] flee at the shaking[6] of a leaf.

[God] can give his people courage, [or] he can break their resolution, cause 'em to alter, however strong. God's purposes are more fixed than theirs.

Whatever their endeavors, [however they] lay themselves out never so much, not only in preparation but action, [though they] exert themselves [with] great vigor, like a storm against the wall; [yet God orders it] that his people shall be like a rock against the raging sea. He that is their wall and bulwark, is stronger than rocks of adamant.

Whatever their hope is, however fair things may appear, [God can frustrate them]. [So it was with] Pharaoh. [Their hopes are like a] "dream

---

5. In revising for re-preaching, JE deleted the reference to Jehoshaphat and the Scripture prooftext.

6. MS: "shaken."

of a night vision." Is. 29:7–8, "And the multitude of all the nations that fight against Ariel, even all that fight against her and her munition, and that distress her, shall be as a dream of a night vision. It shall even be as when an hungry man dreameth, and, behold, he eateth; but he awaketh, and his soul is empty: or as when a thirsty man dreameth, and, behold, he drinketh; but he awaketh, and, behold, he is faint, and his soul hath appetite: so shall the multitude of all the nations be, that fight against mount Zion."

Notwithstanding all those things, [they are] likely to be utterly confounded and broken in pieces. [They shall be] broken in their measures. Things [are] so ordered, that shall entirely render their consultations and schemes vain, {and} otherwise than they thought. [There shall arise] events that they made no provision for, course of things such as they never calculated. [Their] counsels [shall be] all disconcerted.

Their strength is like to be broken. "[The] arms [of the wicked] shall be broken," Ps. 37:17. Their courage [is like to be] broken. [Their courage] doth "faint because of you" [Josh. 2:9]. Their fortresses and weapons [are like to be] broken. Their union one with another [is like to be] broken. Is. 19:2–3, "And I will set the Egyptians against the Egyptians: and they shall fight every one against his brother, and every one against his neighbor; city against city, and kingdom against kingdom. And the spirit of Egypt shall fail in the midst thereof; and I will destroy the counsel thereof: and they shall seek to the idols, and to the charmers, and to them that have familiar spirits, and to the wizards." Their wishes and hopes [are like to be] broken, their hearts broken, [and] themselves utterly destroyed and broken in pieces.

[We have] many remarkable instances in Scripture. [So we have] instances of the experience of our nation. {And we have instances} in the experience of this land.[7]

Application

I. Hence learn the reason why the church of God never has been and never will be destroyed by her enemies, but that finally all that war with her shall be confounded. Zech. 12:2–4, "Behold, I will make Jerusalem a cup of trembling unto all the people round about, when they shall be in the siege both against Judah and against Jerusalem. And in that day

---

7. In revising for re-preaching, JE deleted this paragraph.

will I make Jerusalem a burdensome stone for all people: all that burden themselves with it shall be cut in pieces, though all the people of the earth be gathered together against it. In that day, saith the Lord, I will smite every horse with astonishment, and his rider with madness: and I will open mine eyes upon the house of Judah, and will smite every horse of the people with blindness."

II. What has said may well engage us of this land to do what in us lies, that God may be with us who are now engaged with so many enemies that are round about us in the war that we are engaged in.[8]

Our enemies are numerous. The nation to which we are especially exposed, are much greater than our own nation; and they have strengthened themselves by the alliance of many tribes of Indians that have joined with them, and have already taken up arms against us. And they are industriously endeavoring to strengthen themselves by some other alliances, to draw other nations of Indians over to their interests, and particularly are using all means that they can devise to bring over those numerous western tribes of Indians, that have always hitherto been in a friendship with us. It seems that they leave no stone unturned, are using their utmost craft and subtilty, and spare no pains nor cost, and stick at no lies to beget and cherish in them jealousies of us, and embitter them against [us], and to engage them to them. And they are a people famed above all nations in the world for their craft and subtilty, and now seem to be exercising their subtilty to their utmost

The antichristian kingdoms are noted above all societies of mankind for their subtilty, which is particularly taken notice of in the prophecies of Scripture. Dan. 7:8, "I considered the horns, and, behold, there came up among them another little horn, before whom there were three of the first horns plucked up by the roots: and, behold, in this horn were eyes like the eyes of man, and a mouth speaking great things." [V.] 20, "And of the ten horns that were in his head, and of the other which came up, and before whom three fell; even of that horn that had eyes, and a mouth that spake very great things, whose look was more stout than his fellows."

And the French nation are noted for this beyond any other nation belonging to the antichristian kingdoms. They are a people noted for their foresight, care and vigilance in making preparations for war, and were abundant in their preparations for war against us, even while it was

---

8. In revising for re-preaching, JE deleted "who are now engaged with so many enemies that are round about us."

yet a time of peace; and particularly in building fortresses whereby they have great advantages against us.

And doubtless they are now exerting themselves to their utmost to gird and strengthen themselves, and are taking counsel and laying schemes for their own defense and our annoyance. What their counsels, plots and designs are, we know not.

Now therefore, we eminently need to have God with us, who is the Lord of armies, who knows {their counsels, plots and designs}. Therefore now it greatly concerns us to seek this great benefit.

And here, let us particularly consider several things further to excite us to do what in us lies, that God may be with us.

First. How much we have had lately to convince us of the dependence of a people on God in war, in the whole series of events relating to the expedition {against Cape Breton}.

How fair a prospect was it thought there was {for success}; how much otherwise did things appear, in very many respects, than was expected. How many unthought of incidents {were there} that we never foresaw, nor provided for, and if God had not provided for 'em, [would have been our ruin]. How many critical seasons and junctures and incidents were there in the course of that affair that were not foreseen, wherein if things had happened but a little otherwise than they did, would have been our ruin as to that affair.

And that they happened as they did, was evidently not owing to us. {It was not owing to} any foresight {on our part}, or provision {we made}. If the expedition had been a little delayed by bad weather; if it had not wonderfully happened that the government at home were stirred up just at that time when they had no knowledge {of the events, or} if this had been a little later; if the naval force {that was sent} had been a little longer delayed by contrary winds or any means; if [it] had not unexpectedly met a vessel at sea that prevented their first coming to Boston; if by any means the design had been discovered; if the small pox had [broken out amongst us]; if the enemy had not been strangely intimidated and caused to flee and leave one of their strongest fortresses; if their leaving that fortress had not been discovered quite so soon; if they had come out to repossess themselves {of the fortress} a little sooner; if it had not been extraordinary weather, such as never [was before seen]; if the men of war that was coming {to relieve the fortress} had, by the favor of foggy weather or by any other means, got into the harbor; if they had not been prevented storming the city after it had been determined soon after their arrival; if the army that [was] designed for their relief had arrived seasonably; if our army had not been supplied with stores from the enemy: by these things, and many others, God has remarkably shown us how the events of war are determined by God, are dependent on him.

In all these things and others that might be mentioned, the whole affair was visibly brought over and over into the hands of God. Things were not foreseen nor provided for.

We shall therefore be very stupid if we don't see our dependence, and ben't sensible of our need of God's help in the affair of war for the future.

Second. Consider how much there is to encourage us to seek to God, that he would be with us and help us in the war we are now engaged [in].

1. It may be considered that those that we are at war with, do belong to the antichristian kingdoms, that are appointed to destruction. ['Tis the beast that] goeth into perdition, [and is the] son of perdition [2 Thess. 2:3]. Rev. 17:8, "The beast that thou sawest was, and is not; and shall ascend out of the bottomless pit, and go into perdition: and they that dwell on the earth shall wonder, whose names were not written in the book of life from the foundation of the world, when they behold the beast that was, and is not, and yet is." V. 11, "And the beast that was, and is not, even he is the eighth, and is of the seven, and goeth into perdition."

'Tis true, they are strong, numerous, rich and politic. These things were foretold. But the same prophecies do foretell its destruction.

2.[9] There is ground in Scripture to suppose that the policy of Antichrist shall never prevail to overcome the Protestant church.

[So the pouring out of the] fifth vial, [or] "throne" in original [Rev. 16:10].

Policy and craft is the light of Babylon [Dan. 8:25]; [they are] as true wisdom. [The] Egyptians [were blinded]. [So the] Sodomites [were struck blind], Gen. 19:11. [So the] city wherein Elisha was defended, 2 Kgs. 6:18. [And] Elymas the sorcerer [Acts 13:8–11].

So God defended the children of Israel from Pharaoh. [But the enemies of God's people shall] "grope at noonday as in the night," Job [5:]14, etc.

3. There is all reason to suppose that the time of the destruction of Antichrist is now drawing near.

---

9. Points 2 and 3 are moved here from LL. 15v.–16r.

Third. So that really an encouragement may be drawn from their power and grandure, as they are remarkable fulfillments of the same prophecies that foretell his destructions, and so are confirmations [of them].

God himself has undertaken to destroy. Rev. 18:8, "Therefore shall her plagues come in one day, death, and mourning, and famine; and she shall be utterly burned with fire: for strong is the Lord God who judgeth."

'Tis abundantly revealed; 'tis sworn for the comfort of the church. Dan. 12:7, "And I heard the man clothed in linen, which was upon the waters of the river, when he held up his right hand and his left hand unto heaven, and sware by him that liveth for ever that it shall be for a time, times, and an half; and when he shall have accomplished to scatter the power of the holy people, all these things shall be finished." Rev. 10:5–6, "And the angel which I saw stand upon the sea and upon the earth lifted up his hand to heaven, and sware by him that liveth for ever and ever, who created heaven, and the things that therein are, and the earth, and the things that therein are, and the sea, and the things which are therein, that there should be time no longer."

[Antichrist] shall be destroyed by the instrumentality of man, and that not only in the use of spiritual but temporal weapons. Rev. 13:10, "He that killeth with the sword [must be killed with the sword]." Ch. 17:16–17, "These shall hate the whore."

Fourth. What great encouragement God has lately given in his providence to seek that he would be with us in the present war.

[What great encouragement has God given,] in so remarkably appearing [in the late expedition], notwithstanding our great provocation.

It seems to be manifest hereby to be a special season of mercy, [an] accepted time, time wherein God is mer[ciful].[10] There are such seasons.

To speak of God after the manner of men: God appears remarkably forward and disposed. There is a voice in his providence, a very plain and loud one. He has declared to us how ready he is, shown us what the benefits are of his presence, shown us what he is ready to do, [and] which side his inclination is to be of (to speak of him after the manner of men).

He has been of our side. God is not apt to change sides, not apt to depart from and forsake a visible people.

A work [of] God is commonly very slow about [manifesting itself]. First, [it comes] to the threshold; Ezek. 9:3, "And the glory of the God of

---

10. Conjectural reading.

Israel was gone up from the cherub, whereupon he was, to the threshold of the house." Then, ch. 10:18, "the glory of the Lord departed from off the threshold of the house." Then, ch. 11:23, "the glory of the Lord went up from the midst of the city, and stood upon the mountain which is on the east side of the city." Hos. 11:8–9, "How shall I give thee up, Ephraim? how shall I deliver thee, Israel? how shall I make thee as Admah? how shall I set thee as Zeboim? mine heart is turned within me, my repentings are kindled together. I will not execute the fierceness of mine anger, I will not return to destroy Ephraim: for I am God, and not man; the Holy One in the midst of thee: and I will not enter into the city."

God has appeared on our side, and he won't change sides, unless we as it were force him and drive him away.

For *Direction* what we should do, in order to God's being with us in the present war.

Four things:

1. Fear him.

He that is thus mighty, [is] the Lord of armies, that does what he will in the armies. [He] disposes the events. It becomes us to fear him, rather than men.

This direction is given in the context, vv. 12–13: "Say ye not, A confederacy, to all them to whom this people shall say, A confederacy; neither fear ye their fear, nor be afraid. Sanctify the Lord of hosts himself; and let him be your fear, and let him be your dread."

Therefore if we would have God with us, stand in awe of God, his commands, {his} threatenings. And take heed that we don't offend him; put away every abomination. The congregation in the wilderness feared men, [but] Caleb and Joshua feared God.

2. We must show gratitude to him for what he has done for us.

Not only by praising him with our lips, but rendering again. If we fail of this, it will be a thing of a dark aspect.

There are many instances in Scripture of God's greatly refusing ingratitude after he has remarkably appeared for his people in war, and they han't rendered again; instances of God's soon turning to be their adversary, and fighting against them. The first I shall take notice of is that mentioned, Is. 63:9–10, "In all their affliction he was afflicted, and the angel of his presence saved them: in his love and in his pity he redeemed them; and he bare them, and carried them all the days of old. But they rebelled, and vexed his holy Spirit: therefore he was turned to be their enemy, and he fought against them." The next I shall mention is that of the same people, after they came into Canaan.[11] Another remarkable instance is that of Gideon. Judg. 8:27, "And Gideon made an ephod thereof, and put it in his city, even in Ophrah: and all Israel went thither a whoring after it: which thing became a snare unto Gideon, and to his house." V. 34, "And the children of Israel remembered not the Lord their God, who had delivered them out of the hands of all their enemies on every side." Another [instance is] David, [and another] Amaziah. 2 Chron. 25:14, etc., "Now it came to pass, after that Amaziah was come from the slaughter of the Edomites, that he brought the gods of the children of Seir, and set them up to be his gods, and bowed down himself before them, and burned incense unto them. Wherefore the anger of the Lord was kindled against Amaziah, and he sent unto him a prophet, which said unto him, Why hast thou sought after the gods of the people, which could not deliver their own people out of thine hand?"

3. Seeking God.

God will be inquired of for great and signal mercies. Earnestly call upon God, and seek him in all duties appointed to that end.

If ye seek him, he will be found of you. 2 Chron. 15:2, "The Lord is with you, while ye be with him; and if ye seek him, he will be found of you; but if ye forsake him, he will forsake you." Is. 45:19, ['tis] not a vain thing to seek God. Jer. 29:12–13, "Then shall ye call upon me, and ye shall go and pray unto me, and I will hearken unto you. And ye shall seek me, and find me, if ye shall search for me with all your heart."

4. Trusting in God.

A people after great success are in danger. [Do] not trust in an arm of flesh. We have many instances of the fatal issue of this. [And we have many instances] of the happy and glorious issue of a trust in God in war. [So] Caleb and Joshua, Deborah, Gideon, David [and] Jehoshaphat, 2 Chron. 20:12, Heb. 11:32–34.

---

11. JE cites here the same texts as he cites for Gideon, below, so we can surmise that he meant to cite some other place or places, including Josh. 7, on the sin of Achan. LL. 18–19 are made of a discarded letter from Rev. Edward Billing of Cold Spring to the Church of Northampton (C72).

The Church of Christ Built on a Rock

March 13, 1746

THIS CONTEST BETWEEN FRANCE and Britain covered a myriad of battlegrounds. The New England volunteers were still flush with their victory at Louisbourg having expelled the French from the fort as well as the shipping lanes of the North Atlantic. Britain moved to support this victory by supporting the colonists financially as well as deploying troops and supplies to make sure they could hold this territorial gain. The machinations of war on the continent continued to cycle through shifting alliances in order to find an equilibrium between France and Britain. However, the contest that dominated British headlines—and imaginations—was the French backed rebellion in Scotland. Charles Edward Stuart, a Catholic with a claim to the British throne, landed in Scotland in the fall of 1745 to lead a rebellion against the Hanoverian George II. With the backing of French troops and supplies, this "Young Pretender's" cause gained momentum in the Scottish highlands capturing the towns of Moidert, Athol, Perth, Berwick-upon-Tweed, and threatening to take the cities of Edinburgh and Glasgow. The British and French contested territory on the continent, in the new world, and now, even on the British mainland.

This contest between Britain and France ran deeper than military units or even national entities. These military contests were absorbed into a larger religious contest between Britain and her "Protestant Interest" and the Catholicism of France and Spain. King George reflected this spiritual contest in his call for recruits to fight the Young Pretender: "Go fight for your Religion, and my Kingdom; and remember Charles, there is no Faith to be kept with Hereticks."[1] This spiritual contest saturated the rhetoric of kings and clergy alike. Since the middle of the sixteenth century, the French embedded Jesuit missionaries with the Native groups along the frontier of North America, winning many converts to Catholicism and allies who aided the French economically and militarily. Economic, territorial, religious, and rhetorical—the contest between French Catholics and British Protestants consumed colonial life in the New World.

In *The Church of Christ Built on a Rock*, Edwards engaged in another contest between Protestants and Catholics: a fight for the meaning of a Biblical text. Preaching on a seminal Catholic text, Matthew 16:18, Edwards sought to "wrest this text wholly out of the abusive hands of [what] the Papists have asserted." Challenging Catholic interpretation, Edwards claimed that the "rock" upon which the church is built does not apply solely to the apostle Peter, as Catholicism claims. Instead, this is a reference to all the prophets and apostles as suggested by Ephesians 2:20.

Edwards continued to demonstrate from Scripture that the gates of hell cannot stand against the church of God—not an individual or even the society of God's people. Here, Edwards shifted the focus from the prophets and apostles to Christ himself. It is the person and work of Christ that provides the assurance that nothing can defeat the people of God. Edwards demonstrated this principle with copious Biblical illustrations of God's people in the Old Testament. He highlighted these Biblical references to illustrate this theological truth to the military struggles of New England in 1746. God always worked to fulfill his promises and this is especially true when "Zion" is threatened by her enemies.

Having claimed victory in the contest over the interpretation of Matthew 16, Edwards shifted back to a spiritual battlefield. The church can participate in prevailing over her enemies, first, by ensuring that they belonged to the true church of Christ. This called Northampton to embrace Edwards's particular brand of Protestant, revivalist piety. The only security to which New England could cling was the superintendence of God. Yet, according to Edwards, one was to "take heed" and "do our part"—a recurring theme of spiritual duties[2]—to ensure such a security. Edwards's preaching participated in the grand contest between Protestantism and Catholicism.

1. *Boston Gazette*, January 7, 1745/46.

2. Reflected in the sermons *The Church of Christ Built on a Rock* and *The Duties of Christians in a Time of War*.

* * * * *

This sermon was edited for the Jonathan Edwards Center by Ken Minkema. The manuscript is ten duodecimo-sized leaves of mixed paper. At the top of the first page, Edwards inscribed, "Fast March. 13. 1745,6 / occasiond by the Rebellion."

The Church of Christ Built on a Rock

Matthew 16:18

Upon this rock will I build my church; and the gates of hell shall not prevail against it.

WE HAVE AN ACCOUNT in the 13th verse, [that Jesus asked his disciples, "Whom do men say that I the Son of man am"?]. What Simon Peter answered is the occasion of the words of the text: ["Thou art the Christ, the Son of the living God," v. 16]. We have Christ's reply in the 17th, 18th and 19th verses: "And Jesus answered and said unto him, Blessed art thou, Simon Barjona: for flesh and blood hath not revealed it unto thee, but my Father which is in heaven. And I say also unto thee, That thou art Peter, and upon this rock I will build my church; and the gates of hell shall not prevail against it. And I will give unto thee the keys of the kingdom of heaven: and whatsoever thou shalt bind on earth shall be bound in heaven: and whatsoever thou shalt loose on earth shall be loosed in heaven."

1. [Here is] a great promise concerning his church: "the gates of hell shall not prevail against it"; that is, those that issue out from those gates, Satan and his angels, those powerful and vast enemies of God's church.

2. A reason [is] implied {in} the strength of its foundation: {it is} built upon a rock.

Opinions of divines have been various concerning what it is that he speaks of when he says, "this rock." Some Protestant divines suppose that what Christ refers to when he says, "this rock," is not Peter but {himself}. They are lead to this by the church of Rome's abuse of the words. They suppose {an apostolic succession starting with Peter}. And therefore many Protestant divines, to wrest this text wholly out of the abusive hands of the Papists, have asserted that {Christ is the foundation of the church}.[1]

But there seems to be no difficulty in allowing that it is Peter that Christ means, when he says, "upon this rock I will build my church." For if this be his meaning, it would be unreasonable to understand anymore by it, than what is plainly asserted in Eph. 2:20, "built on the foundation of the prophets and apostles." [This is a] subordinate foundation {of the church}. Rev. 21:14, "And the wall of the city had twelve foundations, and in them the names of the twelve apostles of the Lamb." And it seems very plain that this is what is nextly intended. {So} Cephas, John 1:42.

And yet it is true that Christ is the only foundation, the only bottom foundation. I Cor. 3:11, "no other foundation can any man lay." And yet others may be secondary foundation {of the church}. 'Tis as 'tis in a building. 1 Pet. 2:4–5, "a spiritual house." And if we understand the words as nextly respecting Peter, yet it comes [to] much the same thing. [Propositions.]

I. Show how the church of Christ is built upon a rock.

II. How that therefore the gates of hell never have, and never will, prevail against it.

I. How {the church of Christ is built} upon a rock.

In general, it is so, as it is built on Christ. This is the foundation which God hath laid in Zion. Is. 28:16, "Behold, I lay in Zion [for a foundation a stone, a tried stone, a precious corner stone"]. This foundation is not a sandy foundation, but a rock, as it is a strong and immoveable and sure foundation. The church is built on Christ, and so on a strong and sure foundation, as it is built on the eternal purpose which God purposed in Christ Jesus. Eph. 3:11, "purposed in Christ Jesus." Eph. 1:4, "chosen us in him."

The church stands on this foundation. 2 Tim. 2:19, "The Lord knoweth them." This is a strong [foundation], built on Christ, as it is built on the eternal, unchangeable love of Christ. Christ loved the church from eternity. Jer. 31:3, "[I have loved thee with an] everlasting love." The church is built on this. 1 John 4:19, "because he first loved us." ['Tis a] strong foundation. John 13:1, "he loved [them] to the end."

[The church is] built on Christ, as built on the eternal promise which God promised in Christ Jesus. We read of this eternal promise, Tit. 1:2.

---

1. See, for example, Poole, *Annotations upon the Holy Bible*, on Matt. 16:18; Henry, *Exposition of All the Books*, 5:114; and Doddridge, *Family Expositor*, 1:545.

God promised his Son from eternity that [the elect shall stand]. This is the foundation on which the church is built, on this ground; the saints are called on this ground, {according to the promise}.

['Tis] a strong foundation, built on Christ, as it is built on the worthiness of Christ. This is the fountain of His faith. This is the ground of all the benefits.

This is a strong foundation. That stone that {the builders rejected} is a sure foundation, because it is a precious corner stone. ['Tis] built on Christ, as 'tis built on God's election of Christ. ['Tis] built on a strong foundation in this respect.

['Tis] built on Christ, as it is built on the purchase of Christ, [on the] prayer and intercession of Christ. ['Tis] built on the blood of Christ.

[The church is] built on Christ, as built on the doctrines and promises of Christ as delivered to us by the apostles and prophets in the holy Scriptures. This is the Word of Christ, which is in many respects the foundation, and on which the church is built. {This is a strong foundation}.

And in this respect principally it is that the church is said to be built on Peter and on other apostles. This is a strong foundation.

['Tis] built on Christ, as it is built on the power of Christ. [This is a] strong foundation.

II. How the gates of hell never have prevail[ed], and never will prevail, against the church.

First. I would show how this is true concerning the particular members of the church.

Second. [I would show how this is true] concerning the church collectively, taken as a body or society.

First. The gates of hell never have prevailed, and never can prevail, against any one particular member {of the church}. [They] never will prevail against any one member {of the church}, so as to overthrow it, so as to hinder its eternal glory. [The] church is constituted of a very great multitude. [There are] members of different degrees: different degrees of grace, different degrees in other respects, but {all part of the church}. Every individual member is built on a Rock. Everyone [is] chosen in Christ. [The] promises [are] made to everyone in Christ Jesus. Christ [was] elected and appointed {a surety} for every one. Christ loved [them]. Gal. 2:20, "[I live by the faith of the Son of God, who] loved me." [Christ] redeemed [and] purchased every one—"gave himself for me"—takes care of every one, as much as if there was but one. Is. 27:12, "[and ye shall be] gathered one by one, [ye children of Israel]." [One is] not overlooked among so great a multitude. In times of great danger {and calamity}, God seals his servants, every one, in his forehead, Rev. 7, at the beginning.

So that the whole church of God, with respect to every member, great and small, shall be preserved. The gates of hell never prevails against any member of the church, in the following respects:

1. [The gates of hell] never prevails to hinder the conversion of one of the elect church. There are great endeavors.

2. {The gates of hell never prevail so as} to draw away one to a total apostasy from Christ. [They] never can destroy that principle of grace, [or] quench the smoking flax. Satan has a great spite. [But he] can't draw off {believers} from a belief of the gospel, [so as] entirely and finally to embrace any fundamental error. Matt. 24:24, "if it were possible, they shall deceive the very elect." [So] Peter: [Christ] prayed for him,[2] "that thy faith fail not."

[The gates of hell shall not] draw away their hearts from Christ, [so as to] alienate their affections. [Their] love [shall not] wax cold [Matt. 24:12]. [They shall remain] virgins [Matt. 25].

[The gates of hell shall not draw them] away from the practice of holiness into ways[3] of wickedness. [The elect shall be supported, so they] cannot sin.

Great are the endeavors of the gates of hell. [They have] great subtilty, [and are] unwearied.

Reasons

[The church is] built on Christ. [They shall] in no wise [be] cast out. John 10:27–28, "My sheep hear my voice, and I know them, . . . none shall pluck them out of my hand."

[They] have the promise of Christ for a foundation of their perseverance. 1 Thess. 5:23–24, "Faithful is he that hath called you."

[They have the] merits of Christ: [his] intercessions, election [and] eternal promise.

[They are] united to a risen Savior.

3. [The gates of hell shall not prevail against the church,] so as to hinder their progress in a way of holiness and final victory over sin.

---

2. MS: "them."

3. MS: "into among way."

Philip. 1:6, "being confident of this very thing, [that he which hath begun a good work in you will] carry it on."

4. [The gates of hell shall not prevail against the church, so as] to procure their damnation, or hinder their everlasting glory. [The devil] finds means to destroy great multitudes. Satan thirsts for their blood, as a hungry lion. If he has as it were actually convinced 'em into his den—Cant. 4:8, "the lions' dens, and from the mountain of leopards"—yea, if they are actually between the teeth {of the lion, yet they} shall be rescued, 1 Sam. 17:35.

God will take care when the saints come to die. [The devils will] gnash with their teeth, [but God] will take care at the day of judgment.

Secondly. The gates of hell never have prevailed, and never will prevail, against the church as a society or collective body, maintained through successive generations, in these two respects:

1. So as ever to extirpate the church out of the world; or,

2. So as to hinder her finally obtaining that glorious victory over all her enemies, and that possession of the whole earth, which God has promised her.

1. The gates of hell never have, and never will, prevail against the church, so as wholly to root out [the church], so but that God evermore has had a church in the world, from the first founding it after the fall, and will have to the end of the world.

The church of God in the world is often in Scriptures called God's and Christ's kingdom, by way of eminency; 'tis his part. And the Scripture reveals this difference between Christ's kingdom and other kingdoms [of] that [worldly] nature: his is an everlasting kingdom. Other religions are overthrown; heresies fail, [and] the worship of false gods. But that God's church never should be extirpated {out of the world}, this is a truth abundantly manifest from the Scriptures. Ps. 72:5, "[They shall] fear thee as long as the sun and moon endure, throughout all generations." V. 7, "In his days shall the righteous flourish; and abundance of peace so long as the moon endureth." V. 15, "And he shall live, and to him shall be given of the gold of Sheba: prayer also shall be made for him continually; and daily shall he be praised." V. 17, "is name shall endure for ever: his name shall be continued as long as the sun: and men shall be blessed in him: all nations shall call him blessed." Ps. 102:25, etc., "Of old hast thou laid the foundation of the earth: and the heavens are the work of thy hands. They shall perish, but thou shalt endure: yea, all of them shall wax old like a garment; as a vesture shalt thou change them, and they shall be changed: but thou art the same, and thy years shall have no end. The children of thy servants shall continue, and their seed shall be established before thee." Ps. 145:4, "One generation shall praise thy works to another, and shall declare thy mighty acts." V. 13, "Thy kingdom is an everlasting kingdom, and thy dominion endureth throughout all generations." Is. 9:6–7, "For unto us a child is born, unto us a son is given: and the government shall be upon his shoulder: and his name shall be called Wonderful, Counselor, The mighty God, The everlasting Father, The Prince of Peace. Of the increase of his government and peace there shall be no end, upon the throne of David, and upon his kingdom, to order it, and to establish it with judgment and with justice from henceforth even for ever." Is. 51:7–8, "Hearken unto me, ye that know righteousness, the people in whose heart is my law; fear ye not the reproach of men, neither be ye afraid of their revilings. For the moth shall eat them up like a garment, and the worm shall eat them like wool: but my righteousness shall be for ever, and my salvation from generation to generation." Is. 54:15–17, "Behold, they shall surely gather together, but not by me: whosoever shall gather together against thee shall fall for thy sake. Behold, I have created the smith that bloweth the coals in the fire, and that bringeth forth an instrument for his work; and I have created the waster to destroy. No weapon that is formed against thee shall prosper; and every tongue that shall rise against thee in judgment thou shalt condemn. This is the heritage of the servants of the Lord, and their righteousness is of me, saith the Lord." [Is.] 59:21, "As for me, this is my covenant with them, saith the Lord; My spirit that is upon thee, and my words which I have put in thy mouth, shall not depart out of thy mouth, nor out of the mouth of thy seed, nor out of the mouth of thy seed's seed, saith the Lord, from henceforth and for ever." Ch. 66:9, "Shall I bring to the birth, and not cause to bring forth? saith the Lord: shall I cause to bring forth, and shut the womb?" Jer. 33:17 to the end,

Be not a terror unto me: thou art my hope in the day of evil. Let them be confounded that persecute me, but let not me be confounded: let them be dismayed, but let not me be dismayed: bring upon them the day of evil, and destroy them with double destruction. Thus said the Lord unto me; Go and stand in the gate of the children of the people, whereby the kings of Judah come in, and by the which they go out, and in all the gates of Jerusalem; and say unto them, Hear ye the word of the Lord, ye kings of Judah, and all Judah, and all the inhabitants of Jerusalem, that enter in by these gates: thus saith the Lord; Take heed to yourselves, and bear no burden on the sabbath day, nor bring it in by the gates of Jerusalem; neither carry forth a burden out of your houses on the sabbath day, neither do ye any work, but hallow ye the sabbath day, as I commanded your fathers. But they obeyed not, neither inclined their ear, but made their neck stiff, that they might not hear, nor receive instruction. And it shall come to pass, if ye diligently hearken unto me, saith the Lord, to bring in no burden through the gates of this city on the sabbath day, but hallow the sabbath day, to do no work therein; then shall there enter into the gates of this city kings and princes sitting upon the throne of David, riding in chariots and on horses, they, and their princes, the men of Judah, and the inhabitants of Jerusalem: and this city shall remain for ever. And they shall come from the cities of Judah, and from the places about Jerusalem, and from the land of Benjamin, and from the plain, and from the mountains, and from the south, bringing burnt offerings, and sacrifices, and meat offerings, and incense, and bringing sacrifices of praise, unto the house of the Lord. But if ye will not hearken unto me to hallow the sabbath day, and not to bear a burden, even entering in at the gates of Jerusalem on the sabbath day; then will I kindle a fire in the gates thereof, and it shall devour the palaces of Jerusalem, and it shall not be quenched. Dan. 7:14, "And there was given him dominion, and glory, and a kingdom, that all people, nations, and languages, should serve him: his dominion is an everlasting dominion, which shall not pass away, and his kingdom that which shall not be destroyed." Ps. 109:25, etc., "I became also a reproach unto them: when they looked upon me they shaked their heads. Help me, O Lord my God: O save me according to thy mercy: that they may know that this is thy hand; that thou, Lord, hast done it. Let them curse, but bless thou: when they arise, let them be ashamed; but let thy servant rejoice. Let mine adversaries be clothed with shame, and let them cover themselves with their own confusion, as with a mantle. I will greatly praise the Lord with my mouth; yea, I will praise him among the multitude. For he shall stand at the right hand of the poor, to save him from those that condemn his soul."

['Tis] implied that the church as a society on the earth, in the enjoyment of ordinances and means of grace, shall continue to the end of the world. Eph. 4:11–13, "And he gave some, apostles; and some, prophets; and some, evangelists; and some, pastors and teachers; for the perfecting of the saints, for the work of the ministry, for the edifying of the body of Christ: till we all come in the unity of the faith, and of the knowledge of the Son of God, unto a perfect man, unto the measure of the stature of the fulness of Christ."

That prophecy, Jer. 31:35–36, "Thus saith the Lord, which giveth the sun for a light by day, and the ordinances of the moon and of the stars for a light by night, which divideth the sea when the waves thereof roar; the Lord of hosts is his name: If those ordinances depart from before me, saith the Lord, then the seed of Israel also shall cease from being a nation before me for ever," {implies that the church shall} never cease to be a nation. [This is] is true both of Israel according to the flesh, and also the spiritual Israel.

[Christ] promised to be with his ministers to the end of the world, in teaching and baptizing. Matt. 28:19–20, "Go ye therefore, and teach all nations, baptizing them in the name of the Father, and of the Son, and of the Holy Ghost: teaching them to observe all things whatsoever I have commanded you: and, lo, I am with you always, even unto the end of the world. Amen."

Great have been the endeavors that have been used by the gates of hell {to extirpate the church, which} was since the church was first set up in the world. All the powers of hell have been engaged. We read of the war there is [to be], in Rev. 12. This continued, unwearied, inveterate opposition {of the gates of hell}, is a contingence of that curse upon the serpent, Gen. 3:15, "And I will put enmity between thee and the woman, and between thy seed and her seed; it shall bruise thy head, and thou shalt bruise his heel." There is a very great army. The devils are spirits of great strength; [they] possess arts[4] of great subtilty. And there is a very great army: the number is figuratively represented, Rev. 9:16, "two hundred thousand thousand."

[The devils] act with united strength and subtilty. It torments the devil to see the church of God standing. [Satan] uses all manner of endeavors. [He] endeavors to prevent the church's being upheld, by striving to hinder the conversion of sinners, fighting against grace in the saints, introducing corruption into the church of God, broaching and propagating heresies. Innumerable have been the heresies, infidelity and false religions, leading off gradually from the Word of God as their rule, leading men off from ordinances of the gospel, propagating false religion instead of true experimental piety. In this way he hath often [endeavored] by promoting immorality and profaneness, by stirring up open opposition

---

4. Conjectural reading where the words are poorly formed.

against the church of God, filling the princes and nations of the world with a hatred to it, and stirring them to oppose it by war and persecution. [Satan] endeavors to root out the church, by killing all, [through] open war, massacres, secret plots, by wearing out the saints with lingering torments.

Never [was] any society or sect of men so persecuted; no sect of men [has] ever suffered so much from their fellow creatures. But yet God has ever upheld his church. The church has been like a weak and tender plant growing out of the earth: not a strong tree, but as a reed. {The church has} often been bruised. But {God has ever upheld her}.

The open opposition began with Cain. When the inhabitants of the earth were multiplied afterwards, Satan seemed almost to swallow up the church of God by the increase of idolatry and heathenism: stirring up Laban [Gen. 29], stirring up Esau [Gen. 27]. Great were the endeavors of the gates of hell against the church in Egypt: by stirring up Pharaoh to destroy the children [of Israel], by cruel bondage, by prevailing ignorance and idolatry among the Israelites. Ezek. 20:5, etc.,

And say unto them, Thus saith the Lord God; In the day when I chose Israel, and lifted up mine hand unto the seed of the house of Jacob, and made myself known unto them in the land of Egypt, when I lifted up mine hand unto them, saying, I am the Lord your God; in the day that I lifted up mine hand unto them, to bring them forth of the land of Egypt into a land that I had espied for them, flowing with milk and honey, which is the glory of all lands: then said I unto them, Cast ye away every man the abominations of his eyes, and defile not yourselves with the idols of Egypt: I am the Lord your God. But they rebelled against me, and would not hearken unto me: they did not every man cast away the abominations of their eyes, neither did they forsake the idols of Egypt: then I said, I will pour out my fury upon them, to accomplish my anger against them in the midst of the land of Egypt.

Ch. 23:3, "And they committed whoredoms in Egypt; they committed whoredoms in their youth: there were their breasts pressed, and there they bruised the teats of their virginity." So ch. 24:14, "I the Lord have spoken it: it shall come to pass, and I will do it; I will not go back, neither will I spare, neither will I repent; according to thy ways, and according to thy doings, shall they judge thee, saith the Lord God."

After the children of Israel were gone forth {out of Egypt, the devil sought to oppose them} by stirring up Pharaoh to pursue {them}. Ex. 15:9, "The enemy said, I will pursue, I will overtake, I will divide the spoil;

my lust shall be satisfied upon them; I will draw my sword, my hand shall destroy them." [So also by] stirring up Amalek,[5] drawing the people away to idolatry at Mt. Sinai, by hardening the hearts of that wicked generation, and stirring them up from time to time to such perverse behaviors: [to choose one] among them, to make 'im a captain; the opposition of Sihon and Og [Deut. 29:7]; corrupting them in the matter of Peor [Num. 31:16]. [So the devil sought to oppose the church by] stirring up such a mighty opposition of the nations of Canaan, from time to time promoting idolatry in Israel in the time of the Judges, stirring up the neighboring nations mightily to oppose Israel.

[So] in his endeavors to extirpate the true religion in the times of the kings: [in] Ahab's time, Manasseh's time. The rest of the land [was] almost lost by Sennacharib's war. [So] Zarah the Ethiopian, 2 Chron. 14:9, etc., "And there came out against them Zerah the Ethiopian with an host of a thousand thousand, and three hundred chariots; and came unto Mareshah. Then Asa went out against him, and they set the battle in array in the valley of Zephathah at Mareshah. And Asa cried unto the Lord his God, and said, Lord, it is nothing with thee to help, whether with many, or with them that have no power: help us, O Lord our God; for we rest on thee, and in thy name we go against this multitude. O Lord, thou art our God; let no man prevail against thee. So the Lord smote the Ethiopians before Asa, and before Judah; and the Ethiopians fled." [So the] Ammonites and Moabites and Edomites, 2 Chron. 20, v. 12, "we have no might against this great company." [So] Rabshakeh and his army [2 Kgs. 18].

[God preserved them] in the time of the Babylonish captivity, [and] after their return, preserving them from the continual plots of the Samaritans and governors on their side the River Euphrates. [So] in Esther's time. [And] afterwards often, especially in the time of Antiochus Epiphanes.

When true religion ran very low, and the church of God was greatly reduced by the overspreading of the principles of Pharisees and Sadducees, God sent John the Baptist, who was followed by Jesus Christ. Satan made a dreadful attack on the church of Christ at the time of Christ's last sufferings [and] afterwards, in the great persecutions of the Jews, mimicking the works of the Spirit of God by the works of a false spirit; by

---

5. See Gen. 17, Judg. 6.

the many heresies; by the Inquisition [and] violent persecutions; by the Arian heresy.⁶

But the greatest opposition that ever Satan made against the Christian church, and that by which he prevailed most and for the longest time, and came the nearest to wholly rooting of it out, was that which was made by Antichrist. But God upheld [her].

About the same time that Antichrist first appeared in the world, Mahomet appeared and broached his imposture.

Since the Reformation, very great endeavors have been used to extirpate⁷ the Protestant religion out of the world, which the Papists call "The Northern Heresy."

But never perhaps was so grand a scheme laid by the Papists' powers to overthrow the Protestant church, as in the time of King James the II of England, the present Pretender's pretended father.

[And] as the church never has been as yet overthrown—it has stood {all of these attempts}—so, we may be assured, it never will be. There is yet mighty opposition to be expected.

2. The gates of hell can't prevail so against the church, as to prevent its finally obtaining that glorious victory over all her enemies, and that possession of the whole earth that God has promised.

'Tis with the church in the world, as 'tis with grace in the hearts of the saints.

Application

[I.] What has been said, should bid us to acknowledge and adore the faithfulness [of God]. We have Christ's promise in the text. I have mentioned many other promises, and we have observed how God has hitherto fulfilled [them].

God's faithfulness in those things is the more conspicuous, by reason of the church's weakness: [they are] commonly small, few in numbers, chiefly of the poorer sort. [They are] in times of the greatest opposition without any secular power, without temporal advantages. [They are] like the people of Israel in Deborah's time, like a little fire, a spark enkindled from heaven and ever maintained. The church has been like a weak and

---

6. Named after Arius (250–336 CE), who was condemned at the Council of Nicea (325 CE) for arguing that the Son was created by Father, and was therefore inferior.

7. MS: "Extirpart."

tender plant growing out of the earth,[8] not like a strong tree, but like a small reed. [The church has] been often bruised, but never broken. So is that fulfilled, Is. 42:3, [he] will not break the bruised reed. It has been often like the burning bush in Mt. Sinai, like Moses in the river, like the lamb in the paw of the lion and the bear that David delivered. The faithfulness and immutability of God will appear that more conspicuous in thus preserving his church, if we consider how miserable those are that the church is constituted of.

Again, the faithfulness of God to his church in thus preserving it, will appear the more wonderful if we consider the dangers the church has often been in: how dreadful the storms, [on the] brink of ruin. [Their enemies] often swallowed them down in their own imagination. [The church has] been like Shadrach, Meshach [and Abednego] in the burning fiery furnace [Dan. 3]. God has remarkably fulfilled that promise, Is. 43:2, "when thou passest through the waters, [I will be with thee]." [The church has] been like Noah's ark, like the ship where Christ was, [like] Daniel in the lions' den.

Yea, sometimes the church has to appearance been overcome and swallowed up. Enemies have triumphed [over her]. [So in] Nebuchadnezzar's time; so in Diocletian's time;[9] so in the darkest times of papacy. Rev. 11:7, etc., "And when they shall have finished their testimony, the beast that ascendeth out of the bottomless pit shall make war against them, and shall overcome them, and kill them. And their dead bodies shall lie in the street of the great city, which spiritually is called Sodom and Egypt, where also our Lord was crucified. And they of the people and kindreds and tongues and nations shall see their dead bodies three days and an half, and shall not suffer their dead bodies to be put in graves. And they that dwell upon the earth shall rejoice over them, and make merry, and shall send gifts one to another."

But then it has proved otherwise: suddenly, a great revival [occurred], like Jonah in the whale's belly, like the corn that was cut down in Hezekiah's time. Is. 37:30, etc., "And this shall be a sign unto thee, Ye shall eat this year such as groweth of itself; and the second year that which springeth of the same: and in the third year sow ye, and reap, and plant vineyards, and eat the fruit thereof. And the remnant that is escaped of the house of Judah shall again take root downward, and bear

---

8. See the sermon on Jonah 4:6–7, no. 805, Jan. 1746, for an exploration of this theme but applied to an individual.

9. Roman Emperor who instigated persecution of Christians starting in 302 CE.

fruit upward: for out of Jerusalem shall go forth a remnant, and they that escape out of mount Zion: the zeal of the Lord of hosts shall do this."[10]

Again, the faithfulness {of God has been} the more wonderful, if we consider the unworthiness of the church.

II. Hence we may learn how happy a society the church of God is: how highly favored of God, that thus has the most high God for her refuge, her strength, that none of her enemies can prevail [against], though so many [and] so great.

{We may learn how happy a society the church of God is,} that God has actually appeared so wonderfully for her defense. And how happy is every member of this society, which never can be overthrown. There is no other such societies. As to those societies which have depended on the most noted of the false gods, [they have been overthrown]. There have been other societies that have been protected with the greatest human strength, cities with walls as it were up to heaven. But no other society has such a foundation, such strong bulwarks. It may well be said of the church of God, as Ps. 48:12–14, "Walk round about Jerusalem, count the towers."

III. What great encouragement there is, for those who have the interest of Zion at heart, to hope [and] pray for her preservation at such times as when her overthrow is especially attempted by her enemies. We are often directed to pray for the restoration, peace and prosperity of the church of God. What we have heard, affords us great encouragement so to do. Though God has promised {that the enemies of the church shall not prevail}, yet 'tis his revealed will that it should be done in answer to the prayers of the church. Rev. 8:3, etc., "And another angel came and stood at the altar, having a golden censer; and there was given unto him much incense, that he should offer it with the prayers of all [the] saints." [So,] as God delivered Jonah out of the belly of hell, in answer to prayer. God often brings his church into great straits, for that end, to bring her to look to him and earnestly to seek his face. Hos. 5:15, "in their affliction they will seek me early." There ought to be this sort of evidence in opposition to the violence of Satan, as Jacob [Gen. 33].

The present great attempt made by the powers of hell and the church of Rome against the Protestant religion, in {attempting to set up the

---

10. See the sermon on Is. 37:31, no. 811, Mar. 1746.

Pretender}, should have this effect in all that love Zion, and prefer it to their chief joy: to awaken them to cry the more earnestly to God, not only that this attempt may be defeated, but that God would speedily bring on that glorious victory {of his church over her enemies}. The present dispensations of providence ought to be looked upon as a loud call of God to his people to do this: for God waits, that he may be gracious.

[*Directions*]

Before I conclude, I would mention two or three things by way of *Direction*, with respect to the duties that should properly attend our praying for the church of God, that the gates of hell may not prevail against it.

1. We ought to give diligence, to make it sure to ourselves that we are some of the true church of Christ.

2. We should take heed to ourselves, that the devil don't prevail against it.

3. [We should] do our part, that the devil don't prevail against that part of the church of God to which we more especially belong. Particular parts of the church of God may fail, [and] oftentimes [have] failed [in] particular towns, cities, kingdoms, yea, vast regions of the face of the earth. The church of Ephesus was warned, Rev. 2:5, "Remember therefore from whence thou art fallen, and repent, and do the first works; or else I will come unto thee quickly, and will remove thy candlestick out of his place, except thou repent." Every church should take the warning: we at this day especially, when the threatening aspects of divine providence are such as they are. We should do our part, that the devil don't prevail against this part of the church of God by apostasy, leading us on to such degrees of wickedness as to provoke God to remove our candlestick {out of its place}. This we should do, by doing our utmost to suppress iniquity, to promote [godliness] by keeping our garments pure, and by being blameless and harmless as the sons of God "in the midst of a crooked and perverse nation," and by shining amongst them [Philip. 2:15].

The People of God Going Forth to War

June 1746

FRENCH CATHOLIC ENCROACHMENT MUST have seemed stifling by the late Spring of 1746. The French-backed Scottish rebels defeated the forces of the king at Falkirk in January, prompting King George II to appoint his son, Duke of Cumberland, hero of Dettingen, commander of the armies in the north. Developments on the continent were so fluid, despite the considerable attention given it in the *Boston Gazette*, progress must have been hard to observe in this contest with the French. The *Gazette's* description of Catholicism as a "profane and ostentatious system of iniquity" demonstrated a colonial attachment to Protestant British identity.[1] Encroachment of French and Native forces into the Hudson River Valley became the most immediate threat to Northampton and her citizens.

Descriptions of Native ambushes in the *Gazette* focused on the swiftness, cruelty, and proximity of such attacks. One such "depredation" visited three men from Saratoga, killing one, capturing another, and the third escaped to tell the tale. The papers described these attacks as "daring and insolent" because they happened to colonists at work on their farms "in sight of their settlements."[2] From April to June, eighteen persons were killed and taken (including four "negroes") and over one hundred houses burnt and cattle taken.[3] Despite their new and formidable outpost at the mouth of the St. Lawrence, New York and New England never anticipated peace.

1. *Boston Gazette*, April 29, 1746.
2. *Boston Gazette*, June 3, 1746.
3. *Boston Gazette*, June 10, 1746.

By the end of June, the *Boston Gazette* reported on a letter from the Duke of Newcastle that promised to ease New England's fears. The king had ordered an expedition to oust the French from their foothold in North America.[4] The colonies were to raise men and monies to execute the invasion plan of 1690. Troops were to gather in Albany to move against Montreal while another force gathered in Boston to sail to Quebec. Edwards's uncle, Col. Stoddard, promoted this plan and enthusiastically set about to recruit a sufficient force to achieve their freedom from "popish tyranny."

Edwards implored his congregation to support this measure in his text from Nehemiah encouraging Israel to "fight for your brethren, your sons, and your daughters, your wives, and your houses." In many ways, this sermon reflected the interests of *Duties of Christians in a Time of War* by offering a defense of military action. Military action is not merely lawful but a duty when defending one's homes and religion. Edwards even touched on the principle of proportionality in war: "The greater [the] trial, [the] greater manifestations of the degree of good principle, [the] greater exercise of regard to duty." This duty is owed to God, to one's country, and to one's self.

This defense of just warfare transitions in the Application to a call to arms. God's people are to "exert and expose" themselves in warfare and are not called upon "indolently to lie still and suffer. Because we are safest in the way of our duty." Edwards continued to warn parents not to prevent their children from serving or allow husbandry and private business to interfere with military service because, "'tis to be feared they would not be in God's way nor in the way of his blessing."

Edwards preached this sermon in support of the proposed expedition to Canada because it was a means by which he could promote his religious program.[5] In collaboration with his uncle, Col. Stoddard, Edwards promoted military action because the removal of Catholic forces to the north would allow his brand of revivalism to expand into new territories furthering his cosmic vision for the Protestant Empire.

* * * * *

This sermon was edited for the Jonathan Edwards Center by Ken Minkema. The manuscript is fourteen duodecimo-sized leaves of mixed paper. Edwards wrote at the top of the first page, "preceding the Expedition to Canada June 1746."

4. *Boston Gazette*, June 24, 1746.
5. Cf. Cuthbert, "More Swiftly Propagating the Gospel," 153–68.

The People of God Going Forth to War[1]

Nehemiah 4:14

And I looked, and rose up, and said unto the nobles, and to the rulers, and to the rest of the people, Be not ye afraid of them: remember the Lord, which is great and terrible, and fight for your brethren, your sons, and your daughters, your wives, and your houses.

WE HAVE AN ACCOUNT in the foregoing verses [of how the Samaritans, under Sanballat and Tobiah, conspired to attack the Jews as they rebuilt the walls of Jerusalem, and of Nehemiah's arming the people]. In the words of the text, we may observe:

1. The duty that Nehamy[2] recommends to the people on this occasion, viz., fighting with their enemies.

2. To whom the duty is recommended: "[to the nobles, and to the rulers, and to the rest of the people]."

3. Who are spoken of, as those that they should have a regard to in the performance: in the first place, to God; nextly mentioned are this people; then those persons and things they were more immediately interested in.

Doctrine

When a people of God are molested and endangered by an injurious and bloody enemies, for them cheerfully to exert and expose themselves in a

---

1. Also referred to as "Preceding the Expedition to Canada, June 1746."
2. The familiar form of the name "Nehemiah."

war tending to their defense and safety, is a good work and a duty they owe to God, their country, and themselves.

I. I would show that war, in such a case, is lawful and a duty.

II. I shall take notice of some things that do show, that for persons in such a case cheerfully to exert and expose themselves, it may especially be said to be a good work.

III. [I] would observe particularly, how it is a duty that persons in such a case owe to God, to their country and themselves.

I. I would show, in the general, that when a people are molested and endangered by an injurious and bloody enemy, it is lawful and a duty for them to engage in a war, tending to their own defense.

II. [I shall] take notice of some things that show it to be especially a good work for a people of God, when they are molested and endangered {by an injurious and bloody enemy}, cheerfully to exert and expose themselves in a war, tending to their defense and safety.

First. It appears from the nature of the work.

Now here, I would observe, that there are two things that do especially render a work that is agreeable to duty, and done for a right end, eminently a good work. And,

1. [When] the self-denial that attends it is great.
2. When the good or benefit it tends to is great.

1. When duty is performed from a right spirit, with great self-denial, it renders it eminently a good work.

The greater trial [there is in a duty, the] greater manifestations of the degree of good principle, [and the] greater exercise of regard to duty, the more it shows how much men are influenced by good,[3] and how far they are carried beyond self, and are devoted and give up themselves to duty. And hence, the greater difficulty and self-denial {there is in a duty}, the more acceptable to God {is it}, and the greater reward; as is abundantly manifest in Scripture, where a great and distinguished reward is often promised to great degrees of self-denial and suffering in the ways of duty, and from a right regard to duty. Matt. 5:10–12, "Blessed are they which are persecuted for righteousness' sake: for theirs is the kingdom of heaven. Blessed are ye, when men shall revile you, and persecute you, and

---

3. MS: "Conscience a good."

shall say all manner of evil against you falsely, for my sake. Rejoice, and be exceeding glad: for great is your reward in heaven: for so persecuted they the prophets which were before you." Matt. 19:29, "And every one that hath forsaken houses, or brethren, or sisters, or father, or mother, or wife, or children, or lands, for my name's sake, shall receive an hundredfold, and shall inherit everlasting life." 2 Tim. 2:11, "It is a faithful saying: If we suffer with him, we shall also live with him." 1 Pet. 4:13, "But rejoice, inasmuch as ye are partakers of Christ's sufferings; that, when his glory shall be revealed, ye may be glad also with exceeding joy."

But now that duty which is spoken of in the Doctrine, viz., persons' cheerfully exerting and exposing themselves {in a war tending to their defense}, is a work often attended with much difficulty and self-denial. If persons in such a war lose their lives complying with this work from a proper regard to their duty, 'tis one way of doing this great and eminent[4] Christian duty that Christ[5] recommends, 1 John 3:16, "[we] ought to lay down our lives for the brethren"; and so a fulfillment of that new command of Christ, John 13:34, "[That ye love one another]."

2. Another thing that renders a duty performed with a proper regard to duty, to be eminently a good work, is when it is a work that tends to great good and benefit.

All good works are not equally good, and one reason is more good [than another]. And so a man does more good by it, more fruit is brought forth. There is a more plentiful harvest of good fruits and consequences. To do good, and to do works materially good, are the same thing. And consequently, the more good persons do in what they do, and the more good what they do has a tendency to, the more eminently good is the work. As he that by his charity relieves a great number {of poor, the more he relieves, the more eminently good is the work}. As in evil works, the more hurt is done {to a greater number of people}, the more mischief, the more wicked the work. God is pleased to distinguish those of his servants with the most eminent rewards, that with a proper regard to their duty to him, do the most good: for they serve him the most; they bring forth the most fruit. [God] rewards men "according to the fruit of their doings," Jer. 17:10.

But this work that is spoken of in the Doctrine, is on this account eminently a good work. These things do show the work spoken of in the Doctrine to be a good work, especially when persons are voluntary in it,

---

4. The middle of this word is missing due to MS damage.
5. Conjecture for MS damage.

and do exert and expose themselves of their own free will from a regard to their duty, and not as being forced or pressed. Thus it appears from the nature of the work.

Second. The work spoken of {in the Doctrine}, appears to be a good [work], and in some respects eminently so, by the manifestations God has from time to time given in[6] his Word of his special approbation of it.

With what high encomiums are they spoken of by the Spirit of God in the song of Deborah, that {was made after the death of Sisera and the defeat of the Canaanites}. The people then were greatly molested; Judg. 5:6–7, "In the days of Shamgar the son of Anath, in the days of Jael, the highways were unoccupied, and the travelers walked through byways. The inhabitants of the villages ceased, they ceased in Israel." [They] could not attend their business, v. 11. [Jabin king of the Canaanites] mightily oppressed Israel, ch. 4:3. There was then a loud call, and many did cheerfully {offer themselves}. And how highly are they {praised}, ch. 5:2. Particular notice is taken who they were, and it is rewarded by the Spirit of God to their everlasting honor throughout all generations, vv. 14–15. What a note of honor [is] put on Jael, v. 24, "Blessed above women shall Jael the wife of Heber the Kenite be, blessed shall she be above women in the tent."

And what a special note of approbation have we of the behavior of the two tribes and [an] half, and left on record {in Scripture}. Josh. 22, at the beginning, "Then Joshua called the Reubenites, and the Gadites, and the half tribe of Manasseh, and said unto them, Ye have kept all that Moses the servant of the Lord commanded you, and have obeyed my voice in all that I commanded you: ye have not left your brethren these many days unto this day, but have kept the charge of the commandment of the Lord your God. And now the Lord your God hath given rest unto your brethren, as he promised them: therefore now return ye, and get you unto your tents, and unto the land of your possession, which Moses the servant of the Lord gave you on the other side Jordan."

And how are the names of those that exerted and exposed themselves in war for David, after he had long been molested and endangered by his injurious and bloody enemies, [recorded], 1 Chron. 12:1–13. [They] exposed themselves to difficulties and dangers; v. 8, "And of the Gadites there separated themselves unto David into the hold to the wilderness

---

6. MS: "to."

men of might, and men of war fit for the battle, that could handle shield and buckler, whose faces were like the faces of lions, and were as swift as the roes upon the mountains." V. 15, "These are they that went over Jordan in the first month, when it had overflown all his banks; and they put to flight all them of the valleys, both toward the east, and toward the west." What an high expression was there of the approbation of the Spirit of God of their behavior in the time of it; v. 18, "Then the spirit came upon Amasai, who was chief of the captains, and he said, Thine are we, David, and on thy side, thou son of Jesse: peace, peace be unto thee, and peace be to thine helpers; for thy God helpeth thee." The names of some are here recorded with great honor, that helped David against the band of the rovers; v. 21, "And they helped David against the band of the rovers: for they were all mighty men of valor, and were captains in the host." Those that came to David to help out, are spoken of with honor, and those "that had understanding of the times, to know what Israel ought to do"; v. 32, "And of the children of Issachar, which were men that had understanding of the times, to know what Israel ought to do." And God has been pleased to cause the names of those persons {that exerted themselves}, to be enrolled {in the Scriptures}.

And so 'tis recorded how the people[7] denied themselves in Nehemiah's[8] time, and what hardships and dangers they exposed themselves to, [to] resist the injurious enemies—how they held a weapon in one hand; [how they endured] extraordinary fatigue; denied themselves their usual meat[9] and sleep; never put off their clothes, day nor night—in the chapter wherein is the text.

III. [I will] show how the duty spoken of in {the Doctrine}, is a duty they[10] owe to God, their country and themselves.

First. ['Tis a duty that men owe] to God, as 'tis a duty he requires. [This is] one means God has appointed for the suppressing[11] iniquity, [the] defense of human society, and the defense of his church.

[God has] appointed {military leaders}, as he has appointed civil magistracy. Military officers in such a case are God's ministers, in the

---

7. The first half of this word is missing due to MS damage.
8. The beginning of this word is missing due to MS damage.
9. This word is a conjecture where the MS is damaged.
10. MS: "we."
11. Conjectural reading of a poorly written word.

same sense that it is said of the civil magistrate in Rom. 13:4, "he is the minister of God to thee for good"; [v.] 6, "they are God's ministers, attending continually upon this very thing."

And as the duty spoken of, is attended often with special self-denial, so 'tis[12] a duty that is especially to his honor, when performed from regard to him.

Second. ['Tis a] duty that men owe to their country. [We] ought to love [our] neighbors as ourselves, and accordingly to do our part.

Third. {'Tis a duty that men owe} to themselves, as they are members of the society [that is] injured and endangered. Especially is it commonly so in some parts of a professing land.

Application

I proceed now to apply this Doctrine to the case of the people of God in this land, and particularly in this part of the land, with regard to our present circumstances, as grievously molested {by an injurious and bloody enemy}; and especially with regard to the present call given in divine [providence] to the people of this land, to exert themselves in the proposed expedition against Canada.

To be sure, the case that is signified in the text and Doctrine, is eminently the case of this land at this day. You have heard that in such a case, it is a good work and a duty {that is required of us}. Therefore, as we are professing Christians and a covenant people of God, we ought seriously to consider of what we have heard, and be careful that we don't fail of so great a duty that is required of us.

And here, let us consider the remarkable loudness of the call of providence to this land at this very time, cheerfully and vigorously to exert themselves. This will appear from many considerations:

If we consider how greatly this land has been molested.

And it will further appear, if we consider how notoriously injuriously [our enemies have treated us].

And particularly this will appear, if it be considered how greatly and cruelly, and how unjustly, we are oppressed by our enemies at this time. [They] have been applied to from time to time. Our enemies, in some

---

12. Conjectural reading of a word where the MS is damaged.

respects, have greater advantages to exert their cruelty, {by virtue of} a strong fortress on our border,[13] and do greatly improve it.

We seem to be especially called at this time, {because} the enemy this year, and at this time in particular, do press hard upon us.[14] And then we have a special call at this time, as now we are called upon, by the authority of the nation, {who are the} ministers of God, which, it may be, will not be anymore {heeded}.

As the call is extraordinary by reason of our extraordinary necessity, so {too by reason of our} opportunity {for it}: never did divine providence seem to open such a door: [not] in the first expedition, [nor] in the second.[15] We have good evidence that the authority of the nation are now sincere {in their intentions}.[16]

Now [we] have special advantage in our hands that we never had before, in that we are possessed of Cape Breton. [This is a] season of special advantage by reason of the present circumstances of the French nation.[17] Another circumstance especially tending to encourage us, is {the appearance of providence} in the appointment of the Admiral[18] {to lead the expedition}. Another {circumstance tending to encourage us, is} that so much that appertains to the affair, is betrusted in the hands of our Governor.[19]

The call to us in this part of the land especially seems to be very loud. The land never had such a call, never such a door opened, [or] so fair an opportunity.

And although providence did in some respect remarkably frown upon many of our soldiers the last year, that went on the expedition

---

13. Probably a reference to Fort St. Frédèric, at Crown Point, or to Montreal.

14. Fort No. 4 (at present-day Charlestown, N.H.) was attacked in both May and June 1746, and raids occurred at Keene, N.H., and from Albany to Schenectady, N.Y.

15. The first was the aborted campaign against Quebec in 1712, and the second, the successful campaign to take Louisburg in 1745, mounted by New England forces but with essential cooperation from the British navy.

16. The British Secretary of State had promised British troops for the attack, and promised arms, supplies, and compensation for colonial forces, including booty.

17. France, along with many of the nations of Europe, was involved in The War of Austrian Succession, with theatres stretching from the West Indies to India. This made their shipping especially vulnerable to the British navy and privateers; in 1747, JE would begin recording French ships sunk and taken in "Notes on the Apocalypse" (WJE 5:253–84).

18. Commodore Peter Warren, who had led the attack against Cape Breton the year before.

19. Governor William Shirley.

against Cape Breton, particularly in the sore sickness and mortality;[20] yet it is to be considered that that was a judgment especially from the hand of God. We are in the hands of God at home. We can't hide ourselves from the sword of the destroying angel. We are not called upon indolently to lie still and suffer {harm} because {it will mean having to exert ourselves}.

We are safest in the way of our duty. Some may be ready to say, there were other difficulties that our soldiers met with, that went in the expedition the last year, that they did not expect,[21] that were not so immediately from the hand of God.[22] Yet, have we any reason to conclude that the case will be the same? [The] circumstances of the expedition, to be sure, will in many respects be very different. And though it be true, that it may be so {that there will be risk}, yet we are called to run no ventures. All things are in the hands of God. There is no business whatsoever that men are more called to run ventures in. Herein consists very much of the self-denial {spoken of in the Doctrine}.

Joab spoke well, and as became a captain of the Lord's host, when he said, as in 2 Sam. 10:12, "Be of good courage, and let us play the men for our people, and for the cities of our God: and the Lord do that which seemeth him good." And God in his providence manifested his approbation of that speech of Joab, and that behavior of him and the people, that is agreeable thereto. There must be in all difficult and self-denying duties, a resignation as to the consequences.

There is no special reason for us to suppose that a like sickness and mortality {will occur this time, or} like other difficulties; however, we are safest in the way of duty. And besides, we should take heed, that while we look at the misfortune that befell many of our soldiers {in the last expedition} through our sinful abuse of God's mercies, {that} we don't wholly overlook the extraordinary encouragement that God gives us.

If the people of this land should, by an extraordinary backwardness, neglect this opportunity, and should abide at home in our tents, to attend our husbandry and attend private business, 'tis to be feared they would not be in God's way, nor in the way of his blessing. How does the Spirit of God stigmatize those in Israel that did so, with a note of everlasting

---

20. After the fall of Louisburg, an epidemic broke out among the English; shortly after the capitulation, nearly 1500 men were down with fever and dysentery, and by the spring of 1746 nearly 900 occupying English had died.

21. MS: "Expec."

22. Perhaps referring, among other reasons for discontent, to the reneged-upon promise of booty to New Englanders who volunteered for the Cape Breton campaign.

disgrace, to remain on record against them to all generations? Judg. 5:16–17, "Why abodest thou among the sheepfolds, to hear the bleatings of the flocks? For the divisions of Reuben there were great searchings of heart. Gilead abode beyond Jordan: and why did Dan remain in ships? Asher continued on the sea shore, and abode in his breaches."

Men, in such a case as that which is now before us, should conscientiously take heed that they don't neglect doing what God calls them to, lest God should resent it, and they should not be in the way of a blessing. Moses tells the two tribes and an half, that if they did not do their part in the war that Israel had to engage in, {their sin would find them out}. Num. 32:21–23, "And will go all of you armed over Jordan before the Lord, until he hath driven out his enemies from before him, and the land be subdued before the Lord: then afterward ye shall return, and be guiltless before the Lord, and before Israel; and this land shall be your possession before the Lord. But if ye will not do so, behold, ye have sinned against the Lord: and be sure your sin will find you out." See also v. 27.

Those that [are] now called to exert themselves {in a war tending to their defense and safety}, have an extraordinary opportunity of doing an eminently good work. Perhaps they never will have another opportunity so much to serve God and their generation in their lives. It is worth the while to be born for such a service.

If the expedition should be succeeded, and they should with others be a means of its success, how great a good indeed will they be the instruments of, how great a blessing to the country, saving multitudes of ours. Future generations will have occasion to honor their memory. Persons that are the instruments of such a work, are in Scripture dignified by the honorable name of "saviors." Neh. 9:27, "in the time of their trouble, when they cried unto thee, thou heardest them from heaven; and according to thy manifold mercies thou gavest them saviors, who saved them out of the hand of their enemies." Such persons are to be looked upon as great benefactors to the public, instruments of saving their country, of redeeming many of our poor captives."[23]

This seems to be a great opportunity that God gives us, for delivering this land from that which has been one of the sorest scourges. If we neglect it, therefore, is there not danger of bringing the like effects of God's displeasure upon us, which Ahab brought on himself? 1 Kgs. 20:42,

---

23. At this time, there were estimated to be nearly a hundred and fifty captives from New England, taken to Canada during previous raids and conflicts by the French and Canadian Indians.

"Thus saith the Lord, Because thou hast let go out of thy hand a man whom I appointed to utter destruction, therefore thy life shall go for his life, and thy people for his people." Benhadad had been a sore scourge to Israel. God says to Ahab, "thy life shall go for his life." And if we neglect {to exert ourselves}, and the expedition should fail of success, is there not reason to fear that multitudes of our lives {shall be lost}? The consequence probably will be very dismal: and how can such as have had any hand {in the effort}, have any comfort in the consideration? Ahab repented, 1 Kgs. 20:43, "he went to his house heavy, and much displeased"; and so may we.

It may be further considered, that if those that enlist themselves in this service are the instruments of {God}, they will not only be the instruments of great good to this land and nation, but will be the instruments of the overthrow of a considerable part of mystical Babylon. 'Tis to be hoped that the time of her overthrow is approaching. A blessing is pronounced on those that should have an hand in the overthrow of old Babylon, that had cruelly oppressed [the people of Israel]. Ps. 137:8–9, "O daughter of Babylon, who art to be destroyed; happy shall he be, that rewardeth thee as thou hast served us. Happy shall he be, that taketh and dasheth thy little ones against the stones." But a much greater[24] blessing may be expected.

And parents will be in the way of a blessing, in showing a proper readiness that their children should expose themselves in such an important service to God and their country. Let it be considered, that we have abundantly given up our children. It is worth [our while] to bring forth children to offer 'em up to God in so great a service, and to be the instrument of so much good, as we may reasonably hope through the blessing of God that {they will be so}.

And they that cheerfully engage {in this service}, and go forth {to be instruments of good}, may hope, through the protection and blessing of God, after enduring the hardships and dangers of the expedition, and after a glorious victory and conquest of that land of our enemies, to[25] return with that blessing that Joshua gave to the two tribes and an half after {they had had kept the commandment of God}. Josh. 22[:8], "And he spake unto them, saying, Return with much riches unto your tents, and with very much cattle, with silver, and with gold, and with brass, and with iron, and with very much raiment: divide the spoil of your enemies with your brethren."

24. MS: "much a greater."
25. MS: "Enemies of to."

The Fall of the Antichrist

July 10, 1746

THE ANTICIPATION OF THE momentous expedition to rid North America of the French loomed so large that there was scarce a mention of the conflict on the continent in the July 1 edition of the *Gazette*. This edition of the *Gazette* led with the speech of Governor Shirley who equated the threat of the French in Canada to that of the ancient Carthaginians.[1] Shirley continued to invoke the memory of the failed 1690 expedition which had been foiled due to a series of providences and highlighted the continued molestation that resulted from this failure. Shirley implied that another failure to remove the French from North America would prolong this molestation.

This edition concluded with three reminders. First, the *Gazette* announced that the colonial volunteers would be commanded by European officers. This announcement may have invoked bad memories of the expedition to the West Indies, yet it also signaled London's commitment to supporting the expedition and ensuring its success. New England had transcended the provincial and became part of the Imperial machine. Second, Boston received "advice" that Indians had killed four men and captured three on its frontier. The Catholic threat was not a distant idea but imminent; not benign but deadly. Finally, a reward was offered for the return of a recent deserter from a naval ship. Volunteer soldiers must understand the seriousness of their duty.

Amidst this uncertainty, Edwards used this sermon to provide a measure of certainty for his parishioners. Edwards long understood

---

1. *Boston Gazette*, July 1, 1746.

Catholicism, and specifically French Catholicism, through an apocalyptic lens. But now, as the expedition to Canada materialized with London's support, Edwards saw the fall of French Canada as the harbinger of the fall of the Biblical antichrist. This sermon claimed, in no uncertain terms, that the pope and his clergy were the antichristian powers to which John referred in his Apocalypse. Furthermore, the pope's downfall was guaranteed by the authority of God.

Edwards continued to describe the manner of the antichrist's fall. The chief means was the spiritual sword in the form of the word of God, "sharper than any two-edged sword" (Heb. 4:12). Yet, Edwards presented the role of temporal sword as a parallel mechanism for bringing about the antichrist's fall. Not because the spiritual sword was insufficient, but because it was the means of the word of God. Warfare and judgments were to be the vehicle for the fall of the antichrist because it was only fitting that the antichrist be destroyed by the same means as their oppression.

In the Application, Edwards presented several means by which the citizens of Northampton could participate in the fall of the antichrist. First, they should seek his destruction through prayer. This was a means of wielding the spiritual sword, yet not the only means. Second, Northampton should enthusiastically lend her support to the expedition to Canada, personally and materially. This wielding of the temporal sword ensured the expulsion of the French Catholics from Canada, and eventually the downfall of the papacy itself. The connection between the spiritual and temporal sword is reflected in Edwards's allusion to the "sixth vial." Mentioned in Revelation 16, this final vial of God's judgments involved the drying up of the River Euphrates, which Edwards understood as the evaporation of papal resources leading the forces of Christ to triumph. The capture of Louisbourg and the impending expedition to Montreal and Quebec would deprive Catholicism's signal nation from its considerable resources removing her ability to wage war in support of the papacy. Edwards saw this expedition as a significant milestone in the advance of the gospel.

* * * * *

This sermon was edited for the Jonathan Edwards Center by Ken Minkema also known as "Fast on Occasion of the Expedition to Canada." The manuscript is ten duodecimo-sized leaves of mixed paper. At the top of page one Edwards wrote, "Fast on Occasion of the Expedition to Canada

July 10 1746." The text is very sketchy. Leaves 8–9 are made from an undersized scrap on which is written a discarded prayer bid.

The Fall of the Antichrist

Revelation 17:11

And the beast that was, and is not, even he is the eighth,[1] and is of the seven, and goeth into perdition.

1. The subject spoken of.[2]
    2. What is here predicated of him, with regard to his end.

[The] Subject

that I would now insist upon from these words is,
The fall of Antichrist.
    I. [I would] observe some things by way of introduction.
    II. Proceed directly to treat of the subject.

I. [I would observe some things by way of introduction.]
First. Under what names, representations [and] characters Antichrist and the antichristian society is exhibited and foretold in Scripture.
Second. Who it is that these names, {representations and characters} are to be ascribed it, or who these prophecies are fulfilled in.

First. Under what names.
1. "Little horn," Dan. 7:8, 11, 20–21, 24–26.

---

1. MS: "eight."
2. See "Exposition on the Apocalypse," in loc. (WJE 5:119), and *Humble Attempt* (WJE 5:399, 401), for JE's glosses on this verse.

2. The "man of sin" and "son of perdition," by the apostle Paul, 2 Thess. 2:3. There is all reason to think this is the same. The Apostle speaks of the same apostasy again, 1 Tim. 4:1, "Now the Spirit speaketh expressly, that in the latter times some shall depart from the faith, giving heed to seducing spirits, and doctrines of devils." This is undoubtedly the same.

3. "Antichrist," 1 John 2:18. [This is] the same [as he] "[who] opposeth [and exalteth himself above all that is called God" (2 Thess. 2:4)]. [The Apostle] speaks of that which they had heard of before.

4. The kingdom of Antichrist [is represented by] the beast with seven heads and ten horns, [one of whose heads was wounded to death but which was] revived, spoken of, Rev. 13, three first verses. [So] in the text and context. The same {names} as {he is called} in Daniel, [ch. 7], "ten horns," "ten kings," v. 24; so. Rev. 17:12. The time [is] the same, v. 5, Dan. 7:25.

5. The church of Antichrist [is represented] by the woman on the beast.[3]

"Babylon the Great," so the woman is called. Rev. 14:8.

Spiritual Sodom, and Egypt, Rev. 11:8.

['Tis] the same. The time [is] the same

The antichristian clergy [is] the second beast, Rev. 13:11, that exhibits the false doctrines and false miracles [of the church of Rome].

The same that the apostle Paul [speaks of], vv. 13–14, "[he] doeth great wonders."

The "false prophet," Rev. 19:20.

This [is] the same with the beast.

II. Who it is that is meant by these names and representations, or who {it is} they[4] belong to.

Answer. The Pope of Rome with his clergy, church and kingdom. ['Tis] exceedingly manifest by the text and context:

"[And there are seven kings]": 1. Kings. 2. Consuls. 3. Tribunes. 4. Decemvirs. 5. Dictators. 6. Emperors. 7. Popes.[5]

[So] the description in the 7th [chapter] of Daniel.

---

3. See JE on Rev. 17:3, WJE 5:126.

4. MS: "who —— are to they[-]."

5. These titles identify for JE the successive types of the seven kings; see WJE 5:127, on Rev. 17:10.

The description {given by the} apostle Paul, 2 Thess. 2. 1 Tim. 4[:1–3], Rev. 13.

The second beast is the clergy, [which is] evidently the same with the false prophet, ch. 19. [So] the description in the 18th chapter, and elsewhere, which I have no time {to explain in this discourse}.[6]

[II.] Having thus {observed some things by way of introduction}, I come now more directly to the subject, viz., the fall of Antichrist.

First. The certainty
Second. The means of it
Third. [The] manner
Fourth. [The] time.

First. The fall of Antichrist is certain.

['Tis] often foretold, with the circumstances of it. ['Tis] declared once and again in the first prophecy, Dan. 7, v. 11, "I beheld then because of the voice of the great words which the horn spake: I beheld even till the beast was slain, and his body destroyed, and given to the burning flame." Vv. 25–26, "And he shall speak great words against the most High, and shall wear out the saints of the most High, and think to change times and laws: and they shall be given into his hand until a time and times and the dividing of time. But the judgment shall sit, and they shall take away his dominion, to consume and to destroy it unto the end." The certainty of it [is] emphatically represented in the words of the text; so in the 8th verse. [Antichrist is] called by the Apostle "the son of perdition" [2 Thess. 2:3], with the particular circumstances, Rev. 18. The same [is] declared twice, with its exact limitation, with the most solemn oath of the Son of God: once under the Old Testament, and once in the New; Dan. 12, Rev. 10. ['Tis called the] "times of the gentiles," Luke 21:24. In Rev. 18:8, it is represented as sure as that God is able to destroy her.

Second. [The] means.

[They are] principally two, viz., a spiritual, and a temporal sword.

1. Chiefly, the spiritual sword, that proceeds out of the mouth of Christ. Rev. 19:15, "And out of his mouth goeth a sharp sword, that with it he should smite the nations." We read of the same sword, ch. 1:16, "and out of his mouth went a sharp two-edged sword." Is. 49:2, "He hath made

---

6. On Rev. 18, see WJE 5:120–22.

my mouth [like a sharp sword]." This is the Word of God; [the] spiritual sword is the Word of God. Eph. 6:17, "the sword of the Spirit, which is the word of God." ['Tis] "sharper than any two-edged sword," Heb. 4:12. So we read, ch. 14:6–8, "And I saw another angel fly in the midst of heaven, having the everlasting gospel to preach unto them that dwell on the earth, and to every nation, and kindred, and tongue, and people, saying with a loud voice, Fear God, and give glory to him; for the hour of his judgment is come: and worship him that made heaven, and earth, and the sea, and the fountains of waters. And there followed another angel, saying, Babylon is fallen, is fallen, that great city, because she made all nations drink of the wine of the wrath of her fornication."

2. A temporal sword.

[There] will be great temporal judgments. The time of introducing {the glorious times of the church, is} often in the prophecies spoken of as a time of great judgments on {Antichrist}, to be executed in this world. [There will be] great judgments in this world visible to all, not only to the saints, but to the nations of the earth: her friends, men of the world. Rev. 18:9–10, "And the kings of the earth, who have committed fornication and lived deliciously with her, shall bewail her, and lament for her, when they shall see the smoke of her burning, standing afar off for the fear of her torment, saying, Alas, alas that great city Babylon, that mighty city! for in one hour is thy judgment come." Vv. 15, etc., "The merchants of these things, which were made rich by her, shall stand afar off for the fear of her torment, weeping and wailing, and saying, Alas, alas that great city, that was clothed in fine linen, and purple, and scarlet, and decked with gold, and precious stones, and pearls!"

That those judgments shall be very much by a temporal sword, as God's judgments on Jerusalem for crucifying Christ were, is especially manifest by two things:

(1) ['Tis] threatened that Antichrist shall suffer by the same means, which they have made use of to destroy others. Rev. 13:10," He that leadeth into captivity shall go into captivity: he that killeth with the sword must be killed with the sword."

(2) That the kings of the earth shall destroy her. Rev. 17:16, "[And the ten horns which thou sawest upon the beast, these shall hate the whore, and shall make her desolate and naked, and shall eat her flesh, and burn her with fire]."

Third. [The] manner.

[It will consist in the] following things:

1. [Antichrist shall be] totally [destroyed].

This, many of the expressions imply. Dan. 7:11, "I beheld then because of the voice of the great words which the horn spake: I beheld even till the beast was slain, and his body destroyed, and given to the burning flame." V. 26, "But the judgment shall sit, and they shall take away his dominion, to consume and to destroy it unto the end." [There is] the like reduplication[7] of expressions, 2 Thess. 2:8, "And then shall that Wicked be revealed, whom the Lord shall consume with the spirit of his mouth, and shall destroy with the brightness of his coming." [So there is an] accumulation of expressions. Rev. 17:16, "make her desolate and naked, and shall eat her flesh, and burn her with fire." Ch. 18:21, "And a mighty angel took up a stone like a great millstone, and cast it into the sea, saying, Thus with violence shall that great city Babylon be thrown down, and shall be found no more at all."

2. [Antichrist shall be] suddenly [destroyed].

Rev. 18:10, "in one hour is thy judgment come." V. 17, "For in one hour so great riches is come to naught." V. 19, "for in one hour is she made desolate."

3. [Antichrist shall be destroyed] very terribly.

Dan. 7:11, "I beheld even till the beast was slain, and his body destroyed, and given to the burning flame." So Rev. 17:16. Rev. 18:6–8, "Reward her even as she rewarded you, and double unto her double according to her works: in the cup which she hath filled fill to her double. How much she hath glorified herself, and lived deliciously, so much torment and sorrow give her: for she saith in her heart, I sit a queen, and am no widow, and shall see no sorrow. Therefore shall her plagues come in one day, death, and mourning, and famine; and she shall be utterly burned with fire: for strong is the Lord God who judgeth her." V. 15, "The merchants of these things, which were made rich by her, shall stand afar off for the fear of her torment, weeping and wailing." V. 18, "[And cried when they saw the smoke of her burning, saying, What city is like unto this great city!]" V. 2, "[And he cried mightily with a strong voice, saying, Babylon the great is fallen, is fallen, and is become the habitation of devils, and the hold of every foul spirit, and a cage of every unclean and hateful bird]."

---

7. Conjectural reading for a poorly written word.

[It shall be] with violence. V. 24, "And in her was found the blood of prophets, and of saints, and of all that were slain upon the earth." Ch. 16:19–21, "And the great city was divided into three parts, and the cities of the nations fell: and great Babylon came in remembrance before God, to give unto her the cup of the wine of the fierceness of his wrath. And every island fled away, and the mountains were not found. And there fell upon men a great hail out of heaven, every stone about the weight of a talent: and men blasphemed God because of the plague of the hail; for the plague thereof was exceeding great." Ch. 19:20–21, "And the beast was taken, and with him the false prophet that wrought miracles before him, with which he deceived them that had received the mark of the beast, and them that worshipped his image. These both were cast alive into a lake of fire burning with brimstone. And the remnant were slain with the sword of him that sat upon the horse, which sword proceeded out of his mouth: and all the fowls were filled with their flesh." Ch. 14, latter end, "And another angel came out from the altar, which had power over fire; and cried with a loud cry to him that had the sharp sickle, saying, Thrust in thy sharp sickle, and gather the clusters of the vine of the earth; for her grapes are fully ripe. And the angel thrust in his sickle into the earth, and gathered the vine of the earth, and cast it into the great winepress of the wrath of God. And the winepress was trodden without the city, and blood came out of the winepress, even unto the horse bridles, by the space of a thousand and six hundred furlongs."

4. [Antichrist shall be destroyed] with most evident and very marvelous manifestations of the hand of God.

[God shall destroy Antichrist "with the] brightness of his coming," [2 Thess. 2:8]; [with] voices of thunders and lightnings, Rev. 16:18; [with] great magnificence, Rev. 19[:11–16],[8]

And I saw heaven opened, and behold a white horse; and he that sat upon him was called Faithful and True, and in righteousness he doth judge and make war. His eyes were as a flame of fire, and on his head were many crowns; and he had a name written, that no man knew, but he himself. And he was clothed with a vesture dipped in blood: and his name is called The Word of God. And the armies which were in heaven followed him upon white horses, clothed in fine linen, white and clean. And out of his mouth goeth a sharp sword, that with it he should smite the nations: and he shall rule them with a rod of iron: and he treadeth the winepress of

8. It is a matter of conjecture how much of the chapter JE would have quoted, but these verses seem best to fit his point.

the fierceness and wrath of Almighty God. And he hath on his vesture and on his thigh a name written, KING OF KINGS, AND LORD OF LORDS."

All nations shall see his glory. Is. 42:13, "The Lord shall go forth as a mighty man, he shall stir up jealousy like a man of war: he shall cry, yea, roar; he shall prevail against his enemies." [The] destruction of Pharaoh [was] a type of it. [The] nations shall be awed, Rev. 19.

5. [The destruction of Antichrist shall be] attended with exceeding great Revelations in the state of the world of mankind.

Rev. 16:18, "And there were voices, and thunders, and lightnings; and there was a great earthquake, such as was not since men were upon the earth, so mighty an earthquake, and so great." "The stone that [was] cut out of the mountains without hands, and that it brake in pieces the iron, the brass, the clay, the silver, and the gold" [Dan. 2:45]. Dan. 2:34–35, "Thou sawest till that a stone was cut out without hands, which smote the image upon his feet that were of iron and clay, and brake them to pieces. Then was the iron, the clay, the brass, the silver, and the gold, broken to pieces together, and became like the chaff of the summer threshingfloors; and the wind carried them away, that no place was found for them: and the stone that smote the image became a great mountain, and filled the whole earth."

Fourth. [The] time.

[1. I] observe that there is something concerning it, certain and precisely and plainly fixed, viz., the continuance of Antichrist from his first rest. ['Tis mentioned] very often. Twice in the Old Testament: Dan. 7:26, "But the judgment shall sit, and they shall take away his dominion, to consume and to destroy it unto the end"; and 12:7, "And I heard the man clothed in linen, which was upon the waters of the river, when he held up his right hand and his left hand unto heaven, and sware by him that liveth for ever that it shall be for a time, times, and an half; and when he shall have accomplished to scatter the power of the holy people, all these things shall be finished." [And] very often in the New: Rev. 11:2, "forty-two months"; [v.] 3, "two witnesses, [and they shall prophesy 1260 [days]"; Rev. 12:6, "1260 days"; [v.] 14, [the] woman in the wilderness, "time, [and] times, and half a time"; ch. 13:5, "forty-two months."

2. [There is] something uncertain, viz., where the beginning, and so the end, of this duration is to be fixed.

[There are] several decrees: [by] Cyrus; Darius, Ezra 6; Artaxerxes, Ezra 7; Artaxerxes by Nehemiah, Neh. 2.[9]

Use

Use [I] is of *Exhortation* to all, to seek this destruction of Antichrist. Don't let us look on ourselves as unconcerned in those prophecies. This is unbecoming Christians. Seek it in two ways:

First. By praying for it.

Scripture represents this as very much the matter of the prayer and faith of the Christian church. Here is the portions [spoken of].[10] [The church should be] in travail. Earnest prayer preceded the destruction of old Babylon; Jer. 29:10, etc.,

For thus saith the Lord, That after seventy years be accomplished at Babylon I will visit you, and perform my good word toward you, in causing you to return to this place. For I know the thoughts that I think toward you, saith the Lord, thoughts of peace, and not of evil, to give you an expected end. Then shall ye call upon me, and ye shall go and pray unto me, and I will hearken unto you. And ye shall seek me, and find me, when ye shall search for me with all your heart. And I will be found of you, saith the Lord: and I will turn away your captivity, and I will gather you from all the nations, and from all the places whither I have driven you, saith the Lord; and I will bring you again into the place whence I caused you to be carried away captive.

Second. To do what in us lies, in our places, and as called of God, tending to it. Means that Christians should use in order to it, are of two sorts, according to the twofold means that the prophecies do show God will make use of: spiritual and temporal.

1. They should do those things of a spiritual nature that have a tendency to it, promoting the interest of religion in the Protestant church, endeavoring to promote a revival of religion.

---

9. JE viewed these decrees as part of the process of the gradual deliverance and restoration of the children of Israel from the Babylonian Captivity. Cyrus's decree allowed for a partial restoration of the Jews from captivity; Darius's decree for the reconstitution of the Jewish state; and Artaxerxes's decree allowed for the complete reestablishment of the Jews in Palestine. On Ezra 7–8, see "Notes on the Apocalypse," *WJE* 5:216, 398, 404; and "Blank Bible" entry on Ezra 7, *WJE* 24:418.

10. Possibly a reference to the Ezekiel's prophecy of the portions, Ezek. 47:13, 48:21, 29.

2.[11] Christians should seek the overthrow of Antichrist by using temporal means, when called in providence to a temporal war with antichristian powers.

Motive. What a Captain you will follow in it, Rev. 19, "[THE KING OF KINGS, AND THE LORD OF LORDS]."

Use II. What has been observed, may animate and encourage us in seeking God and trusting in him, and in other respects doing our duty with relation to the great affair which is the special occasion of the appointment of this day, viz., the intended expedition against Canada.

The country {of Canada} belongs to the kingdom of Antichrist, the most considerable part of that kingdom in those northern parts of America. God has already much weakened the antichristian interest. If that land was subdued, {it would} open a door for the introducing the gospel into that dark land. Not only so, but [for] the instruction of the Indians. [It would] open a door for the bringing all North America {under the gospel}, which is a considerable part of the world.[12]

[*First.*] We have much to encourage us to hope for great things to be done for the pulling down the kingdom of Satan, and the setting up the kingdom of Christ in America. [We have much to encourage us,] in the extraordinary {late} stirrings of his Spirit {in this land}; and further to animate us {to such things as} tend to diminish and weaken the kingdom of Antichrist in general, as it will weaken the kingdom of France, the greatest power that supports Antichrist. [It will] dry up a considerable

---

11. MS: "1."

12. The bid reads:

Reuben Cors and his wife Desirs that
Gods nam might be praisd in this this ———
Congration for his goodnes to hour in presaring
the Life of mother and Child in anouer of Destrest
and given hour safe Delevrance thay all so Desier
prais that god would parficit his begon goodnes to
them. and that god would give them grace to Live
acorden to so grait a marsy marcy
thare parence . Desires the same ————————

Reuben and Sarah Corse had a son, Ebenezer, born on July 1, 1746, but he did not live out the month, dying on July 25. Trumbull, "History of Northampton: Genealogies," typescript, Forbes Library, Northampton, vol. 3, p. 155.

stream of their wealth. [It will] deliver this part of the church of God, from the sufferings they have endured from Antichrist.

Therefore, certain, here is much to engage us to seek {the pulling down of Antichrist}. And there is surely much in what has been observed on the subject we have been upon, to encourage us both in praying to God for success in this undertaking, and also vigorously exerting and cheerfully exposing ourselves in using the proper means in order to it.

Second. How joyful an event it will be to the church of God. Rev. 18:20, "Rejoice over her, thou heavens, [and ye holy apostles and prophets; for God hath avenged you on her]."

Third. How glorious [will be] the consequences. [Then will be the] calling in the kingdom of Christ. Dan. 7, three last verses:[13] "And he shall speak great words against the most High, and shall wear out the saints of the most High, and think to change times and laws: and they shall be given into his hand until a time and times and the dividing of time. But the judgment shall sit, and they shall take away his dominion, to consume and to destroy it unto the end. And the kingdom and dominion, and the greatness of the kingdom under the whole heaven, shall be given to the people of the saints of the most High, whose kingdom is an everlasting kingdom, and all dominions shall serve and obey him." [The will be the] marriage of the Lamb; Rev. 19:7, "Let us be glad and rejoice, and give honor to him: for the marriage of the Lamb is come, and his wife hath made herself ready." Ch. 20, [the] binding of Satan. [And the] spiritual reformation of the world, a long-continued, holy reign, and reign of the church on earth.

Fourth. [This will be] the way to have a share in the joy and triumph of the church of God, and glorious consequences.

Fifth. What encouragements there are: what was observed of the certainty of his fall; in that God has done so much towards the fall of Antichrist already.

What encouragements there are that the time is approaching. Antichrist has reigned so long; so many things [have been] fulfilled: all {has been fulfilled} but the two last vials. [And it has been] so long since the last {vial was} fulfilled.[14]

---

13. I.e., Dan. 7:25–27, since v. 28 is a conclusion that JE seems not to intend to be included.

14. In *Humble Attempt*, published in 1747, JE agrees with Moses Lowman that the fifth vial was poured out at the beginning of the Reformation, and states that "it is now about 220 years since the fifth vial began to be poured out." WJE 5:383, 421.

The Scripture represents {that it will} come swiftly. The church of God here [has] so long expected [it]. [So in the] late extraordinary things, [and the] extraordinary spirit of prayer stirred up of late.

An earnest seeking of God preceded the destruction of old Babylon, and the deliverance of the church then ensnared. Jer. 29:10, "[For thus saith the Lord, That after seventy years be accomplished at Babylon I will visit you, and perform my good word toward you, in causing you to return to this place]."

The Sovereignty of God's Mercy

August 1746

THE ENTHUSIASM OVER THE planned expedition to Canada waned in the face of two other developing situations. It was expected that France would not allow the loss of Louisburg without a challenge. In early May, reports emerged from France that a squadron of ships prepared to sail form Brest to support the French cause in North America. London and Boston interpreted this move as an attempt to recapture fortress Louisburg and scrambled to reinforce the outpost. This possibility caused Gov. Shirley and the Duke of Newcastle to reprioritize their military objectives. The expedition to Canada could not be successful if the British lost their foothold on Cape Breton. Therefore, considering these developments, the British shifted their resources to Louisburg and the eastern frontier.

Yet, in the mother country, there emerged a more significant threat to Britain's Protestant Interest. The rise of the Jacobite movement swelled in the highlands of Scotland. These Scottish rebels rallied around Charles Edward Stuart, the son of the Stuart Catholic heir to the British throne, James Edward Stuart. James (the "Pretender"), sent his son, Charles (the "Young Pretender"), supported by Catholic French troops to reclaim the British throne and restore the Catholic House of Stuart.

New Englanders read with horror as accounts of French troops landing on British soil appeared in the *Boston Gazette*. News of the rebel army taking Perth[1] and Berwick-upon-Tweed[2] served as a cautionary tale warning New England of the consequences of French intervention. The

---

1. *Boston Gazette*, November 5, 1746.
2. *Boston Gazette*, January 7, 1745/46.

landing of French troops in Britain, the emergence of a rebel army, the rebel victory at Falkirk, the leadership of the Duke of Cumberland—all of these events drove the conflict to a head at Culloden. The battle was fought on April 16th, 1746 and reports ran in the *Boston Gazette* by July 15th. This was a decisive victory where the Duke of Cumberland broke the Jacobite rebellion and all but ended the French Catholic threat to the crown. The House of Peers highlighted the "Value and Extent of that happiness which this execrable Rebellion was formed to take from us, our holy religion, our laws and liberties." It is understandable that New England—and Edwards—would have understood their own situation in the same terms.

Edwards identified this victory as a "grace" in his sermon *The Sovereignty of Mercy*. Mercy, according to Edwards, differed from judgment in that God's judgments are not arbitrary, they are applied according to a rule. Yet mercies are given, not according to a rule, but according to God's pleasure and will, or grace. This constitutes the core of God's sovereignty: his ability to exercise and withhold mercy as he wills. These mercies may be exercised on individuals or societies and may come in temporal and spiritual forms. One of these temporal advantages God bestows is "victory in war." Edwards understood Cumberland's victory at Culloden to have been rooted in God's special mercy.

Northampton's inference from this doctrine was that their situation was also one of dependence on mercy. First, they were dependent on mercy for their personal salvation. Furthermore, these mercies should be sought on behalf of both the land (New England) and the nation (British Empire). But Edwards also included a warning. Though he acknowledged that God sometimes exercised mercy on wicked people, one should not abuse this doctrine by relying on this uncommon mercy. Edwards, in *The Sovereignty of God's Mercy*, outlined a program for New England's spiritual posture in their engagement with French forces.

* * * * *

This sermon was edited for the Jonathan Edwards Center by Ken Minkema. Also known as "Thanksgiving for Victory over the Rebels," the manuscript is twelve duodecimo-sized leaves of mixed paper. Edwards titled it, "Thanksgiv[ing] for victory over the / Rebels Aug 1746." Re-preaching notations at the front of the sermon state, first in the left margin, "Novem. 1754 +," and, above the scripture text, "St.," for Stockbridge. A "+" sign appears at the beginning of the Application, which suggests that this section was what he re-preached. It is not clear whether these relate to one and the same re-preaching occasion, or to two, perhaps one to the Indians and one to the English congregation. The year 1754 marked the beginning of the French and Indian War in the colonies, and the month of September saw deadly raids on Stockbridge, so Edwards chose to re-preach on this topic under quite different circumstances from the first time. In revising for re-preaching, he made additions and deletions, which are indicated in the notes.

The Sovereignty of God's Mercy

Exodus 33:19

And will be gracious to whom I will be gracious, and will show mercy on whom I will show mercy.

We have an account, in the foregoing context, of those things that were wonderful displays of God's mercy, both to Moses and to the congregation of Israel. The words of the text come in as a reason.

1. What kind of divine acts are here spoken of, viz. showing mercy.

2. The ground of these acts, {viz.,} his own sovereign will and pleasure.

Subject

The sovereignty of God's mercy.

I. What we are to understand by the sovereignty of God's mercy.

II. How mercies that [God] bestows differ from the judgments that he executes, with respect to sovereignty.

III. Consider how the sovereignty of God is exercised in the various mercies he bestows.

I. What we are to understand by the sovereignty of mercy.

The sovereignty of mercy is God's showing mercy according his mere will and pleasure, without subjection, obligation or dependence in the exercises of his mercy.

First. God's mercy's being sovereign, implies his being without subjection in the exercises {of his mercy}.

Second. [It implies his being without] obligation, merit, or stated rule [in the exercises of it].

Third. {It implies his being without} dependence [in the exercises of it].

II. How the mercies that God bestows, differ from the judgments that he executes with respect to the sovereignty that is exercised therein.

God's executing judgment is not an arbitrary sovereign act, as his showing mercy. [God] does it as a judge, and not as a sovereign. God don't show mercy as a judge. A judge, so far he acts the part of a judge, never acts an arbitrary part. [He] has respect to a rule prescribed. God, in showing mercy, don't act the part of judge.

But yet the sovereignty of God is, in several respects, exercised about the executing of judgment. 'Tis so in the following respects:

First. God acts the part of a sovereign in appointing the subordinate rule of judgment.

Second. God acts the part of a sovereign in leaving men to commit sin, so as to expose themselves to punishment by the rule {of judgment}.

Third. The sovereignty of God is exercised in the withholding mercy from those whom he executes judgment upon.

There are two things from God, with respect to the judgments God executes on sinners, viz., something negative, which is withheld by mercy or not bestowing mercy; and something positive, viz., the executing punishment. One is the consequence of the other. Now with respect to the former, viz., {withholding mercy}, God acts as a sovereign. Therefore it is said, Rom 9:18, "he hath mercy on whom he will have mercy, and whom he will he hard[eneth]." But not with respect to the latter: for in punishing sinners, God acts as a judge by a prescribed or appointed rule, and he determines no punishment but what the rule points forth and limits. But in determining whether to show mercy or no, God don't act as a judge as limited by any rule but his own pleasure.

The law directs the judge with regard to the punishment to be adjudged, unless mercy be shown by the sovereign. But the law don't direct the sovereign when to show mercy, and when not: that is at his mere pleasure, provided mercy ben't shown in a way inconsistent with the law. The rule of judgment declares what punishment the sinner shall suffer that han't obtained mercy. But the rule of judgment don't declare what sinner shall obtain mercy, and what not.

God, so far as he acts as a judge, is limited and directed by a prescribed rule, viz., the law; and in punishing sin, he always acts as a judge. But the rule or law, don't oblige God always to act as a judge. Therefore, as a sovereign he may determine whether to show mercy, or withhold it. He acts as a sovereign in determining not to establish a new subordinate rule of judgment in favor {of the sinner}. [He acts as a sovereign] in determining not to give the sinner an interest in a new subordinate rule.

But God's showing mercy is different[1] from God's executing judgment, with respect to sovereignty, in the following respects:

1. The exercises of mercy to the sinners are without merit.
2. [The exercises of mercy to the sinners are] without the limitations or direction of a declared rule. If there be no rule, there can be no judgment.
3. {God is} thus sovereign in the exercises of mercy, both in what is negative, and also what is positive. I observed that there is something negative, viz., withholding deserved judgments; and {something positive}; and that [one is the consequence of the other]. God, in executing judgment, exercises sovereignty only in what is negative.

III. How the sovereignty of God is exercised in the various exercises of his mercy.
First. [To] mankind.
Second. [To] particular persons.[2]
Third. [To] people.
Fourth. [To] times.

First. God is sovereign in the mercies he bestows on mankind in general.

---

1. MS: "differs."

2. Pts. 2 and 3 in this outline are reversed from the original, to correspond with the discussion of the points below.

All mankind on the face of the whole earth are, while living in this world, in many respects the subjects of mercy. 'Tis said, God's tender mercies "are over all thy works" [Ps. 145:9]. All that wherein the present state of mankind differs from a state of damnation, is mercy. God is sovereign in all.

In all, [mankind] are distinguished from fallen angels, and that they are so, is owing only to God's mere good pleasure. 'Tis owing to God's sovereign mercy that the execution of the deserved punishment is forborne, that there is a possibility of salvation, another surety provided, [and] another opportunity and time of probation. God is sovereign in the temporal mercies bestowed on mankind in general. None of them [are] deserved.

Second. God exercises his sovereignty in distinguishing[3] one man from another, in the mercies he bestows.

1. In temporal mercies, in the innumerable differences made, as [in] temporal, natural endowments: birth, education, place of abode, station, {worldly} power, wealth, honor, outward possessions, preservation, continuance of life, particular good things, [and] special deliverances.

2. As to spiritual advantages: opportunities, talents, [and] advantages.

3. [In the] exercises of particular [mercies].

The people of the kingdom of Judah [were] worse [than all others]. Ezek. 23:11, "And when her sister Aholibah[4] saw this, she was more corrupt in her inordinate love than she, and in her whoredoms more than her sister in her whoredoms." And 16:46–48, "And thine elder sister is Samaria, she and her daughters that dwell at thy left hand: and thy younger sister, that dwelleth at thy right hand, is Sodom and her daughters. Yet hast thou not walked after their ways, nor done after their abominations: but, as if that were a very little thing, thou wast corrupted more than they in all thy ways. As I live, saith the Lord God, Sodom thy sister hath not done, she nor her daughters, as thou hast done, thou and thy daughters."

4. In the bestowment of saving mercies.

Here, more especially, God's sovereignty appears. God is in some respect obliged to bestow them, as [they are] all promised to his Son. But then, these two things must be noted: 1. [God is] not properly obliged to the sinner. 2. It was all through sovereign mercy that {God was} obliged to his Son.

3. MS: "distinguished."

4. In Ezekiel's vision, the sisters Aholah the elder and Aholibah the younger stand for the kingdoms of Israel and Judah.

Here, [I will] show particularly:

(1) How God manifests his sovereignty in the mercy that he bestows on sinners, in and at their conversion.

(2) [How God manifests his sovereignty in the mercy he shows] to his saints after their conversion.

(1) [How God manifests his sovereignty in the mercy that he bestows on sinners, in and at their conversion.]

(2) {How God manifests his sovereignty} in saving mercies bestowed on the saints.

These are all sovereign, but yet not in the same manner. The difference may appear by noting the two following things:

1. There are some things appertaining to the saving mercies that God bestows, that he has obliged himself to bestow by his promises to them. But yet,

2. Those mercies are not the less originally of free and sovereign grace, because it is altogether of God's sovereignty that he became obliged. Notwithstanding the manner of giving, viz., giving them by promise, [they are] not the less free, because the promises [are] altogether free and sovereign. Mercy don't appear the less, but the greater, for its being given in this manner.

3. The saving mercies {of God to the saints}, in other respects, are such as God has in no respect obliged himself concerning them: [such as] the degree, the times, the means, [and] the manner. "[The] wind[5] bloweth where it listeth" [John 3:8]. Thus God is sovereign in the mercies by which he distinguishes one man from another.

Third. God is sovereign in the mercies he bestows on nations and peoples.

1. Spiritual [mercies]. Calling a people to be his covenant people, when sunk into great degrees of wickedness. [When their] "fathers [dwelt] on the other side the flood [. . . they served other gods]," Josh. [24:2, 14–15]. [So] Israel in Egypt, [the] calling of the gentiles, [and the] reviving of religion in the later days.

2. Temporal [mercies]: withholding judgments, patience, in the outward advantages and prosperity he bestows, advantages in [temporal affairs, and] victory in war.

But here, for the better understanding, three things must be noted:

---

5. In revising for reproaching, before this sentence JE inserted, "In these Respects the."

(1) [God] don't, in all his temporal dispensations of outward things towards a people, proceed in a way of mere sovereignty, but is wont to punish vice [and] reward virtue. Ps. 94:10, [he] "chastises the heathen."

(2) There is difference between a covenant people and others. Amos 3:2, "You only have I known."

(3) As to a covenant people, there is very much sovereignty oftentimes exercised as to temporal mercies that are bestowed. God threatens, but the threatenings are not positive and absolute as the threatenings of the covenant of works, with regard to particular persons. [The threatenings] signify no more than that this will be his usual manner. But they don't bind God.

Sometimes, God is pleased in this respect to go out of his usual manner.[6] Sometimes [he] bestows great temporal mercies on a very wicked people. We have instances of it in Scripture.[7] [God bestowed mercy] a long time on that stiff-necked congregation in the wilderness. [God continued to bestow mercy on] Saul, after he was rejected by God from being king, [in the] great victory by Jonathan; afterwards, after he had spared Agog; [and] when Goliath was slain.[8] [God continued] great mercies from time to time for the apostate Ten Tribes, though they never returned. [God continued] great public mercies on that wicked king Ahab and his wicked people: [in] plenty after a famine, [in] remarkable deliverances [and] victories, 1 Kings, 20th chapter. Benhadad besieged Samaria and swore, "[The gods do so unto me, and more also, if the dust of Samaria shall suffice for] handfuls [for all the people that follow me," 1 Kgs. 20:10, yet Ahab defeated him]. Again, [the children of Israel were like] "two little flocks of kids" [before the Syrians, yet defeated them, 1 Kgs. 20:27]. [God granted a] great victory to Jehoram, a wicked king of the apostate Ten Tribes, over the Moabites, 2 Kings, 3rd chapter; and again miraculously delivered the army of the Syrians into his hands, 2 Kings, ch. 6, smiting the army with blindness; and again miraculously delivered him and Samaria, when greatly distressed, ch. 7. Wicked King Jehoash, king of Israel, had three successive conquests over the Syrians, ch. 13:17–19.[9] [So] Manasseh, [who had] the longest reign of any of the kings.

Thus I have shown how God exercises his sovereignty in the mercies he bestows on nations.

6. In revising for re-preaching, JE deleted this word and inserted "way."
7. In revising for re-preaching, JE deleted and rewrote this phrase.
8. In revising for re-preaching, JE deleted this sentence.
9. In revising for re-preaching, JE deleted the numerals of the verses and inserted, "latter Part of the Chap."

Fourth. {God exercises his sovereignty}, as to the times wherein he will especially bestow mercy.

The day of the gospel is more remarkably a day of mercy, than the time of the old testament. God brought on that dispensation when he pleased.

Application

I.[10] [*Use* of] *Information.*

First. This shows the glory of God's mercy.

[God's mercy is] without subjection, [without] constraints, [not subject to] the will of another, without obligation, without dependence, not attracted [by any object], [and] self-moved. [This] shows how abundant the benevolence and grace is, that is in the heart of God. [There is] no mercy like this.

Second. How absolutely and universally dependent we are on God in the affair of our salvation.

II. [*Use* of] *Caution*, not to abuse this Doctrine, to presume on mercy and encourage yourselves in sin.

Many abuse the Doctrine. There is much in the Doctrine, rightly considered, to deter men from sin. God is not obliged to show mercy. [Nothing] can oblige him afterwards. [He is] not obliged to show you so much mercy as others.

[We must] not abuse past experiences we have had of God's sovereign mercy. [We must] not abuse the experiences we have had of sovereign mercy in public benefits. Extraordinary temporal mercies, though sometimes bestowed on a very wicked people, yet, unless followed with repentance, surely will not be continued. {Mercy was continued for a} long time on that stiff-necked congregation, but {God eventually gave them over}. [It was not only so with] Saul, but [also with] Ahab, [the] Ten Tribes, and yet longer on the kingdom of Judah. Therefore, if the public mercies we have experienced, wherein God has so much manifested the sovereignty of mercy, don't lead us to repentance, [we can expect our temporal mercies will not be continued].

---

10. A "+" sign written by JE in the left margin suggests that he re-preached the Application as one of the occasions indicated at the head of the sermon.

III. [*Use* of] *Exhortation*.

First. To all, to seek that they may see the sovereignty of God with respect to them, in order to fit them to be the subjects of mercy.

Second. Let us hence be exhorted to thankfulness for the mercies we enjoy.

Let us consider in how many respects we are the subjects of sovereign mercy: [mercy] to our land, to our nation. [The] sovereignty of mercy shows the abundant cause we have of thankfulness.

Third. Let the people of God be excited and encouraged to pray for mercies to the public societies they belong to, and to the world of mankind.

Walking Righteously, Speaking Uprightly

October 16, 1746

REPORTS OF A FRENCH fleet sailing to recapture Louisburg circulated through the *Gazette* for months. Despite the victory of the British forces at Culloden, the French backed Scottish rebellion had set New England on edge. The planned expedition dislodging the French from Canada began to take shape: a commission at Albany finally secured a commitment from the Six Nations as well as a seventh, the Mississauga, to take up the hatchet against the French,[1] Massachusetts approved an additional £10,000 for the expedition,[2] five sloops sailed from New Jersey to join the expedition[3] while troops from the Jerseys marched through New York *en route* to Albany,[4] and one hundred additional Native forces arrived in Albany.[5]

Yet the optimism from the battle of Culloden and the progress of these preparations must have been tempered by a foreboding. Combined Native and French attacks continued along the Hudson River Valley. The September 9th edition of the *Boston Gazette* reported that Fort Massachusetts had burned with none escaping. When a detachment from Fort Pelham arrived at the fort, they found only scattered, smoldering sticks remaining with some Indians fluttering about, plundering what was left. A letter From Rev. John Norton survived, stuck in the crotch of the well,

1. *Boston Gazette*, September 9, 1746.
2. *Boston Gazette*, September 16, 1746.
3. *Boston Gazette*, September 23, 1756.
4. *Boston Gazette*, September 16, 1746.
5. *Boston Gazette*, September 23, 1746.

to give an account of the incident. Furthermore, news of the killing and scalping of a sergeant as he was hunting appeared in the pages of the September 30th edition of the *Gazette*. Northampton would not enjoy peace.

But the news which unnerved New England the most was the rumors concerning the progress of the French fleet from Brest. Rumors of its progress trickled across the news pages as early as July 29, when the *Gazette* published a report of a French fleet sailing for Louisburg. Rumors came from as far as Utrecht and Amsterdam building a sense of anxiety about its progress. Finally, in early October, Capt. Cobb reported sighting ten French ships, "four of them very large" along with about forty tents on shore with "a great number" of masts for the transports and store-ships accompanying the French fleet. The Brest fleet had arrived in Jebucta.[6]

Edwards used this sermon to both assuage the fears of his congregation as well as prepare them for the unknown challenges ahead. The text explicitly employed nautical terms—tackles, masts, sails, etc.—emphasizing God's control over naval affairs. God has made promises for the defense in a time of war for the person and people for those who *Walk Righteously and Speak Uprightly*. Edwards's list of the promises to the righteous began with military success and concluded with the forgiveness of iniquity. This rhetorical approach demonstrated Edwards's pastoral heart by beginning with the concerns that weighed most heavily on the heart of his congregation to lead them to Edwards's central concern: personal piety.

Framing these promises as "mercies" allowed Edwards to extend his thought from *The Sovereignty of God's Mercy*. However, Edwards warned that the conditions for enjoying these mercies are the opposite of New England's situation. New England had "fierce and cruel" people with a "strange tongue" amidst their "weak habitations." New England needed defense, as described by Edwards, "we are lame." As the French prepared to execute their counter-attack, New England's spiritual weakness exacerbated their strategic weaknesses. New England stood in need of God's mercies. Therefore, Edwards exhorted his congregation to righteous action so they could enjoy the protection of God. In the same way that it is folly to neglect military defenses, it is so much more foolish to neglect the defense of one's spiritual posture. One seeking such defense needed to forsake one's sin, pursue righteousness of word and deed, and consider the defense God provided in the past.

6. This was a transliteration of the Mi'kmaq name "Jipugtug." It has also been rendered in the English as Chebucto. It is modern-day Halifax harbor.

*****

This sermon was edited for the Jonathan Edwards Center by Ken Minkema. The manuscript is twenty-one duodecimo-sized leaves of mixed paper, including one leaf with a child's writing exercise, and a discarded prayer bid. Edwards headed the booklet, "Fast, Octob. 16, 1746, On Occasion of the Arrival of the French Fleet, etc." He re-preached this in July 1756, most likely at Stockbridge. There are a few minor alterations for re-preaching.

Walking Righteously, Speaking Uprightly

Isaiah 33:19 to the End

Thou shalt see a fierce people, a people of a deeper speech than thou canst perceive; of a stammering tongue, that thou canst not understand. Look upon Zion, the city of our solemnities: thine eyes shall see Jerusalem a quiet habitation, a tabernacle that shall not be taken down; not one of the stakes thereof shall ever be removed, neither shall any of the cords thereof be broken. But there the glorious Lord will be unto us a place of broad rivers and streams; wherein shall go no galley with oars, neither shall gallant ship pass thereby. For the Lord is our judge, the Lord is our lawgiver, the Lord is our king; he will save us. Thy tacklings are loosed; they could not well strengthen their mast, they could not spread the sail: then is the prey of a great spoil divided; the lame take the prey. And the inhabitant shall not say, I am sick: the people that dwell therein shall be forgiven their iniquity.

THREE THINGS ARE TREATED of in this chapter:
    1. God's dealings with the open enemies of his people, wherein there is a more immediate respect to the people of Assyria, that came up against the land of Judah and the inhabitants of Jerusalem in Hezekiah's time; but ultimately a respect to the destruction of the open enemies of the Christian church in the days of the gospel. God's dealings with these, in their destruction, is spoken of in the 1st verse: "Woe to thee that spoilest, and thou wast not spoiled; and dealest treacherously, and they dealt not treacherously with thee! when thou shalt cease to spoil, thou shalt be

spoiled; and when thou shalt make an end to deal treacherously, they shall deal treacherously with thee." Vv. 3–4, "At the noise of the tumult the people fled; at the lifting up of thyself the nations were scattered. And your spoil shall be gathered like the gathering of the caterpillar: as the running to and fro of locusts shall he run upon them." [V.] 7, "Behold, their valiant ones shall cry without: the ambassadors of peace shall weep bitterly."

2. God's merciful dealing with those in Israel that walk righteously.

3. His dealing with hypocrites, and the professors of religion that live wickedly. God's dealings with the righteous {are spoken of}, v. 2: "O Lord, be gracious unto us; we have waited for thee: be thou their arm every morning, our salvation also in the time of trouble." [Vv.] 5–6, "The Lord is exalted; for he dwelleth on high: he hath filled Zion with judgment and righteousness. And wisdom and knowledge shall be the stability of thy times, and strength of salvation: the fear of the Lord is his treasure." And God's different dealings with hypocrites and the righteous, are spoken of interchangeably, from the 8th verse to the end of the chapter. From the 8th verse to the end of the 14th, God's dealings with the wicked {and those that are open enemies of God's people}, are spoken of:

The highways lie waste, the wayfaring man ceaseth: he hath broken the covenant, he hath despised the cities, he regardeth no man. The earth mourneth and languisheth: Lebanon is ashamed and hewn down: Sharon is like a wilderness; and Bashan and Carmel shake off their fruits. Now will I rise, saith the Lord; now will I be exalted; now will I lift up myself. Ye shall conceive chaff, ye shall bring forth stubble: your breath, as fire, shall devour you. And the people shall be as the burnings of lime: as thorns cut up shall they be burned in the fire. Hear, ye that are far off, what I have done; and, ye that are near, acknowledge my might.

And then, in the 15th, 16th, and the former part of the 17th verse, {God's dealings} with those that walk righteously {are spoken of}. And in the latter part of the 17th and the 18th (verses, God's dealings} with those that live wickedly {and profess religion, are spoken of}. And then again, from thence to the end, in those verses that have been read as the foundation of my present discourse, God's gracious dealings with those of God's professing people that behave righteously, {are spoken of}.

The Method

in which I would discourse from those words at this time, is this:

[*Observation*] I. I would observe who they are, to whom the promises in the text are made.

Obs. II. What promises are here made to such. And then,

[*Obs.*] III. For Application, [I] shall observe how applicable those things are to our present circumstances in this land, and how that those blessings here promised, are the very blessings we need at this day. And,

[*Obs.*] IV. [I] shall endeavor to enforce these things as arguments, to persuade to those qualifications and duties to which these promises are made.

I. Who they are, that are {those to whom the promises in the text are made}.

The promises in the text are made in the form of a speech, directed to a person, signified by the words "thou"—"Thou shalt not see a fierce people"—{and} "thine"—"thine eyes shall see Jerusalem a quiet habitation." Now these words are manifestly relative to something that had been spoken of before; and if we look back to the 15th verse, we shall see who this is that God speaks to, and makes those promises to: "He that walketh righteously, and speaketh uprightly." The person here spoken of, is set in opposition to sinners in Zion and hypocrites,[1] spoken of in the preceding verse. The person to whom these promises are made, is not only one that is outwardly one of Israel, and pretends to be a worshipper of the true God, and comes before God as his people comes and sit before him as his people, and joins in the public ordinances of his worship; but a person whose fruits are agreeable to such a profession.

Now the good fruits that are brought forth in life and conversation, are of two sorts, viz., good fruits in behavior, and in speech. These two kinds of good fruits, are here spoken of under those two expressions: "He that walketh righteously, and speaketh uprightly." They to whom those promises are made, bring forth fruit answerable to their profession in their behavior: they walk righteously, or, as it is in the text, "walk in righteousness."

---

1. See *Sinners in Zion*, WJE 22:262–84.

[*First*.] The word "righteousness," as it is commonly used in Scripture, is put for all manner of virtuous, pious and right behavior, both to God, our neighbor, and ourselves, in obedience to all the commands of God, including all that is included by the Prophet. Micah 6:8, "He hath showed thee, O man, what is good; and what doth the Lord require of thee, but to do justly, and to love mercy, and to walk humbly with thy God?" And all that [is] included by those expressions of the Apostle. Titus 2:12, "Teaching us that, denying all ungodliness and worldly lusts, [we should] live righteously, soberly, and godly."

He that walks righteously, and speaks uprightly, he behaves himself with all proper reverence and devotion towards God; gives him that honor in his behavior that he requires. He renders to God the things that are God's; he is strict in the observation of the holy sabbath, and neglects no duty of the worship of God that is required of him; and strives to promote the honor of God, according to his talents and opportunities. He performs all duties of justice towards men. He is just in his dealing, is careful to render to everyone his due. He performs all relative duties. He is careful to give honor[2] to his superiors, and to walk with justice, humanity and condescension to his inferiors.

He behaves himself agreeable to the duties required of him, in the relations he stands in in the family he belongs to. If he be a parent, {he is observant of the duties of a parent}. If the person be in a married state, then he or she is observant of the duties {of a spouse}. If the person stands in the relation of a child, [then he or she is observant of the duties of a child; and] if a servant, [then those of a servant]. He is one that performs duties required of him towards his rulers, leading a quiet and peaceable life in submission to lawful authority.

If he be one that is in authority, [he is observant of his duties as a ruler]. If he be an officer, either civil or ecclesiastical, [he is observant of his duties as an officer]. He is one that behaves himself meekly, peaceably and charitably; studies the things that make for peace; endeavors, if it be possible,[3] as much as lies in him, [to edify];[4] is of a forgiving spirit; governs his spirit, [is] not soon angry, and will not suffer the sun to go down {on his wrath [Eph. 4:26]}.

---

2. In revising for re-preaching, JE changed this to read "due honor."
3. MS: "possibly."
4. This insert is based on Rom. 14:19, which JE alludes to in the former clause.

[He] is of a merciful behavior {towards his fellow creatures}, is of a public spirit, is universally of a benevolent spirit, seeks the good of mankind, treats all courteously and kindly, [and is] ready to bear others' burdens.

[He] behaves himself humbly and modestly, in honor praises others, as though others were better than himself.

He is one that behaves himself truly and faithfully. He hates guile and deceit, and is careful to fulfill his promises. [He] behaves him[self] chastely, avoids all lewd and lascivious behavior.

[He] is temperate, {is} patiently contented with his lot, avoiding a covetous and envious behavior. [He bows] submissively under the adverse dispensations of divine providence. Thus, they to whom the promises in the text are made, walk righteously, or bring forth the fruits of righteousness in their behavior.

[*Second.*] They to whom the promises in the text are made, bring forth the fruits of righteousness, not only in their behavior but in their speech. They "walk righteously, and speak uprightly." Great part of the wickedness that is committed in the world, is committed with the tongue; by this, men are guilty of lying, bearing false witness, perjury, treachery and deceitfulness towards their neighbor. By this member of the body, men vent their malice and hatred one towards another, in reviling one another, slandering and judging, censuring [and] backbiting one another. The sin that is committed in contentions among neighbors in towns and churches, is principally by the tongue. The exercises and manifestation of the pride of the heart, is very much by the tongue: hereby, men manifest their high conceit of themselves, and their contempt of their fellow creatures. By this also is vented the lust of uncleanness, in lascivious speeches, lewd songs and the like. 'Tis principally by the tongue that men tempt one another to sin, and join together in iniquity, and stir up and influence each others' corruptions. By this, men show the vanity of their mind, [and in] idle, vain conversation.

The corruption of the heart having so great vent by the tongue, hence the apostle James observes, Jas. 3:6–8, "And the tongue is a fire, a world of iniquity: so is the tongue among our members, that it defileth the whole body, and setteth on fire the course of nature; and it is set on fire of hell. For every kind of beasts, and of birds, and of serpents, and of things in the sea, is tamed, and hath been tamed of mankind: but the tongue can no man tame; it is an unruly evil, full of deadly poison." Men generally show what they are, by the manner of their using their tongues. For as Christ observes, Matt. 12:34, "out of the abundance of the heart the mouth speaketh"; and therefore says that by our words we shall be justified, v. 37. And the Wise Man says, "Life and death are in the power of the tongue," Prov. 18:21. And to the like purpose, the apostle James observes, on the one hand, "if any man offend not in word, the same is a perfect man. Jas. 3:2, "If any man offend not in word, the same is a perfect man, and able also to bridle the whole body." And on the other hand, that if any man seem to be religious, {but does not bridle his tongue, his religion is vain}. Jas. 1:26, "If any man among you seem to be religious, and bridleth not his tongue, but deceiveth his own heart, this man's religion is vain."

Now he to whom the promises in the text are made, is one that bridles the tongue. He not only walketh righteously, but speaketh uprightly. He not only conscientiously avoids these forementioned sins of the tongue, but he uses his tongue to virtuous and pious purposes. He is a person of strict veracity {in speech}, without guile and deceit.

He is pure and chaste in his conversation. His speech is "with grace, seasoned with salt," Col. 4:6. His speech is not vain, but solid and profitable, and "to the use of edifying" [Eph. 4:29]. In his tongue is "the law of kindness," as the expression is, Prov. 31:26. And there is an agreement between his tongue and his heart, as the expression of speaking uprightly denotes. There is such an agreement in the profession he makes of religion, in what he says in prayer and praise, and in his conversation amongst men. He don't speak with a flattering and deceitful tongue.

Thus those to whom the promises in the text are made, in general do bring forth the fruits of righteousness in speech and behavior. They "walk righteously, and speak uprightly."

[*Third.*] In what follows, several particular instances of a right behavior are mentioned, that do more especially relate[5] to rulers, though not only to them.[6]

He "despiseth the gain of oppressions": he is one who, if he has power and authority in his hands, will not abuse {his power} to oppress; nor will he take any advantage to extort, or to enrich himself, or advance his own interest with the spoils of his neighbors. He "despiseth [the gains

---

5. MS: "Related."
6. In what follows, JE expounds on the clauses of Is. 33:15.

of oppression]." [He] don't look on such gain worthy to be called gain; esteems it nothing worth, and worse than nothing.

[He] "shaketh his hands from holding bribes": [he] does the part of an impartial judge, loves justice, hates unrighteousness, is sensible of his own liableness to be blinded by self-interest, and therefore strictly avoids the snare; not only refuses a bribe, but abhors [it].

[He] "stoppeth his ears from hearing of blood": [he] abhors cruelty, will hear no suggestion of any such thing, will hear nothing tending to move or excite to any acts of that nature.

[He] "shutteth his eyes [from seeing evil]": herein, [he] imitates God himself, who is of purer eyes, can neither bear to hear of or see iniquity, shuts his eyes from beholding the objects of lust, [is] careful to avoid all temptation. [He] hates and shuns the appearance of evil, treats sin as men are wont to treat those things that they bear an exceeding detestation of, and antipathy against.

Of such a character are those to whom the promises in the text are made; which may be understood as indefinite promises made to particular persons of such a character, but as promises made more particularly and determinately to a people of such qualities, or in any whom such virtues and such a behavior prevails. 'Tis evident the promises in the text are especially made to a people as a people, by [the] 21st [and] 22nd verses: "But there the glorious Lord will be unto us a place of broad rivers and streams; wherein shall go no galley with oars, neither shall gallant ship pass thereby. For the Lord is our judge, the Lord is our lawgiver, the Lord is our king; he will save us"; and [the] 24th verse, "[And the inhabitant shall not say, I am sick: the people that dwell therein shall be forgiven their iniquity]."

I come now, in the

II. [Second] place, to consider the promises themselves that are here made to such.

Here are promised to such as {walk righteously, and speak uprightly}:

First. Defense in time of war.

Second. Success in war in conquering, and taking the spoil of enemies.

Third. Health.

Fourth. Plenty.

Fifth. That mercy which makes way for all these, [viz.,] forgiveness of their iniquities.

First. Defense and safety from enemies in a time of war.

Of which promise, we may observe the following circumstances:

1. Who will be the author of this defense: Jehovah.

2. In what relation he will appear to a righteous people, in thus defending them and giving them safety: [as a] judge [who will] plead [their] cause [as a] righteous cause, [and as a] lawgiver.

3. What enemies they shall be defended from.

4. [What they shall be] particularly preserved from: the enemy's ships and naval forces.

5. [Their] habitation is weak: tabernacle.

6. The degree of safety: [Zion shall] not "see a fierce people"; "not one of the stakes [thereof shall ever be removed]"; [the] ships shall not pass.

7. The great quietness and tranquility that shall be the consequence.

8. One means whereby God will defend them: [by] strangely weakening the power of enemies and confounding them in their attempts. The

Second thing promised, is success and victory in war, and taking the spoil of enemies.

Two circumstances:

1. That the victory and spoil that shall be taken, shall be very great.

2. That this victory shall be obtained by those that are very weak and insufficient of themselves. [The]

Third thing promised, [is] health. "[The inhabitant shall not say, I am sick]." [The]

Fourth thing, [is] plenty. "[The glorious Lord will be unto us a place of] broad rivers and streams." By which may well be under[stood] a plenty, both spiritual and temporal. Rivers, and streams of water, are often in Scripture put for both of these.

[So] temporal [plenty]. Therefore, the drying up the waters of a city or kingdom, is in Scripture put for taking away their wealth and temporal supplies. Is. 15:6–7, "For the waters of Nimrim shall be desolate: for the hay is withered away, the grass faileth, there is no green thing. Therefore the abundance they have gotten, and that which they have laid up, shall they carry away to the brook of the willows." Hosea 13:15, "Though he be fruitful among his brethren, an east wind shall come, the wind of the

Lord shall come up from the wilderness, and his spring shall become dry, and his fountain shall be dried up: he shall spoil the treasure of all pleasant vessels." Jer. 50:37–38, "A sword is upon their horses, and upon their chariots, and upon all the mingled people that are in the midst of her; and they shall become as women: a sword is upon her treasures; and they shall be robbed. A drought is upon her waters; and they shall be dried up: for it is the land of graven images, and they are mad upon their idols."

[So]⁷ spiritual [plenty]. Is. 43:20, "I give waters in the wilderness, and rivers in the desert, to give drink to my people, my chosen"; Ps. 46:4. Spiritual [plenty is] especially intended, because God himself will be as a river.

A peculiar circumstance of this plenty is here mentioned, viz., that it shall be without any calamity attending it. It was a great convenience to great cities, to be built on the banks of some great river. But there was this inconvenience attended it: {the cities were vulnerable to its enemies}. Prov. 10:22, "The blessing of the Lord maketh rich, and he addeth no sorrow with it."

Fifthly, and lastly. That mercy is promised, which makes way for all these other blessings, viz., forgiving the iniquities of such a people. Which seems to intimate that the words of the text, as a prophecy, have a special respect to God's professing people, who had much corrupted themselves, and were now remarkably reformed, religion having greatly revived among them.

God often promises this mercy of forgiveness to professing people on their repentance and reformation, however corrupt they have been. Is. 1:16–18, "Wash ye, make ye clean; put away the evil of your doings from before mine eyes; cease to do evil; learn to do well; seek judgment, relieve the oppressed, judge the fatherless, plead for the widow. Come now, and let us reason together, saith the Lord: though your sins be as scarlet, they shall be as white as snow; though they be red like crimson, they shall be as wool." Jer. 31:33–34, "But this shall be the covenant that I will make with the house of Israel; After those days, saith the Lord, I will put my

---

7. The leaf from which this portion of the sermon was made was originally used for a child's writing exercise, which appears perpendicularly along the left side of the page:
   [—-] Psalm 59

---

1 Save Me O god by thy and Judg
By thy Strength Hear my
O God by the

law in their inward parts, and write it in their hearts; and will be their God, and they shall be my people. And they shall teach no more every man his neighbor, and every man his brother, saying, Know the Lord: for they shall all know me, from the least of them unto the greatest of them, saith the Lord: for I will forgive their iniquity, and I will remember their sin no more."[8]

This mercy makes way for all other mercies and blessings. 'Tis therefore often connected, in God's promises, with promises of other blessings. Jer. 33:8–9, "And I will cleanse them from all their iniquity, whereby they have sinned against me; and I will pardon all their iniquities, whereby they have sinned, and whereby they have transgressed against me. And it shall be to me a name of joy, a praise and an honor before all the nations of the earth, which shall hear all the good that I do unto them: and they shall fear and tremble for all the goodness and for all the prosperity that I procure unto it."

Particularly, this mercy is often connected with the removing of sickness, or healing of diseases. Ps. 103:2, "[Bless the Lord, O my soul, and forget not all his benefits]"; Matt. 9, beginning: "Son, be of good cheer, thy sins [be forgiven thee]." Jas. 5:14–15, "and if he have committed sins, they shall be forgiven."

III. To show how suitable those promises are to our present circumstances in this land, and in this part of the land.

It is now a time of war with us. We need defense. The circumstances under which this mercy is promised, are opposite to our particular circumstances and present needs. We are exposed to a people of a strange language, of a deeper speech than we can perceive, and to us of a stammering tongue that we cannot understand, a fierce and cruel [people]. [We] are afraid of being invaded by 'em, and are so exposed, that if they should come against us, they could hardly fail of, honorably speaking, greatly distressing us. But here it is promised, they shall not come nigh; [we shall] "not see [a fierce people]." Our habitations are weak, like a tent or tabernacle, not a strong building, easily broken down. But {we have} "a quiet habitation." We need this quietness. [We] have been greatly disturbed, and are so still.

---

8. The last two Scripture references are written in a slightly different ink from the rest of the sermon, and may have been a later addition, but the difference is slight enough to warrant inclusion here.

We particularly need defense from the naval forces of our enemies. A great naval force is come against us, as is implied [vv. 21–23]. We are lame. We therefore need to have God remarkably interpose, to hinder and consume 'em. [We] need the blessing of health; [we] need both temporal and spiritual provisions; we greatly need forgiveness of our iniquities: the mercy that is here spoken of, as that which makes way {for salvation [v. 22]}.

IV. To apply and enforce these things as arguments, to persuade to the qualifications and duties to which these promises have been made.

I have observed what the promises [are], and how the mercies here promised are the very mercies that are suited to our present circumstances, and are the very mercies that we now stand in special and extraordinary need of. Every one of them are mercies that the present state of this land, and the present state of this part of it in particular, do especially require, and most of them the very mercies that this[9] day is set apart {to observe}. And God, in the context, has told us what a people must do. God himself, who is the governor {of the world}, has told us the way.

This land has rarely been in so distressing circumstances, and never in this generation was so threatened, and had such dark clouds hanging over it. Our enemies never had such advantages against us, at least in some respects. Never were so great preparations made. And we in this place are nearly concerned, not only as we are a part of the nation, and part of the country that is thus annoyed and threatened; but we ourselves are particularly in danger. The enemy doubtless are able to raise such a force as shall be sufficient {to spoil us}. They are much acquainted [with the region], acquainted with the woods and country about, [and] know the way to us. What they have done seems to show an aim at something below the line, of sorts, that we have had on our frontiers. There has appeared very much a disposition to exert themselves. They have lately opened their own way; their own behavior shows how they look upon it.

There has been very much to stir 'em up and animate 'em of late: {such as} our preparations against them, {then} our disappointment,[10] {then} their success [in sending] the fleet.

---

9. MS: "mercies they that."

10. Referring to the aborted English plans to invade Canada in the summer of 1746.

Their present behavior appears threatening. It would be no wonder, if they should attempt to do some greater thing than ever they have done yet. These things show our great need of those mercies.

And we have now heard what is incumbent on us. Each one [is] to consider his ways. [We are to] turn from all our evil ways, to walk righteously and speak uprightly, to bring forth the fruits of righteousness, both in speech and behavior; to hearken to the commands of God, deny all ungodliness; to forsake our profaneness and neglect of God and Christ, and the great things of the eternal world, [the] profanation of [the] sabbath, [and] neglect of family prayer. [We are to] make religion our business. [We are to] forsake our worldliness, forsake our injustice,[11] uncleanness, [and] youthful vanities;[12] forsake all our bitterness and grudges one against another, and follow the things that make for peace: making restitution,[13] confessing faults one to another, forgiving injuries, do[ing] works of love, mutual kindness and mercy. [We are to] forsake our narrowness of spirit, and seek the public good, with care and exactness to perform relative duties: parents taking up Joshua's resolution,[14] applying themselves with the greatest care and diligence to the religious education {of their children}, reviving family government; forsaking all our fraud, deceit, oppressions and unfaithfulness in our dealing, and neglecting to render our just dues; rulers, both civil and ecclesiastical, as for God, {ruling} as ministers of God, as fathers of the people; inferiors rendering due honor to superiors, and rulers in church and state, not increasing their[15] burden, but strengthening, assisting, [and] encouraging; turning from all ways of sinning committed with the tongue, particularly {the sins of} evil-speaking and backbiting, [instead of] using our tongues to glorify God, and bless and edify men, endeavoring that our conversation one with another may be profitable, and sweetened with love.

And one thing I cannot neglect to speak of as a special duty, that a people in such circumstances as we are in owe to God and ourselves, i.e., using proper preemptives for our own safety. The contrary would be tempting God, like casting ourselves down from the pinnacle [of the

---

11. In revising for re-preaching, JE drew a line in the left margin besides the preceding part of this sentence.

12. In this passage, JE is rehearsing themes from sermons earlier in the year. See the sermon on Eph. 5:5–7 (no. 838).

13. See the sermon on Luke 19:8–9 (no. 823).

14. See the two sermons on Josh. 24:15 (no. 807 and 815).

15. I.e., "inferiors," or the general populous.

temple].¹⁶ David was eminent for his trust in God for defense from his enemies, but yet dwelt in a strong fortress. God promised Israel, that if they would be obedient to him, he would enable 'em to subdue their enemies, and take their strong cities; but {they must also build} bulwarks against it, {until they are subdued}. Deut. 20:20, "thou shalt build bulwarks against the city that maketh war with thee, until it be subdued." God promised Joshua and the children of Israel [that they would take] Ai, but [commanded them to "take all the people of war" and to lay an ambush, Josh. 8:2].

We have warning against the folly of neglecting of proper means of defense from enemies, in the example of the people of Laish. Judg. 18:7, "Then the five men departed, and came to Laish, and saw the people that were therein, how they dwelt careless, after the manner of the Zidonians, quiet and secure; and there was no magistrate in the land, that might put them to shame in anything; and they were far from the Zidonians, and had no business with any man." This animated 'em; vv. 9–10,¹⁷ "And they said, Arise, that we may go up against them: for we have seen the land, and, behold, it is very good: and are ye still? be not slothful to go, and to enter to possess the land. When ye go, ye shall come unto a people secure, and to a large land: for God hath given it into your hands; a place where there is no want of anything that is in the earth." See the consequences, vv. 27–28: "And they took the things which Micah had made, and the priest which he had, and came unto Laish, unto a people that were at quiet and secure: and they smote them with the edge of the sword, and burnt the city with fire. And there was no deliverer, because it was far from Zidon, and they had no business with any man; and it was in the valley that lieth by Bethrehob. And they built a city, and dwelt therein." And God has lately given us a remarkable warning in our own nation.¹⁸

And it has been a thing frequently observed in history, that when God has intended destruction to a people, he has left 'em to be infatuated, so as either to do that which tends greatly to expose 'em to their enemies, or strangely to neglect the proper means of their defense from their enemies. It was an old observation, even among the heathen, *Quos Jupiter perdit prius infatuat*.¹⁹ However, we ought not to use those means,

16. Apparently a reference to the devil's tempting of Jesus, Matt. 4:5, Luke 4:9.

17. The MS appears to read "Is 15 11," apparently a mistake on JE's part. The verses quoted seem to refer to what he intends.

18. Probably a reference to the unsuccessful Jacobite Rebellion.

19. "Those whom Jupiter destroys he formerly loved." One of the very rare

as trusting in the means any more than Joshua {did}, but as part of the duty.

[I will] mention some *Motives*, to persuade all thus to forsake their sins, and walk righteously and speak uprightly.

First. This is the easiest and cheapest course we can take for our security and defense. We may turn from our sins to God, without any expense to us of anything that is truly valuable. And although, as I said before, a part of our duty {will} be to use necessary means {of defense from enemies}, and this can't be done without cost; yet this is the way to save expense {to us of anything truly valuable}, under a more valiant Captain.[20]

Second. There is no way so sure. Hereby, we shall have the Lord for our judge. [There is] none so able, on the account of knowledge [and] power. [He is the] God of the sea and dry land; [he] "breaks the ships of Tarshish," Ps. 48:7.

Third. Without this way, all others will be in vain. Prov. 11:21, "Though hand join in hand, the wicked shall not be unpunished: but the seed of the righteous shall be delivered."

Fourth. Let us consider how ready God has shown himself to appear [on] our side, and to help us in the present war. [Consider the] year past. [God has] done things of the nature of the things promised. [We have made] prey of great spoil. {Though we are as} the lame, [yet we have] strangely weakened and confounded our enemies. Some things that we now hear of God's dealings with the great force that our enemies have sent over the seas, [are] very agreeable {to God's appearing on our side}.

[*Objection.*] But here possibly, some persons be ready to object, and say, "But what will it signify for me alone to turn from my sins, and to take utmost care to walk righteously and speak uprightly, if others don't? If still there be no general reformation, as there is no prospect at present, how little influence will my reforming have? If the people don't reform as a people, still we shall not be entitled to those promises; and if general

occasions when JE employs Latin in a sermon.
20. I.e., Christ.

judgments come, I may, notwithstanding my own personal {reformation}, be involved among the rest."

Answer 1. There never will be a general reformation, unless particular persons reform. God sometimes does bring [it] about, whereby a people are saved from judgments [by the act of one person].

[*Answ.*] 2. If you do thoroughly {reform}, you know not how much influence you may have on others. Examples {have} great influence. The example of one person that is thorough {can have influence}, especially if he be eminent, and [observes] the strictness of religion. Hereby, a testimony is borne {for reformation} in the most effectual manner. Hereby, matter of conviction is held forth. When professors of religion live loosely, unchristianly, {this} tends greatly to harden {others}. But when {they live strictly}, it has a great tendency to convince and awaken. Christ directs his disciples to see to it, that their light may so shine {before men, that} others, seeing their good works, [may glorify God, Matt. 5:16].

[*Answ.*] 3. God has oftentimes great respect to a few persons, that are thorough in a religious and virtuous walk and conversation. God did not probably destroy the old world, till there {were no righteous left but Noah and his family}. As wicked as the generality of the inhabitants of Sodom were, yet if there had been ten, [God would have spared them, Gen. 18:20–33]. God has a great respect to a little thorough religion and virtue among a people. Such are [God's] blessings. What respect had God to Potiphar [Gen. 39]. Such {persons} are as walls and bulwarks, are powerful in their prayers. If any do his will, him he hears. As princes that have power with God and with men, sometimes someone {eminent in righteousness} is more of a defense than a whole army: "[the] chariots of Israel, and the horsemen [thereof," 2 Kgs. 2:12, 13:14]. If you [will be thus thorough], this will add to the number, and this adds to the strength.

[*Answ.*] 4. God sometimes in his providence remarkably distinguishes such as {are thorough in religion}, in a time of public calamity and destruction. [So] Noah {was distinguished from the rest of the old world, and} Lot {from the rest of the people of Sodom, and} Caleb, Joshua, [and] Jeremiah. Jer. 40, at [the] beginning,

The word that came to Jeremiah from the Lord, after that Nebuzaradan the captain of the guard had let him go from Ramah, when he had taken him being bound in chains among all that were carried away captive of Jerusalem and Judah, which were carried away captive unto Babylon. And the captain of the guard took Jeremiah, and said unto him, The Lord thy God hath pronounced this evil upon this place. Now the

Lord hath brought it, and done according as he hath said: because ye have sinned against the Lord, and have not obeyed his voice, therefore this thing is come upon you. And now, behold, I loose thee this day from the chains which were upon thine hand. If it seem good unto thee to come with me into Babylon, come; and I will look well unto thee: but if it seem ill unto thee to come with me into Babylon, forbear: behold, all the land is before thee: whither it seemeth good and convenient for thee to go, thither go.

[So] the Christians in Jerusalem. God knows how [to distinguish such].

[*Answ.*] 5. If such {as are distinguished in a time of calamity}, seem to be involved {in religion}, yet it shall certainly go well with them. Infinite power and infinite wisdom is on their side; nothing shall happen to 'em, but what shall be best for 'em. God orders every circumstance; the hairs of their head are all numbered. Enemies [have] no more power, in any respect, than[21] their heavenly Father gives them. God, who is able, takes thorough care of 'em.[22] He can influence the hearts of enemies, deliver out of their hands, [and] turn seeming calamities in[to] prosperity. There is God's faithful promise, Is. 3, at the beginning: God threatens {Jerusalem and Judah with ruin}, then says, 10th verse, "Say ye to the righteous, it shall be well." Such shall surely dwell on high; God is their refuge, sure hiding place. Thousands shall fall at their side, and ten thousand [at their right hand, Ps. 91:7]. [God shall] deliver 'em from the power of the sword, cover 'em with his feathers; wherever they are, [God] will be a sanctuary to 'em. God is for 'em, and none can be effectually against 'em. [They shall be] "in league with the stones" [Job 5:23]. [They shall] make their enemies to be at peace, [they shall] be at home in God. [They] belong to the church of God, and that will ever be safe. God will fulfill that [promise] to Zion, spoken of, 20th [and] 21st verses of the text: "[Look upon Zion, the city of

---

21. MS: "that."

22. The paper that comprises the following portion of the sermon is a discarded prayer bid, which reads:
Ebenezer Ferry and his wife desire that
thanks may be given to god in this Congregation
for So far recovering her and and one of their Children
from their Late Illness as that She She is able to
Come to the house of god
they desire that the Present marcy and the Late
Afliction they are the Subjects of may work for
their Spiritual good

our solemnities: thine eyes shall see Jerusalem a quiet habitation, a tabernacle that shall not be taken down; not one of the stakes thereof shall ever be removed, neither shall any of the cords thereof be broken. But there the glorious Lord will be unto us a place of broad rivers and streams; wherein shall go no galley with oars, neither shall gallant ship pass thereby]." [They have "a] strong city; salvation will God appoint for walls and bulwarks" [Is. 26:1]. That will be fulfilled, Ps. 46[:4–5], "[There is a river, the streams whereof shall make glad the city of God, the holy place of the tabernacles of the Most High. God is in the midst of her; she shall not be moved: God shall help her, and that right early]."

[*Answ.*] 6. Your virtue will have the greater reward for its singularity. This will be the glory of it. [It will be the] greater evidence of the sincerity [and] strength of it. It is spoken of by God as a circumstance attending Noah's virtue, that rendered it peculiarly acceptable to him, that he was righteous in that generation. Gen. 7:1, "And the Lord said unto Noah, Come thou and all thy house into the ark; for thee have I seen righteous before me in this generation." And great was his reward.

So that that objection can be [no] just objection against our turning, whether others {turn} or no. God will take care, that it shall be well with you. He'll be a cover and shield to you, your sure defense and mighty Redeemer. He will bless you, and you shall be blessed; you shall be carried on eagles' wings, and nothing shall by any means hurt you.

God's People in Danger

November 27, 1746

DESPITE THE SUCCESSES THE British enjoyed over the past months, New England still found itself in a precarious position. The celebration for the victory at Louisburg and the breaking of the Jacobite rebellion was now tempered by many realities. First, the French proposed articles of peace seeking the restitution of Cape Breton to France. Second, combined Native and French groups sat encamped outside Annapolis Royal preparing for an assault. Third, French allied Native groups killed sixteen men outside of Saratoga and the British mustered a poor response. But the most threatening news reported in Boston was the sighting of the French Fleet off the coast of Canada. The Brest squadron left the port of Jebucta and sailed in support of the defense against the British expedition.

Foreboding turned to thanksgiving when this fleet found itself in confusion. According to Thomas Hutchinson's *History of Massachusetts*, the commander of the squadron, Duke D'Anville, died of apoplexy while harbored in Jebucta. Then, a sickness swept through the French sailors diminishing their numbers to half strength. Finally, a cold storm swept in, separating the fleet and exposing it to British capture.[1] This series of providences became the occasion for Edwards's thanksgiving sermon *God's People in Danger*.

Edwards began with a text describing the position of Israel in Hezekiah's time. Sennacharib threatened Israel and prepared to launch attacks against her. Israel was in a weak position because she had been cut down for some time: she lost her lands across the Jordan, she was small

---

1. Hutchinson, *History of Massachusetts*, 2:384–85.

compared to her enemies, and Israel suffered from debilitating corruption. Yet God still intervened to deliver his people as he had done many times before. As Edwards noted, God had the power to overcome Israel's enemies and acted with the "immediate hand of heaven" to do so. This deliverance was rooted in more than just the welfare of his own people but in a desire for his own glory. But this deliverance had an eye to the future "reviving of his church" and the "flourishing of religion."

Edwards then transitioned from Israel's position during the reign of Hezekiah to New England's position with France. Edwards elucidated a long list of comparisons using the formula, "as Sennacharib" went "so we" will do likewise. This comparative formula connected New England with the Biblical drama. France's designs to defeat the British became the occasion for France's own defeat. From this comparison, Edwards drew a series of improvements for the people of Northampton. God's manner of dealing with his people, evidenced in the confusion of the French fleet, should lead one to praise God, to trust in God, and to hope and pray for the revival of God's church. Edwards summarized this in a theme that has appeared throughout his war sermons: "To do what in us lies that a revival of religion may be the event and issue of these wonderful [dispensations]." Edwards exhorted his people to actively participate in the outcome of military battles through their fulfillment of spiritual duties.

* * * * *

This sermon was edited for the Jonathan Edwards Center by Ken Minkema. Also known as "Thanksgiving after the Confusion of the French Fleet that Came to Jebucta," the manuscript is eighteen duodecimo-sized leaves of mixed paper. Edwards headed the booklet, "Thanksgiving Novem. 27. after the Confusion of the French Fleet that Came to Jebucta." One of the pieces of paper (L. 13) used to construct the sermon is a discarded letter cover, with the address sheared on the left side: "To / [the] Revrend Mr Jonathan Edwards / [Minr] of the Gospel at North hampton / [in] new England / To the Care of the Revrend / [Mr Th]omas prince Minr of the Gospel / [in Bosto]n in N:E: Containg under this / [a?] Letter to the said Mr prince and [?] Mr John Moorhead." At points throughout the manuscript, a previous owner drew penciled lines alongside some of the heads, and still another made brief descriptive comments on the front and back page.

God's People in Danger

Isaiah 37:28–38[1]

But I know thine abode, and thy going out, and thy coming in, and thy rage against me. Because thy rage against me, and thy tumult, is come up into mine ears, therefore will I put my hook in thy nose, and my bridle in thy lips, and I will turn thee back by the way by which thou camest. And this shall be a sign unto thee, Ye shall eat this year such as groweth of itself; and the second year that which springeth of the same: and in the third year sow ye, and reap, and plant vineyards, and eat the fruit thereof. And the remnant that is escaped of the house of Judah shall again take root downward, and bear fruit upward: for out of Jerusalem shall go forth a remnant, and they that escape out of mount Zion: the zeal of the Lord of hosts shall do this. Therefore thus saith the Lord concerning the king of Assyria, He shall not come into this city, nor shoot an arrow there, nor come before it with shields, nor cast a bank against it. By the way that he came, by the same shall he return, and shall not come into this city, saith the Lord. For I will defend this city to save it for mine own sake, and for my servant David's sake. Then the angel of the Lord went forth, and smote in the camp of the Assyrians a hundred and fourscore and five thousand: and when they arose early in the morning, behold, they were all dead corpses. So Sennacherib king of Assyria departed, and went and returned, and dwelt at Nineveh. And it came to pass, as he was worshipping in the house of Nisroch his god, that Adrammelech and Sharezer his sons smote him with the sword; and they escaped into the land of Armenia: and Esarhaddon his son reigned in his stead.

---

1. JE's call-out is for vv. 28–39, but ch. 37 has only 38 verses.

What has now been read, consists partly of prophecy, from the 28th to the 35th verse; and partly of history, giving an account of a wonderful dispensation, whereby the prophecy was fulfilled. That part which [is] prophetical, is part of the message that God sent to Hezekiah and the people of Jerusalem, by Isaiah the prophet, on occasion of the threatening, insulting letter that was sent by Rabshakeh, the captain of the host of Assyria, to Hezekiah. God, in this message which he sends to Hezekiah on this occasion, encourages him and his people with promises of protection and deliverance unto them, and denunciations of confusion to their enemies. And in the 36th verse, we have an account of the wonderful and immediate hand of heaven against these enemies of God's people, by which this prophecy was fulfilled.

The Method

In which, by divine help, I would discourse from that part of God's Word that has been now read, is this: in the Explication, I would,

I. Observe what is here declared, concerning the danger God's people were in, in Hezekiah's time.

II. What is here set forth concerning their deliverance.

And then, by way Application, [I] shall, first, observe how applicable these things are to God's late dispensation towards this land, with other English settlements in America; second, show what improvement we are lead [to], by this part of Scripture, to make of these dispensations of providence towards us.

I. I would take notice of the things that are here signified concerning the danger that God's people were in.

And with respect to this, we may observe the following things, that are either declared or pointed forth to us in the words:

First. Who the enemy are, by which God's people were brought into danger: Sennacharib, king of Assyria.

When it said, vv. 28–29, "But I know thine abode, and thy going out, and thy coming in, and thy rage against me. Because thy rage against me, and thy tumult, is come up into mine ears, therefore will I put my hook in thy nose, and my bridle in thy lips, and I will turn thee back by the way by which thou camest," respect is had to him. This appears by the preceding context, vv. 21, etc.; and he is expressly mentioned in the 33rd and 34th verses: "Therefore thus saith the Lord concerning the king of Assyria, He shall not come into this city, nor shoot an arrow there, nor come before it with shields, nor cast a bank against it. By the way that he came, by the same shall he return, and shall not come into this city, saith the Lord." He was a very potent enemy, the greatest monarch in the world, very proud and haughty, one that had great successes of late, of which he boasts, [and] one that sought universal empire.

Second. The preparations and attempts that he made against God's people: [he] formed an expedition with vast preparation.
[He] sent a vast armament, more than 185,000 [men].

Third. The spirit with which the enemies of God's people made this attempt: with a spirit of rage and arrogance. "[I know thy] rage," v. 28.
[They] came with a fierce, violent and cruel spirit, threatening to make them "drink their own dung, and drink their own piss," ch. 36:12. [They] came with a design of destroying the land, ch. 36:10. [Sennacherib came with] a great spirit of arrogance and insolence, manifested in his great, swelling words and haughty speeches, called his "tumult"; v. 29, "Because thy rage against me, and thy tumult, is come up into mine ears."
The enemies of God's [people] acted as people [who] were exceeding proud of their strength and numbers and former victories, and had a great confidence in their own strength, and acted as though they were sure of victory; and therefore behaved themselves in a most haughty and insulting manner, vaunting themselves, triumphing before the victory, showing the highest degree of scorn and contempt of Hezekiah and his people: and not only a contempt of them, but of the Lord their God, as appears by Rabshakeh's insolent speeches and messages. Ch. 36:4, "And Rabshakeh said unto them, Say ye now to Hezekiah, Thus saith the great king, the king of Assyria, What confidence is this wherein thou trustest?" [V.] 9, "How then wilt thou turn away the face of one captain of the least of my master's servants, and put thy trust on Egypt for chariots and for horsemen?" And by his reply, when Eliakim [said to Rabshakeh], vv. 11–12, "Speak, I pray thee, unto thy servants in the Syrian language; for we understand it: and speak not to us in the Jews' language, in the ears of the people that are on the wall. But Rabshakeh said, Hath my master sent me to thy master and to thee to speak these words? hath he not sent me to the men that sit upon the wall, that they may eat their own dung, and

drink their own piss with you?" He is not afraid to declare, that he did not think that their God could deliver 'em. Vv. 18–20, "Beware lest Hezekiah persuade you, saying, The Lord will deliver us. Hath any of the gods of the nations delivered his land out of the hand of the king of Assyria? Where are the gods of Hamath and Arphad? where are the gods of Sepharvaim? and have they delivered Samaria out of my hand? Who are they among all the gods of these lands, that have delivered their land out of my hand, that the Lord should deliver Jerusalem out of my hand?" And in the 10th and following verses of this chapter [36:10–13]:

> Thus shall ye speak to Hezekiah king of Judah, saying, Let not thy God, in whom thou trustest, deceive thee, saying, Jerusalem shall not be given into the hand of the king of Assyria. Behold, thou hast heard what the kings of Assyria have done to all lands by destroying them utterly; and shalt thou be delivered? Have the gods of the nations delivered them which my fathers have destroyed, as Gozan, and Haran, and Rezeph, and the children of Eden which were in Telassar? Where is the king of Hamath, and the king of Arphad, and the king of the city of Sepharvaim, Hena, and Ivah?

Fourth. We may observe the weak and defenseless circumstances that the people were in, when they were thus invaded and threatened.

They were very small and weak, in comparison of their enemies. [They] had been exceedingly reduced already, by their enemies having prevailed so far against [them]; as is signified here in that sign that God gave 'em, containing a symbolical representation of their circumstances. V. 30, "And this shall be a sign unto thee, Ye shall eat this year such as groweth of itself; and the second year that which springeth of the same: and in the third year sow ye, and reap, and plant vineyards, and eat the fruit thereof."

The people of Israel had been as it were cut down, as a field of wheat is by the reapers, and only some small remnant or gleanings of them left. {They are} spoken of as a remnant that had escaped a general destruction. Vv. 31–32, "And the remnant that is escaped of the house of Judah shall again take root downward, and bear fruit upward: for out of Jerusalem shall go forth a remnant, and they that escape out of mount Zion: the zeal of the Lord of hosts shall do this." So they are also spoken of, ch. 37:4, "It may be the Lord thy God will hear the words of Rabshakeh, whom the king of Assyria his master hath sent to reproach the living God, and will reprove the words which the Lord thy God hath heard: wherefore lift up thy prayer for the remnant that is left."

First, God began to cut Israel short in the days of Jehu by Hazael, in subduing the country beyond Jordan. 2 Kgs. 10:32, etc., "In those days the Lord began to cut Israel short: and Hazael smote them in all the coasts of Israel; from Jordan eastward, all the land of Gilead, the Gadites, and the Reubenites, and the Manassites, from Aroer, which is by the river Arnon, even Gilead and Bashan." And afterwards, utterly destroying all the country of the Reubenites and Gadites and half-tribe of Manasseh, by Pul and Tilgathpilneser. 1 Chron. 5:26, "And the God of Israel stirred up the spirit of Pul king of Assyria, and the spirit of Tilgathpilneser king of Assyria, and he carried them away, even the Reubenites, and the Gadites, and the half tribe of Manasseh, and brought them unto Halah, and Habor, and Hara, and to the river Gozan, unto this day." And then destroyed all the remaining country of the Ten Tribes, by Shalmanaser {king of Assyria}, so that there remained only {the two tribes of Judah} [2Kgs. 18]. And now Sennacharib had come up against all the fenced cities of the remaining kingdom of Judah, and had taken them, and had subdued almost all the country but Jerusalem. Ch. 26:1, "Now it came to pass in the fourteenth year of king Hezekiah, that Sennacherib king of Assyria came up against all the defensed cities of Judah, and took them." So that the remaining people might well be represented as the remnant of standing corn after the reaping of a field.

The people were so small and weak in comparison of their enemies, that Rabshakeh greatly insults 'em on that account. Ch. 36, vv. 8–9, "Now therefore give pledges, I pray thee, to my master the king of Assyria, and I will give thee two thousand horses, if thou be able on thy part to set riders upon them. How then wilt thou turn away the face of one captain of the least of my master's servants, and put thy trust on Egypt for chariots and for horsemen?" And Hezekiah owns the weakness of the people, and their insufficiency to resist so great strength, comparing it to the weakness of a woman in travail, that han't strength to bring forth. Ch. 37:3, "And they said unto him, Thus saith Hezekiah, This day is a day of trouble, and of rebuke, and of blasphemy: for the children are come to the birth, and there is not strength to bring forth."

And then God's people were very small and weak, and like the gleanings of a field after reaping, in another respect, viz., as the church of God had been greatly diminished and as it were cut down by their spiritual enemies. [There was] prevailing corruption. [During the] reign of wicked

King Ahaz, {the people of Israel were subjected to the Assyrians}. This also greatly weakened them, and exposed 'em to their enemies.

II. To observe what is here set forth, concerning the deliverance of God's people from the destruction they were threatened with.

First. God's sufficiency to deliver his people, and to disappoint and confound their enemies.

God's sufficiency, in two respects, is set forth in this part of Holy Writ that we are upon:

1. The sufficiency of his knowledge. V. 28, "But I know thy abode, and thy going out, and thy coming in, and thy rage against me." The designs {of God} were probably kept secret from the Jews.[2]

The sufficiency of his power, is intimated in the figure of speech used. V. 29, "[I will] put my hook in thy nose, and my bridle in thy lips, and I will turn thee back by the way by which thou camest."

2. The degree in which God would defend his people in Jerusalem, and disappoint their enemies. He would prevent their fulfilling any part of their design against Jerusalem.

[He] would not suffer 'em so much as to begin any warlike operations—their hands should be held {from shedding blood}—nor enter on their hostile enterprises. [They] should be sent back without having performed anything. [Their] expedition should be wholly in vain. Vv. 33–34, "Therefore thus saith the Lord concerning the king of Assyria, He shall not come into this city, nor shoot an arrow there, nor come before it with shields, nor cast a bank against it. By the way that he came, by the same shall he return, and shall not come into this city, saith the Lord."

Third. The means by which God accomplished this: by the immediate hand of heaven.

No human [was] made use of. [No] looked-for help [came] from Egypt. Ethiopians threatened 'em, but it was not these [that defeated the enemies of God's people].

[God accomplished this by] sending a great mortality among them. There are some remains of this account in the heathen histories.

They intended to destroy {God's people}, but are themselves destroyed. They vaunted themselves against the God of Israel, as though he

---

2. Unusually, in the MS, JE renders the word "Jews" all in capitals.

could not deliver. But they found him stronger, not like those other gods they mention. [God] showed them how weak and frail [they were], but weak and ashes. [God will] look on him that "is proud, and abase him," Job 40:11.

Fourth. The manner of God's disappointing and confounding their enemies.

And here are three things signified, concerning the manner {with which God's disappoints and confounds them}: with contempt, with irresistible power, [and] with great reluctance in them. [These are] all signified in the figure of speech, v. 29. God dealt with this haughty, violent monarch, as men are wont to deal with a wild, unruly, headstrong horse: bring 'em to rule with bit and bridle. Or as men will manage a wild bull or boar, or other unruly beast that they are going to lead to a place of slaughter, that will not willingly be led or governed: putting a hook through the nose {of the beast}, that sensible, tender part; forcing them, however unwilling, with strength of hand and intolerable pain, compelling them to follow, let 'em fret and rage never so much. Or as men make a fish to follow their line, by a hook in their mouths, whereby they are drawn, with a strength they can't resist, and surely against their wills, out of their element, where they want [to remain].

Thus God lead back Sennacherib, though he was like leviathan in the waters. Thus the figure here used, with respect to the king of Assyria, seems very similar to that used with respect to the king of Egypt, in Ezek. 29:3–5, comparing him to a dangerous leviathan in the waters:

Speak, and say, Thus saith the Lord God; Behold, I am against thee, Pharaoh king of Egypt, the great dragon that lieth in the midst of his rivers, which hath said, My river is mine own, and I have made it for myself. But I will put hooks in thy jaws, and I will cause the fish of thy rivers to stick unto thy scales, and I will bring thee up out of the midst of thy rivers, and all the fish of thy rivers shall stick unto thy scales. And I will leave thee thrown into the wilderness, thee and all the fish of thy rivers: thou shalt fall upon the open fields; thou shalt not be brought together, nor gathered: I have given thee for meat to the beasts of the field and to the fowls of the heaven.

The leviathan is represented as exceeding proud, and full of rage and tumult, in Job 41. "[He is a king over the children of] pride," [v.] 34. His contempt of those that oppose him, [is described], vv. 27–29: "He esteemeth iron as straw, and brass as rotten wood. The arrow cannot make him flee: slingstones are turned with him into stubble. Darts are counted as stubble: he laugheth at the shaking of a spear." [His] tumult, v. 31: "[He maketh the deep to boil like a pot: he maketh the sea like a pot of ointment]." "Who can discover the face of his garment? or who can come to him with his double bridle," v. 13. Thus was the king of Assyria.

But God can govern him, and turn him out of his course, as easily as men are wont to do a small fish, with a hook in their chaws. The history is agreeable to this. In the midst of his haughtiness and vanity, rage and insolence, God sends in one night {a great mortality}, only as it were by sending a blast upon him; see v. 7 of the chapter.

Fifth. The ground or spring of this exercise of mercy towards his people: a regard to his own glory, and his servant David, v. 35.

Sixth. Who they were whose welfare God had a special respect to in this wonderful dispensation: viz., Zion, or his church and chosen people, vv. 31–32.

"Zion" [is] a common appellation, to signify the church. By "the remnant of Jerusalem," or Zion, is often intended the elect. So it used elsewhere in that Book of Isaiah. So it is used, Is. 1:9, "Except the Lord of hosts had left unto us a very small remnant, we should have been as Sodom, and we should have been like unto Gomorrah." Is. 10:21–22, "The remnant shall return, even the remnant of Jacob, unto the mighty God. For though thy people Israel be as the sand of the sea, yet a remnant of them shall return: the consumption decreed shall overflow with righteousness." So this [is] explained by the Apostle; Rom. 9:27–28, "Esaias also crieth concerning Israel, Though the number of the children of Israel be as the sand of the sea, a remnant shall be saved: for he will finish the work, and cut it short in righteousness: because a short work will the Lord make upon the earth," with Rom. 11:5.

Seventh. What future happy event God had in view in this wonderful dispensation: viz., the future reviving of his church, and flourishing of religion.

Vv. 30–31, "And this shall be a sign unto thee, Ye shall eat this year such as groweth of itself; and the second year that which springeth of the same: and in the third year sow ye, and reap, and plant vineyards, and eat the fruit thereof. And the remnant that is escaped of the house of Judah shall again take root downward, and bear fruit upward." The meaning of these words is this: [the church shall revive again as it were out of its own ashes, and flourish again like a plant after it had been seemingly destroyed and past recovery].[3]

This was the reason why God did such wonderful things {for the people of Israel}, because he had designs of great future mercy in view to his church. {And so} God, by this great temporal mercy, had in view great mercies of an higher nature, viz., great spiritual mercies, [and the] glorious reviving of religion.

There is probably here a regard to various accomplishments {of God's designs of future mercy to the church}.

Eighth. [I shall] observe how God represents his heart as being engaged in this matter: v. 32, "the zeal of the Lord of hosts shall do this."

[This is] to represent that God will not be slack, [but] will be thorough, [will] do [it] effectually; and to represent the greatness of his favor, the greatness of his displeasure against the enemies of his people, the greatness of his regard to the glory of his name, his great regard to the Mediator, the spiritual David, [and his] regard to his covenant. [This represents] how much his heart was upon these future glorious events, that were spoken of as what God had in view: the future intended revival.

Application

In the Application, I shall, as has been proposed,

First. Consider how applicable the things that have been observed in this place of Scripture, are to God's late dispensations towards this land, and other English settlements in America.

Second. What improvement we are lead to make, {by this part of Scripture, of these dispensations of providence towards us}.

First. [How applicable the things that have been observed in this place of Scripture, are to God's late dispensations towards this land, and other English settlements in America.]

As {the children of Israel} were brought into danger by Sennacherib, the most potent monarch of all in the nations with which Israel had to do,

---

3. This insert is based on JE's entry on Is. 37:30–31 in the "Blank Bible," WJE 24:668; see also the Explication of the sermon on Is. 37:31 (no. 811), where JE states "that this remnant shall flourish again, after it seems to be in a great measure cut down." Generally, JE viewed such promises as prophecies of future revivals of the church.

so [we are brought into danger by the king of France]. Sennacherib was a monarch of great ambition [and] haughtiness of spirit; so the French monarchs have been noted of late, above all other princes of Europe, for {their ambition and haughtiness}.

As {Sennacherib} aimed at universal empire, {so does the French monarch}. [Sennacherib] made war purely for the enlargement of his dominions; so [do the French].

As he was of a violent and cruel disposition towards the church of God—"[I know . . . thy] rage against me"—so [the king of France is of a violent and cruel disposition towards the church of God]. As {Sennacherib} sought the overthrow of the church {of God}, so {the king of France seeks her overthrow}.

[As Sennacherib was] one that was lifted up with his successes, [and] boasts, v. 25, "I have digged, and drunk water; and with the sole of my feet have I dried up all the rivers of the besieged places"; so {the French king boasts} of his having besieged and taken so many strong cities of late.

Sennacherib was used as a scourge to other nations in the hands of God, to chastise them for their sins. Vv. 26–27, "Hast thou not heard long ago, how I have done it; and of ancient times, that I have formed it? now have I brought it to pass, that thou shouldest be to lay waste defensed cities into ruinous heaps. Therefore their inhabitants were of small power, they were dismayed and confounded: they were as the grass of the field, and as the green herb, as the grass on the housetops, and as corn blasted before it be grown up." So [the king of France is used as a scourge to us].

And as King Sennacherib, though he did not go in person against Jerusalem, yet sent a very great military force against it under Rabshakeh, who was doubtless one of the nobles of his kingdom; so {the king of France has sent} a very great military force {against us}, the greatest by far that ever [was seen]—and this under the command of one of the peers of France.[4] Consider the many French and Indians that were to have joined 'em here.[5]

And as {Sennacherib was} in a great rage, so {the French monarch} seems to have been with very much of a spirit of revenge. As [Sennacherib was] come with a design of utter destruction, so it seems, by what we are informed, {that the king of France intended the utter destruction of the English}.

4. I.e., the commanding admiral of the expedition, the Duc D'Anville.

5. Arcadian colonists and Indian tribes—however hesitantly—were on hand to meet the French forces when they arrived.

As {Sennacherib} seemed to be very confident, {and} triumphed before the victory, so it seems to have been [with the French], by some accounts we have of the great things they had in view, and by some things we hear of their confident expectations in France. And also by some things we have heard of our enemies in Canada, their boasting and seeming to depend upon it, that we were going to be invaded and destroyed: and not only New England, but the whole nation subjected to a popish power.

And as the people of Jerusalem were weak {and defenseless}, so we [are weak and defenseless].

And as it had been a very corrupt time in Israel, the church of God greatly weakened and diminished, {and there remained} but a remnant; so [it has been a corrupt time with us].

As the designs {of the Assyrians} were kept secret {from the people of Israel}, but [God] knew their abode; so it was here.

As God defended {the people of Israel} in such a degree that {the Assyrians succeeded in} no part of their design, {and they could} not enter on any military enterprise; {so it was here}.

Though they were come to the place, yet {God declared that the Assyrians would} not "shoot an arrow, nor come before it with shields, nor cast a bank against it." The expedition against Jerusalem [was] wholly in vain, {and they were} sent back without performing anything. So [it was here].

As it was by the immediate hand of heaven—no human arm [was raised], though they had looked to Egypt and Ethiopia, "[the land] shadowing with wings, ch. 18, at [the] beginning—so [it was here]. And it [was] very remarkably so ordered, that there should be no human arm {raised against the French}. Human strength was prepared, {and we} had been employed; we looked for help, as the Jews looked to Egypt. And 'tis very strange, when we consider the preparation, that no human help was sent. Human preparations for defense were making here, and at Louisburg, and at Annapolis; but a remarkable hand of heaven [rose] against them: storms, [with] sickness before they came, [and] after they were come; awful frowns; their chief man, the Duke d'Anville, {taking his life}; and then, sickness and death still prevailing: as God turned back Sennacherib's army by a great mortality. God {drove them away} with great manifestations of his indignation and contempt, forcing them [back], though with great reluctance after all their boasting and great preparations, and insolent threatenings and triumphing before the victory. The indignation and irresistible hand of God forced 'em to quit their purpose, drove 'em back, [like an] unruly beast, [with] bridle [and] hook.

So {God manifested} an awful and most visible hand {against our enemies}, exceedingly vexing and discouraging [them], as appears by their behavior, their chief men laying violent hands on themselves.[6] God so ordered it, that Sennacherib's sons killed him; but these were made to kill themselves. Instead of killing us, as they intended, God followed 'em with the like curse that he did Ahithophel who, being famed for his subtilty, {ended by} seeing his counsels turned into foolishness, {and} killed himself [2 Sam. 17].

So the [French], famed for their subtilty, come with a design of destroying us; {but their designs are} but are an occasion of the destruction of our enemies and their friends, that they expected to assist 'em in destroying us, by bringing a mortal sickness among 'em, by which multitudes of the Cape Sable and St. John's Indians have been swept away.[7] Our friends, that we expected from England to help us to destroy our enemies, failed; but our enemies themselves, are made the occasion of it.

Some of their ships were cast away in coming over, and others, some of the quickest and strongest, kept back, and either shipwrecked or driven away; and others, they are brought to burn themselves. Thus, either the immediate hand of heaven, or their own hands, are brought to do that which we hoped for an English fleet to do.

If their weak circumstances had been known, the fleet we had at Louisburg might have [attacked them]. But we were not suffered to have any hand {in our enemy's defeat}; as was said in another case, "Ye had not need to fight in this battle," 2 Chron. 20:17.

When, after they had met with all those discouragements, they continued still in a design of going against Annapolis, {and} being very loath to go way and do nothing, and violently set like a wild beast not to yield to command, God continued his hook in their nose. And after they had sailed out of their place of rendezvous, {they were struck by a violent gale, and put away for the West Indies}.[8] Thus they were forced to yield {to

---

6. Not only did the Duc D'anville reportedly commit suicide, but his successor, Vice Admiral d'Estourmel, did as well.

7. Unknowingly, the French had spread contagion to their Indian allies by giving them blankets that had been used by infected soldiers and sailors. Reportedly, some 150 natives died as a result. *Boston Evening Post*, Nov. 3, 1746.

8. This insert is based on language in the *Boston Evening Post* for Nov. 3, 1746, p. 2,

command}, like a fish to the hook of the fisherman; thus they were turned back, as an headstrong horse by the bridle in his lips.

And as God declares in that place of Scripture that we are upon, that the grand spring {of this exercise of mercy towards his people}, and foundation of that wonderful exercise of divine mercy towards Jerusalem, [was regard to his own glory, and to his servant David]; so there is abundant evidence in this case that {God's exercises of mercy towards this land} can have no other ground.

I come now to the

Second thing in the Application, viz., to show what improvement this part of God's Word leads us to make of this remarkable dispensation of divine providence.

1. It leads us to praise God, and give all the glory unto him of this deliverance, and of all our preservations and successes in war. The text shows us the weakness of God's people in Jerusalem, the disproportion between their strength and {that of their enemy}; and it also shows the unworthiness {of God's people}, by reason of the great corruptions {among them}.

And I have observed how, in these respects, it has been with us {of late}. The text shows what a great deliverance {this was}: from a great enemy, [with] great armament, [and] great destruction intended. [The] nation's destruction seemed to be very near. So have we {reason to be thankful for so great a deliverance}.

The text shows how sufficient God is.

[The] text shows {us} the completeness of the deliverance; so [is our deliverance complete].

The text shows how remarkably God delivered the Jews by himself, without human help; so I have observed, [we have been delivered without human help].

The text shows how the spring of that wonderful mercy [was God's regard to his own glory, and to his servant David]; so [is the spring of God's late mercy to us].

The text shows that God's heart was engaged; so [God's heart was engaged here].

Now all these things lead us to give the praise to God, and him alone, and to praise him with all our hearts, answerably to the greatness, importance and wonderfulness of the mercy [he has shown]. If they had

---

a newspaper to which JE had relatively quick access.

succeeded, how terrible would the consequences have been! It is God alone that hath prevented it.

God has not called us to fight. He has appointed other work instead of fighting, viz., to praise God; as it was in Jehoshaphat's time, when {Judah was} invaded by the Moabites and Ammonites. 2 Chron. 20:17, "Ye shall not need to fight in this battle: set yourselves, stand ye still, and see the salvation of the Lord with you, O Judah and Jerusalem: fear not, nor be dismayed; tomorrow go out against them: for the Lord will be with you." [V.] 24, "And when Judah came toward the watch tower in the wilderness, they looked unto the multitude, and, behold, they were dead bodies fallen to the earth, and none escaped." [V.] 26, "And on the fourth day they assembled themselves in the valley of Berachah; for there they blessed the Lord: therefore the name of the same place was called, The valley of Berachah, unto this day."

The text especially shows what cause God's saints have to praise him; [it] shows that God had a special respect to them.

2. The words of the text lead us to improve the late remarkable deliverance, so as to trust in him, in God, and him alone, for future preservations and success in the present war.

The text shows the weak and defenseless circumstances [of the people of Israel, who were] like the dry stubble. So, it has been observed, we are weak. Therefore, we ought not to trust in ourselves.

The text shows us God's sufficiency, knowledge, [and] power, and God's providence towards {his people, and} shows it in this case of[9] deliverance, and in the success he gave us. [God is] able to save, without human help.

God's dealings with us, also show us the sufficiency of his mercy, as well as his dealings with Hezekiah and the inhabitants of Jerusalem: that when we are become so corrupt, and God's church and the state of religion among us is so low, so [God will] wonderfully appear for us, [and] grant us so complete a deliverance by his own invincible and extraordinary {power}, that he should be tender of us, as of the apple of his eye. God has shown us abundantly, that he is the God of armies.

3. That part of God's Word that we are upon, leads us to make this improvement of {God's late dispensations towards this land}: to hope and pray for the revival of religion and of God's church.

---

9. MS: "&."

The text shows, that God had this happy event in view. These wonderful {dispensations} seem to be tokens for good, as though it were a day of mercy, and God was about to show great mercy, and to cause it to be with his church—at least that part of it that is here in America—agreeable to that which God gave for a sign to Hezekiah. At least we may be reasonably encouraged to hope for it, by these marvelous appearances of divine mercy, and we ought to be stirred up earnestly to pray for it.

4. We ought to do what in us lies, that a revival of religion may be the event and issue of these wonderful (dispensations}.

For us to hope and pray {for revival of religion}, without using proper endeavors, will be but a tempting God. These dispensations have a great tendency both to encourage us to endeavor, and also, as one would think, to constrain us.

This dispensation {of God was} so wonderful and affecting, and so soon following another that was also exceeding remarkable,[10] that we must be exceeding stupid and ungrateful indeed, if we still go on {in our corrupt ways}, and there be no remarkable alteration in us {as a result}. And if such great and remarkable mercies have no good effect upon us, we have reason to fear that mercy will be turned into wrath, and those remarkable mercies will cease, and be followed with no less signal and remarkable judgments.

---

10. Possibly a reference to the defeat of the Young Pretender and his forces earlier in the year.

Continuing Unawakened Under Divine Chastisements

August 1747

OVER THE SUMMER OF 1747, the *Boston Gazette* reported a number of natural phenomena. Earthquakes, violent storms, and lightning strikes served as troubling signs. Most notably, the August 18th edition of the *Gazette* reported on a "tempest" that hit Plymouth, several lightning strikes burning barns, and news of a lightning strike on a church in Milford, Connecticut, during service, killing three people. The war with the French had not been progressing as successfully as New England had hoped and prayed and news of these storms may have reflected New England's attitudes towards the tide of war.

New England had good reason to be concerned. Over the course of the summer, small attacks on frontier settlements became more common, culminating with a major assault on Fort Saratoga. Intelligence from friendly Indians revealed a force of four thousand French and Indians descending on the Carrying Please (Fort Edward). Experienced scouting teams, such as that of Indian chief Hendrick, came under ambush, forcing his retreat to Fort Saratoga. The British situation became so precarious, Mohawk warriors fighting on behalf of the British signed a treaty of neutrality with France leaving frontier settlements exposed. By the middle of August, Fort Saratoga was surrounded and French and Indians parties enjoyed free range over much of the wilderness between the Hudson River and Connecticut River Valley.

CONTINUING UNAWAKENED UNDER DIVINE CHASTISEMENTS

Warfare touched Northampton on August 27th, 1747. While threshing grain in his own barn, a party of sixteen Indians attacked and killed Elisha Clark of Southampton, shooting him seven times, scalping him, and covering his body under straw.[1] News reports of French and Indian control of the frontier now began to look like a daily reality for the citizens of Northampton, exacerbating long-standing fears over their precarious frontier position. Warfare was more than a military problem for Edwards's congregation, it was a pastoral problem.

Sunday, August 30th, Edwards responded with the sermon *Continuing Unawakened Under Divine Chastisements*. Edwards did not treat this tragedy as the result of poor strategy or flaws in the defensive works of the town, but the consequence of the town's "backslidings." A people who don't mind the chastisements of God put themselves in the way of destruction. However, Edwards seemed less interested in merely assigning blame for these calamities as he was impressing upon his congregation the lessons of such a tragedy. The advance of the French near Saratoga as well as the incursion of Indians into Northampton's backyard should drive the one towards a "speedy awakening." Edwards designed this sermon to not just promote his brand of evangelical piety, but to offer a measure of hope and assurance to a congregation mourning in fear of the future.

* * * * *

This sermon was edited for the Jonathan Edwards Center by Ken Minkema. The manuscript is nineteen duodecimo-sized leaves. Edwards wrote at the head of the sermon, "after Elisha Clark was Kill'd Aug. 1747."[2]

---

1. Trumbull, *History of Northampton*, 2:155.
2. Clark was killed by Indians at his farm on the outskirts of Southampton, August 27, 1747.

Continuing Unawakened Under Divine Chastisements

Isaiah 9:13–14

For the people turneth not to him that smiteth him, neither do they seek the Lord of hosts. Therefore the Lord shall cut off from Israel heads and tail, branch and root in one day.

1. THE PROVOCATIONS OF Israel: their obstinacy under chastisements and corrections.
    2. What they exposed themselves to by it: viz., utter destruction.

Doctrine

When men are so regardless of divine chastisements and corrections as to continue unawakened and unreclaimed by them, it brings 'em into great danger of utter destruction.

    The adverse dispensations of providence that men are the subjects of, are of two kinds: viz., those that are for correction, and those that are for destruction.

    I would here show how those are distinguis[hed][1] one from the other, and then give the reasons of the Doctrine.

    I. I would show how adverse dispensations {of providence} that are for correction, and those that are for destruction, are different.

---

1. MS damage.

First. As to those afflictive dispensations of providence that are for correction, the following things may be noted concerning them:

1. In them, God afflicts in measure.

Is. 27:7–9, "Hath he smitten him, as he smote those that smote him? or is he slain according to the slaughter of them that are slain by him? In measure, when it shooteth forth, [thou wilt debate with it: he stayeth his rough wind in the day of the east wind. By this therefore shall the iniquity of Jacob be purged; and this is all the fruit to take away his sin; when he maketh all the stones of the altar as chalkstones that are beaten in sunder, the groves and images shall not stand up.]"

2. [Adverse dispensations] are wont to be mingled with merciful dispensations of providence.

Not only is God's mercy manifested in the circumstances [and in] the measure, [but they have] oftentimes some special mercies.

So it is wont to be both in God's dealings with particular persons, and towards a people.

[So] towards persons. [I shall] exemplify this in two instances: Jacob, [and] David.

[So] a people, [as] Israel.

God, by thus intermingling some special mercies, testifies {his love for them}.

3. Oftentimes those afflictions that {are for correction}, are such as have a special tendency to the good of those that are the subjects of them.

Oftentimes [they have a tendency] so as plainly to point forth the particular sin by which they have provoked God, tending to lead 'em to reflect on themselves for it, and repent of it.

[So] Jacob, [when he] deceived his father; [and when he was] deceived by Laban [Gen. 29]; [and when he was deceived] by his own children [Gen. 37]. [So] David, [when] guilty of adultery, {he was} secretly corrected by his own sons, {and then} openly and in the sight of the sun. And [so] his son Amnon [2 Sam. 13]. [David] caused Uriah to be slain [2 Sam. 11]; [so his] own sons were slain. One of them[2] sought to kill him, his own father.

[God] often corrects by taking away those enjoyments that they most idolized. [He takes away the] enjoyment {that has been most} abused. [So] Absalom. Hos. [2:9], "Therefore will I return, and take away [. . .] my wool and my flax."

---

2. I.e., Absalom.

[God will] meet with and cross the lust that has most prevailed: pride, worldliness, [or] sensuality.

[God will] hinder, disappoint and entangle them in an ill way, so naturally tending to bring 'em to reflect on themselves. Hos. 2:6–7, "[I will] hedge up thy way with thorns, [and make a wall, that she shall not find her paths. And she shall follow after her lovers, but she shall not overtake them; and she shall seek them, but shall not find them: then shall she say, I will go and return to my first husband; for then was it better with me than now.]"

[God will] show 'em the vanity of that which they most trusted in. [So the people of] Egypt.

4. [Oftentimes adverse dispensations are] attended with other means to reclaim, and with special opportunities and advantages to return.

[God will] wait [for them], uses other means, [other] counsels {to reclaim them}, as when a father corrects [his children]. So it was when God corrected Israel.

[Adverse dispensations are attended] oftentimes with a degree of the striving of God's Spirit. So it was in Israel; Is. 63:9–10, "[In all their affliction he was afflicted, and the angel of his presence saved them: in his love and in his pity he redeemed them; and he bare them, and carried them all the days of old. But they rebelled, and] vexed his Holy Spirit." [So it was] before Jerusalem's first destruction, [and in] Josiah's time, [and] before her last destruction.

Secondly. The other kind of adverse dispensations, are the judgments God brings on men for their destruction.

Of these, the following things may be noted:

1. They are not attended with such special mercies as are often wont to attend [other dispensations].

Hos. 1:6, "[And she conceived again, and bare a daughter. And God said unto him, Call her name Loruhamah: for I will no more have mercy upon the house of Israel; but I will utterly take them away.]" Zech. 11:6, "[For I will no more pity the inhabitants of the land, saith the Lord: but, lo, I will deliver the men every one into his neighbor's hand, and into the hand of his king: and they shall smite the land, and out of their hand I will not deliver them.]"

[So it was with the] Jews in the apostles' days.

2. [They] are not attended with those advantages for repentance and pardon.

[God] often removes their candlestick out of its place. Amos 8:11, "[Behold, the days come, saith the Lord God, that I will send a famine in the land, not a famine of bread, nor a thirst for water, but of hearing the words of the Lord.]"

[They are] not attended with the strivings of the Spirit of God. [The people] are given over to judicial hard[ness]. [So it was with] the Jews, [and with] Saul, [and] Judas.

3. Those judgment that are for destruction, are not of that salutary tendency as that {other kind of dispensation}; but, on the contrary, do either bring on destruction, or are the forerunner of it.

4. There is not that merciful care used in these judgments with regard to their measure, as is in the other kind.

Thus I have briefly, as I proposed, shown how these two kinds of afflictive dispensations of providence, viz., those that are for correction, and those that are for destruction, are distinguished [one] from the other. The Doctrine teaches us that when men under the former of these, viz., those that are for correction, are so regardless of God's hand as to continue unawakened and unreclaimed, it greatly exposes them to the latter, viz., to those judgments that are for utter destruction.

Obstinacy and irreclaimableness, manifested in this way, is often spoken of in the Word of God as what has this dreadful issue. So in Is. 1:5, "Why should ye be stricken any more? ye will revolt more and more: the whole head is sick, and the whole heart faint." Vv. 7–8, "Your country is desolate, your cities are burned with fire: your land, strangers devour it in your presence, and it is desolate, as overthrown by strangers. And the daughter of Zion is left as a cottage in a vineyard, as a lodge in a garden of cucumbers, as a besieged city." Jer. 2:30, "In vain have I smitten your children; they received no correction: your own sword hath devoured your prophets, like a destroying lion." And Jer. 5:3, etc.,

O Lord, are not thine eyes upon the truth? thou hast stricken them, but they have not grieved; thou hast consumed them, but they have refused to receive correction: they have made their faces harder than a rock; they have refused to return. Therefore I said, Surely these are poor; they are foolish: for they know not the way of the Lord, nor the judgment of their God. I will get me unto the great men, and will speak unto them; for they have known the way of the Lord, and the judgment of their God: but these have altogether broken the yoke, and burst the bonds. Wherefore a lion out of the forest shall slay them, and a wolf of the evenings shall spoil them, a leopard shall watch over their cities: every one that goeth out thence shall be torn in pieces: because their transgressions are many, and their backslidings are increased. How shall I pardon thee for this? thy children have forsaken me, and sworn by them that are no gods: when I had fed them to the full, they then committed adultery, and assembled themselves by troops in the harlots' houses. They were as fed horses in the morning: every one neighed after his neighbor's wife. Shall I not visit for these things? saith the Lord: and shall not my soul be avenged on such a nation as this?"[3]

Zeph. 3:1–2, "Woe to her that is filthy and polluted, to the oppressing city! She obeyed not the voice; she received not correction; she trusted not in the Lord; she drew not near to her God."

And the same is confirmed by Scripture examples: Israel in the wilderness, [the] Ten Tribes, [the] people of Judah and Jerusalem, [and the] Jews in the apostles' times.

[II. Reasons of the Doctrine.] Upon three accounts:

First. The greatness of the provocation given, and guilt contracted.

In those corrective dispensations of providence, the great and holy God, besides strictly forbidding sin, and the testimonies he gives of his hatred of it in his Word, does in a more sensible manner testify his abhorrence, [and] shows his displeasure [of sin].

[Sin] tends therefore greatly to provoke [God].

Would not a parent or master [be provoked by the continued disobedience of a child or servant]?

Second. When men continue {in sin}, it greatly increases their hardness of heart, and ripens them for destruction.

[They] revolt more and more.

Third. When [men continue in sin], there appears to be no remedy.

These corrective {dispensations} are commonly some of the last means God uses.

God before instructs, and {uses means and counsels to reclaim them}, and by these dispensations manifests [his displeasure], testifies [his wrath].

---

3. Here, vv. 3–9 of the chapter are quoted, though JE may have intended to quote more or less.

Hereby [he] gives 'em warning. [He] shows 'em their dependence on him, showing 'em how they are in his hands, [and] can't help themselves. [He] shows 'em the evil of sin, the folly and unprofitableness [of it].

[Such a dispensation] has a tendency to take off the heart from the object of their lusts. [It] takes away those things that tended to stupefy. And, as it was observed, afflictive[4] dispensations that are for correction, are often wont to be such as have a special tendency {to the good of those that are the subjects of them}.

And it was also observed that God was wont to intermingle mercy [with adverse dispensations]. [God has] a merciful care with regard to the measure [of those afflictions]. [He] intermingles some special mercies. He hereby shows [their dependence on him].

And it was further observed that {afflictive dispensations are often} attended with special opportunities given {to return}. [They come with the] strivings of his Spirit.

Therefore, [those that continue in sin] appear to be past remedy. Such {in Scripture} are spoken of as past remedy, Is. 1.

[They are] those whose wickedness is past re[medy]—not that it is beyond Omnipotence {still to reclaim them}. But [commonly 'tis not so].

Those whose sin is thus past remedy, are greatly exposed to destruction, as is manifest by 2 Chron. 36:15–17. "And the Lord God of their fathers sent to them by his messengers, rising up betimes, and sending; because he had compassion on his people, and on his dwelling place: but they mocked the messengers of God, and despised his words, and misused his prophets, until the wrath of the Lord arose against his people, till there was no remedy. Therefore he brought upon them the king of the Chaldees, who slew their young men with the sword in the house of their sanctuary, and had no compassion upon young man or maiden, old man, or him that stooped for age: he gave them all into his hand."

Application

Use of *Warning* to all, to take heed that they don't thus expose themselves to destruction, even by continuing so regardless of divine chastisements and corrections, as to continue unawakened and unreclaimed by them.

Consider,

---

4. MS: "afflictions."

First. What our backslidings and departures from God have been in this place.

There has been a time within the memory of most of those here present, wherein the town in general seemed to be greatly affected and moved with things of religion, of all sorts. [There was] a general awakening; [there was] an appearance of an almost universal engagedness in the things of religion; an appearance of great regard to the worship and ordinances of God.

[There was] a reformation, diligence in religious duties, [in] religious conversation, [in] religion in the house of God, [and in] families.

How full was this place about five or six years ago. [We had] great affection, love, admiration, praise, great joy, [and] great zeal. Many that formerly {were converted have come} greatly to lament past backslidings. [What] great resolutions [they made], what solemn promises and vows.

But how greatly are we gone away backward. How little appearance of awakening {has there been among us}. How little appearance of engagedness in religion. [We are] taken up about other things. What a return to those things that were, for a season, reformed [have we seen]: [a return] to a worldly spirit and behavior. What lamentable contentions [have we seen], what prevalence of youthful vanity, what a different face on our public assemblies, what a sad drop of religious conversation, what little appearance of religion in occasional meetings of young or old, what a coldness with regard to private religious meetings. How little appearance of a work of conversion [has there been amongst us], what outbreakings of gross sin.

How much do we fall short of living answerably to those great discoveries, that great love. [How we fall short in] admiration, [in] gratitude.

Second. What different things might God justly have expected from us, that have been saved.

If it was not to be expected {that we could maintain} affections always to the same height, yet [we should have] continued to behave ourselves as a holy people, remarkably so, that we should have distinguished ourselves.

Seeing there was such an appearance and profession of religion {amongst us, it was to be expected} that we should have adorned religion. We drew the eyes of multitudes; [we] were as a city set on an hill.[5]

---

5. Referring to the 1734–35 revival, and the notoriety brought by *A Faithful Narrative*.

[God could have justly expected] that [we were] in some measure answerable to the discoveries [we had], answerable to that love {shown us in the outpouring of God's Spirit}, answerable to that resolution that was professed, answerable to the promises that since we promised.

[It might be expected] that we should remarkably have differed from whatever appeared amongst us before. [We should have been] a far better sort of people, of a more Christian spirit, more highly prizing the ordinances, improving sabbaths. [God might have justly expected that we were] answerable to the great mercies we supposed we received, [being] more kind one to another.

If we do impartially consider, we may be sensible we have been far otherwise than God has justly expected.

Third. Let it be considered what chastisements and corrections we have been the subjects of, since we have thus departed from God, and failed of answering his expectations from us, especially within this few years.

What public calamities have we shared in! We formerly long enjoyed the blessing of peace, [and] the many great advantages that attend it: spiritual advantages, temporal advantages, free enjoyment of the good land that God had given, [and] opportunity to provide settlements. [We formerly were] more in the enjoyment of this great blessing in the time of those great awakenings and extraordinary religious appearances. But when we had in a great measure quenched the Spirit, [we were] alarmed with the news of war with the French nation.[6] Henceforward, [you have] been deprived of our former freedom and quietness, deprived of the free enjoyment of your estates, driven off from many of your lands. [You] could not go to and fro with that safety and quietness, as formerly. [You] have been put to great expense, often taken off from your ordinary business. [You have been] from time to time disquieted and put into an uproar by the alarms of war, by which many have been put into a great fright. [You] have been put to a great deal of trouble by night and by day, in performing the necessary military duties for the common defense and safety.[7] Many have been called to such service, one place and another, wherein they have been obliged to suffer hardship and jeopard their lives.

---

6. In 1744, the War of the Austrian Succession began in Europe, with operations in the American theater.

7. Northampton residents enlisted for the Cape Breton campaign, and also served locally to protect the town, as in May 1746 when watchtowers were built around the town's perimeter, and in August 1746, when Edwards' house was forted in and

You have [been] hindered from making that provision for the settlement of your families in the land which God has given us, that otherwise might have been by purchasing and cultivating lands in new settlements.

We have often had the uncomfortable, sorrowful news to hear of one and another.

And we suffer with the rest of the land in that miserable and forlorn state that the land is in with respect to a medium of trade, occasioning innumerable calamities.

And God of late has visited us in this place with mortal sicknesses, and frequent instances of death, from year to year, in somewhat of an unusual manner. The year before last, in the winter, five or six of our young men {who were} at Cape Breton, {died of mortal disease}. [So it was] the last year, and now this year, very lately.

And the week past, God has testified against us in a very awful dispensation that is of a new kind, i.e., different from what {we had suffered before}.

Fourth. What special and wonderful mercies we have had intermingled [with afflictions].

'Tis a time of God's awful frowns and chastisement, a time of far greater calamity than what formerly was; but yet {these are afflictions} we share with the nation.[8] But God has distinguished us here in America, in the success given to our arms, marvelously protecting us from the fleets of our enemies by sea, {as in} the last year, [and] now again this year.[9]

{God has marvelously protected us} from armies by land, from time to time: an army after the beginning of the war with France; another army after that, that our captives that are now returned inform of; [and] another army this year. And remarkable has been the hand of heaven in protecting particular settlements and forts. [This has been] taken notice of by our enemies themselves.

[God has been] restraining our enemies, that they have done us no more mischief. And how wonderful is his mercy, in procuring deliverance to our captives.

Thus wonderfully has God in his wrath remembered mercy. [He] shows his great readiness, [that he is] disposed to mercy, [and] delights in it. [God] says concerning us, as concerning Ephraim of old, Hos. 11:8–9,

---

quartered with soldiers.

8. I.e., Great Britain.

9. Referring to the campaign against Louisburg, and the French fleet sent to relieve it that was wrecked off Chebucto.

"How shall I give thee up, Ephraim? how shall I deliver thee, Israel? how shall I make thee as Admah? how shall I set thee as Zeboim? mine heart is turned within me, my repentings are kindled together. I will not execute the fierceness of mine anger, I will not return to destroy Ephraim: for I am God, and not man; the Holy One in the midst of thee: and I will not enter into the city."

It appears by these things, that hitherto God's judgments are of the nature of correction, and not for destruction; [he is] waiting to be gracious, drawing with the cords of a man. Hos. 11:4, "I drew them with cords of a man, with bands of love: and I was to them as they that take off the yoke on their jaws, and I laid meat unto them."

Such as these have been God's wonderful dealings with us; such as have been represented, have been our obligations, [in] mercies [shown, and] profession [made]. And such {have been God's dealings with us in} our backslidings, and such {have been his} corrections [and] dealings with us in this town in particular. Such {have been} his wonderful mercies. And as was said of old, Is. 5:4, "What could have been done more to my vineyard," so {it could be said of us today}. What will become of us, if we [continue in sin]? May it not well be said of us, as it was of Israel of old, 2 Chron. 36:16, "there was no remedy"?

Let these things be seriously and sedately considered. If there be a God in heaven that governs the world, surely he must be exceedingly provoked {by our continuing regardless of divine chastisements and corrections}. Hitherto, we have remained so far insensible {of God's corrections}, that {we have remained} unawakened and unreclaimed.

Now some particular persons may [be awakened and reclaimed], but [there is] no appearance of any such thing in the people as a people, nothing general, no remarkable alteration in the face of things.

'Tis no time of reformation. So it is in the land, and so it is here in this place. Now if things still go on thus, what can be expected by wise and rational persons to be the end of it?

Let each one consider what is like to become of his own soul. Let Christless persons consider.

I confess, it appears most reasonable to suppose that, before very long, there will be a great alteration one way [or] other: either a time of great awakening {and} great mercy, or a time of great and dreadful destruction. Yea, probably there may be both: great mercy to some, terrible destruction to others.

There are many things that seem to give great hopes. But then it seems most probable {that God will show mercy} on a new generation. God sometimes wonderfully preserves a people, because he designs mercy to their posterity, Is. 65:8–9.

God is not to be limited. But this is most agreeable to the analogy of his dispensation. God may remarkably favor the land, and protect it, from a design of mercy to the rising generation, and yet execute awful [on the people], as he did of old in the wilderness. There may be a gleaning of the risen generation, as {'tis said}, Is. 17:4–6.[10] "And in that day it shall come to pass, that the glory of Jacob shall be made thin, and the fatness of his flesh shall wax lean. And it shall be as when the harvestman gathereth the corn, and reapeth the ears with his arm; and it shall be as he that gathereth ears in the valley of Rephaim. Yet gleaning grapes shall be left in it, as the shaking of an olive tree, two or three berries in the top of the uppermost bough, four or five in the outmost fruitful branches thereof, saith the Lord God of Israel."

I am sure the state of things is such as may well be exceeding alarming to all such as yet in their sins, and such as, notwithstanding all the very many and very loud calls of God in his Word and in his providence, are still going on in a careless {state, and} are not awakened or reclaimed. If such persons do not speedily awaken, and consider seriously and in good earnest, it is exceeding likely God will make them eternally most terrible monuments of his vengeance in their utter, remediless, and most peculiarly awful destruction.

---

10. MS cites ch. 17.

A Strong Rod Broken and Withered

June 1748

IT IS HARD TO overstate the role John Stoddard played in Northampton. Son of Reverend Stoddard, Col. Stoddard served as an officer in the militia, narrowly escaping his station at Deerfield in February of 1704. Stoddard continued to serve as town selectman, town moderator, and justice of the peace for Northampton. His reliability in town politics led to his election as representative to the General Assembly, his appointment as Justice of the Inferior Court of Pleas, and selection for the Governor's Council. In the Assembly, he served as commissioner of Indian Affairs, was responsible for deciding bills of credit, boundary disputes, and was the standard-bearer for the "court party" in support of the Governor. From his beginnings as a lieutenant in Deerfield, Stoddard progressed to the rank of colonel, first serving as the executive officer for Samuel Partridge, commander of the western forces, before assuming those duties himself. At the outbreak of King George's War, one of Governor Shirley's first dispatches was to Col. Stoddard, first commissioning him to raise a company of troops, supervise the construction of a line of defensive block-houses, and then sent him to negotiate the assistance of the Six Nations at Albany. Shirley wrote to Stoddard, "I will take care of your own Interest: and approve much of your scheme for carrying on the War, I shall govern myself very much by it."[1]

Similarly, it is hard to overstate the relationship Edwards had with Col. John Stoddard, his uncle. When young Edwards came to Northampton, he stayed under the same roof as his uncle John learning the ropes of

---

1. Shirley, *Correspondence*, 128.

ministry from the patriarch of the family, Solomon Stoddard. After Reverend Stoddard died, uncle John became more than just a benefactor and confidant of the young pastor. Col. Stoddard became a full participant of the evangelical awakenings even penning a defense of the religious movement. Stoddard supported the religious innovations of his nephew and supported a series of pay raises over the course of two decades.

So when Stoddard passed away June 19, 1748, it was a loss for Edwards, Northampton, and all New England. In this eulogy, Edwards argues that godly civil magistrates are a blessing to society and their removal is a divine judgment. Edwards took time to offer a very personal picture of the esteemed leader, extolling not only his civil positions but his integrity, largeness of heart, and piety. Edwards gives a very personal evaluation of the colonel stating that experimental religion was a part, not just of his understanding, but of his experience. Stoddard would converse freely about religion and with some, "he was very intimate." This picture suggests that Stoddard was not merely an observer to the religious revivals, nor merely an adherent, but an enthusiastic promoter to Edwards's brand of evangelical piety.

Edwards believed that ministers and magistrates collaborate to advance the gospel and in Stoddard, Edwards had an enthusiastic collaborator. Col. Stoddard supported Edwards's opposition to the ordination of Robert Breck, he supported the Stockbridge mission where Edwards would later serve, and he supported Edwards's vision for the defeat of the French antichristian kingdom through his plan to invade Canada. The loss of a leader like Stoddard was to be lamented. However, Edwards's description of Stoddard stood as an example to which the people of Northampton should aspire.[2]

* * * * *

This sermon was edited by Wilson Kimnach for the *Works of Jonathan Edwards* and is also known as "On Occasion of the death of Col. Stoddard." The manuscript of *A Strong Rod Broken* is a duodecimo booklet of twenty-six leaves, written in double columns on a mixture of old letter covers and fan papers. Edwards titled it, "On Occasion of the death of Col. Stoddard, June 1748." The manuscript and first edition of the sermon are very close in form, including the unusual Application without

---

2. For a more thorough examination of the life of Col. John Stoddard, see Cuthbert, "'Your Most Humble Servant.'"

separately numbered uses. There are a few brief passages deleted in the manuscript, most of which nevertheless appear in similar wording in the printed text.

As is the case for all sermons published by Edwards himself, the text of the sermon below is taken from the first edition: "A Strong Rod broken and withered./ A/ Sermon/ Preach'd at Northampton, on the Lord's-Day, June 26. 1748./ On the Death of/ The Honourable/ John Stoddard, Esq;/ Often a Member of his Majesty's/ Council,/ For many Years Chief Justice of/ the Court of Common Pleas for/ the County of Hampshire,/ Judge of the Probate of Wills, and/ Chief Colonel of the Regiment, &c./ Who died at Boston, June 19. 1748, in the 67th Year of/ his Age./ By Jonathan Edwards, A.M./ Pastor of the first Church in Northampton./ Boston:/ Printed by Rogers and Fowle for J. Edwards in Cornhill./ 1748." A quote from Dan. 4:35 follows the title. The twenty-nine-page booklet is a small quarto.

A Strong Rod Broken and Withered

Ezekiel 19:12

Her strong rods were broken and withered.

IN ORDER TO A right understanding and improving these words, these four things must be observed and understood concerning them.

1. Who she is that is here represented as having had strong rods, viz., the Jewish community, here as often elsewhere, is called the people's mother. She is here compared to a vine planted in a very fruitful soil (v. 10). The Jewish church and state is often elsewhere compared to a vine; as Ps. 80:8 ff., Is. 5:2, Jer. 2:21, Ezek. 15 and 17:6.

2. What is meant by "her strong rods," viz., her wise, able and well-qualified magistrates or rulers. That the rulers or magistrates are intended is manifest by v. 11: "And she had strong rods for the scepters of them that bear rule." And by rods that were STRONG must be meant such rulers as were well qualified for magistracy, such as had great abilities and other qualifications fitting them for the business of rule. They were wont to choose a rod or staff of the strongest and hardest sort of wood that could be found, for the mace or scepter of a prince; such an one only being counted fit for such an use; and this generally was overlaid with gold.

It is very remarkable that such a strong rod should grow out of a weak vine: but so it had been in Israel, through God's extraordinary blessing, in times past. Though the nation is spoken of here, and frequently elsewhere, as weak and helpless in itself, and entirely dependent as a vine, that is the weakest of all trees, that can't support itself by its own strength, and never stands but as it leans on or hangs by something else that is stronger than itself; yet God had caused many of her sons to be strong rods fit for scepters; he had raised up in Israel many able and excellent princes and magistrates in days past, that had done worthily in their day.

3. It should be understood and observed what is meant by these strong rods being "broken and withered," viz., these able and excellent rulers being removed by death: men's dying is often compared in Scripture to the withering of the growth of the earth.

4. It should be observed after what manner, the breaking and withering of these strong rods is here spoken of, viz., as a great and awful calamity, that God had brought upon that people. 'Tis spoken of as one of the chief effects of God's fury and dreadful displeasure against them; "But she was plucked up in fury, she was cast down to the ground, and the east wind dried up her fruit, her strong rods were broken and withered; the fire hath consumed them." The great benefits she enjoyed while her strong rods remained, are represented in the preceding verse; "And she had strong rods for the scepters of them that bear rule, and her stature was exalted among the thick branches; and she appeared in her height with the multitude of her branches." And the terrible calamities that attended the breaking and withering of her strong rods, are represented in the two verses next following the text; "And now she is planted in the wilderness, in a dry and thirsty ground; and fire is gone out of a rod of her branches, which hath devoured her fruit." And in the conclusion in the next words, is very emphatically declared the worthiness of such a dispensation to be greatly lamented; "so that she hath no strong rod to be a scepter to rule; this is a lamentation, and shall be for a lamentation."

That which I therefore observe from the words of the text, to be the subject of discourse at this time, is this,

[Doctrine]

When God by death removes from a people those in place of public authority and rule that have been as strong rods, 'tis an awful judgment of God on that people, and worthy of great lamentation.

In discoursing on this proposition, I would
I. Show what kind of rulers may fitly be called "strong rods."
II. Show why the removal of such rulers from a people by death is to be looked upon as an awful judgment of God on that people, and is greatly to be lamented.

I. I would observe what qualifications of those who are in public authority and rule may properly give 'em the denomination of "strong rods."

First. One qualification of rulers whence they may properly be denominated "strong rods," is *great ability for the management of public affairs.* When they that stand in place of public authority are men of great natural abilities, when they are men of uncommon strength of reason and largeness of understanding; especially when they have remarkably a genius for government, a peculiar turn of mind fitting them to gain an extraordinary understanding in things of that nature, giving ability, in an especial manner, for insight into the mysteries of government, and discerning those things wherein the public welfare or calamity consists, and the proper means to avoid the one and promote the other; an extraordinary talent at distinguishing what is right and just, from that which is wrong and unequal, and to see through the false colors with which injustice is often disguised, and unravel the false and subtle arguments and cunning sophistry that is often made use of to defend iniquity; and when they have not only great natural abilities in these respects, but when their abilities and talents have been improved by study, learning, observation and experience; and when by these means they have obtained great actual knowledge; when they have acquired great skill in public affairs, and things requisite to be known, in order to their wise, prudent and effectual management; when they have obtained a great understanding of men and things, a great knowledge of human nature, and of the way of accommodating themselves to it, so as most effectually to influence it to wise purposes; when they have obtained a very extensive knowledge of men with whom they are concerned in the management of public affairs, either those that have a joint concern in government, or those that are to be governed; and when they have also obtained a very full and particular understanding of the state and circumstances of the country or people that they have the care of, and know well their laws and constitution; and what their circumstances require; and likewise have a great knowledge of the people of neighbor nations, states, or provinces, with whom they have occasion to be concerned in the management of public affairs committed to them; these things all contribute to the rendering those that are in authority fit to be denominated "strong rods."

Second. When they have not only great understanding, but *largeness of heart, and a greatness and nobleness of disposition*, this is another qualification that belongs to the character of a strong rod.

Those that are by divine providence set in place of public authority and rule are called "gods," and "sons of the Most High" (Ps. 82:6). And therefore 'tis peculiarly unbecoming them to be of a mean spirit, a disposition that will admit of their doing those things that are sordid and vile; as when they are persons of a narrow, private spirit, that may be found in little tricks and intrigues to promote their private interest, will shamefully defile their hands, to gain a few pounds, are not ashamed to nip and bite others, grind the faces of the poor, and screw upon their neighbors; and will take advantage of their authority or commission to line their own pockets with what is fraudulently taken or withheld from others. When a man in authority is of such a mean spirit, it weakens his authority, and makes him justly contemptible in the eyes of men, and is utterly inconsistent with his being a strong rod.

But on the contrary, it greatly establishes his authority, and causes others to stand in awe of him, when they see him to be a man of *greatness of mind*, one that abhors those things that are mean and sordid, and not capable of a compliance with them; one that is of a *public spirit*, and not of a private narrow disposition, a man of honor, and not a man of mean artifice and clandestine management, for filthy lucre, and one that abhors trifling and impertinence, or to waste away his time, that should be spent in the service of God, his king, or his country, in vain amusements and diversions, and in the pursuit of the gratifications of sensual appetites; as God charges the rulers in Israel, that pretended to be their great and mighty men, with being "mighty to drink wine, and men of strength to mingle strong drink" [Is. 5:22]. There don't seem to be any reference to their being men of strong heads, and able to bear a great deal of strong drink, as some have supposed: there is a severe sarcasm in the words; for the Prophet is speaking of the "great men," princes and judges in Israel (as appears by the verse next following) which should be "mighty men, strong rods," men of eminent qualifications, excelling in nobleness of spirit, of glorious strength and fortitude of mind; but instead of that they were "mighty" or "eminent" for nothing but gluttony and drunkenness.

Third. When those that are in authority are endowed with much of a spirit of government, this is another thing that entitles them to the denomination of "strong rods." When they not only are men of great understanding and wisdom in affairs that appertain to government, but have also a peculiar talent at using their knowledge, and exerting themselves in this great and important business, according to their great understanding in it; when they are men of eminent fortitude, and are not afraid of the faces of men, are not afraid to do the part that properly belongs to them as rulers, though they meet with great opposition, and the spirits of men are greatly irritated by it; when they have a spirit of *resolution and activity*, so as to keep the wheels of government in proper motion, and to cause judgment and justice to run down as a mighty stream; when they have not only a great knowledge of government, and the things that belong to it in the theory, but it is as it were natural to them to apply the various powers and faculties with which God has endowed them, and the knowledge they have obtained by study and observation, to that business, so as to perform it most advantageously and effectually.

Fourth. Stability and firmness of integrity, fidelity and piety, in the exercise of authority, is another thing that greatly contributes *to*, and is very essential *in* the character of a strong rod.

When he that is in authority is not only a man of strong reason and great discerning to know what is just, but is a man of strict integrity and righteousness, is firm and immovable in the execution of justice and judgment; and when he is not only a man of great ability to bear down vice and immorality, but has a disposition agreeable to such ability; is one that has a strong aversion to wickedness, and is disposed to use the power God has put into his hands to suppress it; and is one that not only opposes vice by his authority, but by his example; when he is one of *inflexible fidelity*, will be faithful to God whose minister he is, to his people for good, is immovable in his regard to his supreme authority, his commands and his glory; and will be faithful to his king and country; will not be induced by the many temptations that attend the business of men in public authority, basely to betray his trust; will not consent to what he thinks not to be for the public good, for his own gain or advancement, or any private interest; is one that is well principled, and is firm in acting agreeably to his principles, and will not be prevailed with to do otherwise through fear or favor, to follow a multitude, or to maintain his interest in any on whom he depends for the honor or profit of his place, whether it be prince or people; and is also one of that *strength of mind*, whereby he rules his own spirit. These things do very eminently contribute to a ruler's title to the denomination of a "strong rod."

Fifth. And lastly, it also contributes to that strength of a man in authority, by which he may be denominated a "strong rod," when he is in *such circumstances*, as give him advantage for the exercise of his strength for the public good; as his being a person of honorable descent, of a distinguished education, his being a man of estate, one that is advanced in years, one that has long been in authority, so that it is become as it were natural for the people to pay him deference, to reverence him, to be influenced and governed by him, and submit to his authority; his being extensively known, and much honored and regarded abroad; his being one of a good presence, majesty of countenance, decency of behavior, becoming one in authority; of forcible speech, etc. These things add to his strength and increase his ability and advantage to serve his generation in the place of a ruler, and therefore in some respect serve to render him one that is the more fitly and eminently called a "strong rod."

I now proceed,
II. To show that when such strong rods are broken and withered by death, 'tis an awful judgment of God on the people that are deprived of them, and worthy of great lamentation.
And that on two accounts,

First. By reason of the many *positive benefits* and blessings to a people that such rulers are the instruments of.

Almost all the prosperity of a public society, and civil community does, under God, depend on their rulers. They are like the main springs or wheels in a machine; that keep every part in their due motion, and are in the body *politic*, as the vitals in the body *natural*, and as the pillars and foundation in a building. Civil rulers are called the "foundations of the earth" (Ps. 82:5 and 11:3).

The prosperity of a people depends more on their rulers than is commonly imagined. As they have the public society under their care and power, so they have advantage to promote the public interest every way; and if they are such rulers as have been spoken of, they are some of the greatest blessings to the public. Their influence has a tendency to promote their wealth, and cause their temporal possessions and blessings to abound. And to promote virtue amongst them, and so to unite them one to another in peace and mutual benevolence, and make them happy in society, each one the instrument of his neighbor's quietness, comfort and prosperity; and by these means to advance their reputation and honor in the world; and which is much more, to promote their spiritual and eternal happiness. Therefore the Wise Man says, Eccles. 10:17, "Blessed art thou, O land, when thy king is the son of nobles."

We have a remarkable instance and evidence of the happy and great influence of such a strong rod as has been described, to promote the universal prosperity of a people, in the history of the reign of Solomon, though many of the people were uneasy under his government, and thought him too rigorous in his administrations: see 1 Kgs. 12:4. "Judah and Israel dwelt safely, every man under his vine and under his fig tree, from Dan even to Beersheba, all the days of Solomon" (1 Kgs. 4:25). "And he made silver to be among them as stones for abundance" (10:27). "And Judah and Israel were many, eating and drinking and making merry" [1 Kgs. 4:20]. The Queen of Sheba admired, and was greatly affected with the happiness of the people, under the government of such a strong rod. 1 Kgs. 10:8–9, says she, "Happy are thy men, happy are these thy servants, which stand continually before thee, and that hear thy wisdom! Blessed be the Lord thy God, which delighted in thee to set thee on the throne of Israel: because the Lord loved Israel for ever, therefore made he thee king, to do judgment and justice."

The flourishing state of the kingdom of Judah, while they had strong rods for the scepters of them that bare rule, is taken notice of in our context; "her stature was exalted among the thick branches, and she appeared in her height with the multitude of her branches" [Ezek. 19:11].

Such rulers are eminently the ministers of God to his people for good. They are great gifts of the Most High to a people, and blessed tokens of his favor, and vehicles of his goodness to them, and therein images of his own Son, the grand medium of all God's goodness to fallen mankind; and therefore all of them are called, "sons of the Most High." All civil rulers, if they are as they ought to be, such strong rods as have been described, will be like the Son of the Most High, vehicles of good to mankind, and like him, "will be as the light of the morning, when the sun riseth, even a morning without clouds, as the tender grass springing out of the earth, by clear shining after rain" [2 Sam. 23:4]. And therefore when a people are bereaved of them they sustain an unspeakable loss, and are the subjects of a judgment of God that is greatly to be lamented.

Second. On account of the *great calamities* such rulers are a defense from. Innumerable are the grievous and fatal calamities which public societies are exposed to in this evil world, which they can have no defense from without *order and authority*. If a people are without government, they are like a city broken down and without walls, encompassed on every side by enemies, and become unavoidably subject to all manner of confusion and misery.

Government is necessary to defend communities from miseries from within themselves; from the prevalence of intestine discord, mutual injustice and violence. The members of the society continually making a prey one of another, without any defense one from another. Rulers are the heads of union in public societies, that hold the parts together; without which nothing else is to be expected than that the members of the society will be continually divided against themselves, every one acting the part of an enemy to his neighbor, every one's hand against every man, and every man's hand against him; going on in remediless and endless broils and jarring, till the society be utterly dissolved and broken in pieces, and life itself, in the neighborhood of our fellow creatures, becomes miserable and intolerable.

We may see the need of government in societies by what is visible in families, those lesser societies, of which all public societies are constituted. How miserable would these little societies be, if all left to themselves, without any authority or superiority in one above another, or any head of union and influence among them? We may be convinced by what we see of the lamentable consequences of the want of a proper exercise of authority and maintenance of government in families, that yet are not absolutely without all authority. No less need is there of government in public societies, but much more, as they are larger, a very few may possibly, without any government, act by concern, so as to concur in what shall be for the welfare of the whole; but this is not to be expected among a multitude, constituted of many thousands, of a great variety of tempers and different interests.

As government is absolutely necessary, so there is a necessity of strong rods in order to it: the business being such as requires persons so qualified; no other being sufficient for, or well capable of the government of public societies: and therefore those public societies are miserable that have not such strong rods for scepters to rule; Eccles. 10:16, "Wo to thee, O land, when thy king is a child."

As government, and strong rods for the exercise of it, are necessary to preserve public societies from dreadful and fatal calamities arising from among themselves; so no less requisite are they to defend the community from foreign enemies. As they are like the pillars of a building, so they are also like the walls and bulwarks of a city: they are under God the main strength of a people in a time of war, and the chief instruments of their preservation, safety and rest. This is signified in a very lively manner in the words that are used by the Jewish community in her lamentations, to express the expectations she had from her princes, Lam. 4:20, "The breath of our nostrils, the anointed of the Lord, was taken in their pits, of whom we said, Under his shadow we shall live among the heathen." In this respect also such strong rods are sons of the Most High, and images or resemblances of the Son of God, viz., as they are their saviors from their enemies; as the judges that God raised up of old in Israel are called, Neh. 9:27: "Therefore thou deliveredst them into the hand of their enemies, who vexed them; and in the time of their trouble, when they cried unto thee, thou heardest them from heaven; and according to thy manifold mercies, thou gavest them saviors, who saved them out of the hand of their enemies."

Thus both the prosperity and safety of a people, under God, depends on such rulers as are strong rods. While they enjoy such blessings, they are wont to be like a vine planted in a fruitful soil, with her stature exalted among the thick branches, appearing in her height with the multitude of her branches; but when they have no strong rod to be a scepter to rule, they are like a vine planted in a wilderness, that is exposed to be plucked up, and cast down to the ground, to have her fruit dried up with the east wind, and to have fire coming out of her own branches to devour her fruit.

On these accounts, when a people's strong rods are broken and withered, 'tis an awful judgment of God on that people, and worthy of great lamentation: as when King Josiah (who was doubtless one of the strong rods referred to in the text) was dead, the people made great lamentation for him: 2 Chron. 35:24–25, "And they brought him to Jerusalem, and he died, and was buried in one of the sepulchers of his fathers, and all Judah and Jerusalem mourned for Josiah. And Jeremiah lamented for Josiah; and all the singing men and singing women spake of Josiah in their lamentations, to this day, and made them an ordinance in Israel; and behold they are written in the lamentations."

Application

I come now to apply these things to our own case, under the late awful frown of divine providence upon us, in removing by death that honorable person in public rule and authority, an inhabitant of this town, and belonging to this congregation and church, who died at Boston the last Lord's day.

He was eminently a *strong rod* in the forementioned respects. As to his natural abilities, strength of reason, greatness and clearness of discerning, and depth of penetration, he was one of the first rank: it may be doubted whether he has left his superior in these respects, in these parts of the world. He was a man of a truly great genius, and his genius was peculiarly fitted for the understanding and managing of public affairs.

And as his natural capacity was great, so was the knowledge that he had acquired, his understanding being greatly improved by close application of mind to those things he was called to be concerned in, and by a very exact observation of them, and long experience in them. He had indeed a great insight into the nature of public societies, the mysteries of government, and the affairs of peace and war: he had a discerning that very few have of the things wherein the public weal consists, and what those things are that do expose public societies, and of the proper means to avoid the latter and promote the former. He was quick in his discerning, in that in most cases, especially such as belonged to his proper business, he at first sight would see further than most men when they had done their best; but yet he had a wonderful faculty of improving his own thoughts by meditation, and carrying his views a greater and greater length by long and close application of mind. He had an extraordinary ability to distinguish right and wrong, in the midst of intricacies, and circumstances that tended to perplex and darken the case: he was able to weigh things as it were in a balance, and to distinguish those things that were solid and weighty from those that had only a fair show without substance, which he evidently discovered in his accurate, clear and plain way of stating and committing causes to a jury, from the bench (as by others hath been observed) he wonderfully distinguished truth from falsehood, and the most labored cases, seemed always to lie clear in his mind, his ideas properly ranged—and he had a talent of communicating them to everyone's understanding, beyond almost anyone, and if any were misguided it was not because truth and falsehood, right and wrong were not well distinguished.

He was probably one of the ablest politicians that ever New England bred: he had a very uncommon insight into human nature, and a marvelous ability to penetrate into the particular tempers and dispositions of such as he had to deal with, and to discern the fittest way of treating them, so as most effectually to influence them to any good and wise purpose.

And never, perhaps, was there a person that had a more extensive and thorough knowledge of the state of this land, and its public affairs, and of persons that were jointly concerned with him in them: he knew this people, and their circumstances, and what their circumstances required: he discerned the diseases of this body, and what were the proper remedies, as an able and masterly physician. He had a great acquaintance with the neighboring colonies, and also the neighbor nations on this continent with whom we are concerned in our public affairs: he had a far greater knowledge than any other person in the land of the several nations of Indians in these northern parts of America, their tempers, manners and the proper way of treating them, and was more extensively known by them, than any other person in the country: and no other person in authority in this province, had such an acquaintance with the people and country of Canada, the land of our enemies, as he.

He was exceeding far from a disposition and forwardness to intermeddle with other folks' business; but as to what belonged to his proper business, in the offices he sustained, and the important affairs that he had the care of, he had a great understanding of what belonged to them. I have often been surprised at the length of his reach, and what I have seen of his ability to foresee and determine the consequences of things, even at a great distance, and quite beyond the sight of other men. He was not wavering and unsteady in his opinion: his manner was never to pass a judgment rashly, but was wont first thoroughly to deliberate and weigh an affair; and in this, notwithstanding his great abilities, he was glad to improve the help of conversation and discourse with others (and often spake of the great advantage he found by it); but when, on mature consideration, he had settled his judgment, he was not easily turned from it by false colors and plausible pretenses and appearances.

And besides his knowledge of things belonging to his particular calling as a ruler, he had also a great degree of understanding in things belonging to his general calling as a Christian. He was no inconsiderable divine: he was a wise casuist, as I know by the great help I have found from time to time, by his judgment and advice in cases of conscience, wherein I have consulted him: and indeed I scarce knew the divine that I ever found more able to help and enlighten the mind in such cases than he. And he had no small degree of knowledge in things pertaining to experimental religion; but was wont to discourse on such subjects, not only with accurate doctrinal distinctions, but as one intimately and feelingly acquainted with these things.

He was not only great in speculative knowledge, but his knowledge was *practical*, such as tended to a wise conduct in the affairs, business and duties of life; so as properly to have the denomination of wisdom, and so as properly and eminently to invest him with the character of a wise man. And he was not only eminently wise and prudent in his own conduct, but was one of the ablest and wisest counselors of others in any difficult affair.

The greatness and honorableness of his disposition, was answerable to the largeness of his understanding: he was naturally of a great mind: in this respect he was truly the "son of nobles" [Eccles. 10:16]. He greatly abhorred things which were mean and sordid, and seemed to be incapable of a compliance with them. How far was he from trifling and impertinence in his conversation? How far from a busy, meddling disposition? How far from any sly and clandestine management to fill his pockets with what was fraudulently withheld, or violently squeezed from the laborer, soldier or inferior officer? How far from taking advantage from his commission or authority, or any superior power he had in his hands? Or the ignorance, dependence or necessities of others to add to his own gains with what property belonged to them, and with what they might justly expect as a proper reward for any of their services? How far was he from secretly taking bribes offered to induce him to favor any man in his cause, or by his power or interest to promote his being advanced to any place of public trust, honor or profit? How greatly did he abhor lying and prevaricating? And how immovably steadfast was he to exact truth? His hatred of those things that were mean and sordid was so apparent and well known, that it was evident that men dreaded to appear in anything of that nature in his presence.

He was a man remarkably of a public spirit, a true lover of his country, and greatly abhorred the sacrificing the public welfare to private interest.

He was very eminently endowed with a "spirit of government." The God of Nature seemed to have formed him for government, as though he had been made on purpose, and cast into a mold, by which he should be every way fitted for the business of a man in public authority. Such a behavior and conduct was natural to him as tended to maintain his authority, and possess others with awe and reverence, and to enforce and render effectual what he said and did, in the exercise of his authority. He did not bear the sword in vain: he was truly a terror to evil doers. What I saw in him often put me in mind of that saying of the Wise Man, Prov. 20:8, "The king that sitteth in the throne of judgment scattereth away all evil with his eyes." He was one that was not afraid of the faces of men; and everyone knew that it was in vain to attempt to deter him from doing what, on mature consideration, he had determined he ought to do. Everything in him was great, and becoming a man in his public station. Perhaps never was there a man that appeared in New England, to whom the denomination of a "great man" did more properly belong.

But though he was one that was great among men, exalted above others in abilities and greatness of mind, and in place of rule, and feared not the faces of men, yet *he feared God*. He was strictly conscientious in his conduct, both in public and private. I never knew the man that seemed more steadfastly and immovably to act by principle, and according to rules and maxims, established and settled in his mind by the dictates of his judgment and conscience. He was a man of strict justice and fidelity; faithfulness was eminently his character: some of his greatest opponents, that have been of the contrary party to him in public affairs, yet have openly acknowledged this of him, that he was a faithful man. He was remarkably faithful in his public trusts: he would not basely betray his trust, from fear or favor: it was in vain to expect it, however men might oppose him or neglect him, and how great soever they were. Nor would he neglect the public interest, wherein committed to him, for the sake of his own ease, but diligently and laboriously watched and labored for it night and day. And he was faithful in private affairs as well as public: he was a most faithful friend; faithful to anyone that in any case asked his counsel: and his fidelity might be depended on in whatever affair he undertook for any of his neighbors.

He was a noted instance of the virtue of temperance, unalterable in it, in all places, in all companies, and in the midst of all temptations.

Though he was a man of a great spirit, yet he had a remarkable government of his spirit; and excelled in the government of his tongue. In the midst of all provocations he met with, with the multitudes he had to deal with, and the great multiplicity of perplexing affairs in which he was concerned, and all the opposition and reproaches he was at any time the subject of; yet what was there that ever proceeded out of his mouth that his enemies could lay hold of? No profane language, no vain, rash, unseemly and unchristian speeches. If at any time he expressed himself with great warmth and vigor, it seemed to be from principle and determination of his judgment, rather than from passion: when he expressed himself strongly and with vehemence, those that were acquainted with him and well observed him from time to time, might evidently see it was done in consequence of thought and judgment, weighing the circumstances and consequences of things.

The calmness and steadiness of his behavior in private, particularly in his family, appeared remarkable and exemplary to those who had most opportunity to observe.

He was thoroughly established in those religious principles and doctrines of the first fathers of New England, usually called the "doctrines of grace," and had a great detestation of the opposite errors of the present fashionable divinity, as very contrary to the Word of God, and the experience of every true Christian. And as he was a friend to truth, so he was a friend to vital piety and the power of godliness, and ever countenanced and favored it on all occasions.

He abhorred profaneness, and was a person of a serious and decent spirit, and ever treated sacred things with reverence. He was exemplary for his decent attendance on the public worship of God. Whoever saw him irreverently and indecently lolling, and laying down his head to sleep, or gazing and glaring about the meeting house in time of divine service? And as he was able (as was before observed) to discourse very understandingly of experimental religion, so to some persons with whom he was very intimate, he gave intimations sufficiently plain, while conversing of these things, that they were matters of his own experience. And some serious persons in civil authority, that have ordinarily differed from him in matters of government, yet on some occasional close conversation with him on things of religion, have manifested an high opinion of him as to real experimental piety.

As he was known to be a serious person, and an enemy to a profane or vain conversation, so he was feared on that account by great and small. When he was in the room, only his presence was sufficient to maintain decency; though many were there that were accounted gentlemen and great men, who otherwise were disposed to take a much greater freedom in their talk and behavior, than they dared to do in his presence.

He was not unmindful of death, nor insensible of his own frailty, nor did death come unexpected to him. For some years past he has spoken much to some persons of dying, and going into the eternal world, signifying that he did not expect to continue long here.

Added to all these things, that have been mentioned to render him eminently a "strong rod," he was attended with many circumstances which tended to give him advantage for the exerting of his strength for the public good. He was honorably descended, was a man of considerable substance, had been long in authority, was extensively known and honored abroad, was high in the esteem of the many tribes of Indians in the neighborhood of the British colonies, and so had great influence upon them above any other man in New England. God had endowed him with a comely presence, and majesty of countenance, becoming the great qualities of his mind, and the place in which God had set him.

In the exercise of these qualities and endowments, under these advantages, he has been as it were a father to this part of the land, on whom the whole county had, under God, its dependence in all its public affairs, and especially since the beginning of the present war.[1] How much the weight of all the warlike concerns of the county (which above any part of the land lies exposed to the enemy) has lain on his shoulders, and how he has been the spring of all motion, and the doer of everything that has been done, and how wisely and faithfully he has conducted these affairs, I need not inform this congregation. You well know that he took care of the county as a father of a family of children, not neglecting men's lives, and making light of their blood; but with great diligence, vigilance and prudence, applying himself continually to the proper means of our safety and welfare. And especially has this his native town, where he has dwelt from his infancy, reaped the benefit of his happy influence: his wisdom has been, under God, very much our guide, and his authority our support and strength, and he has been a great honor to Northampton, and ornament to our church.

He continued in full capacity of usefulness while he lived; he was indeed considerably advanced in years, but his powers of mind were not sensibly abated, and his strength of body was not so impaired, but that he was able to go long journeys, in extreme heat and cold, and in a short time.

But now this "strong rod is broken and withered," and surely the judgment of God therein is very awful, and the dispensation that which may well be "for a lamentation." Probably we shall be more sensible of the

---

1. I.e., "King George's War," one of several installments of the French and Indians wars. "Present" is a suggestive usage, indicating JE's sense of a continuum of conflict.

worth and importance of such a strong rod by the want of it. The awful voice of God in this providence is worthy to be attended to by this whole province, and especially by the people of this county, but in a more peculiar manner by us of this town. We have now this testimony of the divine displeasure, added to all the other dark clouds God has lately brought over us, and his awful frowns upon us. 'Tis a dispensation, on many accounts, greatly calling for our humiliation and fear before God; an awful manifestation of his supreme, universal and absolute dominion, calling us to adore the divine sovereignty, and tremble at the presence of this great God; and it is a lively instance of human frailty and mortality: we see how that none are out of the reach of death, that no greatness, no authority, no wisdom and sagacity, no honorableness of person or station, no degree of valuableness and importance exempts from the stroke of death. This is therefore a loud and solemn warning to all sorts to prepare for their departure hence.

And the memory of this person who is now gone, who was made so great a blessing while he lived, should engage us to show respect and kindness to his family. This we should do both out of respect to him and to his father, your former eminent pastor, who in his day was in a remarkable manner a father to this part of the land in spirituals, and especially to this town, as this his son has been in temporals. God greatly resented it, when the children of Israel did not show kindness to the house of Jerubbaal that had been made an instrument of so much good to them: Judg. 8:35, "Neither showed they kindness to the house of Jerubbaal, according to all the good which he had showed unto Israel."

Part 3

War Spreads to the Colonies

Warring With the Devil

April 1754

EDWARDS'S SETTLEMENT IN STOCKBRIDGE brought a new series of challenges. In addition to the challenges of frontier living, Edwards bore the burden of instructing the Mohican tribe in the Bible, the basics of a British education, as well as the standards of British culture. Most colonists took issue with the Mohican's lax, nomadic lifestyle that did not reflect British political or social structures. One area of Native life with which Edwards took no issue was their warrior ethos. The Mohicans of Stockbridge had cooperated with British military efforts for some time. In 1747, Maj. Ephraim Williams led a group of Stockbridge Indians on a supply mission to Albany. On the way, they spotted a French and Indian party watching their movements from atop a bald mountain. Ensign Kunkapot, a Stockbridge leader, led a scouting party chasing these French and Indian soldiers a considerable distance.[1] Edwards's ministry in Stockbridge sought to incorporate the Mohicans into the British "Protestant Interest."

In the spring of 1754, there was a "storm rising in the west." The journals of George Washington's failed diplomatic mission were printed in the *Boston Gazette*, news of French activity abounded from the Kennebec River to the Carrying Place below Lake George.[2] In response, Governor Shirley issued a call to recruit six new companies.[3] The machinations of war were beginning to crank in anticipation of another widespread conflict. This time, the conflict would involve Pennsylvania and Virginia

1. *Boston Gazette*, June 9, 1747.
2. *Boston Gazette*, April 16, 1754.
3. *Boston Gazette*, April 23, 1754.

as well as New York and New England. These preparations gave Edwards the opportunity to draw on the Mohican warrior ethos in his sermon, *Warring with the Devil*.

Delivered in April 1754, Edwards drew on this warrior ethos to push them towards a uniquely British version of spirituality. Comparing the devil to a strong man waging war, Edwards argued that the Stockbridge, in effect, have allowed this strong man to defeat them, a condition unacceptable for the Native warrior. They have been defeated through several Native practices: strong drink, idleness, wandering about, lax parenting, and fear. In order to win this war, one must imitate the practices of Christ who is stronger than the devil. Edwards even challenged their virile sensibilities: "What slaves are you! How you are held fast!"

This sermon, like so many Edwards preached in Northampton, sought to draw on the martial experience of his congregation to move them towards deeper levels of spiritual commitment. In this case, the spirituality Edwards promoted was inextricably tied up in notions of British life: strict parenting, agriculture, a hard work ethic, and moderation. Parting from their practices, according to Edwards, was to defeat the devil, whereas continuing in these ways would be to accept defeat.

* * * * *

This sermon was edited for the *Works of Jonathan Edwards* by Wilson Kimnach. The unstitched four-leaf octavo manuscript is written in double columns, much of it in outline form. There is no textual commentary or formal statement of doctrine, but six propositions follow the initial text. The lengthy Application is formally identified and is more fully developed, though still very much in outline. The sermon is dated, "St[ockbridge] Ind[ians]. April. 1754." The first four pages of the manuscript are written on a folded letter draft to Andrew Oliver, Esq., Commissioner for Indian Affairs in Boston, requesting the delivery of Gideon Hawley's salary. The second four pages are written on the folded leaf of a disbound commonplace book (not Edwards'), leaves from which are frequently found in sermons of this period. Never having been bound together, the two bifolds became separated in the archive and are now reunited in print (catchword and context providing the linkage). The manuscript is in the Edwards Papers of the Trask Library, Andover Newton Theological School.

Warring With the Devil

Luke 11:21–22.

When a strong man armed keepeth his palace.

THE DEVIL IS AN enemy that is like a strong man armed. [He is an] enemy to God [and an] enemy to men.

Always carrying on a war.

A strong enemy.

[He is] armed: his arms [are] men's lusts.

II. The devil lives in wicked man as in his house. A man's house is his own; he has it in possession [with all] his goods: [he] lives there [and] rules over [it].

Inference. How miserable [is one whose house is taken from him and possessed by another, evil being].

III. While Christ lets men alone, the devil keeps 'em quiet and secure in their sins.

IV. Christ is stronger than the devil.

V. When a sinner is converted, Christ fights with the devil [and] overcomes [him].

VI. When a sinner is converted, he turns the devil out of his house where he lived, and takes possession himself.

Application

Exhortation. To such as are going on in sin, to come to Christ. I would have you Indians consider how it is with you. Your whole nation was formerly under the power of that strong man armed, and now you are brought under the gospel. Consider how much has been done [for you]. And yet, how is it with many of you still? How the devil keeps you under his power! What slaves are you! How you are held fast! You sometimes take up resolutions [to change your ways, but] some that are in the church [are still overwhelmed by the devil's devices]. We have had meetings about it, time after time. Consider the sorrowful consequences of it. Means of grace do you no good. [Drink] ruins your health: many die, [and] you do hurt one to another. [You] are uncomfortable [before your pastor and among your fellows at our meetings]. What an example is here set before your children! You are kept a poor, miserable people: what you get you lay out, a great deal of it, for rum. Your families suffer [much][1] by it.

I'll tell you how I think it comes to pass. One thing is your idleness: young men don't work; [they] live upon their relations. Some of you don't like it, but you durst not tell your mind.

Another thing [is] want of prayer.

Another thing is your wandering so much about.

[Another thing is your] want of keeping good order and government in your families: children rule their parents. Parents don't [really] bring up their children. When they are children, they go to school and are kept orderly; but as soon as they are grown up, they begin to love to drink {and} wander about. [They] serve the devil more and more.

[Another thing is that] you are too much afraid one of another.

[There are] some bring rum to sell to others to get a little money. A number of women [do this]: they are the devil's servants, [and they] do it for the devil. They don't care how many they make drunk with it. Hence it comes to pass, we every now and then hear 'em go howling about [the] streets. Their money will do 'em no good that is got in such ways as these. Some of those are in the church. Some of 'em are grown old.

You see the Indians die faster than others.

It may be you will say, "The English are as bad."

It may be you will say, "What shall I do?"

Now, consider: are you not miserable slaves [to the] worst of masters? Consider what must become of you if you thus continue under the power of the devil. You must have your part with him, [for you] shall be given up to his power. [There will be] no other pay for your service: none to deliver [you], none to pity [you]. [You] can't run away [from hell, and you] can't die. These things are certain.

---

1. Conjecture for MS damage.

God Is He Who Orders

March 5, 1755

THE SHADOW OF WAR loomed so large in the Connecticut River Valley that this was Edwards's second message on the topic in as many days. While the previous day's message was delivered to the entire Stockbridge congregation, this message was delivered before a private fasting event. This suggests that many within Stockbridge were particularly concerned about the coming of wide-spread war to the frontier. And they had good cause to worry. Recent editions of the *Gazette* included the speeches of other colonial governors including Horatio Sharpe of Maryland[1] and Arthur Dobbs of North Carolina as well as news from Virginia and Pennsylvania outlining the French and Indian threat to their colonies. Correspondence from the Earl of Holderness instructed each colony to act to preserve its own territory and the London proprietors grew nervous about French and Native encroachment on their lands.[2] This was not the first time war swept through New England and the *Gazette* reported that the previous experiences of war were so "fresh in every body's memory I need not repeat them."[3]

This sermon echoed the theme of his previous on March 4th, *The Enemies of God Confounded and Broken in Pieces*, expressing a confidence in the ultimate purposes of God. Supporting his idea that war is chiefly spiritual, Edwards argued that God is the one who orders all things and is, therefore, in control of the outcome of war. This should be

1. *Boston Gazette*, February 4, 11, 1755.
2. *Boston Gazette*, February 4, 18, 1755.
3. *Boston Gazette*, October 1, 1754.

an encouragement to the residents of Stockbridge, Native or British, because God is stronger than the strongest man, mightier than the mightiest army, and has the ability to preserve his people.

God's control extends from the global—"armies by land and ships by sea"—as well as the personal—even the inclinations of one's heart. If God can control everything from nations and kings down to "body and soul," then God can control the outcome of wars. This theological claim was designed to offer encouragement to an apprehensive frontier town. Furthermore, it sought to cultivate a trust in such an all-powerful God as the best way to ensure one's protection.

* * * * *

Edited for the Jonathan Edwards Center by Roy Paul also known as "Private Fast for Our Defense from the Enemy to the Stockbridge Indians." The manuscript is six octavo-sized leaves. Edwards constructed this booklet from a discarded seventeenth-century commonplace book, around the entries of which he writes his text. The title and date at the head of the sermon are Edwards's.

God Is He Who Orders[1]

2 Chronicles 20:6

And said, O Lord God of our fathers, art not thou God in heaven? and rulest not thou over all the kingdoms of the heathen? and in thine hand is there not power and might, so that none is able to withstand thee?

Doctrine

God is he that orders all things in a time of war.

[God orders things] just as he pleases. And all defense and success in war is from him.

I. In a time of war, he sees and knows all things concerning the affair.

[God] knows who is in the right.

[There is] always one side in the wrong.

[God knows] what it is that moves 'em, whether good principles [or bad].

[God knows] all the designs of the enemy

[Their] plots.

[The things] they keep secret.

Knows all that they do.

Sees in darkness.

Sees all the hiding places in the minds.

---

1. "Private Fast for Our Defense from the Enemy, March 5, 1755, to the Stockbridge Indians."

All under the whole heaven.
Knows when a people are most in danger.
Never sleeps.

II. God's wisdom is above all that cunning and craftiness that men use in a time of war.
Many are very subtil and crafty.
Are² very cunning in their schemes and plots for the carrying on the war.
By their craftiness, they often deceive others and lead 'em into a snare.
Sometimes a nation in a time of war have very cunning rulers and great men.
[They] take counsel.
Use all their cunning.
But God is wiser.
They are as little children and fools.
[God] knows how to disappoint.
[God knows how to] lead 'em into the pits they have digged for others.
Men have no wisdom or understanding but what God has given 'em.
Makes wiser than the beasts.³
Makes some men wiser than others.

III. Sometimes the devil leads men to make war
[The devil is] cunninger than men.
God's wisdom is above.
God's strength is above the strength of men.
[Above the] strongest men.
The greatest armies.
All their strength put together.
[God] gave 'em their strength.
Men are but little worms.
All nations before him are as nothing.
[The] strongest armies as chaff before a strong wind.
As dry straw before devouring fire.

2. MS: "have."
3. MS: "beat."

God made the world.
Manages the sun, moon and stars.
Manages the sea.
Can shake the world in pieces.

IV. God has all things in his hands.
All nations.
All kings.
Made every man, body & soul, and all are his.
The greatest nations and armies as much in his power as one little child.
Their hearts [are in his hands].
He can turn them.
He directs all their thoughts
Lead to right thoughts.
Armies by land and ships at sea [are in God's hands].
[The] weather [is] of his ordering.
[God can] sink their ship.
Their hearts are in his hands.
Give courage.
Direct their thought in the time of the fight.
Can make 'em disagree one with another.
Has men's health in his[4] hands.

---

4. MS: "their."

In the Name of the Lord of Hosts

July 1755

THE SUMMER OF 1755 brought war to the frontiers of New England and to the center of the town of Stockbridge. Because Edwards was the pastor, his house was centrally located in town, making it an ideal location for a fortified home. That summer, a palisade encircled the Edwards homestead and it became a military garrison, providing food and lodging to the militia stationed there (at the Edwards's family expense).[1] Preparations accelerated throughout the colonies as Braddock began his march to the Ohio River,[2] Connecticut raised one thousand troops for the capture of Crown Point to which Massachusetts added five hundred more.[3] Military action in the east seemed to progress successfully with the capture of Fort Beausejour and the surrender of St. John's Fort practically driving the French out of Nova Scotia.[4]

As Edwards preached this sermon in July of 1755, Col. Ephraim Williams prepared to march a unit of Stockbridge Indians to Albany in support of the British cause. At least one Stockbridge received a British commission and joined a group of about fifty Mohicans.[5] At Albany, Generals Shirley and Johnson vied for their services. Initially, Johnson convinced them to join his expedition to Crown Point, however, when it became apparent that Johnson had no specific mission for them, they

---

1. Frazier, *Mohicans*, 109.
2. *Boston Gazette*, June 9, 1755.
3. *Boston Gazette*, June 23, 30, 1755.
4. *Boston Gazette*, July 14, 1755.
5. Most likely Joseph Cheeksunkun. Frazier, *Mohicans*, 112.

joined Shirley's expedition to Oswego and Fort Ontario.[6] When Shirley enlisted the services of one hundred Oneidas en route, the Stockbridge returned to Albany where they would help recruiting other Natives whereas some would be employed by Captain Robert Rogers and his ranger company. Most would see action at the battle of Lake George on September 8th, 1755 in what was described at the time as the greatest battle in American history. Edwards did not merely draw on martial themes for this sermon, he preached to warriors who would participate in war.

This sermon uses the story of David and Goliath to set up a spiritual dichotomy: those who trust in God and those who don't. Since God orders all things, he is the one who can bring victory. Those who trust in themselves dare God to expose the folly of their trust by bringing defeat. To demonstrate his power, God often foils the strength of men and their armies, forts, and wisdom.[7] Therefore, the only sure way to victory, according to Edwards, was fighting in God's name which entailed both a trust in God and a trust in God's ways for victory.

Edwards offered some practical advice for these Native warriors: to "forsake sin" and to trust in God. Edwards continued by offering words of encouragement. Even though the French have many advantages, their religion disadvantages them. Edwards thought that "papism" was contrary to God's word and detestable to God, therefore, God was not willing to fight for them. Edwards concluded by reminding the Stockbridge that Christ has already conquered the devil as David conquered Goliath. As in so many other sermons, Edwards's message combined his call to a deeper personal piety with the martial task at hand. It exhorted the Mohican warriors to adopt Edwards's brand of evangelical piety as an essential part of their war-making practices.

* * * * *

Edited by Wilson Kimnach for the *Works of Jonathan Edwards*, also known as "([To the] Stockbridge Indians on Occasion of the Expedition to Crown Point, Etc." The octavo sermon booklet consists of six leaves and is written in double columns. The paper appears to be remnants

---

6. Frazier, *Mohicans*, 114–15.

7. Braddock suffered his defeat on July 9th. It is unclear when this sermon was preached during the month of July or if it was preached with a knowledge of Braddock's death. However, if Edwards did preach this sermon with a knowledge of Britain's defeat at the Ohio River, it would explain the ominous tone during an optimistic period as well as give Edwards's warning some force.

from another person's commonplace book. At the top of the first page is the inscription, "St[ockbridge] Ind[ians] on Occasion of the Expedition to Cr[own] Point &c. July 55." Edwards changed "June" to "July" in the heading, apparently correcting a simple mistake.

In The Name of the Lord of Hosts[1]

1 Samuel 17:45–47

Then David said to the Philistine, Thou comest to me with a sword, and with a spear, and with a shield: but I come unto thee in the name of the Lord of hosts . . . This day will the Lord deliver thee into mine hand; and I will smite thee, and take thine head from thee; . . . for the battle is the Lord's, and he will give you into our hands.

[Doctrine]

[In two propositions:]

I. *For men to trust in themselves when they go to war is the way for 'em to be overcome by their enemies.* [Neither] their strength, courage, [and] wisdom, [nor their] numbers, forts, [and] weapons of war [will be sufficient for their victory]. Such men as trust [in these things] take that upon them which belongs to God. He takes [it] upon him[self] to order all things that belong to the effect and events of war. It belongs to him, as king of the whole world. [God is] king over all nations, [for they are] all made by him. Men that trust in themselves make gods of themselves. God will make men to know that he is king in these matters. Such men make God angry, as they don't give him the honor that belongs to him. They do foolishly, because they trust in that that is very weak. Man [is] but a worm. The wisdom of men goes but a little way. It becomes us to

---

1. "[To the] Stockbridge Indians on Occasion of the Expedition to Crown Point, Etc., July 1755."

be sensible of our ignorance. Men's strength often proves insufficient [to their needs]: their wisdom, [their] biggest armies, [and] their forts [often fail them]. [Even the] strongest nations, greatest cities, [and] strongest kingdoms [fail]: God brings 'em to nothing. All depends on the life of man, and what is man's life? It shows pride [to depend upon ourselves]. God abhors the proud; [he] delights to confound them and bring 'em low.

II. *To go to fight against our enemies in God's name is the way to overcome our enemies.* Going to war in God's name implies these three things:

First. Going to war when God allows us to go [to] war, and calls us to it in [his] providence.

Second. Going to war trusting in God.

Third. Walking in God's ways.

This is the way, for then they choose him for their king; then they follow this captain. He is willing to be the king and captain to them that choose him and follow [him]. He takes care of 'em as his people: a king is to take care [of his people], to be a father to 'em. So is God. Christ is willing to be a captain to them that choose him. He looks on their armies as his armies. This is the way [for you to go], because God is a just and righteous God. He sees when one nation does wrong to another. He is a merciful God.

Application

I. [*Exhortation.*] To forsake sin.

II. [*Exh.*] To trust in God and pray to God, [and] not to trust in ourselves. [Do] not trust in men: cursed is he that trusts in men, like the dry tree.² Happy is he that trusts in the Lord, [for he is] like a tree that grows by a river. We have great encouragement to trust in God in this war we are now engaged in with our enemies.

First. 'Tis not we that begin the war. Our cause is just. [Our enemy have acted] contrary to their agreement [with us].

---

2. The image of the dry (or dead) tree is one that would have had immediate meaning for the forest-dwelling Indians, but tree images were also among JE's favorite biblical nature images (or types) from prophecies and parables. See his references in the "Images" table (WJE 11:141).

Second. Our enemies seem to trust in themselves. They have been making great preparations [for war] in time of peace, [both] by sea and [by] land. [They have been] telling lies [to] draw off nations of Indians from the English, [and they] send Indians in time of peace to kill us. [They] come against us as Goliath did against David. [That is, they are] very proud.

Third. The religion of the Papists, that they are of, is contrary to God's word, and what he hates.[3] The Pope [is an impostor; Papists] pray to images, [and] pray to [the] Virgin Mary. [They] pray to dead men. [The] Pope contrived for his[4] people to get away money from the people [by selling them] pardon [for] sin. [They] pretend that in another world there is a fire that is on this side hell, where their people lie a great while, [until they are released by the church's intervention]. [They] won't let the people have the Bible.

Fourth. We should consider what Christ has done for us. [He has] conquered the devil [and the] armies of hell like David.

[III.] *Exh.* To be much in prayer to God that he would help us. How miserable we should be if we shall be overcome by the French.

[IV.] *Exh.* Put away all sin. How happy they are that have God on their side! He sees all that the enemy are doing. He is strong. God can easily [bring victory in battle for those who trust in him].[5]

---

3. MS: "<& what He hates> is what G. hates."
4. MS: "the."
5. Of the six leaves in the sermon booklet only about four and one half are used, and there are blank columns among those leaves, as well as crossed-out writings by another hand.

God's People Tried By a Battle Lost

August 28, 1755

THROUGHOUT THE SUMMER OF 1755, enthusiasm over Britain's inevitable victories grew throughout the colonies. The *Boston Gazette* reported the arrival of General Braddock along with several regiments from England and Ireland. And just in time. France had occupied the "Forks," the strategic confluence of the Allegheny and Monongahela rivers to form the Ohio River which threatened to connect France's territories along the Mississippi with those in Canada. Britain planned on driving a wedge between these territories, severing communications and supplies and allowing the British to pivot north, taking the French forts of Niagara and Crown Point before removing the French from Montreal and Quebec. This had been the vision of the British colonies since King William's War in 1690 and now it seemed as if Britain was on the verge of realizing this vision.

However, Braddock's mission proved disastrous, challenging not only the physical safety of New England, but the spiritual interpretation of their position. This defeat strengthened France's position, exposing Pennsylvania and Virginia to direct attacks and emboldening French and Indian troops along the Hudson River Valley. It was so deflating to New England's morale, it received a mere passing mention in the *Boston Gazette*.[1] This defeat was so unique that Edwards could not recycle a previous sermon, instead, he had to present a framework within which his British and Native congregation could make sense of this improbable

---

1. *Boston Gazette*, August 11, 1755. For a more thorough treatment of how news of this defeat spread, see Preston, *Braddock's Defeat*, 282–83.

defeat. While Edwards delivered a new sermon, *God's People Tried by a Battle Lost* draws heavily on the martial themes of his previous sermons.

Referencing the theme of *The Sovereignty of God's Mercy*, Edwards highlighted the role of God's pleasure in Britain's defeat: God will have mercy on whom he will have mercy. He continued to claim, drawing on *Christ, Lord of Hosts*, that God is the Lord of the Host or armies and determines the outcome of battles. God often, according to Edwards, throws even the best prepared armies into confusion reflecting the themes of *Enemies Confounded and Broken*. Edwards reminded his congregation, drawing on *The Church of Christ Built on a Rock*, that God promised that "the enemies of God's church never shall prevail against [the one true church]." Themes of humility, repentance, "the accursed thing," and "vigor" echo the language of previous sermons. While this sermon was written specifically for the occasion of Braddock's defeat, it summarized many of the themes Edwards developed over the past fifteen years.

This sermon also emphasized the role that defeat plays in the plan of God. Oftentimes, God allows defeat to motivate his people to "relinquish all other dependence and to look to him for help." While this evangelical call has a personal element, Edwards emphasized the corporate duty to oppose and defeat antichristian kingdoms. This sermon used the occasion of Braddock's defeat to provide his congregation a warning, calling them into deeper expressions of piety. Yet this sermon reminds the people of God of the ultimate encouragement: dependence on and confidence in God alone is never misplaced.

* * * * *

This sermon was edited by Wilson Kimnach for the *Works of Jonathan Edwards*, also known as "Fast After General Braddock's Defeat." The sixteen leaves of the duodecimo manuscript are composed of old letter paper (good stock). The manuscript is written in double columns, some heads are left undeveloped, and the whole is written in an apparently hasty hand. The last one and a half leaves are blank. The formal structure of the sermon is loose, the Doctrine consisting of four propositions rather than a formal statement of doctrine; the Application has no head divisions whatsoever, and there are no subheads in the entire sermon. The sermon is titled, "Fast after Gen. Bradocks defeat. Aug. 28. 1755." Both physical and internal evidence indicate that the sermon was preached to the English congregation.

God's People Tried By A Battle Lost

Psalms 60:9–12

Who will bring me into the strong city?[1]

1. THE CIRCUMSTANCES THAT God's people were in: [they were] brought into great trouble by a defeat in war. Psalms 60:1–3, "O God, thou hast cast us off, thou hast scattered us, thou hast been displeased; O turn thyself to us again. Thou hast made the earth to tremble; thou hast broken it: heal the breaches thereof; for it shaketh. Thou hast showed thy people hard things: thou hast made us to drink the wine of astonishment."

2. The thing they needed under those circumstances: deliverance and victory. And in order to this, getting possession of the strongholds of their enemies.

3. Here is declared whence this help is not to be had.

4. On whom David and God's people had their dependence in this affair.

[Doctrine]

[In four propositions:]

I. *If God be pleased to forsake a people, and not to go forth with their armies, defeat and confusion is like to [be] the consequence.* In such a case,

---

1. JE only quoted the opening of Ps. 60:9. The remainder of the passage reads: "who will lead me unto Edom? Wilt not thou, O God, which hadst cast us off? and thou, O God, which didst not go out with our armies? Give us help from trouble: for vain is the help of man. Through God we shall do valiantly: for he it is that shall tread down our enemies."

the increase of numbers, the strength of armies, the greatness of the preparation made of arms and warlike stores, the valor and experience of officers, the exercise of the greatest human wisdom in laying the plan of operation, and the greatest vigilance and care in the execution are like to be in vain. The Psalmist, in speaking of the circumstances of God's people and the defeats they had met with, does not ascribe it to the want of sufficient numbers or [military preparation], but [to the absence of God's help]. The Wise Man observes, Eccles. 9:11, "The race is not to the swift, nor the battle to the strong."

The event of warlike enterprises and attempts is absolutely dependent on God's power and pleasure. The very being of the warriors is from God, and his are all their warlike talents, strength and fortitude of mind. All war-like preparations are from his stores—materials that he has made—and things which God has made he keeps in his hands; [he] don't dismiss 'em and leave 'em independent.

The success of warlike undertakings depends on innumerable circumstances and events that are purely providential, and can't be foreseen and be provided against by human preventions. God is wont, especially, to make his hand visible in this affair. He takes upon him to order the events of war in such a manner that it shall be plain that all depends on his sovereign will. God orders all things, but in some things he is wont to make his interposition and disposal more visible than [in] others; and this in particular may be observed: the more important any affair is, 'tis fit it should be so [transacted] in order to the maintaining of God's due honor as King of the universe. We see in earthly kingdoms [that] kings will commit the lesser affairs of their kingdoms to others, but reserve [to themselves] the affairs of greatest importance; and particularly, the affairs of war and peace are earthly kings wont [to take upon themselves]. The affair of war is one of the most important of all the affairs of the universe: the state of the world of mankind principally depends upon it.

God calls himself very often the Lord of hosts and armies, and he will be acknowledged as supreme in these affairs; [for he] is jealous of his honor, as [he] was in the case of the war with the Midianites in the time of Gideon. And God has abundantly made it appear in his providence in all ages that unless he be with a people in this affair and go forth with their armies, nothing is to be expected but that they will be utterly defeated and confounded.

It appears in this that when human strength and preparation and expectations have been greatest, there very commonly has been the greatest disappointment and confusion. This appears both in sacred and profane history: Pharaoh's chariots and horsemen, Midianites, Zerah the Ethiopian, Ammonites and Moabites and others in Jehoshaphat's time, [and] Sennacherib's army; and not only the enemies of God's people, but in God's people themselves, as when they went against Ai, [and] against the Benjamites. Profane history [. . .].[2] Especially when men have shown great confidence in their strength, [there has been great disappointment]. Thus it has been in all ages in times past, and 'tis in vain to expect that it should be otherwise for time to come. Is. 8:9–10, "Associate yourselves and ye shall be broken in pieces."

II. *Disappointments and defeats in war commonly bring a people into distress.* Thus, in the text, God's people cry to God as in great trouble. Attended with the loss of many lives, [the] loss of much of a people's substance dispirits them and weakens their courage. [It also] encourages the enemy [and] invites 'em on—victory is sweet—increases their numbers, increases their wealth and warlike stores, [and] gives the enemy time to strengthen themselves.[3]

One defeat makes way for another. The more frequent victories and defeats are, the more easily are they obtained, [leaving the weakened party] exposed to a total conquest. The conquest of towns, cities and countries is very commonly attended with distresses and calamities that are inexpressible. [The experience is] elegantly described [in] Lam. 5:1, 16, "Remember, O Lord, what is come upon us: consider, and behold our reproach. . . . The crown is fallen from our head: woe unto us, that we have sinned!" Those things tend to bring a people into distress as hereby a people's all is brought into danger: danger of losing their liberties, all their civil privileges, all their temporal possessions, and very often their spiritual, too.

'Tis by this, chiefly, God has executed judgments on sinful nations: [from their sins] their great calamities have come. 'Tis principally by this means that kingdoms and nations have been overthrown and brought to utter ruin from age to age. It was by defeats in war that all those nations and kingdoms that were of old, that we read of in Scripture, have been brought to desolation. By this the great monarchies of the world [have

---

2. JE left the heading undeveloped.

3. In the action, the French not only routed the English but captured much military equipment; moreover, the English supply train destroyed equipment rather than risk its capture, further weakening the English.

been destroyed]. By this many beautiful and magnificent cities have [been] brought to that state that is described and represented concerning Babylon; Is. 34:11, "But the cormorant and the bittern shall possess it; the owl also and the raven shall dwell in it: and he shall stretch out upon it the line of confusion, and the stones of emptiness."[4]

III. *It becomes a people after defeats in war to relinquish all other dependence and to look to him for help.*[5] It especially becomes a people in such circumstances to relinquish [trust in their own preparations], for by such defeats God shows their vanity. This is what appears [to be] the lesson taught; and therefore, then, God expects a conviction and acknowledgment of it agreeable to what is said in the text: "vain is the help of man."

And it becomes a people in such circumstances to look to God for help, for by such defeats he shows that 'tis he and not they that determines the event. Then [he] in his providence says, as in Ps. 46:10, "Be still, and know that I am God." How or by which means God says this is expressed in the two foregoing verses: "Come, behold the works of the Lord, what desolations he hath made in the earth. He maketh wars to cease unto the end of the earth; he breaketh the bow, and cutteth the spear in sunder; he burneth the chariot in the fire." The people of God in the text, having been defeated in war, express themselves as being now sensible that God alone can give victory: "Who will bring me into the strong city?" As Jehoshaphat says, 2 Chron. 20:12, "O our God, wilt thou not judge them? for we have no might against this great company that cometh against us; neither know we what to do: but our eyes are upon thee." There is encouragement for a people to look to God [for help], though they have been defeated [recently], because though God has manifested himself angry with them and in his anger has forsaken 'em and cast 'em off, yet there is forgiveness with him, [that he may be feared (Ps. 130:4)].

And 'tis no certain sign that God intends [to] give a people up into the hands of the enemy, or that he don't intend that in the general they shall have success in their war, that they have met with a great defeat in the beginning. God may have a merciful design in it, to fit 'em for the success he intends [ultimately], to humble [them first, and to] make [them]

---

4. JE deletes: "when a People are brought into Trouble by a defeat in war it tends to prepare em for Gods Help as such a state of them tends to convince em of the need of it and to bring em."

5. MS: "him."

sensible [of his power, in order to] teach 'em where their dependence is. 'Tis common that when a people first begin a war, they go forth with much self-confidence: [but] such is the heart of man that it stands in need of a work of humiliation to fit [it] for any great prosperity; otherwise, [it] can't bear prosperity. [People] often need this to fit [them] for success in war; otherwise, [they] would assume all the glory [and] sacrifice to their own nature. [Thus,] God's way is first to prepare men's hearts and then cause their[6] ears to hear. Ps. 10:17, "Lord, thou hast heard the desire of the humble: thou wilt prepare [their heart, thou wilt cause thine ear to hear]." Defeat tends to prepare for God's help, [and to] convince [people] of their need of it.

God often, in his infinite wisdom, chooses such a time for the bestowment of some great salvation on a person or people, when their circumstances look most dark. Such a state shows the value and necessity of the mercy he is about to bestow: in such a state men's weakness most appears, but [God] often takes such times when men's weakness most appears most to glorify his power. If they are but made sensible of their weakness and dependence, [their outlook may become] agreeable to that; II Cor. 12:10, "When I am weak, then am I strong." And though a people may seem really to become weak and may be brought under great disadvantage by a defeat in war, and the enemy [seem] to have gained great advantage, yet if a people repent and put away the accursed thing, and look to God for help, there is no reason to despair: God's power is sufficient for them. In such a case, he can soon retrieve their affair and turn the scale; [he] can quickly scatter all the dark clouds and turn seeming disadvantages to advantages. When the children of Israel first began their wars in Canaan, after they had come over Jordan under Joshua, they met with a defeat before Ai. But [as soon as they "put away the accursed thing" (Josh. 7:13), the Lord directed them in the complete overthrow of the forces of Ai]. So the children of Israel, in the beginning of their war with the Benjamites, [were twice defeated before the Lord gave them their victory (Judg. 20:14–48)]. God has appeared for his people when they humble themselves before him and look to him for help, even when brought to the last extremity. [Remember] Shishak (2 Chron. 12:7) [and] Sennacherib (2 Kings, 18th and 19th chapters).

We can't judge what the event of a war will [be] by a defeat in the beginning so much as by observing the operation of it, and the effect the

---

6. MS: "his."

defeat has on the minds of the party that is the subject of such a rebuke from God. There are two things implied in what God's people say in the text relating to their war with their enemies, viz. their own weakness and disadvantage in that [they] had been defeated; and another is the advantage and strength of the enemy, consisting in the strength of their fortifications. But yet you see God's people, notwithstanding these things which are both against them, encourage themselves that God will give courage [to] do valiantly, obtain victory, [and] take the strong city; yea, [they] shall have an easy and most perfect victory, [and shall] tread down their[7] enemies.

So that if a people humble themselves before God for their sins, and repent and look to God for help, there is reason to hope that God will be with them and will retrieve their affairs. They need not be discouraged by past defeats or by any disadvantages, as strength of the enemy. Now just such a people may reasonably encourage themselves that through God they shall do valiantly, and that God will tread down their enemies and bring 'em into their most fortified places, and give 'em the possession of their strongest fortresses.

IV. There is peculiar encouragement for God's people to look to him for help and victory in war, when those that they are at war [with] are public enemies of God's church. Such were those that were spoken of in the text, viz. the Edomites. "Who will bring me into the strong city? who will lead me into Edom?" There was a great and inveterate hatred in the nations of the Edomites against the Israelites. Ezek. 35:5, speaking of the nation of Edom, "Thou hast had a perpetual hatred, and hast shed the blood of the children of Israel by the force of the sword"; so v. 11, "Therefore, as I live, saith the Lord God, I will even do according to thine anger, and according to thine envy which thou hast used out of thy hatred against them; and I will make myself known among them, when I have judged thee." [This is] signified by Esau's and Jacob's struggling together in Rebekah's womb.[8] And in the beginning of the sixty-third chapter of Isaiah, Christ's victory over the enemies of his church in general, and especially over Antichrist, is represented as his victory over Edom. And so it is in Is. 34:5, etc., "For my sword shall be bathed in heaven: behold,

---

7. MS: "our."

8. JE deletes: "In Ps. 137. 7 7 and following a Psalm penned on occasion of the Captiv. into Bab. Edom is and not Babilon is mentioned as the most peculiar Enemy of Gods Chh. v. 7 and following ⸺."

it shall come down upon Idumea, and upon the people of my curse, to judgment. The sword of the Lord is filled with blood, . . . for the Lord hath a sacrifice in Bozrah, and a great slaughter in the land of Idumea. . . . and their land shall be soaked with blood, and their dust made fat with fatness. For it is the day of the Lord's vengeance, and the year of recompenses for the controversy of Zion."

[This is] peculiar encouragement [to us] because 'tis promised that the enemies of God's church never shall prevail against [the true church] (Is. 54:14, etc., Zech. 12:2–3). The church's Redeemer is mighty,[9] that the church shall finally prevail against all his enemies in the most complete and glorious manner [as is] often foretold: Ps. 45[:5], "Through thee will we push down our enemies: through thy name will we tread them under that rise up against us." Ps. 68[:23], "dip thy foot [in the blood of thine enemies]." [Is. 44:12, "The] smith that bloweth in the coals." Is. 41:10, etc., "Fear thee not; for I am with thee: be not dismayed; for I am thy God: I will strengthen thee; yea, I will help thee; yea, I will uphold thee with the right hand of my righteousness. Behold, all they that were incensed against thee shall be ashamed and confounded: they shall be as nothing; and they that strive with thee shall perish. Thou shalt seek them, and shalt not find them, even them that contended with thee: they that war against thee shall be as nothing, and as a thing of nought." Mic. 4:11, etc., "Now also many nations are gathered against thee, that say, Let her be defiled, and let our eye look upon Zion. But they know not the thoughts of the Lord, neither understand they his counsel: for he shall gather them as the sheaves into the floor. Arise and thresh, O daughter of Zion: for I will make thine horn iron, and I will make thy hoofs brass: and thou shalt beat in pieces many people: and I will consecrate their gain unto the Lord, and their substance unto the Lord of the whole earth." [It] was David's encouragement: "for who is this . . . that he should defy the armies of the living God?" [1 Sam. 17:26]. [The] church of God is God's army, and so is often represented [as an army in Scripture]. When Jacob went to meet Esau, [he beheld Esau's tribe as a threatening army, and he marshaled his own people in military formation (Gen. 33:1–8)].

---

9. Here JE interlineated the separate and incomplete phrase, "Hereafter most Glo. appeared," without indicating where it should be inserted.

Application

I come now to apply these things to our present circumstances and God's late dealings with us.

It is now a time distinguished from all others that ever have been, in this respect, that never was a time wherein the civil and religious liberties and privileges of the British plantations in America, and all that is dear to us, was so threatened as at this time. The British and French plantations are so grown [competitors for civil and religious dominion that they] can't subsist together. It has very evidently appeared what the French have aimed at for a long time: to get the possession of the whole [continent west of our settlements]. To that end, they have [been] long laying their scheme and been exerting themselves with most indefatigable industry, and now the affair seems to be come to a crisis. The principal expedient intended has been in [linking their northern and southern settlements by building strongholds in the] Ohio [Valley, to encircle the British plantations].[10]

[We] have lately been defeated in the principal expedition that was concerned for our defense, an expedition wherein was the chief officer over all the British forces in America, and wherein the two nations principally exerted themselves, and from whence they seem to have had their chief expectations. This defeat is attended with many dark circumstances and threatening appearances. This is the second defeat that our forces have had in those parts,[11] which will tend greatly to encourage our enemies, and gives great opportunity to the enemy to strengthen themselves; and the English have in effect greatly strengthened them by supplying them with such large additions to their artillery and other arms, which we have carried into their country at so great expense, and which they have taken from us, now these two years going. [We] strengthen 'em by supplying them with large stores of provision and ammunition.

These repeated defeats will tend mightily to encourage and animate our enemies—there and everywhere—[and] tend to increase the number of our enemies. [This] defeat, accomplished chiefly by the Indians, [is] the greatest victory that ever the Indians obtained over the English, the most notable exploit [under arms], and [they] have obtained the greatest booty

---

10. In a 1751 letter to Speaker Thomas Hubbard, JE had succinctly stated this theory of the French strategy (see WJE 16:399).

11. In July 1754, a force of Virginia militia under Maj. George Washington had been defeated at Fort Necessity in southwestern Pennsylvania.

by it. It renders the success of our other expeditions, yet depending,[12] more doubtful and precarious.

[The defeat of our forces] has brought some of our colonies into great trouble and distress. 'Tis manifest the enemy have a design not only to settle that country, which is sufficient to sustain ten times the number that Canada can support, but they have also a further design, viz. to settle all the continent on the back of our settlements for more than two thousand miles in length, and this will be a great encouragement to the kingdom of France to go on with these designs and prosecute 'em with the utmost vigor. Such dark appearances is this defeat attended with.

And we indeed have no reason to wonder that we meet with such things when we consider what the state of the nation, and of these colonies, is at this day. Vice weakens and enervates men's bodies and minds, but yet the nation seemed to engage in this affair with a self-confident spirit. And if we consider the state of these colonies [. . .].[13]

This defeat is attended with several very humbling circumstances: [the complete overwhelming] of forces the nation seemed chiefly to rely upon, in some respects by a very despicable enemy—a number of barbarous savages. [Also, we have had] the killing of so great a number of the chief officers, whose clothing, armor, treasure, and scalps are fallen into the hand of the enemy to be carried in triumph through the French settlements of America. 'Tis an awful rebuke of the Most High for our pride and vain confidence, most loudly and awfully calling on the whole nation to deep humiliation and repentance.

And as we are called by it to humiliation, so we are very plainly taught where we ought to place our confidence: God shows us by it that vain is the help of man. How much is there in our present circumstances to make us earnest with God for his help in our expeditions! And if humiliation and repentance and a spirit of trust in God be the effect, there is still hope in Israel concerning this thing. We han't reason at all to despair. At the same time that God has thus awfully rebuked us in this defeat, on the one hand, he is on the other hand inviting us to look to him for help by his appearing ready to help in so remarkably succeeding

---

12. The "yet depending" expeditions were those against Crown Point under Gen. William Johnson, begun in August 1755, and against Fort Niagara.

13. One quarter blank column follows "colonies." For JE's description of the British colonial situation and the advances made by the French, see his letter to Joseph Paice, WJE 16, esp. 436–42.

our forces in the eastern parts.[14] He both corrects with his rod and draws us with bonds of love.

And we have this to encourage us: that [the French and the Church of Rome] are open enemies of God's church. They are members of the kingdom of Antichrist, in like manner the enemies of the true church as Edom was the enemy of Israel of old, [which was] plainly spoken of as a type of Antichrist. In the same terms, Is. 34:10, "It shall not be quenched night nor day; the smoke thereof shall go up for ever: from generation to generation it shall lie waste; none shall pass through it for ever and ever." So that our present case is the more parallel with that spoken of in my text. Antichrist is the greatest enemy of God's church that ever was on earth, [and he is] called "the son of perdition" [2 Thess. 2:3]; [but his] destruction is abundantly foretold. [We] have this encouragement: that [his] kingdom has begun to fall, [and it] has been declining [since the Reformation].[15]

Therefore, if we could but now see the consequence of this [defeat as an occasion for] serious reflection, humiliation, [and] a spirit of prayer, there would be great reason to hope, agreeable to that in Solomon's prayer, 1 Kgs. 8:33–34, "When thy people Israel be smitten down before the enemy, because they have sinned against thee, and shall turn again to thee, and confess thy name, and pray, and make supplication unto thee in this house: then hear thou in heaven, and forgive the sin of thy people Israel, and bring them again unto the land which thou gavest unto their fathers." [Also in vv.] 44–45, "If thy people go out to battle against their enemy, whithersoever thou shalt send them, and shall pray unto the Lord toward the city which thou hast chosen, and toward the house that I have built for thy name: then hear thou in heaven their prayer and their supplication, and maintain their cause." And [in] v. [57], "The Lord our God be with us, as he was with our fathers: let him not leave us, nor forsake us."

---

14. A reference to the capture of two French forts in Nova Scotia—Beauséjour and Gaspereau—by Col. Robert Monckton in June 1755.

15. For the biblical texts JE refers to, in which he interprets God's enemies as being compared to Antichrist, see, for example, Ezek. 25:12–14; Amos 1:6, 9; Obad. 1, 8; and Mal. 1:4. JE discusses the overthrow of the kingdom of Antichrist in language very similar to this paragraph in his *History of the Work of Redemption* (WJE 9:468).

Appendix A

Edwards's Martial Timeline

Oct 5, 1703	Jonathan Edwards Born
Fall 1726	Edwards moves to Northampton as Assistant Pastor
Oct 1731	Edwards Preaches *God Glorified in the Work of Redemption*
Dec 1734	Little Revival Begins in Northampton
Aug 1734	Edwards preaches *A Divine and Supernatural Light*
Mar–Aug 1739	Edwards preaches *History of the Work of Redemption*
Oct 1739	War of Jenkin's Ear Declared
Oct 1740	George Whitefield Preaches in Northampton
Feb 1741	*In Seeking Heaven Persons Should Behave as Valiant, Resolute Soldiers*
Feb 26, 1741	*God's Care for His Servants in Time of Public Commotions*
Mar 1741	Siege of Cartagena
July 1741	Edwards preaches *Sinners in the Hands of an Angry God*
Sept 1741	Edwards preaches *Distinguishing Marks*
Dec 1741	*The Curse of Meroz*
Winter 1742	Edwards preaches series that would be published as *Religious Affections*

APPENDIX A

April 1743	*Prepared to Travail and Fight*
June 1743	Battle of Dettingen
Oct 13, 1743	*Christ the Lord of Hosts*
Mar 1744	Britain and France declare war; King George's War begins
May 1744	French attack British settlements at Canso
June 28, 1744	*Sin Weakens a People in War*
July 1744	*The Armor of God*
March 1745	Expedition to Louisbourg leaves Boston
Apr 4, 1745	*The Duties of Christians in a Time of War*
July 1745	Charles Edward Stuart (Bonnie Prince Charlie) lands in Scotland
July 1745	Whitefield visits Northampton
Aug 1745	*An Occasion for Praise and Thanksgiving*
Aug 1745	*As Soldiers in War*
Sept 19, 1745	*The Enemies of God's People Confounded and Broken in Pieces*
Mar 13, 1746	*The Church of Christ Built on a Rock*
April 1746	Battle of Culloden
June 1746	French fleet sails from Brest for Canada
June 1746	*The People of God Going Forth to War*
July 10, 1746	*The Fall of the Antichrist*
Aug 1746	Fall of Fort Massachusetts
Aug 1746	Indian raiding party attacks near Southampton
Aug 1746	*The Sovereignty of God's Mercy*
Oct 16, 1746	*Walking Righteously, Speaking Uprightly*
Nov 26, 1746	*God's People in Danger*
May 1747	French fleet bound for Louisbourg defeated by Admiral Warren
Aug 1747	Elisha Clark of Southampton attacked and killed in his barn
Aug 30, 1747	*Continuing Unawakened under Divine Chastisements*

Oct 1746	David Brainerd dies in Northampton
June 1748	Col. John Stoddard (Edwards's Uncle) dies
June 1748	*A Strong Rod Broken and Withered*
Oct 1748	Treaty of Aix-la-Chappelle signed ending continental and colonial wars
June 1750	Edwards dismissed from Northampton
Feb 1751	Called to minister in Stockbridge
1752; 1753	*Valiant, Resolute Soldiers* re-preached
Apr 1753	Completes *Freedom of the Will*
Sept 1753	Indian raid kills four in Stockbridge
Apr 1754	*Warring with the Devil*
Nov 1754	*The Sovereignty of God's Mercy* re-preached
Mar 4, 1755	*Enemies Confounded and Broken* re-preached
Mar 5, 1755	*God Is He Who Orders*
Mar 1755	*Sin Weakens a People in War* re-preached
July 1755	Braddock defeated on the Monongahela
July 1755	*The Duties of Christians in a Time of War*
July 1755	*In the Name of the Lord of Hosts*
Aug 1755	Col. Ephraim Williams marches to war with Stockbridge Indians
Aug 28, 1755	*God's People Tried by a Battle Lost*
Sept 1755	Stockbridge attacked, four Englishmen killed
Sept 1755	Battle of Lake George
Nov 1755	*The Armor of God* re-preached
July 1756	*Walking Righteously, Speaking Uprightly* re-preached
Aug 1756	French take Fort Oswego
Sept 1757	Edwards offered presidency of College of New Jersey
Mar 1758	Edwards dies of smallpox vaccinations

Appendix B

Index of Edwards's Martial Letters

THE FOLLOWING LETTERS CONTAIN Edwards's discussion of martial themes with his correspondents both domestic and international. These letters can be found in volume 16 of the Yale Letterpress edition of the *Works of Jonathan Edwards*.

Nov 1745	To a Correspondent in Scotland
May 12, 1746	To the Reverend John McLaurin
Nov 3, 1746	To Esther Edwards
Jan 21, 1746/7	To the Reverend William McCulloch
Sept 23, 1747	To the Reverend William McCulloch
Feb 26, 1755	To Brig. Joseph Dwight
June 3, 1755	To the Reverend Thomas Foxcroft
Sept 4, 1755	To Col. Israel Williams
Sept 5, 1755	To Col. Israel Williams
Dec 11, 1755	To the Reverend John Erskine
Apr 10, 1756	To the Reverend William McCulloch
Oct 9, 1756	To the Reverend Gideon Hawley
Nov 16, 1756	To Lieut. Gov. Spenser Phips et al.

Bibliography

The Boston Gazette, 1739–1775.
Browning, Reed. *The War of Austrian Succession*. New York: St. Martin's Griffin, 2008.
Choi, Peter. *George Whitefield: Evangelist for God and Empire*. Grand Rapids: Eerdmans, 2018.
Cuthbert, Christian. "'More Swiftly Propagating the Gospel': Jonathan Edwards, Col. John Stoddard, and the Invasion of Canada." In *Jonathan Edwards within the Enlightenment: Controversy, Experience, & Thought*, edited by Daniel Gulotta and John Lowe, 153–68. Gottingen: V&R, 2020.
Demos, John. *The Unredeemed Captive: A Family Story from Early America*. New York: Alfred A. Knopf, 1994.
Doddridge, Philip. *The Family Expositor: Or, a Paraphrase and Version of the New Testament*. 6 vols. London: Wilson, 1739–56.
Frazier, Patrick. *The Mohicans of Stockbridge*. Lincoln, NE: Nebraska University Press, 1992.
Grotius, Hugo. *On the Rights of War and Peace*. Abridged version. Translated by William Whewell. Cambridge: Cambridge University Press, 1854.
Henry, Matthew. *An Exposition of all the Books of the Old and New Testament*. 3rd ed. 6 vols. London: Clark et al., 1721–25.
Hutchinson, Thomas. *History of the Colony and Province of Massachusetts-Bay*. 2 vols. Cambridge, MA: Harvard University Press, 1936.
Kidd, Thomas. *The Protestant Interest: New England After Puritanism*. New Haven: Yale University Press, 2004.
Leach, Douglas Edward. *Roots of Conflict: British Armed Forces and Colonial Americans, 1677–1763*. Chapel Hill, NC: University of North Carolina Press, 1986.
Marsden, George. *Jonathan Edwards: A Life*. New Haven, CT: Yale University Press, 2003.
McClymond, Michael, and Gerald McDermott. *The Theology of Jonathan Edwards*. New York: Oxford University Press, 2012.
Parkman, Francis. "A Half-Century of Conflict." In *France and England in North America: Count Frontenac and New France under Louis XIV, A Half-Century of Conflict, Montcalm and Wolfe*, 2:326–828. Library of America. New York: Literary Classics of the United States, 1983.
Peckham, Howard H. *The Colonial Wars, 1689–1762*. Chicago: University of Chicago Press, 1964.
Plank, Geoffery. *Rebellion and Savagery: The Jacobite Rising of 1745 and the British Empire*. Philadelphia: University of Pennsylvania, 2006.

Poole, Matthew. *Annotations Upon the Holy Bible*. London: Parkhurst et al., 1685.
Preston, David. *Braddock's Defeat: The Battle of the Monongahela and the Road to Revolution*. New York: Oxford University Press, 2015.
Shirley, William. *The Correspondence of William Shirley: Governor of Massachusetts and Military Commander in America, 1731–1760*. Vol. 1. Edited by Charles Henry Lincoln. New York: Macmillan, 1912.
Tracy, Patricia. *Jonathan Edwards, Pastor: Minister and Congregation in Eighteenth Century Connecticut Valley*. Amherst, MA: University of Massachusetts Press, 1977.
Trumbull, James Russell. *History of Northampton*. 2 vols. Northampton, MA: Press of Gazette Publishing, Co., 1898.

Scripture Index

Genesis

3:15	239
7:1	302
11:14	203
14	176
17	241n5
18:20–33	300
19:11	225
27	240
29	240, 323
32:2	120
33	244
33:1–8	378
37	323
39	300

Exodus

8:25	43
9:18–25	79
10:8–10	43
10:24, 26	44
12:41	119
14	219
14:12	90
14:21	194
14:28	195n14
15:3	134
15:9	240
17:9–13	176
17:14–16	99
23:27	183

Leviticus

26	173

Numbers

10:36	151
14:7–9	40
14:9	131
22	220
31:16	241
32:20–23	99, 99n6, 256

Deuteronomy

2:15	119
4:7	173
8:16	173
9:22–28	136n4
11:25	183
20:20	298
23:3–4	99
28:7	173
29:7	241
31:6	33
32:4	221
32:10	68
33:26, 27	133
33:29	221

Joshua

2:9	183, 222
5:13–15	90
7 and 8	176
7	228n11

Joshua (continued)

7:12	58
7:13	376
8:2	298
10	194
10:3–4	220
10:12–14	176
11	38
15:63	194, 195n14
22	251
22:8	257
24:2,14–15	279
24:15	297n14

Judges

3:9–10	184
3:15	182
3:27	182
3:27–28	92
4–5	221
5:6–7	251, 256
5:9	182
5:20	121
5:21	195
5:23	88, 98n4
6	241n5
6:14	184
6:34	184
7	176
7:22	195
7:23–24	100n7
8:9	202
8:27	228
8:35	351
11	176
11:29	184
13:25	184
16	176
18:7	298
20:14–48	376
21:10	100n7

1 Samuel

2:32	162
13:5	176
14:6	176
14:23	195
17	176
17:26	378
17:33	205
17:35	236
17:44	131
17:54	191
30	176

2 Samuel

5	176
6:16–23	104
8:5	220
10:12	255
11	323
12:27	191
13	323
17	316
22:3	202
23:4	342
23:5	68
23:21	195

1 Kings

4:20	342
4:25	342
8:33–34	381
10:8–9	342
12:14	342
20:10	280
20:27	219, 280
20:42	256
20:43	257
22:19	120
22:31	59

2 Kings

2:12	300
3:11	176
3:22	195
6:13	123
6:15–16	218
6:18	225
8:44–45	166
10:32	309

13:7–9	280	3:5	101
13:14	300	4:17	112
15	220	8:9–10	105
17:12–15	137	9:27	2:56, 344
17–18	138n8		
17:33–34, 41	77		
18	219, 241	## Esther	
19:14	177		
23	138n11	4:16–17	177
25:25	140		

1 Chronicles

Job

		5:11–13	184
		5:12–13	220
5:26	309	5:12–14	117
12:1–13	251	5:14	225
12:22	119	5:19–22	69
12:23–31	102	5:23	301
28:19	166	23:13–14	219
		38:22–23	194
		40:11	311
		41	311

2 Chronicles

Psalms

12:7	376		
14:9	133, 194, 241		
14:9–12	218		
14:9–15	176	2:7–9	95
15:2	228	7:15–16	195
15:8	180	8:2	119
19	191	9:6–8	96
20	176	10:17	175, 376
20:1	221	11:3	341
20:12	228, 241, 375	18:29	194
20:17	316, 318	18:40–41	220
20:23	195	19:12	52
25:14 etc.	228	24:8	122
35	138n11	32:7	71
35:24–25	344	33:6	120
36:15–17	327	33:10–11	117
36:16	331	33:10–12	220
		33:16	218
		33:16–17	133
## Ezra		34:7	121
		36:12	203
6, 7	268	37:4–5	171
7–8	268n10	37:17	222
9:6	136n4	45:3–4	145
		45:5	378
## Nehemiah		45:10	32
2	268	46	123
2:20	100		

Psalms (continued)

46:1–2	72
46:4	294
46:4–5	302
46:9	221
46:10	375
48:7	299
48:12–13	244
63:1	51
66:18	172
60:9	372n1
68:23	378
72:5	236
76:3–5	71
76:4	221
76:6	123
80:8ff	336
82:5	341
82:6	339
89:34	68
91:4	68
91:7	301
91:11–12	121
94:10	134, 280
102:25	236
103:2	295
103:21	120
109:25	238
110	96
110:1	117
118:9	184
119:111	78
122:3	172
127:1	133
130:4	375
137:7	377n8
137:8–9	257
145:4	237
145:9	278
147:4	120
148:2	120

Proverbs

2:18–19	157
3:6	171
6:26	132
9:17–18	157
10:22	294
11:21	123, 143, 218, 299
13:18	131
16:3	171
16:9	118
16:17	110
18:10	203
18:21	291
19:21	118, 219
20:8	348
23:21	131
28:1	131
28:9	172
28:19	131
30:27	116
31:26	291

Ecclesiastes

9:10	51
9:11	118, 373
9:18	54
10:16	343, 347
10:17	342

Isaiah

1	327
1:9	312
1:15	172, 325
1:16–18	294
2	203
3	301
3:10	68
4:6	80
5:2	336
5:4	331
5:22	339
5:25–27	183
7:18	117
8:9–10	118, 184, 213, 215, 374
9:6–7	237
9:13–14	322
10:21–22	312
13:4	117
15:6	191
15:6–7	293
17:12–13	71

10:5	136	45:19	228
10:6–7	118	47:4	115, 134
10:15	118	49:2	263
17:4–6	332	51:7–8	237
19:2–3	222	52:10	182
19:3–4	220	54	123
25:1–5	191	54:10	69
25:4	80	54:14	378
26:1	133, 302	54:15	220
26:11	79	54:15–17	237
26:20–21	84	54:16	123
27	194	54:16–17	71, 221
27:1	151	57:10	137
27:4	123	58:8–9	145
27:8	65	59:21	237
27:7–9	323	63	227, 377
27:12	235	63:9–10	227, 324
28:15	136	65:8–9	332
28:16	233		
28:15–17	219		
29:7–8	222	## Jeremiah	
29:15	219	2:21	336
30:12–13	128, 129n2	2:30	325
31:3	151	4:11–12	65
32:2	65	4:14	137
33:15	291n6	4:22	54
33:16–17	133	5:3	138, 325
33:19ff	286	9:4–5	140
34:5	377	10:16	115
34:10	381	12:5	84
34:11	375	12:12	136
37:7	118	17:7–8	72
37:26–27	183	17:10	250
37:28–38	305	29:10	268, 271
37:30	243	29:12–13	228
37:31	244n10, 313n3	31:3	233
40:15–17	218	33:17	237
40:26	120	31:33–34	294
41:2	176	31:35–36	239
41:10	378	33:8–9	295
42:3	243	37:10	194
42:13	267	39:11–12	73
43:2	69, 243	40	300
43:20	294	44:15–19	138
44:12	378	48:11–12	79, 144
45:2	133	50:37–38	191, 294
45:5	117	51	195n14
45:7	70	51:20	136
45:12	120		

Lamentations

4:20	344
5:1,16	374

Ezekiel

1	70
2:6	140
9	82, 85
9:3	226
9:4–6	66
15	336
17:6	336
19:11	342
19:12	336
20:5	240
21:27	117
23:11	278
25:12–14	381n15
29:3–5	311
33:13	111
35:5	377
36:26	136n4
37:10	119
47:13	268

Daniel

2:34–35	267
2:45	267
3	74, 74n5, 243
4:27	162
4:35	120, 335
7	270
7:8	223, 261
7:11	263, 265
7:14	238
7:25	262
7:25–27	270n13
7:26	267
8:10,11	119
8:25	225
12	263
12:7	226

Hosea

1:6	324
2:6–7	324
2:9	323
5:15	51, 244
11:4	331
11:8–9	227, 330
13:15	191

Joel

1, 2	116
2:7–8	117–18, 183
2:11	116
2:25	116

Amos

1:6,9	381n15
3:2	134, 280
3:6	70
8:11	325

Obadiah

1, 8	381n15

Jonah

4:6–7	243n8

Micah

4:11	378
6:8	289

Nahum

1:7–10	218

Zephaniah

1:12–13	144
2:1–3	83, 145
3:1–2	326

Zechariah

2:8	68
8:20–22	174n10
9:9	100

11:6	324	15:7	105
12:2–3	378	19:8–9	297
12:2–4	222	19:37–40	100
14	101	21:36	53
		21:20–21	73
		21:24	263
		22:36	159

Malachi

1:4	381n15

Matthew

John

		1:42	233
3:5–6	28	3:8	279
4:5	298	5:39	52
5:10–12	249	7:38–39	72
5:12	75	10:27–28	235
5:16	300	13:1	233
6:24	77, 206	13:34	250
8:8	168	14:13–14	173
9	295	14:19	71
11:12	27, 28, 160, 209	15:7	172
12:25	132	15:16	173
12:30	94, 98	18:36	169
12:34	154, 291		
16	230		
16:18	11, 230, 230, 232, 233n1		

Acts

19:29	250	7:51	139
21:5	100	10:1	168
23	138n9	13:8–12	225
24:35	206	13:45	140
24:24	235	17:5	140
24:12	235	18:12	140
25	235	20:28	69
28:19–20	239	23:17–23, 27–30	168
		28:25	139

Mark

Romans

5:9	121	8:17	39
		8:31	133
		9:27–28	312

Luke

		11:5	312
		11:7	139
2:13	120	13:1–4	168
3:14	168	13:4	167, 253
4:9	298	14:19	289n4
10:18	201		
11:21	151		
11:21–22	357		
12:4	74		
14:26	78		

1 Corinthians

14:31–33	30, 32
3:11	233

1 Corinthians (continued)

9:24	153
9:25–27	47
9:26	46

2 Corinthians

4:4	202
4:17	75
10:4,5	202
12:10	376

Galatians

2:20	234

Ephesians

1:4	233
1:13	84
1:22	70
2:20	230, 233
3:11	233
4:3	172
4:11–13	238
4:15–16	172
4:26	289
4:29	291
5:5–7	297n12
6:11–13	149
6:12	47, 151, 200, 201
6:16	203
6:17	264

Philippians

1:6	236
1:21	74
2:10	117
2:15	245
4:6	171

Colossians

3:3	71
3:14	172
4:6	291

1 Thessalonians

2:14–16	140
5:23–24	235

2 Thessalonians

2	263
2:3	225, 262, 263, 381
2:4	262
2:8	265, 266

1 Timothy

2:8	172
4:1–3	263
4:41	262

2 Timothy

2:3–4	32
2:11	250
2:19	233

Titus

1:2	233
2:12	289

Hebrews

4:12	259
4:12	264
11:30	176
11:32–34	228
12:22	138n10

James

1:26	291
3:2	291
3:6–8	290
4:4	78
5:14–15	295

1 Peter

2:4–5	233
3:13	74

4:13	250	12	121, 239
5:8	53, 151	12:3	151, 201
		12:6	267
2 Peter		12:7	121
		13	262, 263
2:5	79n8	13:10	226, 264
		13:11	262
1 John		14:1	84
		14:8	262
2:15	78	14:13	74
2:18	262	15:3	192
3:16	250	16:10	202, 225
3:22	172	16:16	98
4:19	233	16:18	266–67
5:3	78	17:3	262n3
		17:8	225
Jude		17:10	262n5
		17:12	262
14	151	17:16	264, 265
		17:16–17	226
Revelation		18	263, 263n6
		18:4	95
2:5	245	18:6–8	265
3:10	143	18:8	226, 263
3:12	78	18:9–10	264
3:21	39	18:10	265
5:10	39	18:20	270
7	235	19	267, 269
7:1–3	62	19:7	270
8:3	244	19:11–16	266
9:16	150, 239	19:15	263
10	263	19:20	262
10:5–6	226	21:14	233
11:2	267	22:1	72
11:7	243		
11:8	262		

Subject Index

Abenaki, 175n11, 179, 212
Alexander the Great, 29, 40
Amalekites, 43, 59, 99, 176
Amorites, 38, 176, 194–95
Anakians, 40–41, 48
Annapolis, 163, 175, 189, 303, 315–16
Antichrist, 11, 96, 135, 142, 213, 225–26, 242, 258–59, 261–71, 377, 381, 381n15
Antichristian Kingdoms, 10–13, 17, 213, 223, 225, 261, 334, 371,
Artaxerxes, 268, 268n9
Austrian Succession, 1, 5–6, 7n8, 107, 127, 178, 254n17, 329n6

Babylon, 29, 73–74, 95, 100, 115, 133, 135, 195, 201, 203, 213, 221, 225, 241, 257, 262, 264–66, 268, 268n9, 271, 300–301, 375
Barak, 86–91, 97–99, 102, 182, 191
Battle of Dettingen, 3, 7, 113, 246
Battle of Lake George, 18, 365
Blakeney, Col. William, 5, 25–26, 61, 87
Braddock, Gen. Edward, 2, 4, 16–19, 18n20, 364, 365n7, 370–1, 370n1
Brest, 12–13, 272, 284, 303
Buell, Samuel, 6

Cadiz, 25
Canaan, 33, 38–41, 43, 48–49, 57–59, 89, 98–99, 109, 135, 201, 203, 220, 228, 241, 376
Canaanite, 89, 98–99, 183, 221, 251

Canada, 2, 7, 11–12, 14, 85, 85n14, 174, 185, 187, 247, 248n1, 253, 256n23, 258, 259, 269, 272, 283, 296, 303, 315, 334, 346, 370, 380
Canso, 8, 127, 163, 179
Cape Breton, 2, 8, 12, 178–80, 181n1, 205, 224, 254, 254n18, 255, 255n22, 272, 303, 329n7, 330
Carrying Place, 355
Cartagena, 5–6, 25, 62, 86–87, 107, 141n12, 178
Charles VI, 2n2, 62, 107
Chebucto, (See Halifax)
Clark, Elisha, 3, 13, 155n10, 161n15, 321, 321n2
Constantine, 65
Crown Point, 7, 10, 15–18, 20, 165, 254n13, 364–65, 367n1, 370, 380n12
Culloden, 12, 16–17, 273, 283
Cyrus, 115, 268, 268n9

Deborah, 86–91, 97–99, 102, 182, 191, 194–95, 221, 228, 242, 251
Deism (deist), 29, 141,
Duke of Cumberland, 12, 246, 273
Duke D'Anville, 303, 314n4, 315
Duke of Newcastle, 11, 147, 247, 272

Edomites, 228, 241, 377
Ehud, 92, 182

Falkirk, 246, 273
Fort Duquesne, 17
Fort Massachusetts, 13, 283

399

Fort Ontario, 19, 365
Fort Pelham, 283
Fort Saratoga, 320
French Fleet, 12–13, 16, 19, 283–85, 303–4, 330n9

George II, 7, 10–11, 107, 113, 229, 246
Gideon, 100, 176, 184, 194, 213, 218, 228, 228n11, 373
Goliath, 18, 43, 59, 131, 151, 176, 182, 191, 195, 205, 280, 365, 369
Gooch, Col. William, 5–6, 25, 61

Halifax, 12, 284, 303–4, 330n9
Hawley, Gideon, 356
Hezekiah, 177, 194, 243, 286, 303–4, 306–9, 318–19
Huron, 212

Indian, 4, 7, 10, 13, 16, 18–19, 27, 85n14, 137, 143, 152, 155–56, 155n10, 159–60, 161n15, 165, 175, 185, 213–14, 223, 256n23, 258, 269, 274, 283, 314, 314n5, 316, 316n7, 320–21, 321n2, 333, 346, 350, 350n1, 355–60, 361n1, 364–65, 367n1, 368n2, 369, 370, 379
Iroquois, 212

Jamaica, 5, 16, 25, 61, 86
Jebucto, (See Halifax)
Jebusites, 194–95
Jericho, 90, 119, 129, 176
Jerusalem, 28, 56, 67, 72–3, 78, 82, 96, 100–101, 112, 115, 135, 138n9, 139, 142, 144, 172, 177, 179, 181, 184, 191, 194, 220, 222, 223, 237–38, 244, 248, 264, 286, 288, 300–302 305–6, 308–10, 312, 314–15, 317–18, 324, 326, 344
John the Baptist, 28–29, 59, 168, 241
Johnson, William, 17–19, 364, 380n12
Joshua, 33, 38, 40, 90–92, 99, 119, 176, 194, 220, 227–28, 251, 257, 297, 298–300, 376

King George's War, 4, 8, 333, 350n1
Kunkapot, 355

Louisburg, 163–64, 174n10, 185–86, 195n15, 207, 209–10, 254n15, 255n20, 272, 283, 284, 303, 315–16, 330n9
Lydius, Col. John, 10

Malebois, Marshall, 178, 178n2
Michael (angel), 201, 121
Midianites, 184, 195, 373–74,
Moabites, 92, 99, 176, 182, 195, 241, 280, 318, 374
Mohawk, 3, 147, 212, 320
Mohican Indians, 2–3, 14–16, 18, 355–56, 364–65
Montcalm, Louis-Joseph, 20

Nebuchadnezzar, 73, 74n5, 243
Nineveh, 305,
Nova Scotia, 16–17, 364, 381n14

Oglethorpe, James, 26, 61
Old Pretender, (See Stuart, James Edward)
Oswego, 17, 19, 365

Pepperrell, Col. William, 9, 163, 188n8
Persia, 29, 135
Pharaoh, 43–44, 77, 90, 116, 195, 219, 221, 225, 240, 267, 311, 374
Philistine(s), 43, 59, 131, 135, 176, 191, 195, 205, 367
Pomeroy, Maj. Seth, 20, 163, 179, 188n6
Port Royal, 8
Pragmatic Army, 7, 107, 113

Quebec, 10–11, 16, 20, 212, 247, 254n15, 259, 370
Queen Anne's War, 7, 137, 137n6

Rogers, Cpt. Robert, 19, 335, 365

Sennacherib, 12–13, 177, 194, 305, 307, 309, 311, 313–16, 374, 376,
Shirley, Gov. (Col.) William, 7, 8, 11–12, 15, 17, 19, 127, 147–48, 163, 179, 188n8, 254n19, 258, 272, 333, 355, 364–65
Sisera, 89, 91, 102, 121, 251

Six Nations, 15, 283, 333
Sixth Commandment, 164, 167, 169
Sixth Seal, 65
Sixth Vial, 191n12, 259
St. John's Fort, 316, 364
Stuart, Charles Edward, 10, 12, 137, 229, 242, 245, 272, 319n10 (Bonnie Prince Charlie)
Stuart, James Edward, 10n12, 242, 272
Stockbridge, 2-3, 14, 16-17, 19, 27, 165, 273-74, 285, 334, 355-56, 359, 360, 361n1, 364-65, 367n1
Stoddard, John, 7-8, 10-13, 18, 20, 147-48, 247, 188n6, 333-35, 334n2

Thanksgiving (day of), 113, 163, 179, 303-4
Theresa, Maria, 2, 6, 107

Warren, Commodore Peter, 9, 178, 187-88, 196, 254
Washington, George, 15, 355, 379n11
Wentworth, Gen. Thomas, 86
Whitefield, George, 3, 5, 6n7, 8-9, 26, 61, 80n10, 163, 178
Williams Jr., Col Ephraim, 14, 355, 364
Wolfe, Gen. James, 20,

Xerxes, 133

Young Pretender, (See Stuart, Charles Edward)

Zerah The Ethiopian, 133, 176, 194, 218, 241, 374
Zion, 47, 71, 84, 94-96, 100, 194-95, 201, 210, 215n1, 219, 222, 230, 233, 244-45, 286-88, 288n1, 293, 301, 305, 308, 312, 325, 378

www.ingramcontent.com/pod-product-compliance
Lightning Source LLC
Chambersburg PA
CBHW020604300426
44113CB00007B/508